Resistance Through Rituals

Youth subcultures in post-war Britain

Edited by Stuart Hall and Tony Jefferson

Hutchinson of London
in association with
the Centre for Contemporary
Cultural Studies,
University of Birmingham

Hutchinson & Co (Publishers) Ltd
3 Fitzroy Square, London W1

London Melbourne Sydney Auckland
Wellington Johannesburg and agencies
throughout the world

First published 1975
First published by Hutchinson 1976
© The Centre for Contemporary Cultural Studies,
University of Birmingham

Printed in Great Britain by The Anchor Press Ltd
and bound by Wm Brendon & Son Ltd
both of Tiptree, Essex

ISBN 0 09 127910 0 (cased)
ISBN 0 09 127911 9 (paper)

CONTENTS

INTRODUCTION

This issue of *WPCS* is devoted to post-war youth sub-cultures. We have tried to dismantle the term in which this subject is usually discussed - 'Youth Culture' - and reconstruct, in its place, a more careful picture of the kinds of youth sub-cultures, their relation to class cultures, and to the way cultural hegemony is maintained, structurally and historically. This journal thus pulls together the work of the Centre's Sub-cultures Group over the past three years. This work continues, both within the Centre and in a very fruitful dialogue with others working in the same field. The results and formulations offered are, therefore, part of work-in-progress. They do not pretend to be either final, definitive or 'correct'. We hope they will lead to further work, discussion and clarification and that, on other occasions, some of this can be reflected in the pages of the journal.

Despite the uncompleted nature of the work, we feel that it may be helpful to sketch in a brief history of how the focus of the work has shifted over the period, and how our present position was arrived at. Our starting point, as for so many others, was Howard Becker's *Outsiders* - the text which, at least for us, best signalled the 'break' in mainstream Sociology and the subsequent adoption, by many sociologists working in the fields of deviance, sub-cultural theory or criminology - originally in America, but rapidly, in this country too of what came to be known as an interactionist, and later a 'transactional' or 'labelling' perspective. Our reading of this text - and subsequent British work in this rapidly emerging tradition - and our engagement with the perspective in general was always, however, double-edged: both a sense of exhilaration about the importance of some of the ideas generated by this 'sceptical revolution' (the viewing of social action as *process* rather than as event, for example, and crucially, the idea that deviance was a social creation, a result of the power of some to label **others**) and a sense of unease: a feeling that these accounts, whilst containing many important, new insights, were not comprehensive enough: a feeling, particularly, that deviant behaviour had other origins besides public labelling. This sense of unease was given a concrete empirical and theoretical substance by our subsequent reading of Phil Cohen's seminal paper (published in *WPCS 2*) on youth subcultures and their genesis within the class structure and class cultures of the East End. This settled our feelings of ambiguity and relegated transactional analysis to a marginal position in favour of a concern with the structural and cultural origins of British youth subcultures.

Our subsequent efforts were for some considerable time devoted to filling out the suggestive framework offered by Cohen, initially through papers offering more detailed accounts of particular subcultures - Teds, Mods, Skinheads, etc. - extracts from which

are reproduced in the Ethnographic section.   We also endeavoured
to develop our theoretical position in a number of papers, involving
extensions, revisions and criticisms of Cohen, and these attempts
provided the basis for the theoretical overview presented in this
journal.

In the middle of that work came our involvement in the mugging
project - an involvement which has perhaps been the biggest single
organic influence on the development of our subsequent work, and on
the shaping of the theoretical and methodological position which
we take in this journal.   The project had two major consequences:
politically, it brought a more direct engagement since it stemmed
originally from a concern with a particular, local case; and
theoretically it returned transactionalism to our agenda of work.
Since our initial concern was precipitated by the severity of the
judicial reaction to the Handsworth case, we could, therefore, no
longer simply ignore the question of social reaction, but our
concern in the Subcultures work with structural and historical
forms of analysis meant that we could not regress to a naive
transactionalist perspective.   Our aim became, therefore - and
remains - to explain *both* social action *and* social reaction,
structurally and historically in a way which attempts to do
justice to all the levels of analysis: from the dynamics of
'face-to-face' interactions between delinquents and control agents
to the wider, more mediated, questions - largely ignored by 'pure'
transactionalists - of the relation of these activities to shifts
in class and power relations, consciousness, ideology and hegemony.

A word about presentation.   Much of it - including the long
theoretical overview - arises out of the work of the Sub-Cultures
group.   In keeping with the aims of the Centre - and for good or
ill - this has been collaborative work: the effort to sustain an
ongoing discussion around the key theoretical issues, but also
the collective writing and revision of articles.   Collective work
of this kind is, in practice, extremely difficult to sustain and
by no means always possible: but those who have been involved in
it would like to register, here, their continuing sense of its
rewards, despite the problems attached to it.   A great deal of
empirical work in this field has also been done by Centre members
not directly in the Group: and this issue draws widely on their
work (for example, the studies by Paul Willis and Dick Hebdige).
The work of the group has been presented to and discussed by
Centre members as a whole, and a number of other pieces are
contributed by them.   We have benefited enormously from many
people, who, though outside the Centre, are not only working
along similar lines, but have entered directly into discussion
with us, and given us intellectual support.   On this occasion,
we welcome as contributors to the issue Paul Corrigan, Simon Frith,
Graham Murdock, Robin McCron, Geoff Pearson and John Twohig.
Finally, the issue has been produced by the Group working together

with an Editorial team, and the latter have not only shouldered
the practical load but played a major part in the discussion,
revision and rewriting of articles, etc. (this is partially
but inadequately acknowledged in the otherwise inexplicable
'authorial assignments' at the end of some articles in the issue).

A note on format. The journal begins with an overview article
which, we hope, will set the main themes. Then there is a long
section containing selections from 'ethnographic' work on
different aspects of post-war sub-cultures. The intention here
is, first, to indicate (but by no means exhaustively) the *range*;
second, to provide empirical substantiation; but, third, to
develop, out of the empirical material presented, a theoretical
point, issue or argument which connects with the main themes
outlined in the 'overview'. This is followed by a section of
shorter theoretical articles which pick up and develop some of
the points merely touched on in the overview: the problems of
'style', 'generational consciousness', 'politics' and the
relationship of girls to subcultures.

Finally, Brian Roberts (who, though registered in another
Department, has played a major part in the work of the group)
and Steve Butters (who has a long-standing link with several
areas of the Centre's work) return to questions of methodology.
Steve Butters' piece is an opening attempt, by someone both
familiar with and sympathetically critical of the work of the
Group, to open a critique of its methods of work and the
problematic underlying them.

PHOTOS

Page 84	"	"	Popperfoto
Page 97	"	"	Euan Duff
Page 98	"	"	Camera Press Ltd.
Page 126	"	"	Alan McLean
Page 208	"	"	Alan McLean

CHRONOLOGIES

| Pages | 58 - 59 | Stuart Daniels |
| Pages | 240 - 241 | Jenny Garber |

7

THEORY I

SUBCULTURES, CULTURES AND CLASS

John Clarke
Stuart Hall
Tony Jefferson
Brian Roberts

Our subject in this volume is Youth Cultures: our object, to
explain them as a phenomenon, and their appearance in the post-war
period. The subject has, of course, been massively treated, above all in the mass media. Yet, many of these surveys and analyses seem mainly to have multiplied the confusions and extended
the mythologies surrounding the topic. By treating it in terms
of its spectacular features only, these surveys have become part
of the very phenomenon we want to explain. First, then, we
must clear the ground, try to get behind the myths and explanations which cover up, rather than clarify, the problem. We have
to construct the topic first - partly by demolishing certain
concepts which, at present, are taken as adequately defining it.
Necessarily, this exercise of penetrating beneath a popular
construction must be done with care, lest we discard the 'rational
kernel' along with its over-publicised husk.

The social and political meaning of Youth Cultures is not easy
to assess: though their visibility has been consistently high.
'Youth' appeared as an emergent category in post-war Britain, one
of the most striking and visible manifestations of social change
in the period. 'Youth' provided the focus for official reports,
pieces of legislation, official interventions. It was signified as a social problem by the moral guardians of the society
- something we 'ought to do something about'. Above all, Youth
played an important role as a cornerstone in the construction of
understandings, interpretations and quasi-explanations *about* the
period. As the Rowntree study of the Popular Press and Social
Change suggested:

> Youth was, in both papers /‾the *Daily Express* and the *Daily
> Mirror*/ and perhaps in the whole press of the period, a powerful
> but concealed *metaphor* for social change: the compressed image
> of a society which had crucially changed, in terms of basic
> life-styles and values - changed, in ways calculated to upset

9

the official political framework, but in ways *not yet calculable in traditional political terms* ..

(Smith et. al., 1975)

It would be difficult to sustain the argument that a phenomenon as massively present and visible as 'Youth Culture', occupying a pivotal position in the history and consciousness of the period, was a pure construction of the media, a surface phenomenon only. However, Gramsci warned us that, "in studying a structure, it is necessary to distinguish organic movements (relatively permanent) from movements which may be termed 'conjunctural', and which appear as occasional, immediate, almost accidental". The aim must be to "find the correct relation between what is organic and what is conjunctural" (Gramsci, 1971: 177). The 'phenomenal form' - Youth Culture provides a point of departure, only, for such an analysis. We cannot afford to be blind *to* such a development (as some 'sceptical materialists' of the old left have been, with due respect to the recent debate in *Marxism Today)* any more than we can afford to be blinded *by* them (as some **'vision - ary idealists'** of the new left have at times been).

A. Some definitions

We begin with some minimal definitions. The term, 'Youth Culture', directs us to the 'cultural' aspects of youth. We understand the word 'culture' to refer to that level at which social groups develop distinct patterns of life, and give *expressive form* to their social and material life-experience. Culture is the way, the forms, in which groups 'handle' the raw material of their social and material existence. "We must suppose the raw material of life experience to be at one pole, and all the infinitely complex human disciplines and systems, articulate and inarticulate, formalised in institutions or dispersed in the least formal ways, which 'handle', transmit or distort this raw material, to be at the other" (Thompson, 1960). 'Culture' is the practice which realises or *objectivates* group-life in meaningful shape and form. "As individuals express their life, so they are. What they are, therefore, coincides with their production, both with *what* they produce and with *how* they produce" (Marx, 1970: 42). The 'culture' of a group or class is the peculiar and distinctive 'way of life' of the group or class, the meanings, values and ideas embodied in institutions, in social relations, in systems of beliefs, in mores and customs, in the uses of objects and material life. Culture is the distinctive shapes in which this material and social organisation of life expresses itself. A culture includes the 'maps of meaning' which make things intelligible to its members. These 'maps of meaning' are not simply carried around in the head: they are objectivated in the patterns of social organisation and relationship through which the individual becomes

10

a 'social individual'. Culture is the way the social relations
of a group are structured and shaped: but it is also the way
those shapes are experienced, understood and interpreted.

A social individual, born into a particular set of institutions
and relations, is at the same moment born into a peculiar configuration of meanings, which give her access to and locate her
within 'a culture'. The 'law of society' and the 'law of culture'
(the symbolic ordering of social life) are one and the same.
These structures - of social relationship and of meaning - shape
the on-going collective existence of groups. But they also limit,
modify and *constrain* how groups live and reproduce their social
existence. Men and women are, thus, formed, and form themselves
through society, culture and history. So the existing cultural
patterns form a sort of historical reservoir - a pre-constituted
'field of the possibles' - which groups take up, transform,
develop. Each group makes something of its starting conditions -
and through this 'making', through this practice, culture is
reproduced and transmitted. But this practice only takes place
within the given field of possibilities and constraints (See,
Sartre, 1963). "Men make their own history, but they do not make
it just as they please; they do not make it under circumstances
chosen by themselves, but under circumstances directly encountered,
given and transmitted from the past" (Marx, 1951: 225). Culture,
then, embodies the trajectory of group life through history:
always under conditions and with 'raw materials' which cannot
wholly be of its own making.

Groups which exist within the same society and share some of
the same material and historical conditions no doubt also understand, and to a certain extent share each others' 'culture'.
But just as different groups and classes are unequally ranked in
relation to one another, in terms of their productive relations,
wealth and power, so *cultures* are differently ranked, and stand
in opposition to one another, in relations of domination and
subordination, along the scale of 'cultural power'. The
definitions of the world, the 'maps of meaning' which express
the life situation of those groups which hold the monopoly of
power in society, command the greatest weight and influence,
secrete the greatest legitimacy. The world tends to be
classified out and ordered in terms and through structures
which most directly express the power, the position, the *hegemony*,
of the powerful interest in that society. Thus,

> The class which has the means of material production at its
> disposal, has control, at the same time, over the means of mental
> production, so that, thereby, generally speaking, the ideas of
> those who lack the means of mental production are subject to it
> ... Insofar as they rule as a class and determine the extent and
> compass of an epoch ... they do this in its whole range, hence,
> among other things rule also as thinkers, as producers of ideas,

and regulate the production and distribution of the ideas of
their age: thus their ideas are the ruling ideas of the epoch.

(Marx, 1970: 64)

This does not mean that there is only *one* set of ideas or cultural
forms in a society.   There will be more than one tendency at work
within the dominant ideas of a society.   Groups or classes which
do not stand at the apex of power, nevertheless find ways of
expressing and realising in their culture their subordinate
position and experiences.   In so far as there is more than one
fundamental class in a society (and capitalism is essentially the
bringing together, around production, of two fundamentally
different classes - capital and labour) there will be more than
one major cultural configuration in play at a particular historical
moment.   But the structures and meanings which most adequately
reflect the position and interests of the most powerful class
- however complex it is internally - will stand, in relation to
all the others, as a *dominant* social-cultural order.   The
dominant culture represents itself as *the* culture.   It tries to
define and contain all other cultures within its inclusive range.
Its views of the world, unless challenged, will stand as the most
natural, all-embracing, universal culture.   Other cultural
configurations will not only be subordinate to this dominant
order: they will enter into struggle with it, seek to modify,
negotiate, resist or even overthrow its reign - its *hegemony*.
The struggle between classes over material and social life thus
always assumes the forms of a continuous struggle over the distribution of 'cultural power'.   We might want, here, to make a
distinction between 'culture' and 'ideology'.   Dominant and
subordinate classes will each have distinct cultures.   But when
one culture gains ascendancy over the other, and when the subordinate culture *experiences* itself in terms prescribed by the
dominant culture, then the dominant culture has also become the
basis of a dominant ideology.

   The dominant culture of a complex society is never a homogen-
eous structure.   It is layered, reflecting different interests
within the dominant class (e.g. an aristocratic versus a bourgeois
outlook), containing different traces from the past (e.g. religious ideas within a largely secular culture), as well as emergent
elements in the present.   Subordinate cultures will not always
be in open conflict with it.   They may, for long periods, coexist
with it, negotiate the spaces and gaps in it, make inroads into
it, "warrenning it from within" (Thompson, 1965).   However,
though the nature of this struggle over culture can never be
reduced to a simple opposition, it is crucial to replace the
notion of 'culture' with the more concrete, historical concept
of 'cultures'; a redefinition which brings out more clearly the
fact that cultures always stand in relations of domination - and
subordination - to one another, are always, in some sense, in

struggle with one another.   The singular term, 'culture', can only indicate, in the most general and abstract way, the large cultural configuratións at play in a society at any historical moment.   We must move at once to the determining relationships of domination and subordination in which these configurations stand; to the processes of incorporation and resistance which define the cultural dialectic between them; and to the institutions which transmit and reproduce 'the culture' (i.e. the dominant culture) in its dominant or 'hegemonic' form.

In modern societies, the most fundamental groups are the social classes, and the major cultural configurations will be, in a fundamental though often mediated way, 'class cultures'. Relative to these cultural-class configurations, *sub*-cultures are sub-sets - smaller, more localised and differentiated structures, within one or other of the larger cultural networks.   We must, first, see sub-cultures in terms of their relation to the wider class-cultural networks of which they form a distinctive part. When we examine this relationship between a sub-culture and the 'culture' of which it is a part, we call the latter the 'parent' culture.   This must not be confused with the particular relationship between 'youth' and their 'parents', of which much will be said below.   What we mean is that a sub-culture, though differing in important ways - in its 'focal concerns', its peculiar shapes and activities - from the culture from which it derives, will also share some things in common with that 'parent' culture. The bohemian sub-culture of the *avant-garde* which has arisen from time to time in the modern city, is both distinct from its 'parent' culture (the urban culture of the middle class intelligentsia) and yet also a part of it (sharing with it a modernising outlook, standards of education, a privileged position vis-a-vis productive labour, and so on).   In the same way, the 'search for pleasure and excitement' which some analysts have noted as a marked feature of the 'delinquent sub-culture of the gang' in the working class, also shares something basic and fundamental with it.   Sub-cultures, then, must first be related to the 'parent cultures' of which they are a sub-set.   But, sub-cultures must *also* be analysed in terms of their relation to the dominant culture - the overall disposition of cultural power in the society as a whole.   Thus, we may distinguish respectable, 'rough', delinquent and the criminal sub-cultures *within* working class culture: but we may also say that, though they differ amongst themselves, they *all* derive in the first instance from a 'working class parent culture': hence, they are all subordinate sub-cultures, in relation to the dominant middle-class or bourgeois culture.   (We believe this goes some way towards meeting Graham Murdock's call for a more "symmetrical" analysis of sub-cultures.   See his article below.)

Sub-cultures must exhibit a distinctive enough shape and structure to make them identifiably different from their 'parent' culture.

13

They must be focussed around certain activities, values, certain uses of material artefacts, territorial spaces etc. which significantly differentiate them from the wider culture. But, since they are sub-sets, there must also be significant things which bind and articulate them with the 'parent' culture. The famous Kray twins, for example, belonged both to a highly differentiated 'criminal sub-culture' in East London and to the 'normal' life and culture of the East End working class (of which indeed, the 'criminal sub-culture' has always been a clearly identifiable part). The behaviour of the Krays in terms of the criminal fraternity marks the differentiating axis of that sub-culture: the relation of the Krays to their mother, family, home and local pub is the binding, the articulating axis. (Pearson, 1973; Hebdige, 1974).

Sub-cultures, therefore, take shape around the distinctive activities and 'focal concerns' of groups. They can be loosely or tightly bounded. Some sub-cultures are merely loosely-defined strands or 'milieux' within the parent culture: they possess no distinctive 'world' of their own. Others develop a clear, coherent identity and structure. Generally, we deal in this volume *only* with 'sub-cultures' (whether drawn from a middle or working class 'parent culture') which have reasonably tight boundaries, distinctive shapes, which have cohered around partic-ular activities, focal concerns and territorial spaces. When these tightly-defined groups are also distinguished by age and generation, we call them 'youth sub-cultures'.

'Youth sub-cultures' form up on the terrain of social and cultural life. Some youth sub-cultures are regular and persistent features of the 'parent' class-culture: the ill-famed 'culture of delinquency' of the working-class adolescent male, for example. But some sub-cultures appear only at particular historical moments: they become visible, are identified and labelled (either by themselves or by others): they command the stage of public attention for a time: then they fade, disappear or are so widely diffused that they lose their distinctiveness. It is the *latter* kind of sub-cultural formation which primarily concerns us here. The peculiar dress, style, focal concerns, milieux, etc. of the Teddy Boy, the Mod, the Rocker or the Skin-head set them off, as distinctive groupings, both from the broad patterns of working-class culture as a whole, and also from the more diffused patterns exhibited by 'ordinary' working class boys (and, to a more limited extent, girls). Yet, despite these differences, it is important to stress that, as sub-cultures, they continue to exist within, and coexist with, the more inclus-ive culture of the class from which they spring. Members of a sub-culture may walk, talk, act, look 'different' from their parents and from some of their peers: but they belong to the same families, go to the same schools, work at much the same jobs, live down the same 'mean streets' as their peers and parents. In

[handwritten margin note:] eg Mod T. Boy Skinhea

14

certain crucial respects, they share the same position (vis-a-vis
the dominant culture), the same fundamental and determining life-
experiences, as the 'parent' culture from which they derive.
Through dress, activities, leisure pursuits and life-style, they
may project a different cultural response or 'solution' to the
problems posed for them by their material and social class
position and experience.   But the membership of a sub-culture
cannot protect them from the determining matrix of experiences
and conditions which shape the life of their class as a whole.
They experience and respond to the *same basic problematic* as
other members of their class who are not so differentiated and
distinctive in a 'sub-cultural' sense.   Especially in relation
to the *dominant* culture, their sub-culture remains like other
elements in their class culture - subordinate and subordinated.

   In what follows, we shall try to show why this *double
articulation* of youth sub-cultures - first, to their 'parent'
culture (e.g. working class culture), second, to the dominant
culture - is a necessary way of staging the analysis.   For our
purposes, sub-cultures represent a necessary, 'relatively
autonomous', but *inter-mediary* level of analysis.   Any attempt
to relate sub-cultures to the 'socio-cultural formation as a
whole' must grasp its complex unity by way of these necessary
differentiations.

   'Youth Culture', in the singular and with capital letters, is
a term we borrow from and refer to in our analysis, but which we
cannot and do not *use* in any but a descriptive sense.   It is,
of course, precisely the term most common in popular and journalistic usage.   It is how the 'phenomenon of Youth' in the post-war
period has been most common-sensically appropriated.   It appears
to be a simple and common starting point, a simple concept.
Actually, it presupposes already extremely complex relations.
Indeed, what it disguises and represses - differences between
different strata of youth, the class-basis of youth cultures, the
relation of 'Youth Culture' to the parent culture and the dominant
culture, etc. - is more significant than what it reveals.   The
term is premised on the view that what happened to 'youth' in
this period is radically and qualitatively different from anything
that had happened before.   It suggests that all the things which
youth got into in this period were more significant than the
different kinds of youth groups, or the differences in their
social class composition.   It sustains certain ideological
interpretations - e.g. that age and generation mattered most, or
that Youth Culture was 'incipiently classless' - even, that 'youth'
had itself become a class.   Thus it identified 'Youth Culture'
exclusively with its most phenomenal aspect - its music, styles,
leisure consumption.   Of course, post-war youth did engage in
distinctive cultural pursuits, and this was closely linked with
the expansion of the leisure and fashion industries, directed at
the 'teenage market'.   But the term 'Youth Culture' confuses

15

and identifies the two aspects, whereas what is needed is a
detailed picture of how youth groups fed off and appropriated
things provided by the market, and, in turn, how the market tried
to expropriate and incorporate things produced by the sub-cultures:
in other words, the dialectic between youth and the youth market
industry. The term 'Youth Culture' appropriates the situation
of the young almost exclusively in terms of the commercial and
publicity manipulation and exploitation of the young. As a
concept, it has little or no explanatory power. We must try to
get behind this market phenomenon, to its deeper social, economic
and cultural roots. In short, our aim is to de-throne or
de-construct the term, 'Youth Culture', in favour of a more complex
set of categories. (Part of this demolition work is done in the
article on Style, below.)

We shall try, first, to replace the concept of 'Youth Culture'
with the more structural concept of 'sub-culture'. We then want
to reconstruct 'sub-cultures' in terms of their relation, first,
to 'parent' cultures, and, through that, to the dominant culture,
or better, to the struggle between dominant and subordinate
cultures. By trying to set up these intermediary levels in
place of the immediate catch-all idea of 'Youth Culture', we try
to show how youth sub-cultures are related to class relations,
to the division of labour and to the productive relations of the
society, without destroying what is specific to their content and
position.

It is essential to bear in mind that the topic treated here
relates only to those sections of working-class or middle-class
youth where a response to their situation took a distinctive
sub-cultural form. This must in no way be confused with an
attempt to delineate the social and historical position of
working-class youth as a whole in the period. The great majority
of working-class youth never enters a tight or coherent sub-
culture at all. Individuals may, in their personal life-careers,
move into and out of one, or indeed several, such sub-cultures.
Their relation to the existing sub-cultures may be fleeting or
permanent, marginal or central. The sub-cultures are important
because there the response of youth takes a peculiarly tangible
form. But, in the post-war history of the class, these may be
less significant than what most young people do most of the time.
The relation between the 'everyday life' and the 'sub-cultural
life' of different sections of youth is an important question in
its own right, and must not be subsumed under the more limited
topic which we address here. As Howard Parker reminds us, even
the 'persistent offenders' of the delinquent sub-cultures are
only occasionally preoccupied with illegal or delinquent behaviour
(Parker, 1974). For the majority, school and work are more
structurally significant - even at the level of consciousness -
than style and music (see Graham Murdock's article, below).

16

As Paul Corrigan eloquently testifies, most young working-class boys are principally concerned most of the time with the biggest occupation of all - how to pass the time: the 'dialectics of doing nothing' (see Corrigan's 'Doing Nothing' piece, below).

B. Youth: metaphor for social change

We propose, in this section, to move from the most phenomenal aspects of youth sub-cultures to the deeper meanings, in three stages. We deal, first, with the most immediate aspect - the qualitative *novelty* of Youth Culture. Then, with the most *visible* aspects of social change which were variously held to be responsible for its emergence. Finally, we look at the *wider debate,* to which the debate about Youth Culture was an important, though subsidiary appendage.

We have said that an important element of the concept, 'Youth Culture', was its post-war novelty. The following quotation from Roberts reminds us to be cautious on this account; it could almost be read as referring to any of the distinctive post-war youth culture formations, though what it describes is in fact an Edwardian youth in 'the classic slum':

> The groups of young men and youths who gathered at the end of most slum streets on fine evenings earned the condemnation of all respectable citizens. They were damned every summer by city magistrates and increasingly harried by the police. In the late nineteenth century the Northern Scuttler and his "moll" had achieved a notoriety as widespread as that of any gang in modern times. He had his own style of dress - the union shirt, bell-bottomed trousers, the heavy leather belt, pricked out in fancy designs with the large steel buckle and the thick, iron-shod clogs. His girl-friend commonly wore clogs and shawl and a skirt with vertical stripes.
>
> (Roberts, 1971: 123)

It is vital, in any analysis of contemporary phenomena, to think historically; many of the short-comings in the 'youth' area are due, in part at least, to an absent or foreshortened historical dimension. In the specific area of 'Youth Culture' this historical myopia is perhaps only to be expected, for few historical studies, specifically comparing the post-war situation of youth with their situation in previous periods as yet exist (there is, of course, a growing interest in the social history of childhood and youth, and in leisure and the school, influenced by a social history perspective. Phil Cohen and Dave Robbins' forthcoming volume on sub-cultures will have a strong historical and comparative framework). The Roberts quotation clearly points to this thread of historical continuity which we cannot afford to overlook.

17

On the other hand, there is, also, much evidence to suggest
that there *were* distinctively new historical features in the
1950's which should make us wary of the opposite fault: the
tendency to adopt a static or circular view of history and so
rob the post-war period of its historical specificity. The
significance of the many visible structural and cultural changes
of the post-war period were weighted differently by commentators
and analysts at the time: but, in most calculations, the emergent
'Youth Culture' figured prominently. It was, according to
emphasis, one *product* of these changes, their *epitome,* or, most
sinisterly, a *portent* of future changes. But, whatever the
emphasis, Youth Culture, or aspects of it, was centrally
linked to how these changes were interpreted.

One important set of inter-related changes hinged around
'affluence', the increased importance of the market and consumption, and the growth of the 'Youth-oriented' leisure industries.
The most distinctive product of these changes was the arrival of
Mark Abrams's 'teenage consumer'; relatively speaking, Abrams
saw 'teenagers' as the prime beneficiaries of the new affluence:

> ..... as compared with 1938, their *real* earnings (i.e. after
> allowing for the fall in value of money) have increased by 50%
> (which is double the rate of expansion for adults), and their
> real 'discretionary' spending has probably risen by 100%
> (Abrams, 1959: 9)

It was but a short step from here to the view that teenagers'
collective habits of consumption constituted "distinctive
teenage spending for distinctive teenage ends in a distinctive
teenage world" (Abrams, 1959: 10); in other words, the economic
basis for a unique, self-contained, self-generating Youth Culture.

The second nexus of changes with which Youth Culture came
readily to be identified, as one unfortunate by-product, were
those surrounding the arrival of *mass* communications, *mass*
entertainment, *mass* art and *mass culture.*

Central to this notion was the idea that more and more people
were being submitted (and the passivity implied was not accidental) to ever-more uniform cultural processes. This was the
result of the spread in mass consumption, plus the 'political
enfranchisement' of the masses, and (above all) the growth in
mass communications. The spread of mass communications was
identified with the growth of the press, radio, television,
mass publishing (and not with computers, internal TV and video-
systems, data banks, information storage and retrieval, etc. -
the commercial and managerial 'uses' which provided the real
infrastructure of the 'communications revolution'). For those
interpreting social change within the framework of what came to
be called the 'mass society thesis', the birth of commercial
television in Britain in the mid 1950's was a watershed event.

18

Youth Culture was connected with this set of changes in two ways. Firstly, and most simply, the creation of a truly mass culture meant the arrival of the means of 'imitation' and 'manipulation' on a national scale. The notion that Youth Culture was a result of such 'mindless' imitation by teenagers, fostered by shrewd and 'manipulating' commercial interests, is captured indelibly by the following quotation from Paul Johnson, probably the least perceptive commentator on Youth, in a field distinctive for its bottomless mediocrity:

> Both T.V. channels now run weekly programmes in which popular records are played to teenagers and judged. While the music is performed, the cameras linger savagely over the faces of the audience. What a bottomless chasm of vacuity they reveal. Huge faces, bloated with cheap confectionery and smeared with chain-store make-up, the open, sagging mouths and glazed eyes, the hands mindlessly drumming in time to the music, the broken stiletto heels, the shoddy, stereotyped, 'with-it' clothes: here, apparently, is a collective portrait of a generation enslaved by a commercial machine.
> (Johnson, 1964)

Secondly, and more sophisticatedly, some aspects of the new Youth Culture were seen, portentously, as representing the worst effects of the new 'mass culture' - its tendency to 'unbend the springs' of working class action and resistance. Hoggart, in so many respects our most sensitive recorder of the experiential nuances of working-class culture, has to be counted among the offenders here; for his portrait of the "juke-box boys ..... who spend their evenings listening in harshly lighted milk-bars to the nickelodeons" (Hoggart, 1958: 247) could almost - in its lack of concreteness and 'felt' qualities - have been written by one of the new 'hack' writers he so perceptively analyses:

> The hedonistic but passive barbarian who rides in a fifty-horse-power bus for threepence, to see a five-million-dollar film for one-and-eight-pence, is not simply a social oddity; he is a portent.   (Hoggart, 1958: 250)

The third set of changes which were said to have 'produced' a qualitatively-distinct Youth Culture turned around a hiatus in social experience precipitated by the war. Generally, the argument maintained that the disruptive effects of the war on children born during that period - absent fathers, evacuation and other breaks in normal family life, as well as the constant violence - was responsible for the 'new' juvenile delinquency of the mid 50's, typified by the Teds, which was itself seen as a precursor of a more general tendency towards violence in Youth Culture. Fyvel, for example, whilst not restricting himself to this 'war' explanation, nevertheless does see the Teddy Boys as "Children of an age of violence, born during a world war ...." (Fyvel: 1963, Preface); whilst Nuttall, more simply, identifies

the single fact of the dropping of the first atomic bomb as
responsible for the qualitative difference between the pre-
and post-war generations:

> right ... at the point of dropping bombs on Hiroshima and Nagasaki
> the generations became divided in a very crucial way ... The
> people who had not yet reached puberty ... were incapable of
> conceiving of life with a future ... the so-called 'generation
> gap' started then and has been increasing ever since.
>
> (Nuttall, 1970: 20)

Today

The fourth set of changes which provided an important context
for the 'emergence' of Youth Culture related to the sphere of
education.   This interpretation pin-pointed *two* developments
above all - 'secondary education for all' in age-specific schools,
and the massive extension of higher education.   Many things
were cited as providing the impetus here: the 1944 Education Act
itself, which instituted the primary/secondary division for all;
the expanded 'pool of talent' consequent upon both this reorganisation and the post-war 'bulge';   the meritocratic ideology of
social mobility primarily through the education system;   the
attempts to make a positive correlation between the country's
economic growth-rate and its number of highly-trained personnel;
the increased demand in the economy for technicians and technol-
ogists.   But, for our purposes, the effect was singular.
Quite simply, the increasing number of young people spending an
increasing proportion of their youth in age-specific educational
institutions from the age of eleven onwards - a quite different
situation from the pre-war period when almost half the post-
eleven year olds were still receiving 'secondary' education in
all-age elementary schools - was seen, by some commentators, to be
creating the pre-conditions for the emergence of a specifically
'adolescent society'.   Coleman made the point most explicitly
with his argument that an American high school pupil:

> ... is 'cut off' from the rest of society, forced inwards towards
> his own age group.   With his fellows, he comes to constitute
> a small society, one that has its most important interactions
> *within* itself, and maintains only a few threads of connections
> with the outside adult society.
>
> (Coleman, 1961: 3)

Last, but by no means least, the arrival of the whole range of
distinctive styles in dress and rock-music cemented any doubts
anyone may have had about a 'unique' younger generation.   Here,
as elsewhere, the specifics of the styles and music, in terms of
who was wearing or listening to what, and why, were crucially
overlooked in face of the new stylistic invasion - the image,
depicted weekly in the new 'teenage' television shows as a
'whole scene going'.   Depending on how you viewed this pop-
cultural explosion, either the barbarians were at the gates, or
the turn of the rebel hipster had come at last.   Again, Jeff
Nuttall provides us with the most extravagant and indulgent
example:

> The teddy boys were waiting for Elvis Presley. Everybody
> under twenty all over the world was waiting. He was the super
> salesman of mass distribution-hip ... he was a public butch
> god with the insolence of a Genet murderer ... Most of all he
> was unvarnished sex taken and set way out in the open ... The
> Presley riots were the first spontaneous gatherings of the
> community of the new sensibilities .....
>
> (Nuttall, 1970: 29-30)

These explanations for the appearance of a distinct Youth
Culture emerged out of a much wider debate about the whole nature
of post-war social change. The key terms in this debate were,
of course, 'affluence', 'consensus' and 'embourgeoisement'.
Affluence referred, essentially, to the boom in working class
consumer spending (though it entailed the further, less tenable,
proposition that the working classes not only had more to spend,
but were *relatively* better off). 'Consensus' meant the acceptance by both political parties, and the majority of the electorate, of all the measures - mixed economy, increased incomes,
welfare-state 'safety net' - taken after 1945 to draw people of
all classes together, on the basis of a common stake in the system.
It also entailed the proposition that a broad consensus of views
on all the major issues had developed, including all classes;
and hence the end of major political and social conflicts,
especially those which exhibited a clear class pattern.
'Embourgeoisement' gathered all these, and other social trends
(in education, housing, redevelopment, the move to new towns and
estates, etc.), together with the thesis that working-class life
and culture was ceasing to be a distinct formation in the society,
and everyone was assimilating rapidly towards middle class patterns, aspirations and values. These terms came to be woven
together into an all-embracing social myth or 'explanation' of
post-war social change. Stated simply, the conventional wisdom
was that 'affluence' and 'consensus' together were promoting the
rapid 'bourgeoisification' of the working classes. This was
producing new social types, new social arrangements and values.
One such type was the 'affluent worker' - the "new type of
bourgeois worker", family minded, home-centred, security-
conscious, instrumentally-oriented, geographically mobile and
acquisitive-celebrated in, for example, Zweig's work (Zweig,
1961). Another was the new 'teenager' with his commitment to
style, music, leisure and consumption: to a 'classless youth
culture'.

Thus, for both parents and their children, *class* was seen,
if at all, as being gradually, but inexorably, eroded as society's
major structuring and dynamic factor. Other elements were seen
to be replacing it as the basis of social stratification: status,
a **multiply-differentiated** 'pecking'order' based on a complex
of educational, employment and consumption-achievements; .educa-
tion, the new universally available and meritocratic route by

21

which status, through job success, could be achieved; consumption, the new 'affluence' route through which status, on the 'never-never', could be bought by those failing the meritocratic educational hurdle; and age, above all age. Everything that was said and thought about working class adults was raised to a new level with respect to the working-class young. Born during the war, they were seen as having least experience of and commitment to pre-war social patterns. Because of their age, they were direct beneficiaries of the welfare state and new educational opportunities; least constrained by older patterns of, or attitudes to, spending and consumption; most involved in a guilt-free commitment to pleasure and immediate satisfactions. Older people were, as it were, half-way between the old and the new world. But 'youth' was wholly and exclusively in and of the new post-war world. And what, principally, made the difference was, precisely, their *age*. Generation defined them as the group most in the forefront of every aspect of social change in the post-war period. Youth was 'the vanguard' of social change. Thus, the simple fact of when you were born displaced the more traditional category of class as a more potent index of social position; and the pre-war chasm between the classes was translated into a mere 'gap' between the generations. Some commentators further compounded this myth by reconstituting class on the basis of the new gap: youth *was* a 'new class' (see, for example: Musgrove, 1968; Rowntree and Rowntree, 1968; Neville, 1971).

Yet the whole debate depended crucially on the validity of the three central concepts we started out with – affluence, consensus and embourgeoisement; and here we must begin the task of disentangling the real from the constructed or ideological elements contained in these terms.

In general terms, the reality of post-war improvements in living standards – the real element in 'affluence' – cannot be questioned. The years 1951-64 undoubtedly saw what Pinto-Duschinsky calls, "a steadier and much faster increase $\sqrt{\text{in the}}$ average standard of living$\overline{/}$ than at any other time in this century"; using "any major indicator of performance, the 1950's and the early 1960's were a great improvement on the years between the wars and on the showing of the Edwardian period" (Pinto-Duschinsky, 1970: 56-57). However, this general rise in living standards critically *obscured* the fact that the *relative* positions of the classes had remained virtually unchanged. It was this mythical aspect of affluence, concealed under the persistent and insistent 'never had it so good' ideology, which gradually emerged when poverty – and not just pockets of it – was rediscovered, from the early 1960's onwards.

The massive spending on consumer durables obscured the fact "that Britain lagged behind almost all her main industrial competitors and that she failed to solve the problem of sterling" (Pinto-Duschinsky, 1970: 58; see also Glyn and Sutcliffe, 1972). In fact, Britain's affluent 'miracle' was *constructed* on very shaky economic foundations, "upon temporary and fortuitous circumstances" (Bogdanor and Skidelsky, eds., 1970: 8), on a 'miraculous' historical conjuncture. The Tory policy of "Bread and Circuses" - i.e. "the sacrifice of policies desirable for the long term well-being of a country in favour of over-lenient measures and temporary palliatives bringing in immediate political return" (Pinto-Duschinsky, 1970: 59) or, more succinctly, the promotion of private consumption at the expense of the public sector - was only *one possible response* to this situation, not an *inevitable* outcome.

Consensus, too, in general terms, had a real basis. The war period with its cross-class mobilisations, economic planning, political coalitions and enforced egalitarianism provided a base on which the social reforms of the post-war Labour government could be mounted; and both the war and the post-war reforms provided something of a platform for consensus. Even the old free-market figure, Churchill, returned to power in 1951, had, in his own words, "come to know the nation and what must be done to retain power" (Moran, 1968: 517). In other words, Churchill, and the more astute of the Tory leadership, had come to realise that the success of their 'freedom from controls' anti-austerity programme was crucially predicated upon a 'reformed' capitalism, a socially-mindful capitalism with a 'human face'. Their electoral 'clothes stolen', and "haunted by a composite image of the potential Labour voter as quintessen-tially *petit-bourgeois,* and therefore liable to be frightened off by a radical alternative to Conservatism" (Miliband, 1961: 339), the Labour leadership lost its nerve, and capitulated to 'the consensus'. Official party politics were dominated in the 1950's by "the politics of the centre", whilst "the most vigorous political debates of the 1950's and 1960's were conducted indepen-dently of the party battle" (Pinto Duschinsky, 1970: 73, 74).

However, whilst political consensus (or stalemate) was the overriding feature of the 1950's and early 1960's, the fragility of this consensus was revealed "in the nature of the party struggle" during these years. Despite "the ultimate success of the Tories in retaining office for thirteen years, the political battle was desperately close throughout the whole period" (ibid: 69). In other words, the notion of a political consensus obscu-res the fact that the Conservative survival was predicated con-stantly on the most short-term expediency imaginable (e.g. the 'give-away' inflationary budget.of April, 1955, was followed by a snap April election, which was in turn followed by the deflat-

23

ionary Autumn 'cuts', and the stagnation of 1956). For the
whole thirteen years of Tory rule, despite this vote-catching
'politics of bribery', practically half the electorate voted
against the Tories at each election.   Taken together with the
finding by Goldthorpe and his colleagues, that "the large majority
/of the affluent workers in their study/ were, and generally had
been Labour supporters" (1969: 172), echoing other sociological
enquiries - it is quite possible to read 'consensus' in a
different way: as betokening a waiting attitude by the British
working class (often mistaken at the time for 'apathy') which an
effective lead to the left by Labour at any point in the period
might effectively have crystallised in a different direction
(Goldthorpe et al. themselves make this argument: see, 1969:
190-5).

'Embourgeoisement', the third and final term in our sociological
trinity, was the product of the other two.   As such, it was the
most constructed term of the three, since the frailties of the
other two terms were compounded in it.   Even so, the 'embourgeoisement' notion, too, had some real basis, as even its critics
insisted:

> Our own research indicates clearly enough how increasing
> affluence and its correlates can have many far-reaching
> consequences - both in undermining the viability or desirability
> of established life-styles and in encouraging or requiring the
> development of new patterns of attitudes, behaviour and relation-
> ships.
>
> (Goldthorpe et. al, 1969: 163)

Yet the overriding conclusion of the Cambridge team's research,
which submitted Zweig's "new bourgeois worker" to sociological
scrutiny, only confirmed what their earlier paper had suggested
(Goldthorpe and Lockwood, 1963):

> what the changes in question predominantly entailed was not the
> ultimate *assimilation* of manual workers and their families into
> the social world of the middle class, but rather a much less
> dramatic process of convergence, in certain particular respects,
> in the normative orientations of some sections of the working
> class and of some white-collar groups
>
> (Goldthorpe et. al. 1969: 26)

In other words, 'embourgeoisement', if it meant anything at
all, referred to something very different, and far more limited
in scope, than anything which its more vigorous proponents, such
as Zweig, envisaged.   Even at the time, some of the political
extrapolations made on the basis of the thesis seemed far-fetched,
ideological rather than empirical in character (e.g. Abrams, 1969).
Indeed, looking back at the 'instrumental collectivism' of
Goldthorpe and Lockwood's 'affluent worker' from the perspective
of the later 1960's and 1970's; at the strike-prone nature of the

motor industry, and the 'leadership' which this sector of labour displayed in sustained wage militancy and militant shop-floor organisation, the whole 'embourgeoisement' thesis looks extremely thin and shaky, at least in the terms in which it was currently discussed at the time. (There is something to be said for the view that no student should read the account of the 'affluent worker' at the Vauxhall plant at Luton without setting it cheek by jowl with the experience of the Halewood plant near Liverpool, so graphically described by Huw Beynon, 1973.)

In sum, despite some significant real shifts in attitudes and living patterns, considerably overlaid by the sustained ideological onslaught of 'affluence', what comes through most strongly is the stubborn *refusal of class* - that tired, 'worn-out' category - *to disappear* as a major dimension and dynamic of the social structure.

C. The reappearance of class

The various interpretations of post-war change, enshrined in the holy trinity of affluence, consensus and embourgeoisement, rested on a singular social myth - that the working class was disappearing. This postulate of the 'withering away of class' was challenged from the late 1950's onwards along two main dimensions.

Firstly, there was the rediscovery of poverty and the existence of continual, great inequalities of wealth, opened up by the critiques of the Titmuss Group (Titmuss, 1962), Westergaard (1965) and others. These showed that poverty was a structural not an accidental feature of capitalism, that wealth had been only nominally redistributed and that the main beneficiaries of the Welfare State were, in fact, the middle classes. A very small minority still owned a very large proportion of private wealth; and further, the proportions of national income going to the working and middle classes had remained roughly the same after 1945. A bedmate of the alleged move to equality in wealth - the idea that 'opportunity structures' of society had been thrown open and a new fluid social structure had arisen - was also shown to be an empty promise. Even if relative inequalities between classes had declined, the absolute distribution of life-chances had not. Certainly, changes in the occupational structure had taken place; but, as was again argued, the implications of these changes had been much exaggerated. The number of clerical jobs, for instance, greatly increased, but this was coupled with a decline in the relative status of white collar occupations produced by greater rationalisation and automation. These occupations had been stratified, leading often to a widening of the divisions between clerical 'supervisors' and the clerical

25

'shop-floor'. The increased unionisation and, later, the unexpected militancy of bank clerks, nurses, teachers and local government workers, was one further important development leading in the same direction. At the very least, the recent militancy among such groups suggests that the view that the rise in white collar occupations will lead to a uniform, stable, 'moderate', middle class society is open to question.

Secondly, there was the postulate that power had been diffused via the all-round increase of wealth, the decline in relative inequality, the greater accountability of socially responsible management, and the separation of ownership from managerial control. Allied to this was the thesis that the separation of the sphere of work from the increasingly privatised sphere of home life was leading to a simple 'economic instrumentalism' in worker's attitudes to the unions (devoid of any political content it may have had); indeed, that increasing affluence had led to a permanent pacification of industrial militancy. However, Westergaard, for example, has argued convincingly that, while working class life styles may have changed, the widening of worker's horizons and demands is a potential source of unrest rather than of stability unless the means of fulfilment are given. This is the so-called revolution of rising expectations or what Anderson called "the politics of instrumental collectivism".

Working-class resistance to anti-union and anti-strike legislation in the 1970's, like the sustained demand (through the 1960's into the 1970's) for wages to keep pace with inflation, clearly support this interpretation (though it is important to add that this defensive strategy and wage militancy has, as yet, failed to find clear political expression). In addition, resistance by sections of the working class to the incursions into the localities by property speculators and the redevelopers, and to steadily rising rents, finding its political expression in a community, non-industrial politics rather than in electoral politics and the Labour Party, has also been underplayed, devalued or ignored. Indeed, when the thesis of the 'diffusion of power' is looked at from the perspective, not of the consensual 1950's but of the polarised 1970's, it loses much of its credibility (though the shifts in the patterns of class conflict must not be overlooked). As Westergaard argues:

> ... post-capitalism commentary has been noticeably blind to the sources of actual opposition and latent dissent to the institutions and assumptions of the current social order within the population at large: perennially prone to confuse the institutionalisation of conflict with consensus, and generally incurious about the continuing pressures under which the institutionalisation might loosen, shift or give way. The existence of those pressures should be a constant reminder of the contingent character of the present social structure, and of the limited range of assumptions from which policies conventionally are drawn which envisage little or no basic change in that structure.
>
> (Westergaard, 1974: 38)

26

If we had asked, at the time, 'which social group or category most immediately encapsulates the essential features of these social changes?' we would almost certainly have been given the answer - Youth: the new Youth culture. Even so perceptive an observer as Colin MacInnes could speculate that:

> The 'two nations' of our society may perhaps no longer be those of the 'rich' and the 'poor' (or, to use old fashioned terms, the 'upper' and 'working' classes), but those of the teenagers on the one hand and, on the other, all those who have assumed the burdens of adult responsibility.
>
> (MacInnes, 1961: 56)

Yet, just as the master conceptions of affluence, consensus and embourgeoisement required a more cautious and critical approach, so the evidence upon which the direction and manner of change amongst youth was based requires more detailed analysis and careful interpretation. When we look closely at some of those writers who subscribed to notions such as the generation gap, 'distinctive youth culture', welfare state youth, the 'classlessness' of youth culture, and so on, we find that the evidence they bring forward actually undermines the interpretation of it which they offer. Within the 'classlessness' interpretation, there is often a contradictory stress, precisely upon the class structuring of youth. Perhaps the best example is Abrams's work on "The Teenage Consumer" (quoted previously), which depicts a new, separate culture based on the 'teenage market'. However, if we look more closely, this teenage market is recognised by Abrams himself as having a clear class base. Abrams's 'average teenager' *was* the working class teenager:

> ..... the teenage market is almost entirely working class. Its middle class members are either still at school and college or else only just beginning on their careers: in either case they dispose of much smaller incomes than their working class contemporaries and it is highly probably, therefore, that not far short of 90 per cent of all teenage spending is conditioned by working class taste and values
>
> (Abrams, 1959: 13)

The image of youth often carried with it the threat of 'what could go wrong'. Fyvel explained one problem group - Teddy Boys - predominantly in terms of the dislocation, caused internationally amongst all youth, by the war, increasing materialism, the stress on success, and the influence of the mass media. However his analysis also has a clear class dimension. For instance he says:

> Working-class families are (also) more vulnerable to the socially and psychologically harmful effects of rehousing, as expressed in a break-up of local community life.
>
> (Fyvel, 1963: 213)

27

In fact, Fyvel sees the Teddy Boy as mainly recruited from young unskilled workers whose earnings were too low and irregular for him to take part in the process of embourgeoisement enjoyed by his better-off working class peers (ibid: 122).

It would seem reasonable to assume that the relation between the position of youth (its features and problems) and social class would receive more adequate attention in empirical sociological studies. However in the 1950's and early 1960's there were few such studies, and they largely took as their starting point the rise in delinquency rates. Those that were undertaken were mainly of an 'ecological' nature, focussed on change in working-class neighbourhoods. However the studies by Mays (1954), Morris (1957), Kerr (1958) and others all tended to be concerned with one particular aspect of these class-defined areas - the 'slum culture', and the identification of a number of 'problem families'. Often it was not clear to what degree the rest of the working class held what one writer defined as the values or 'focal concerns' of the slum-violence, excitement, fantasy, etc. (Miller, 1958). More importantly, the class analysis, though now present, was a rather technically-founded 'social' class one, (usually based on the Registrar General's classification) - a static, dehistoricised concept of class. The ecological areas were not sufficiently dynamically placed within the structure of the classes in the city and the class relations in the wider society at the time. Where a wider analysis was outlined it was largely in terms of our old friends, the triumvirate - affluence, consensus and embourgeoisement.

To replace youth within their various class formations does not, as some critics may think, give a simple uni-dimensional explanatory answer to the sub-cultures problem. Indeed explanation becomes more complex and investigation more necessary if the sub-cultures-and-class relationships are explored *without* relying on a global notion of 'the new youth leisure class'. Perhaps the most complex body of theory is the American sub-culture theorisation of the late fifties and early sixties e.g. the work of Albert Cohen (1955), Cloward and Ohlin (1960), and its critique and development in Downes (1966). These writers did indeed try to place delinquent sub-cultures within a larger class framework. Unfortunately, in brief terms, American work envisaged the *individual* youth's class position as one rung on a single status ladder, leading inexorably to middle-class values and goals. The sub-culture problem was then presented as a problem of the disjunction between the (assumed) middle-class *goal* of success and the restricted (working class) *means* for achieving them. A youth group or sub-culture was defined as the result of status-failure, or anxiety because of rejection by middle-class institutions; or as the inability to achieve

28

dominant goals because of blocked opportunities for success.
In short there was an underlying consensual view of society based
on a belief in the American Dream (of success).   'Youth culture'
was a sort of collective compensation for those who could not
succeed.

Significant advances upon sub-cultural theory have recently
been made, especially by Murdock (1973) and Brake (1973).
Following from the traditional theme that sub-cultures arise as
a means of collective "problem solving" they locate youth within
a quite different analysis of class relations from that of
'opportunity structures.'   The major defect in Murdock and
Brake's work is that their central concept - that of "problem"
- is itself taken too unproblematically.   Brake's version of the
formation of sub-culture is neatly summarised in the following
statement:

> Sub-cultures arise (then) as attempts to solve certain problems
> in the social structures, which are created by contradictions
> in the larger society . . . . Youth is not in itself a problem,
> but there are problems created, for example by the conscription
> of the majority of the young into the lower strata of a merito-
> cratic educational system and then allowing them only to take
> up occupations which are meaningless, poorly paid and uncreative.
> Working-class sub-cultures attempt to infuse into this bleak
> world excitement and colour during the short respite between
> school and settling down into marriage and adult-hood.
>   (Brake, 1973: 36)

Murdock's formulation is very similar;

> The attempt to resolve the contradictions contained in the work
> situation through the creation of meaningful styles of leisure,
> typically takes place within the context provided by a sub-culture
> . . . . . Sub-cultures offer a collective solution to the problems
> posed by shared contradictions in the work situation and provide
> a social and symbolic context for the development and reinforcement,
> of collective identity and individual self esteem.
>   (Murdock, 1973: 9)

   Both writers recognise the class basis of youth sub-cultures
but they do not fully work out the implications this has for
the study of youth.   These omissions are due perhaps to the
too-heavy reliance upon the concept of subcultures as "problem
solving".   What we would argue, in general terms, is that the
young inherit a cultural orientation from their parents towards
a 'problematic' common to the class as a whole, which is likely
to weight, shape and signify the meanings they then attach to
different areas of their social life.   In Murdock's and Brake's
work, the situation of the sub-culture's members within an *ongoing*
subordinate culture is ignored in terms of the specific development of the sub-culture.   Thus, a whole dimension of class
socialisation is omitted, and the elements of negotiation and
displacement in the original situated class culture are given
too little weight in the analysis.

The advance made by Murdock and Brake was to reconstruct youth cultures in class terms, thereby dissolving the mythology of a universal youth culture. Also, they stressed the role of style (its appropriation and meaning) in representing youth's class experience. Before turning to our own analysis of youth cultures and class relations we must first discuss the work of Phil Cohen whose suggestive analysis throws light on many of these key points.

D. Subcultures - an imaginary relation

Phil Cohen (1972) also offers a class analysis, but at a much more sophisticated theoretical level, placing the parent culture in a historical perspective, mapping the relations between sub-cultures and exploring the intra-class dynamic between youth and parents. His analysis was based largely on the London East End working-class community, whose strength, he suggested, depended essentially on the mutual articulation of three structures. First, the extended kinship network, which "provides for many functions of mutual aid and support" and "makes for cultural continuity and stability". The kinship system depended, in turn, on the ecological setting - the working class neighbourhood. This dense socio-cultural space "helps to shape and support the close textures of traditional working-class life, its sense of solidarity, its local loyalties and traditions", and thus provides support "with the day to day problems that arise in the constant struggle to survive". Third, there is the structure of the local economy, striking for its diversity as well as for the fact that "people lived and worked in the East End - there was no need for them to go outside in search of jobs". As a result, "the situation of the work place, its issues and interests, remained tied to the situation outside work - the issues and interests of the community".

Cohen, then, in giving a historical context to this portrait of a traditional working class culture, describes the impact of redevelopment and rationalisation on the family, the community and the local economy. Post-war redevelopment and rehousing led to a depopulation of the area, and the break-up of the traditional neighbourhood: this was compounded by speculative development and by a new influx of immigrant labour, producing a further drift of the local work force. The most immediate impact was on the kinship structure - the fragmentation of the traditional 'extended family' and its partial replacement by the more nucleated 'families of marriage'. "This meant that any problems were bottled up within the immediate inter-personal context which produced them; and at the same time the family relationships were invested with a new intensity, to compensate for the diversity of relationships previously generated through neighbours and wider kin ... the working-class family was thus not

only isolated from outside but undermined from within."
(Cohen, 1972: 17).   Redevelopment, in the shape now of the
new East End estates, exacerbated the effects on working-class
family and neighbourhood:

> The first effect of the high-density, high-rise schemes was
> to destroy the function of the street, the local pub, the
> cornershop, as articulations of communal space.   Instead there
> was only the privatised space of the family unit, stacked one on
> top of each other, in total isolation, juxtaposed with the totally
> public space which surrounded it, and which lacked any of the
> informal social controls generated by the neighbourhood.
> (Cohen, 1972: 16)

Alongside this was the drastic reconstruction of the local
economy - the dying of small craft industries, their replacement
by the larger concerns often situated outside the area, the
decline of the family business and the corner shop.   The labour
force was gradually polarised into two groups: the "highly
specialised, skilled and well-paid jobs associated with the new
technology" and "the routine, dead-end, low-paid unskilled jobs
associated with the labour-intensive sections, especially the
service industries".   Cohen argues that the effects of these
changes were most significant for the respectable part of the
East End working class, who found themselves "caught and pulled
apart" by two opposing types of social mobility: upwards into
the ranks of the new suburban working class elite or downwards
into the 'lumpen'.

Perhaps the most significant aspect of this part of Cohen's
analysis is the way in which he picks and redefines certain
key themes in the affluence-consensus-embourgeoisement thesis:
he discards their spectacular and ideological framework, relocates
them within the specific historical relations and situation of
the working class of a particular area, and arrives at a 'thesis',
not about the disappearance or 'embourgeoisement' of a class, but
rather about how wider socio-economic change can fragment,
unhinge and dislocate its intricate mechanisms and defences.
The idea of the 'disappearance of the class as a whole' is
replaced by the far more complex and differentiated picture of
how the different sectors and strata of a class are driven into
different courses and options by their determining socio-
economic circumstances.   This analysis stems from the impact on
the different working-class strata of fundamental economic
forces, but it immediately widens into their social, familial
and cultural consequences.

The changes Cohen discusses had an impact upon *both* the
adult and the young members of the East End working-class community.   Though the response was different according to age, position
in the generational cycle and experience, the basic material and

31

social situation which confronted them - the class problematic -
was the same, for older men and women, for young workers and their
families, and for the working class teenagers.   Cohen traces the
impact of economic and occupational change on the young:

> Looking for opportunities in their father's trades, and lacking
> the qualifications for the new industries, they were relegated
> to jobs as van boys, office boys, packers, ware-housemen, etc.,
> and long spells out of work.   More and more people, young and
> old, have to travel out of the community to their jobs, and some
> eventually moved out to live elsewhere, where suitable work was
> to be found.   The local economy as a whole contracted, and
> became less diverse.
>
> (Cohen, 1972: 18)

He also follows this analysis through to the changed situation of
the young in the family, kinship and neighbourhood situations.

   For Cohen, the working class teenager experienced these
shifts and fragmentations in direct, material, social, economic
and cultural forms.   But they also experienced, and attempted
to 'resolve' them on the ideological plane.   And it is primarily
to this attempted 'ideological solution', that he attributes both
the rise of, and the differentiation between, the different
working class 'youth sub-cultures' of the period:

> The latent function of subculture is this - to express and
> resolve, albeit "magically", the contradictions which remain
> hidden or unresolved in the parent culture.   The succession of
> subcultures which this parent culture generated can thus all be
> considered as so many variations on a central theme - the
> contradiction at an ideological level, between traditional working
> class puritanism, and the new ideology of consumption: at an
> economic level between a part of the socially mobile elite, or
> a part of the new lumpen.   Mods, parkers, skinheads, crombies,
> all represent in their different ways, an attempt to retrieve
> some of the socially cohesive elements destroyed in the parent
> culture, and to combine these with elements selected from other
> class fractions, symbolising one or other of the options confront-
> ing it.
>
> (Cohen, 1972: 23)

   To give one example of how this complex process worked -
Cohen explains the rise of Mods in the following manner:

> ..... the original mod style could be interpreted as an attempt
> to realise, but in an *imaginary relation* the conditions of
> existence of the socially mobile white collar worker.   While
> their *argot* and ritual forms stressed many of the traditional
> values of their parent culture, their dress and music reflected
> the hedonistic image of the affluent consumer.

Cohen's general conclusion is, therefore, that:

> Mods, Parkers, Skinheads, Crombies are a succession of sub-
> cultures which all correspond to the same parent culture and
> which attempt to work out through a series of transformations,
> the basic problematic or contradiction which is inserted in the
> sub-culture by the parent culture. So you can distinguish three
> levels in the analysis of sub-cultures: one is the historical ...
> which isolates the specific problematic of a particular class
> fraction ... secondly ... the sub-systems ... and the actual
> transformations they undergo from one sub-cultural moment to anot-
> her ... thirdly .... the way the sub-culture is actually lived
> out by those who are /its/ bearers and supports.

Cohen's analysis proposes one of the most suggestive interpretations of the relationship between the rise of the sub-cultures
and the fate of a class. It has the merit of placing a social
class formation within a whole historical framework. Its tracing
through of the links between economic and cultural change, the
impact of change on a 'parent' culture, and the response of youth,
is subtle and complex. Certain problems remain unresolved.
The analysis - mainly of the 1950's and early 1960's - needs now
to be extended up to the 1970's. There are problems with
understanding precisely how the impact of certain forces on a
parent culture is filtered through, and differentially experienced
by its youth; and then, how and why this experience is
crystallised into a distinct youth sub-culture. What leads the
Mods to explore an 'upward', the Teds or Skinheads to explore a
'downward' option? How tight is the relation between the *actual*
class composition and situation of those sectors of youth choosing
one or other of these sub-cultural solutions? What accounts
both for the specific sequencing, and the specific forms which
the different sub-cultural formations take? There is also a
question about how 'ideological' youth sub-cultures are understood
as being. In some ways, the most subtle and suggestive parts
of the analysis relate to the way the sub-cultures are shown to
address a common class problematic, yet attempt to resolve by
means of an 'imaginary relation' - i.e. ideologically - the
'real relations' they cannot otherwise transcend. This is a
suggestive proposal - but also one most difficult to test and
refine. The fact that men live, in ideology, an 'imaginary
relation' to the real conditions of their existence is not
something peculiar or limited to sub-cultures. What further
things, then, provoke so highly structured, visible and tightly-
bounded a response? By concentrating on the imaginary,
ideological relation in which sub-cultures stand to the life of a
class, the analysis may now have gone too far in the direction of
reading sub-cultures 'ideologically'. Not enough account is
perhaps taken of the material, economic and social conditions
specific to the 'sub-cultural solution'. Despite these
criticisms, the analysis remains, in our view, one of the most
advanced and sophisticated of available accounts. The proposition
that an 'imaginary relation' lies somewhere near the heart of the
sub-cultures question is a fruitful one which - despite the
problems we find in applying it concretely, we adopt and develop
below.

CLASS & SUBCULTURES: A VERSION OF COHEN'S MODEL

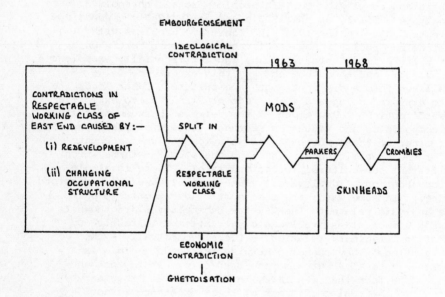

DETERMINATE
CONDITIONS

WORKING CLASS RESPONSES

EMBOURGEOISEMENT

IDEOLOGICAL
CONTRADICTION

1963

1968

CONTRADICTIONS IN
RESPECTABLE
WORKING CLASS OF
EAST END CAUSED BY:—

(i) REDEVELOPMENT

(ii) CHANGING
OCCUPATIONAL
STRUCTURE

SPLIT IN

RESPECTABLE
WORKING
CLASS

MODS

PARKERS

CROMBIES

SKINHEADS

ECONOMIC
CONTRADICTION

GHETTOISATION

E. Dominant and subordinate cultures

The immediate point is to note how *class* has been used by
Cohen to clarify the concept of sub-culture. 'Class' does not
simply *replace* sub-culture in a reductive way. Nor is class
taken as a set of given, 'background', sociological variables.
The relation between class and sub-culture has been placed in a
more dynamic historical framework. The relations *between*
classes, the experience and response to change *within* different
class fractions, is now seen as the *determining* level.
However, the subculture is seen as one specific *kind of response,*
with its own meaning structure - its own "relative autonomy".
Thus, the attempt to think the problem right through to the
level of the social formation as a whole (where class relations
are determining) is done, *not* by repressing but by *retaining*
what is specific about the intermediary concept of 'sub-culture'.
The social formation is not seen as a simple unity (the 'nation,
'the culture'), but as a necessarily complex, differentiated,
antagonistic 'whole'. The further attempt to trace these
general shifts in class relations through to their impact on
particular communities, particular fractions of the class, particular local economies, is a crucial stage of that analysis.

In this section, we discuss briefly some of the broad shifts
in class relations over the period as a whole, before coming
to the specific question of the sub-cultures. This is a necessary
first step, though, by compressing large movements into a short
space, we sacrifice much of what is specific and concrete in
Cohen's analysis of the East End case.

One determining level of change is the way production was
reorganised and modernised in the post-war period; and the impact
of this on the division of labour, on occupational cultures, on
forms of working-class response, defence and resistance. The
war and post-war situation accelerated changes already in train in
the inter-war period. One general result was a widening of the
gap between 'old' and 'new' sectors in the economy - old and new
industries, old and new areas and regions. On the one hand, the
'new' industries, based on modern technical and electronic
processes or tied to the consumer and export drives; on the other
hand, the 'declining' industries, the legacy of the first industrial revolution. The impact of this partial and unplanned
'rationalisation', first on skills and the division of labour,
secondly on the economic life of regions and areas, was profound
but quite "*uneven*". Some areas - the South-East especially -
spurted ahead; others - sometimes whole industries and regions -
were impelled into a long decline. The exact shifts in the
division of labour consequent on this "uneven" development, can't
be charted in detail here - they remain the joker of the much-

shuffled sociological 'pack' of (mainly numerical) representations
of occupational mobility.   Rationalisation certainly introduced
new elements of fragmentation into the labour force.   It also
precipitated a whole 'ideological' debate - North vs. South, the
'cloth cap' vs. the white coat, etc. - which fed straight into
the 'embourgeoisement' thesis, and confused it.   The East End
case, discussed by Cohen, demonstrates its real impact in a
striking way: new economic forces penetrating, in a highly
"uneven" way, into a 'backward' sector and area.   The dockers
caught between the casual labour pool, the state attempts to
'rationalise' and 'modernise' dock work, and the drive for
containerisation is a classic instance of "combined and uneven"
development, biting into a particular locality.

   What matters here is not some general idea of 'social change
and the working-class' but, rather, the particular social and
cultural composition of those sectors of the working-class whose
concrete situation is being restructured by quite specific
economic forces.   Here, changes in the economic mode of
production register on a particular complex of\trades, skills,
workshops, a particular 'mix' of occupational cultures, the
specific distribution of different class strata within them.
The wider economic forces then *throw out of gear* a particular
working-class complex: they dismantle a set of particular
internal balances and stabilities.   They reshape and restructure
the productive basis, which forms the material and social
conditions of life, the 'givens', around which a particular local
working-class culture has developed.   They disturb a particular
historical network of defences and 'negotiations' (again, the
complex history of the formation of the 'East End' is an excell-
ent example).

   These productive relations also form the basis of the
everyday life and culture of the class.   Changes in housing and
in the ecology of the working-class neighbourhood are part of the
same pattern; and the different facets of change react on and
reverberate through each other.   The impact of post-war
redevelopment on traditional working-class neighbourhoods seems
in general to go through three broad phases.   First, the break-up
of traditional housing patterns by post-war re-housing: the new
housing estates and new towns.   The areas left behind decay;
they drift downwards towards the 'urban ghetto' or 'new slum'
pattern, the prey of rack-renting, speculative landlordism and
multiple occupation.   The drift inwards of immigrant labour
highlights and compounds the ghettoising process.   Then some
parts of the ghettoes are selectively redeveloped, through the
combination of planning and speculative property development.
The entry of middle class families 'up-classes' certain neighbourhoods, and "planned development" (the East End scheme is, again,
a classic instance here) redefines the area towards this more
'up-graded', middle-income pattern of life.   Again, these are

not simply forces working abstractly *on* an area.   They
graphically reconstruct the *real* material and social conditions
in which working people live.

   The forces restructuring the working-class neighbourhood
and local economy also had a decisive impact on the structure
of the family.   Those pushed upwards and away in occupational
terms were often also moving to estates and towns which prescribed, in their layout and design, a different, less extended, more
'nucleated' family pattern.   Even estates rebuilt in or near
the old areas have been constructed - more consistently, perhaps,
than their pre-war counterparts - in the image of an 'ideal'
family: that is, a more middle class, 'nuclear' one.   The
working-class family did not 'disappear' under these conditions
nor did working people actively subscribe to the new 'bourgeois'
domestic ideal.   But the family may have become more isolated;
relations between children and parents, or between peers and
siblings were altered, with special effect on younger family
members and on women.   What, in sum, was *unsettled* was the
precise position and role of the working-class family within a
defensive class culture.   What was disturbed was a concrete
set of relations, a network of knowledge, things, experiences -
the *supports* of a class culture.   In these circumstances, too,
the 'new' gained ground precisely because it once again invaded
and undermined alternative patterns of social organisation.

   In the early post-war period, these changes in the intricate
mechanisms and balances of working-class life and culture were
overlaid by the spectacular ideology of 'affluence'.   We know
now what were the limits of its real impact,   its uneven distribution - even in terms of wages and consumption - for most
sections of the working-class.   There was no 'qualitative leap'.
Indeed, 'affluence' assumed the proportions of a full-blown
ideology precisely because it was required to cover over the gaps
between real inequalities and the promised Utopia of equality-
for-all and ever-rising-consumption to come.   By projecting this
ideological scenario, the 'affluence' myth aimed to give the
working-classes a stake in a future which had not yet arrived,
and thus to bind and cement the class to the hegemonic order.
Here, precisely, the ideology of affluence reconstructed the
'real relations' of post-war British society into an 'imaginary
relation'.   This is the function of social myths.   The myth
provided, for a time, the ideological basis of the political
hegemony of the 1950's.   'Affluence' was, essentially, an
ideology of the dominant culture *about* and *for* the working-class,
directed *at* them (through the media, advertising, political
speeches, etc.).   Few working-class people subscribed to a
version of their own situation which so little squared with its
real dimensions.   What mattered, therefore, was *not* the
passive re-making of the working class in the 'affluent' image,
but the *dislocations* it produced - and the responses it provoked.

The full absorption of the Labour Party into its parliamentary-electoral role within the state (the completion of a long histori-cal trajectory) and the partial incorporation into the state apparatus of the trade unions, on the back of an 'affluent' reading of the post-war situation, had *real* political consequences for the working-class, dismantled real defences. **Other** responses were unpredictable and unintended. The overwhelming emphasis in the ideology of affluence on money and consumption may well have had the unintended effect of stimulating an awareness of 'relative deprivation' and thereby contributed to the 'wage militancy' of the 1960's and 70's. The affluent workers in engineering and the motor firms pioneered the shift to work-place power, plant bargaining, shop stewards organisation and 'wage drift' - a militant 'economism' which lasted right into the period of inflation and recession, pulling the 'revolt of the lower paid' behind it. These, too, were responses to 'affluence' which its ideologues neither did nor could foresee.

To locate youth sub-culture in this kind of analysis, we must first situate youth in the dialectic between a 'hegemonic' dominant culture and the subordinate working-class 'parent' culture, of which youth is a fraction. These terms - hegemonic/corporate, dominant/subordinate - are crucial for the analysis, but need further elaboration before the sub-cultural dimension can be introduced. Gramsci used the term "hegemony" to refer to the moment when a ruling class is able, not only to *coerce* a subordinate class to conform to its interests, but to exert a "hegemony" or "total social authority" over subordinate classes. This involves the exercise of a special kind of power - the power to frame alternatives and contain opportunities, *to win and shape consent*, so that the granting of legitimacy to the dominant classes appears not only 'spontaneous' but natural and normal. Lukes has recently defined this as the power to define the agenda, to shape preferences, to "prevent conflict from arising in the first place", or to contain conflict when it does arise by defining what sorts of resolution are 'reasonable' and 'realistic' - i.e. within the existing framework (Lukes, 1974: 23-24). The terrain on which this hegemony is won or lost is **the terrain of the superstructures;** the institutions of civil society and the state - what Althusser (1971) and Poulantzas (1973), somewhat misleadingly, call "ideological state apparat-uses". Conflicts of interest arise, fundamentally, from the difference in the structural position of the classes in the productive realm: but they 'have their effect' in social and political life. Politics, in the widest sense, frames the passage from the first level to the second. The terrain of civil and state institutions thus becomes essentially "the stake, but also the site of class struggle" (Althusser 1971). In part, these apparatuses work 'by ideology'. That is, the definitions of reality institutionalised within these apparatuses come to

constitute a lived 'reality as such' for the subordinate classes
- that, at least, is what hegemony attempts and secures.
Gramsci, using the example of the church, says that it preserves
"the ideological unity of the entire social bloc which that
ideology serves to cement and unify" (Gramsci, 1971: 328).
A hegemonic cultural order tries to *frame* all competing definitions of the world within *its* range.   It provides the horizon of
thought and action within which conflicts are fought through,
appropriated (i.e. experienced), obscured (i.e. concealed as a
"national interest" which should unite all conflicting parties)
or contained (i.e. settled to the profit of the ruling class).
A hegemonic order prescribes, not the specific content of ideas,
but the *limits* within which ideas and conflicts move and are
resolved.   Hegemony always rests on force and coercion, but
"the normal exercise of hegemony on the now classical terrain of
the parliamentary regime is characterised by the combination of
force and consent ... without force predominating excessively over
consent" (Gramsci 1971: 80).   Hegemony thus provides the base
line and the base-structures of legitimation for ruling class
power.

   Hegemony works through ideology, but it does not consist of
false ideas, perceptions, definitions.   It works *primarily* by
inserting the subordinate class into the key institutions and
structures which support the power and social authority of the
dominant order.   It is, above all, in these structures and
relations that a subordinate class *lives its subordination*.
Often, this subordination is secured only because the dominant
order suceeds in weakening, destroying, displacing or incorporating alternative institutions of defence and resistance thrown up
by the subordinate class.   Gramsci insists, quite correctly, that
"the thesis which asserts that men become conscious of fundamental
conflicts on the level of ideology is not psychological or
moralistic in character but *structural and epistemological.*"
(Our italics; Gramsci, 1971: 164.)

   Hegemony can rarely be sustained by one, single class stratum.
Almost always it requires an *alliance* of ruling-class fractions -
a 'historical bloc'.   The content of hegemony will be determined,
in part, by precisely which class fractions compose such a
'hegemonic bloc', and thus what interests have to be taken into
account within it.   Hegemony is not simple 'class rule'.
It requires to some degree the 'consent' of the subordinate class,
which has, in turn, to be won and secured; thus, an ascendancy of
social authority, not only in the state but in civil society as
well, in culture and ideology.   Hegemony prevails when ruling
classes not only rule or 'direct' but *lead*.   The state is a
major educative force in this process.   It educates through its
regulation of the life of the subordinate classes.   These
apparatuses reproduce class relations, and thus class subordination (the family, the school, the church and cultural institutions,
as well as the law, the police and the army, the courts).

The struggle against class hegemony also takes place within these institutions, as well as outside them - they become the "site" of class struggle. But the apparatuses also depend on the operation of "a set of predominant values, beliefs, rituals and institutional procedures ('rules of the game') that operate systematically and consistently to the benefit of certain persons and groups" (Bacrach and Baratz, 1962).

Gramsci believes that, in the Italian state, the dominant classes had frequently ruled without that 'natural social author- ity' which would make them 'hegemonic'. So hegemony cannot be taken for granted - either by the state and the dominant classes, or, for that matter, by the analyst. The current use of the term, to suggest the unending and unproblematic exercise of class power by every ruling class, and its opposite - the permanent and finished incorporation of the subordinate class - is quite false to Gramsci's usage. It limits the historical specificity of the concept. To make that point concrete: we would argue that, though the dominant classes remained massively in command during the 1930's, it is difficult to define them as 'hegemonic'. Economic crisis and unemployment disciplined, rather than 'led', the working classes into subordination in this period. The defeats suffered by the labour movement in the 1920's powerfully contributed to the coercive sway of the former over the latter. By contrast, the 1950's seem to us a period of true 'hegemonic domination', it being precisely the role of 'affluence', as an ideology, to dismantle working-class resistance and deliver the 'spontaneous consent' of the class to the authority of the dominant classes. Increasingly, in the 1960's, and more openly in the 1970's, this 'leadership' has again been undermined. The society has polarised, conflict has reappeared on many levels. The dominant classes retain power, but their 'repertoire' of control is progressively challenged, weakened, exhausted. One of the most striking features of this later period is the shift in the exercise of control from the mechanisms of consent to those of coercion (e.g. the use of the law, the courts, the police and the army, of legal repression, conspiracy charges and of force to contain an escalating threat to the state and to 'law and order'). This marks a *crisis* in the hegemony of the ruling class.

Hegemony, then, is not universal and 'given' to the continuing rule of a particular class. It has to be *won*, worked for, reproduced, sustained. Hegemony is, as Gramsci said, a "moving equilibrium", containing "relations of forces favourable or unfavourable to this or that tendency". It is a matter of the nature of the balance struck between contending classes: the compromises made to sustain it; the relations of force; the solutions adopted. Its character and content can only be established by looking at concrete situations, at concrete

historical moments.   The idea of 'permanent class hegemony',
or of 'permanent incorporation' must be ditched.

In relation to the hegemony of a ruling class, the working-
class is, by definition, a *subordinate* social and cultural
formation.   Capitalist production, Marx suggested, reproduces
capital and labour in their ever-antagonistic forms.   The role
of hegemony is to ensure that, in the social relations between
the classes, each class is continually *reproduced* in its existing
dominant-or-subordinate form.   Hegemony can never wholly and
absolutely absorb the working-class *into* the dominant order.
Society may seem to be, but cannot actually ever be, in the
capitalist mode of production, 'one-dimensional'.   Of course,
at times, hegemony is strong and cohesive, and the subordinate
class is weak, vulnerable and exposed.   But it cannot, by
definition, disappear.   It remains, as a subordinate structure,
often separate and impermeable, yet still contained by the overall
rule and domination of the ruling class.   The subordinate
class has developed its own corporate culture, its own forms of
social relationship, its characteristic institutions, values,
modes of life.   Class conflict never disappears.   English
working-class culture is a peculiarly strong, densely-impacted,
cohesive and defensive structure of this corporate kind.
Class conflict, then, is rooted and embodied in this culture:
it cannot 'disappear' - contrary to the ideology of affluence
- until the productive relations which produce and sustain it
disappear.   But it can be more or less open, more or less formal,
more or less institutionalised, more or less autonomous.
The period between the 1880's and the present shows, not a
single thrust towards incorporation but a marked alternating
rhythm.   It is important to insist that, even when class conflict
is most institutionalised, it remains as one of the fundamental
base-rhythms of the society.

In old and developed industrial capitalist societies, like
Britain, the culture is in fact *covered* by a network of what we
might call 'institutional solutions', which structure how the
dominant and subordinate cultures coexist, survive, but also
struggle, with one another inside the same social formation.
Many of these institutions *preserve* the corporate culture of the
subordinate class, but also *negotiate* its relations with the
dominant culture.   These are the 'negotiated' aspects of a
subordinate class culture.   In work, for example, the line
between workers interests and managerial power, though often
blurred and overlaid by intermediary structures, never disappears.
But it can be very differently *handled,* by each side, from one
workplace to another, or from one historical moment to another.
The informal culture of the workplace, the attempts to exercise
day-to-day control over the work process, the bargaining around
wage minimums from place to place, as well as the 'down-tools',

the walk-out, the strike, the official dispute, the factory
occupation, constitute a whole *repertoire* of working-class responses to the immediate power and authority of management and capital. They are types of counter-hegemonic power. Many of these
strategies - in so far as they do not finally replace the power
of capital over labour - continue to define labour as a corporate
- but *not* as an incorporated - part of capitalist production.
They represent a line of defence of the class, even where these
defences operate within the over-determining framework of
managerial power.

Working-class culture has consistently 'won space' from the
dominant culture. Many working-class institutions represent the
different outcomes of this intense kind of 'negotiation' over
long periods. At times, these institutions are adaptive; at
other times, combative. Their class identity and position is
never finally 'settled': the balance of forces within them
remains open. They form the basis of what Parkin has called
a "'negotiated version' of the dominant system ... dominant values
are not so much rejected or opposed as modified by the subordinate
class as a result of circumstances and restricted opportunities."
... (Parkin, 1971: 92). Often, such 'negotiated solutions'
prevail, not because the class is passive and deferential to
ruling class ideas, but because its perspectives are bounded and
contained by immediate practical concerns or limited to concrete
situations. (This is the material basis and 'rational core' of
working-class 'economism'.) From this arise the *situated
solutions* to problems arising at a wider, more global, level,
beyond the immediate class horizon. In situations where "purely
abstract evaluations are called for, the dominant value system
will provide the moral frame of reference; but in concrete
social situations involving choice and action, the negotiated
version - or subordinate value system - will provide the moral
framework" (Parkin , 1971: 93). Authority, enshrined in the
major institutional orders of society (e.g. the rule of the Law)
may be accepted at an abstract level, but much more ambivalently
handled at the face-to-face level (e.g. attitudes to the police).
English working-class culture is massively orchestrated around
attitudes of 'Us' and 'Them', even when this structured difference
does not lead directly to counter-hegemonic strategies by the
working-class. Recent evidence suggests that the suspicion of
property and property rights remains deeply entrenched in the
class, despite the absence of any concerted thrust to abolish
property relations as such (Moorhouse and Chamberlain, 1974).
Even class institutions like the trade unions, which in this
period were pulled a considerable distance into full collaboration with the state, nevertheless, under slightly different
circumstances (legislation against fundamental trade union
rights and procedures after 1970 by a Conservative Government,
for example) emerged as reluctant defenders of basic working

class rights (Lane, 1974). Thus, in 'good' times as well as 'bad', contrary cultural definitions are *always* in play. These reflect the structural difference between the material position, outlook and everyday life-experience of the different classes. These discrepancies (contradictions) in situation, values and action then provide the real material and historical basis - under the right conditions - for more developed class strategies of open resistance, struggle, and for counter-hegemonic strategies of rupture and transformation. The convergence of these various strategies of negotiation by a subordinate class into a more sustained class politics requires, of course, mobilisation, politicisation and organisation. It is precisely to this distinction that Marx addressed his observations about the movement from a class 'in itself' to a class 'for itself'.

The working-class neighbourhood, which assumes its 'tradition-al' form in and after the 1880's, represents one, distinctive example of the outcome of negotiation between the classes. In it, the different strata of the working-class have won space for their own forms of life. The values of this corporate culture are registered everywhere, in material and social forms, in the shapes and uses of things, in patterns of recreation and leisure, in the relations between people and the character of communal spaces. These spaces are both physical (the networks of streets, houses, corner shops, pubs and parks) and social (the networks of kin, friendship, work and neighbourly relationships). Over such spaces, the class has come to exert those 'informal social controls' which redefine and reappropriate them for the groups which live in them: a web of rights and obligations, intimacies and distances, embodying in its real textures and structures "the sense of solidarity... local loyalties and traditions" (Cohen, 1972). These are the 'rights', not of ownership or force, but of territorial and cultural possession, the customary occupation of the 'sitting tenant'. The institutions are, of course, cross-cut and penetrated by outside forces. The structure of work and workplace, near or far, link the local labour force to wider economic forces and movements. Not far away are the bustling commercial high streets, with their chain stores and supermarkets, linking the home to the wider economy through trade and consumption. Through these structures, the neighbourhood is socially and economically *bounded*. At one level - the horizontal - are all those ties which bind spaces and institutions to locality, neighbourhood, local culture and tradition. At another level - the vertical - are those struc-tures which tie them to dominant institutions and cultures.

The local school is a classic instance of such 'double-binding' (Hall, 1974a: 49-55). It is the *local* school, next to houses, streets and shops where generations of working-class children have been 'schooled', and where ties of friendship,

peer-group and marriage are forged and unmade. Yet, in terms
of vertical relationships, the school has stood for kinds of
learning, types of discipline and authority relations, affirmed
experiences quite at variance with the local culture. Its
selective mechanisms of streaming, 'tracking', eleven-plus, its
knowledge boundaries, its intolerance of language and experience
outside the range of formal education, link the urban working-
class locality to the wider world of education and occupations
in ways which are connective but also, crucially, *disconnective*.
It remains a classic, negotiated, or mediated class institution.
In this context, we can begin to look again and assess differently
the varying strategies, options and 'solutions' which develop in
relation to it: the 'scholarship' boy or girl; the 'ordinary,
average-ability' kids; the 'trouble-makers'; truants and
absentees; the educationally-and-emotionally 'deprived';
the actively mis-educated (e.g. E.S.N-ed black kids).
Similarly, in relation to the leisure activities of the young,
to peer-group culture and association, we must recognise the 'mix'
of resistance and accommodation in, for example: street-corner
culture, with its massively 'masculine' focus; the near-
delinquent group or exploit; the Boys Brigade addict; the
'gang'; the 'football end'; the well-defined sub-culture; and
so on.

   Any one of these strategies in the repertoire developed by
young working-class boys will stand in a complex relation to that
of other 'peers'; to 'adult' strategies and solutions; to
alternative positions in the same age spectrum (e.g. Skinheads
vs. hippies); and to the dominant culture and its repertoire of
control. The strength or absence of any of these strategies
at a historical moment will depend in part on the historical
conjuncture (the balance of forces between domination and subordination; the stable or changing situation of the 'parent'
class, etc.). It will especially produce changes in the
'problematic' of the class - that matrix of problems, structures,
opportunities and experiences which confront that particular
class stratum at a particular historical moment. It will
mirror changes in the material conditions in everyday life
available for construction into the *supports* for one or other
of the collective strategies.

   Negotiation, resistance, struggle: the relations between
a subordinate and a dominant culture, wherever they fall within
this spectrum, are always intensely active, always oppositional,
in a structural sense (even when this opposition is latent, or
experienced simply as the normal state of affairs - what Gouldner
called "normalised repression"). Their outcome is not given
but *made*. The subordinate class brings to this 'theatre of
struggle' a repertoire of strategies and responses - ways of
coping as well as of resisting. Each strategy in the repertoire
mobilises certain real material and social elements: it constructs these into the supports for the different ways the class

44

lives and resists its continuing subordination.   Not all the
strategies are of equal weight: not all are potentially
counter-hegemonic.   Some may even be alternatives - e.g.
working-class politics and certain kinds of working class crime.
We must also recognise that a developed and organised revolutionary working-class consciousness is only *one*, among many
such possible responses, and a very special ruptural one at that.
It has been misleading to try to measure the whole spectrum of
strategies in the class in terms of this one ascribed form of
consciousness, and to define everything else as a token of
incorporation.   This is to impose an abstract scheme on to a
concrete historical reality.   We must try to understand, instead,
how, under what conditions, the class has been able to use its
material and cultural 'raw materials' to construct a whole *range*
of responses.   Some - the repertoire of resistance specific to
the history of one working class - form an immense reservoir of
knowledge and power in the struggle of the class to survive
and 'win space'.   Even those which appear again and again in the
history of the class, are not fixed alternatives (reform vs.
revolution), but *potential* historical 'spaces' used and adapted
to very different circumstances in its tradition of struggle.
Nor can we ascribe particular sociological strata of the class
to particular, permanent positions in the repertoire.   This,
too, is quite a-historical.   It is possible for the 'labour
aristocracy' to provide critical radical leadership;   for the
unorganised or so-called 'lumpen' to organise;   for 'deference
voters' to lose their respect for authority;   for 'affluents'
to be, also, 'militants'; for 'clericals' to strike;   for working
wives and first generation immigrants to take the vanguard
position;   and so on.   In the diagram below, we have tried to
enforce this argument (which, we believe follows directly from
Gramsci's conception of hegemony and corporateness) by a sketch
of one possible part of the strategies of negotiation, conflict
and subordination.   It is offered for illustrative purposes
only - its value lying in the fact that it includes, within one
typology, strategies which belong to the more or less adaptive
poles of the spectrum, strategies developed both within and
outside the formal institutionalisation of class struggle.

F. The subcultural response

We can return, now, to the question of 'sub-cultures'.
Working-class sub cultures, we suggested, take shape on the level
of the social and cultural class-relations of the subordinate
classes.   In themselves, they are not simply 'ideological'
constructs.   They, too, *win space* for the young: cultural space
in the neighbourhood and institutions, real time for leisure and
recreation, actual room on the street or street-corner.   They
serve to mark out and appropriate 'territory' in the localities.
They focus around key occasions of social interaction: the week-

"the naturally Conservative Nation"	"one nation"	"the two sides of industry"	"the parliamentary road"	"equality before the law"	"militancy" "extremism" "holding the nation to ransom"	"subversion" "anarchy"
deference vote	w.c. neighbourhood	Trade Union Membership	Labour Vote	'the Law'	shop steward power	the Left sects
Working Class Tory	'Us' vs. 'Them'	Trade Union Consciousness	Labourism	Crime Delinquency	Militant 'Economism'	Revolutionary Politics

("false consciousness") ... ("normalized repression") .. (ab-normal responses) . (threats to state)

A REPERTOIRE OF NEGOTIATIONS AND RESPONSES

end, the disco, the bank-holiday trip, the night out in the
'centre', the 'standing-about-doing-nothing' of the weekday
evening, the Saturday match.   They cluster around particular
locations.   They develop specific rhythms of interchange,
structured relations between members: younger to older, experienced to novice, stylish to square.   They explore 'focal concerns'
central to the inner life of the group: things always 'done' or
'never done', a set of social rituals which underpin their
collective identity and define them as a 'group' instead of a mere
collection of individuals.   They adopt and adapt material
objects - goods and possessions - and reorganise them into
distinctive 'styles' which express the collectivity of their
being-as-a- group.   These concerns, activities, relationships,
materials become embodied in rituals of relationship and occasion
and movement.   Sometimes, the world is marked out, linguistica-
lly, by names or an *argot* which classifies the social world
exterior to them in terms meaningful only within their group
perspective, and maintains its boundaries.   This also helps
them to develop, ahead of immediate activities a perspective on
the immediate future - plans, projects, things to do to fill
out time, exploits ... They too are concrete, identifiable
social formations constructed as a collective response to the
material and situated experience of their class.

Though not 'ideological', sub-cultures have an ideological
dimension: and, in the problematic situation of the post-war
period, this ideological component became more prominent.   In
addressing the 'class problematic' of the particular strata from
which they were drawn, the different sub-cultures provided for
a section of working-class youth (mainly boys) *one* strategy for
negotiating their collective existence.   But their highly
ritualised and stylised form suggests that they were also *attempts
at a solution* to that problematic experience: a resolution which,
because pitched largely at the symbolic level, was fated to fail.
The problematic of a subordinate class experience can be 'lived
through', negotiated or resisted;   but it cannot be *resolved* at
that level or by those means.   There is no 'sub-cultural career'
for the working-class lad, no 'solution' in the sub-cultural
milieu, for problems posed by the key structuring experiences
of the class.

There is no 'subcultural solution' to working-class youth
unemployment, educational disadvantage, compulsory miseducation,
dead-end jobs, the routinisation and specialisation of labour,
low pay and the loss of skills.   Sub-cultural strategies cannot
match, meet or answer the structuring dimensions emerging in
this period for the class as a whole.   So, when the post-war
sub-cultures address the problematics of their class experience,
they often do so in ways which reproduce the gaps and discrepancies between real negotiations and symbolically displaced
'resolutions'.   They 'solve', but in an imaginary way, problems

Interesting

which at the concrete material level remain unresolved. Thus
the 'Teddy Boy' expropriation of an upper class style of dress
'covers' the gap between largely manual, unskilled, near-lumpen
real careers and life-chances, and the 'all-dressed-up-and-
nowhere-to-go' experience of Saturday evening. Thus, in the
expropriation and fetishisation of consumption and style itself,
the 'Mods' cover for the gap between the never-ending-weekend
and Monday's resumption of boring, dead-end work. Thus, in
the resurrection of an archetypal and 'symbolic' (but, in fact,
anachronistic) form of working-class dress, in the displaced
focussing on the football match and the 'occupation' of the
football 'ends', Skinheads reassert, but 'imaginarily', the
values of a class, the essence of a style, a kind of 'fan-ship'
to which few working-class adults any longer subscribe: they
're-present' a sense of territory and locality which the planners
and speculators are rapidly destroying: they 'declare' as alive
and well a game which is being commercialised, professionalised
and spectacularised. "Skins Rule, OK". OK ? But "in ideology,
men do indeed express, not the real relation between them and
their conditions of existence, but *the way* they live the relation
between them and the conditions of their existence; this presupposes both a real and an *'imaginary'*, *'lived'* relation.
Ideology then, is ... the (over determined) unity of the real
relation and the imaginary relation ... that *expresses a will* ...
a hope, or a nostalgia, rather than describing a reality"
(Althusser, 1969: 233-234).

    Working-class sub-cultures are a response to a problematic
which youth shares with other members of the 'parent' class
culture. But class structures the adolescent's experience of
that problematic in distinctive ways. First, it locates the
young, at a formative stage of their development, in a particular
material and cultural milieu, in distinctive relations and
experiences. These provide the essential cultural frame-works
through which that problematic is made sense of by the youth.
This 'socialisation' of youth *into* a class identity and position
operates particularly through two 'informal' agencies: family
and neighbourhood. Family and neighbourhood are the specific
structures which *form*, as well as frame, youth's early passage
into a class. For example, the sex-typing roles and responsibilities characteristic of a class are reproduced, not only
through language and talk in the family, but through daily
interaction and example. In the neighbourhood, patterns of
community sociality are embedded partly through the structure of
interactions between older and younger kids. (Howard Parker,
1974, has commented on the role of street football as a way in
which younger kids 'learn' a distinctive kind of class sociability.)
These intimate contexts also refer the young to the larger world
outside. Thus it is largely through friends and relations that

the distant but increasingly imminent worlds of work or of face-to-face authority (the rent man, Council officials, social security, the police) are appropriated. Through these formative networks, relations, distances, interactions, orientations to the wider world and its social types are delineated and reproduced in the young.

Class also, broadly, structures the young individual's life-chances. It determines, in terms of statistical class probabilities, the distribution of 'achievement' and 'failure'. It establishes certain crucial orientations towards careers in education and work - it produces the notoriously 'realistic' expectations of working-class kids about future opportunities. It teaches ways of relating to and negotiating authority. For example, the social distance, deference, anxiety and dressing-up of parents in meetings with school teachers may confirm or reinforce the experience of school as essentially part of an alien and external world.

These are only some of the many ways in which the way youth is inserted within the culture of a class also serves to reproduce, within the young, the problematics of that class. But, over and above these shared class situations, there remains something privileged about the specifically *generational experience* of the young. Fundamentally, this is due to the fact that youth encounters the problematic of its class culture in *different sets of institutions and experiences* from those of its parents; and when youth encounters the same structures, it encounters them at *crucially different points* in its biographical careers.

We can identify these aspects of "generational specificity" in relation to the three main life areas we pointed to earlier: education, work and leisure. Between the ages of five and sixteen, education is the institutional sphere which has the most sustained and intensive impact on the lives of the young. It is the "paramount reality" imposing itself on experience, not least through the fact that it cannot (easily) be avoided. By contrast, the older members of the class encounter education in various *indirect* and distanced ways: through remembered experiences ("things have changed" nowadays); through special mediating occasions - parents' evenings, etc.; and through the interpretations the young give of their school experiences.

In the area of work, the difference is perhaps less obvious, in that both young and old alike are facing similar institutional arrangements, organisations and occupational situations. But within this crucial differences remain. The young face the problem of choosing and entering jobs, of learning both the formal and informal cultures of work - the whole difficult transition from school to work. We have already observed how the

49

changing occupational structures of some areas and industries may dislocate the traditionally evolved "family work - career structure" - thus making the transition even more difficult. For the older members of the class, work has become a relatively routine aspect of life; they have learnt occupational identities and the cultures of work, involving strategies for coping with the problems that work poses - methods of "getting by".

In the broader context, the young are likely to be more vulnerable to the consequence of increasing unemployment than are older workers: in the unemployment statistics of the late sixties, unskilled school leavers were twice as likely to be unemployed as were older, unskilled workers. In addition, the fact of unemployment is likely to be differentially *experienced* at different stages in the occupational "career".

Finally, leisure must be seen as a significant life-area for the class. As Marx observed,

> ..... The worker therefore only feels himself outside his work, and in his work feels outside himself. He is at home when he is not working, and when he is working he is not at home. His labour is therefore not voluntary but coerced; it is forced labour. It is therefore not the satisfaction of a need; it is merely the means to satisfy needs external to it.
> (1964: 110-1)

In working-class leisure, we see many of the results of that "warrenning" of society by the working-class discussed above. Leisure and recreation seem to have provided a more negotiable space than the tightly-disciplined and controlled work situation. The working-class has imprinted itself indelibly on many areas of mass leisure and recreation. These form an important part of the corporate culture and are central to the experience and cultural identity of the whole class. Nevertheless, there are major differences in the ways working-class adults and young people experience and regard leisure. This difference became intensified in the 1950's and 1960's, with the growth of the 'teenage consumer' and the reorganisation of consumption and leisure provision (both commercial and non-commercial) in favour of a range of goods and services specifically designed to attract a youthful clientele. This widespread availability and high visibility of Youth Culture structured the leisure sphere in crucially different ways for the young. The equation of youth with consumption and leisure rearranged and *intensified* certain long-standing parent culture orientations; for example, towards the special and privileged meaning of 'freetime', and towards 'youth' as a period for 'having a good time while you can' - the 'last fling'. This reshaping of attitudes from within the class, in conjunction with pressures to rearrange and redistribute the patterns of leisure for the young from outside, served to highlight - indeed to *fetishise* - the meaning of

leisure for the young.   Thus, not only did youth encounter
leisure in different characteristic institutions from their
parents (caffs, discos, youth clubs, 'all nighters', etc.):   these
institutions powerfully presented themselves to the young as
different from the past, partly because they were so uncompromisi-
ngly youthful.

Here we begin to see how forces, working right across a class,
but differentially experienced as between the generations, may
have formed the basis for generating an outlook - a kind of
consciousness - specific to age position: a *generational conscio-
sness*.   We can also see exactly why this 'consciousness', though
formed by class situation and the forces working in it, may
nevertheless have taken the form of a consciousness apparently
separate from, unrelated to, indeed, able to be set over against,
its class content and context.   Though we can see how and why
this specific kind of 'generational consciousness' might arise,
the problem is not resolved by simply reading it once again out
of existence - that is, by re-assigning to youth a clear and
simple class-based identity and consciousness.   This would be
simply to over-react against 'generational consciousness'.
We have suggested that, though a fully-blown 'generational
consciousness' served unwittingly to repress and obscure the
class dimension, it did have a 'rational core' in the very
experience of the working-class young in the period;   the
specificity of the institutions in which post-war changes were
encountered, and above all, in the way this sphere was reshaped
by changes in the leisure market.   It may also have been located
in other, material experiences of the youth of the class in
this period.   A 'generational consciousness' is likely to be
strong among those sectors of youth which are upwardly and
outwardly mobile from the working-class - e.g. Hoggart's
'scholarship boy'.   Occupational and educational change in
this period led to an increase in these paths of limited mobility.
The upward path, through education, leads to a special focussing
on *the school and the education system* as the main mechanism
of advancement: it is this which 'makes the difference' between
parents who stay where they were and children who move on and
up.   It involves the young person valuing the dominant culture
positively, and sacrificing the 'parent' culture - even where
this is accompanied by a distinct sense of cultural disorienta-
tion.   His experience and self-identity will be based around
mobility - something specific to his generation, rather than to
the over-determining power of class.   One of the things which
supports this taking-over of a 'generational consciousness'
by the scholarship boy is, precisely, his cultural isolation -
the fact that his career is different from the majority of his
peers.   The peer group is, of course, one of the real and
continuing bases for collective identities organised around the
focus of 'generation'.   But a sense of generational distinctness
may also flow from an individual's isolation from the typical

51

involvement in kinds of peer-group activities which, though specific to youth, are clearly understood as forming a sort of cultural apprenticeship to the 'parent' class culture. This kind of isolation may be the result of biographical factors - e.g. inability to enter the local football game where football is the primary activity of the peer group; or being a member of a relatively 'closed' and tight family situation. A young person, who for whatever reasons, fails to go through this class-culture apprenticeship, may be more vulnerable to the vicarious peer-group experience provided by the highly visible and widely accessible commercially provided Youth Culture, where the audience as a whole substitutes for the real peer group as one, vast, symbolic 'peer group': "Our Generation".

'Generational consciousness' thus has roots in the real experience of working-class youth as a whole. But it took a peculiarly intense form in the post-war sub-cultures which were sharply demarcated - amongst other factors - by age and generation. Youth felt and experienced itself as 'different', especially when this difference was inscribed in activities and interests to which 'age', principally, provided the passport. This does not necessarily mean that a 'sense of class' was thereby obliterated. Skinheads, for example, are clearly both 'generationally' and 'class' conscious. As Cohen suggested, "sub-culture is ... a compromise solution, between two contra-dictory needs: the need to create and express *autonomy and difference* from parents ... and the need to maintain ... the *parental identifications* which support them" (Cohen: 1972: 26). It is to the formation of these generationally distinct working-class sub-cultures that we next turn.

G. Sources of style

The question of style, indeed, of generational style, is pivotal to the post-war formation of these youth sub-cultures. (The issue is treated at length below in the essay on "Style"; the main points only are summarised at this point.) What concerns us here is, first, how 'class' and 'generational' elements interact together in the production of distinctive group-styles; second, how the materials available to the group are constructed and appropriated in the form of a visibly organised cultural response.

Working-class youth inhabit, like their parents, a distinctive structural and cultural *milieu* defined by territory, objects and things, relations, institutional and social practices. In terms of kinship, friendship networks, the informal culture of the neighbourhood, and the practices articulated around them, the young are already located in and by the 'parent' culture. They also encounter the dominant culture, not in its distant, remote, powerful, abstract forms, but in the located forms and institut-

ions which mediate the dominant culture to the subordinate
culture, and thus permeate it.   Here, for youth, the school,
work (from Saturday jobs onwards), leisure are the key institutions.   Of almost equal importance − for youth above all - are
the institutions and agencies of public social control: the
school serves this function, but alongside it, a range of institutions from the 'hard' coercive ones, like the police, to the
'softer' variants - youth and social workers.

It is at the intersection between the located parent culture
and the mediating institutions of the dominant culture that
youth sub-cultures arise.   Many forms of adaptation, negotiation
and resistance, elaborated by the 'parent' culture in its encounter with the dominant culture, are borrowed and adapted by the
young in *their* encounter with the mediating institutions of
provision and control.   In organising their response to these
experiences, working-class youth sub-cultures take some things
principally from the located 'parent' culture: but they apply
and transform them to the situations and experiences characteristic of their own distinctive group-life and generational
experience.   Even where youth sub-cultures have seemed most
distinctive, different, stylistically marked out from adults
and other peer-group memebers of their 'parent' culture, they
develop certain distinctive outlooks which have been, clearly,
structured by the parent culture.   We might think here of the
recurrent organisation around collective activities ('group
mindedness');   or the stress on 'territoriality' (to be seen
in both the Teddy Boys and Skinheads);   or the particular conceptions of masculinity and of male dominance (reproduced in all the
post-war youth sub-cultures).   The 'parent' culture helps to
define these broad, historically-located 'focal concerns'.
Certain themes which are key to the 'parent culture' are
reproduced at this level again and again in the sub-cultures,
even when they set out to be, or are seen as,'different'.

But there are also 'focal concerns' more immediate, conjunctural, specific to 'youth' and its situation and activities.
On the whole, the literature on post-war sub-culture has neglected the first aspect (what is shared with the 'parent' culture)
and over emphasised what is distinct (the 'focal concerns' of
the youth groups).   But, this second element - which is, again,
generationally very specific - must be taken seriously in any
account.   It consists both of the materials available to the
group for the construction of subcultural identities (dress,
music, talk), and of their contexts (activities, exploits, places,
caffs, dance halls, day-trips, evenings-out, football games,
etc.).   Journalistic treatments, especially, have tended to
isolate *things*, at the expense of their use, how they are borrowed
and transformed, the activities and spaces through which they are
'set in motion', the group identities and outlooks which imprint

53

a style *on* things and objects.   While taking seriously the
significance of objects and things for a sub-culture, it must be
part of our analysis to *de*-fetishise them.

The various youth sub-cultures have been identified by their
possessions and objects: the boot-lace tie and velvet-collared
drape jacket of the Ted, the close crop, parker coats and
scooter of the Mod, the stained jeans, swastikas and ornamented
motorcycles of the bike-boys, the bovver boots and skinned-head
of the Skinhead, the Chicago suits or glitter costumes of the
Bowieites, etc.   Yet, despite their visibility, things simply
appropriated and worn (or listened to) do not make a style.
What makes a style is the activity of stylisation - the active
organisation of objects with activities and outlooks, which
produce an organised group-identity in the form and shape of
a coherent and distinctive way of 'being-in-the-world'. Phil
Cohen, for example, has tried to shift the emphasis away from
things to the *modes* of symbolic construction through which style
is generated in the sub-cultures.   He identified four modes
for the generation of the sub-cultural style: dress, music,
ritual and *argot*.   Whilst not wanting to limit the 'symbolic
systems' to these particular four, and finding it difficult to
accept the distinction (between less and more 'plastic') which
he makes, we find this emphasis on group generation far
preferable to the instant stereotyped association between commod-
ity-objects and groups common in journalistic usage.

Working-class sub-cultures could not have existed without a
real economic base: the growth in money wages in the 'affluent'
period, but, more important, the fact that incomes grew more
rapidly for teenagers than for adults in the working-class, and
that much of this was 'disposable income' (income available for
leisure and non-compulsory spending).   But income, alone, does
not make a style either.   The sub-cultures could not have
existed without the growth of a consumer market specifically
geared to youth.   The new youth industries provided the raw
materials, the goods: but they did not, and when they tried
failed to, produce many very authentic or sustained 'styles' in
the deeper sense.   The objects were there, available, but were
used by the groups in the construction of distinctive styles.
But this meant, not simply picking them up, but actively constructing a specific selection of things and goods *into* a style.
And this frequently involved (as we try to show in some of the
selections in our 'ethnographic' section) subverting and trans-
forming these things, from their given meaning and use, to other
meanings and uses.   All commodities have a social use and thus
a cultural meaning.   We have only to look at the language of
commodities - advertising - where, as Barthes observes, there is
no such thing as a simple 'sweater': there is only a 'sweater

for autumnal walks in the wood' or a sweater for 'relaxing at home on Sundays', or a sweater for 'casual wear', and so on (Barthes, 1971).   Commodities are, also, cultural *signs*. They have already been invested, by the dominant culture, with meanings, associations, social connotations.   Many of these meanings seem fixed and 'natural'.   But this is only because the dominant culture has so fully appropriated them to its use, that the meanings which it attributes to the commodities have come to appear as the only meaning which they can express.   In fact, in cultural systems, there is no 'natural' meaning as such. Objects and commodities do not mean any one thing.   They 'mean' only because they have already been arranged, according to social use, into cultural codes of meaning, which *assign meanings to them*.   The bowler hat, pin-stripe suit and rolled umbrella do not, in themselves, mean 'sobriety','respectability', bourgeois-man-at-work.   But so powerful is the social code which surround these commodities that it would be difficult for a working-class lad to turn up for work dressed like that without, either, aspiring to a 'bourgeois' image or clearly seeming to take the piss out of the image.   This trivial example shows that it is possible to expropriate, as well as to appropriate, the social meanings which they seem 'naturally' to have: or, by combining them with something else (the pin-stripe suit with brilliant red socks or white running shoes, for example), to change or inflect their meaning.   Because the meanings which commodities express are socially given - Marx called commodities "social hieroglyphs" - their meaning can also be socially altered or reconstructed. The interior of the working-class home, as described, say, by Roberts (1971) or Hoggart (1958), represents one such 'reworking', by means of which things are imprinted with new meanings, associations and values which expropriate them from the world which provides them and relocates them within the culture of the working-class.

Working-class youth needed money to spend on expressive goods, objects and activities - the post-war consumer market had a clear economic infrastructure.   But neither money nor the market could fully dictate what groups used these things to *say* or *signify* about themselves.   This re-signification was achieved by many different means.   One way was to inflect 'given' meanings by combining things borrowed from one system of meanings into a different code, generated by the sub-culture itself, and through sub-cultural use.   Another way was to modify, by addition, things which had been produced or used by a different social group (e.g. the Teddy Boy modifications of Edwardian dress, discussed by Tony Jefferson, below).   Another was to intensify or exaggerate or isolate a given meaning and so change it (the 'fetishising' of consumption and appearance by the Mods, discussed by Dick Hebdige;   or the elongation of the

pointed winkle-picker shoes of the Italian style; or the current
'massification' of the wedge-shapes borrowed from the 1940's).
Yet another way was to combine forms according to a 'secret'
language or code, to which only members of the group possessed
the key (e.g. the *argot* of many sub-cultural and deviant groups;
the 'Rasta' language of black 'Rudies'). These are only *some*
of the many ways in which the sub-cultures used the materials
and commodities of the 'youth market' to construct meaningful
styles and appearances for themselves.

Far more important were the aspects of group life which
these appropriated objects and things were made to reflect,
express and resonate. It is this reciprocal effect, between
the things a group uses and the outlooks and activities which
structure and define their use, which is the generative principle
of stylistic creation in a sub-culture. This involves members
of a group in the appropriation of particular objects which are,
or can be made, 'homologous' with their focal concerns, activities, group structure and collective self-image - objects in
which they can see their central values held and reflected.
(This is discussed more fully below, in the paper on 'Style').[1]
The adoption by Skinheads of boots and short jeans and shaved
hair was 'meaningful' in terms of the sub-culture only because
these external manifestations resonated with and articulated
Skinhead conceptions of masculinity,'hardness' and 'working-
classness'. This meant overcoming or negotiating or, even,
taking over in a positive way many of the negative meanings which,
in the dominant cultural code, attached to these things: the
'prison-crop' image of the shaved head, the work-image, the
so-called 'outdated cloth-cap image', and so on. The new
meanings emerge because the 'bits' which had been borrowed or
revived were brought together into a new and distinctive stylistic
ensemble: but also because the symbolic objects - dress, appearance, language, ritual occasions, styles of interaction, music -
were made to form *a unity* with the group's relations, situation,
experiences: the crystallisation in an expressive form, which
then defines the group's public identity. The symbolic aspects
cannot, then, be separated from the structure, experiences,
activities and outlook of the groups as social formations.
Sub-cultural style is based on the infra-structure of group
relations, activities and contexts.

This registering of group identity, situation and trajectory
in a visible style both consolidates the group from a loosely-
focussed to a tightly-bounded entity: and sets the group off,
distinctively, from other similar and dissimilar groups. Indeed,
like all other kinds of cultural construction, the symbolic use
of things to consolidate and express an internal coherence was,
in the same moment, a kind of implied opposition to (where it was

not an active and conscious contradiction of) *other* groups *against* which its identity was defined. This process led, in our period, to the distinctive visibility of those groups which pressed the 'sub-cultural solution' to its limits along this stylistic path. It also had profound negative consequences for the labelling, stereotyping and stigmatisation, in turn, of those groups by society's guardians, moral entrepreneurs, public definers and the social control culture in general.

It is important to stress again that sub-cultures are only *one* of the many different responses which the young can make to the situations in which they find themselves. In addition to indicating the range and variation in the options open to youth, we might add a tentative scheme which helps to make clear the distinction we are drawing between youth's *position* and the cultural options through which particular responses are organised.

We can distinguish, broadly, between three aspects: structures, cultures and biographies. (For a development of this scheme and its application to the situation of black youth, see the extract from *20 Years*, below.) By *structures* we mean the set of socially-organised positions and experiences of the class in relation to the major institutions and structures. These positions generate a set of common relations and experiences from which meaningful actions - individual and collective - are constructed. *Cultures* are the range of socially-organised and patterned responses to these basic material and social conditions. Though cultures form, for each group, a set of traditions - lines of action inherited from the past - they must always be collectively constructed anew in each generation. Finally, *biographies* are the 'careers' of particular individuals through these structures and cultures - the means by which individual identities and life-histories are constructed out of collective experiences. Biographies recognise the element of individuation in the paths which individual lives take through collective structures and cultures, but they must not be conceived as either wholly individual or free-floating. Biographies cut paths in and through the determined spaces of the structures and cultures in which individuals are located. Though we have not been able, here, to deal at all adequately with the level of biography, we insist that biographies only make sense in terms of the structures and cultures through which the individual constructs himself or herself.

H. Rise of the counter-cultures

Up to this point, we have dealt exclusively with working-class youth sub-cultures. And there are some problems in deciding whether we can speak of *middle*-class sub-cultures in the same

U.K.

	political	cultural
1965	CND anti-Vietnam march	Bob Dylan Tour
1966	Vietnam Solidarity Campaign Radical Student Alliance	I.T./OZ/B.I.T./Release
1967	Grosvenor Sq. I L.S.E. Sit-in. Dialectics of	Pirate Radio closed. IT raided Liberation conf. Stones drug arrests. Anti-University of London. Arts Lab.
1968	Grosvenor Sq. II & III. London squatting campaign R.S.S.F. founded Essex/Hornsey/Hull/Birmingham	Legalise Pot Rally. Black Dwarf. Hyde Park Free concerts. Time Out. Apple. Gandalf's Garden. Hair.
1969	Refusal of visas to N.Vietnam delegation - March. Peter Hain/S.T.S.T. 144 Piccadilly squat	Stones in Hyde Park 1st I. of Wight Festival Wootton Report rejected
1970	Garden House, Cambridge Fair Cricket Campaign W.L. Conf. Oxford/W.L. disrupt Miss World.	I. of Wight II. Godspell Yippies on Frost. IT Trial White Panthers. 'Female Eunuch'. 'Play Power'.
1971	Bombs: Carr; Biba; GPO. Angry Brigade arrests. Prescott Purdie Trials. OZ Trial. Mangrove case.	Ink/7 days begin. Nasty Tales seized. Glastonbury Fest. Rainbow opens. Socialist Woman. Festival of Light.
1972	Angry Brigade Trial Finance of Student Unions Issue. Hair privately prosecuted. Hull/LSE sit-ins Stirling.	Blueprint for Survival publ. Spare Rib. Undercurrents. Night Assemblies Bill. Bickershaw/Lincoln Fests.
1973	Grants Demos. Thames Poly. sit-in.	Save Piccadilly/London belongs to the People Campaigns. Last OZ. Alt. Soc. ideas pool
1974	Red Lion Square Demo. Troops Out Movement Chile. Essex.	Windsor Free Fest. CLAP Index of Possibilities F.O.E. paper at Whitehall

A CHRONOLOGY

political	cultural	
1st Nat. Anti-War March. SDS. Watts. Malcolm X assass.	Free University of N.Y.	1965
SNCC - Stokeley Carmichael. SDS anti-war sit ins	Diggers at Haight-Ashbury Kesey Trips Festival	1966
Black Panthers. Riots in Newark/Detroit. Newton jailed. Pentagon March.	First Be-in - San Francisco Monterey Pop Festival.	1967
Democratic Conv. - Chicago Luther King assass. 'Pig for President'. Black students struggle.	Yippies-Festival of Life Warhol/Valerie Solanas (SCUM) 'Revolution for the Hell of it' - Hoffman	1968
Anti-War Moratorium. SDS split - Weathermen bombings. Conspiracy trial. Fred Hampton shot. W.L. People's Park Berkeley Indians occupy Alcatraz	Woodstock Charlie Manson Sinclair of White Panthers in jail. Easy Rider	1969
Panther shoot-outs. Kent State Angela Davis. Support for Panthers at Yale. Nixon/Agnew: War on bums.	Leary in and out of jail - sprung by Weathermen. Manson trial. 'Greening of America'	1970
Last Nat. anti-war March. Attica. Panthers split. George Jackson shot. Seale/ Huggins freed.	Sinclair 'out' aided by Lennon and Ono. Jim Morrison dies. 'We are everywhere' Rubin	1971
Angela Davis acquitted. Nixon back. Panthers 'survival conf' Indians occupy Bureau of Indian Affairs.	Bangla Desh Concert 'Fritz the Cat'	1972
Seale stands for Mayor of Oakland. Soglin-Radical Mayor Wisconsin .Symbionese Liberation Army. Marcus Foster.	Guru J. Leary recaptured - Kabul.	1973
S.L.A. shoot out & Patty Hearst. Watergate - Nixon's free pardon.	Leary recants Prisig - 'Zen and the art of motorcycle maintenance.	1974

way and within the same sort of theoretical framework.   Yet,
not only has the period since the war witnessed the rise of quite
distinctive kinds of 'expressive movements' among middle-class
youth, different from the school or 'student' cultures of the pre-
war period, but, as we get closer to the 1970's, these have
attracted, if anything, *more* public attention - and reaction -
than their working-class counterparts.   We point, of course,
not simply to the growing involvement of middle-class youth with
the commercialised popular culture and leisure associated with
'Youth Culture', but the appearance of quite distinct 'sub-
cultural' currents: the Hippie movement;   the various 'deviant'
drug, drop-out and gay sub-cultures;   the elements of cultural
revolt in the student protest movements, etc.   Most significant
is the widespread cultural disaffiliation of broad sectors of
middle-class youth - the phenomenon of the Counter-Culture.
This has, in turn, been linked with the general radicalisation
and politicisation (and de-politicisation) of some middle-class
youth strata.

   We must note some clear structural differences in the
response of the youth of the different classes.   Working-class
sub-cultures are clearly articulated, collective structures -
often, 'near-' or 'quasi'-gangs.   Middle-class counter-cultures
are diffuse, less group-centred, more individualised.   The
latter precipitate, typically, not tight sub-cultures but a
diffuse counter-culture *milieu*.   Working-class sub-cultures
reproduce a clear dichotomy between those aspects of group life
still fully under the constraint of dominant or 'parent'
institutions (family, home, school, work), and those focussed on
non-work hours - leisure, peer-group association.   Middle-class
counter-culture *milieux* merge and blur the distinctions between
'necessary' and 'free' time and activities.   Indeed, the latter
are distinguished precisely by their attempt to explore 'alternative institutions' to the central institutions of the dominant
culture: new patterns of living, of family-life, of work or
even 'un-careers'.   Middle class youth remains longer than their
working-class peers 'in the transitional stage'.   Typically,
working-class youth appropriate the existing environment, they
construct distinct leisure-time activities around the given
working-class environment - street, neighbourhood, football
ground, seaside town, dance-hall, cinema, bomb-site, pub,
disco.   Middle class youth tend to construct enclaves within the
interstices of the dominant culture.   Where the former represent
an appropriation of the 'ghetto', the latter often make an exodus
to the 'ghetto'.   During the high point of the Counter-Culture,
in the 1960's, the middle-class counter-cultures formed a whole
embryo 'alternative society', providing the Counter-Culture with
an underground, institutional base.   Here, the youth of each
class reproduces the position of the 'parent' classes to which
they belong.   Middle-class culture affords the space and

opportunity for sections of it to 'drop out' of circulation. Working-class youth is persistently and consistently structured by the dominating alternative rhythm of Saturday Night and Monday Morning.

The objective oppositional content of working-class sub-cultures expresses itself socially. It is therefore often assimilated by the control culture to traditional forms of working-class 'delinquency', defined as Hooliganism or Vandalism. The counter-cultures take a more overtly ideological or **political** form.   They make articulate their opposition to dominant values and institutions - even when, as frequently occurred, this does not take the form of an *overtly* political response.   Even when working-class sub-cultures are aggressively class-conscious, this dimension tends to be repressed by the control culture, which treats them as 'typical delinquents'.   Even when the middle-class counter-cultures are explicitly anti-political, their objective tendency is treated as, potentially, political.

Middle-class counter-cultures are a feature of the mid-1960's and after, rather than of the 1950's.   Only a handful of the more intellectual youth was involved in the English counter-part to the 'Beat Movement'.   The post-Beat, 'on-the-road', style was prevalent in and around CND and the peace-movement in the late 1950's - the beatnik/peacenik period, associated with the folk revival and the music of Bob Dylan. The Hippies of the later 1960's were the most distinctive of the middle-class sub-cultures.   Their cultural influence on this sector of youth was immense, and many counter-culture values must still be traced back to their Hippie roots.   Hippies helped a whole quasi-bohemian sub-cultural *milieu* to come into existence, shaped styles, dress, attitudes, music and so on. The alternative institutions of the Underground emerged, basic-ally, from this matrix.   But Hippie culture quickly fragmented into different strands - heads, freaks, street people, etc. It fed both the 'drop-out' and the drug sub-cultures of the period.   It permeated student and ex-student culture.   It was then crosscut by influences stemming from the more political elements among middle-class youth - the student protest movement, radical social work, community action groups, the growth of the left sects and so on.   All these tendencies came to a partial fusion in the period between 1967 and 1970 - the high point of the Counter-Culture.   This formation, too, has fragmented in several directions.   The two most distinctive strands flow, one way, via drugs, mysticism, the 'revolution in life-style' into a Utopian alternative culture; or, the other way, via community action, protest action and libertarian goals, into a more activist politics.   What we have here, in short, is a host of variant strands, connections and divergencies within a broadly defined counter-culture *milieu*, rather than (with the exception of the drug and sexual sub-cultures) a sequence of tightly-defined, middle-class sub-cultures.

Both working-class sub-cultures and middle-class counter-cultures are seen, by moral guardians and the control culture, as marking a 'crisis in authority'. The 'delinquency' of the one and the 'disaffiliation' of the other index a weakening of the bonds of social attachment and of the formative institutions which manage how the former 'mature' into hard-working, law-abiding, respectable working-class citizens, or the latter into sober, career-minded, 'possessively-individual' bourgeois citizens. This is a break in, if not a break-down of, the reproduction of cultural-class relations and identities, as well as a loss of deference to 'betters and elders'. The difference is that where the first was a weakening of control over the youth of a subordinate class, the second was a crisis among the youth of the dominant class. As Gramsci remarked, when a 'crisis of authority' is spoken of, "this is precisely the crisis of hegemony or general crisis of the state".

Juliet Mitchell has argued:

> Each class has aspects of its own culture, which are relatively autonomous. This fact is illustrated by such phrases as 'working class culture','ghetto culture', 'immigrant culture', etc., and by the absent phrase - 'middle class culture'. We talk of middle class mores: manners and habits ... but not of a whole 'culture'. We don't think of 'middle class culture' as something separate - it simply is the overall culture, within which are inserted these isolable other cultures. However, this cultural hegemony by bourgeois thought is not on an absolute par with the domination within the economy by the capitalist class.
> (Mitchell, 1971: 33)

Middle-class counter-culture spearheaded a dissent from their own, dominant, 'parent' culture. Their disaffiliation was principally ideological and cultural. They directed their attack mainly against those institutions which reproduce the dominant cultural-ideological relations - the family, education, the media, marriage, the sexual division of labour. These are the very apparatuses which manufacture 'attachment' and internalise consent. "Women, hippies, youth groups, students and school children all question the institutions which have formed them and try to erect their obverse ..." (Mitchell, 1971: 32). Certainly, some of these groups aimed for a systematic inversion, a symbolic up-turning, of the whole bourgeois ethic. By pushing contradictory tendencies in the culture to extremes, they sought to subvert them, but from the inside, and by a negation. "Its libertarian aspirations appear as a negation of traditional culture: a methodological desublimation" (Marcuse: 1969). This 'negating' of a dominant culture, but from within that culture, may account for the continual oscillation between two extremes: total critique and - its reverse - substantial incorporation.

62

It initiated a profoundly ambiguous 'negative dialectic'.

Once again, this emergent movement among middle-class youth must be located, first, in the dynamic and contradictions peculiar, in this period, to its 'parent' middle-class culture. The middle classes have also been effected by the advancing division of labour under modern capitalist production. We have seen the growth of the intermediate white-collar and lower managerial strata, the rise of new professions alongside the old, a growth in the administrative and 'welfare-state' non-commercial middle classes, and new strata connected with the revolutions in communications, management and marketing. These are what Gramsci called "the organic intelligentsia" of modern capitalism - groups marked out by their "directive and technical capacity", their role as organisers, in the whole expanded sphere of production, of "masses of men ... of the 'confidence' of investors ... and of the customers for his product, etc." (Gramsci, 1971: 5). Schools and universities are the instruments "through which intellectuals of various levels are elaborated ... the more extensive the 'area' covered by education and the more numerous the 'vertical' levels of schooling, the more complex is the cultural world ..." (ibid). The expansion in education was, thus, central to changes in the composition, character and problematic of this class. Hence, a crisis in the youth of this class expressed itself, specifically, as a crisis in the educational and ideological apparatuses.

The relation between intellectual strata and the world of production is "'mediated' by the whole fabric of society and by the complex of super-structures" (ibid.). The culture of 'bourgeois' man, with its intricate emotional restraints and repressions, its regulated tempo of restraint and release, its commitment to the protestant 'ethic' of work, career, competitive achievement and possessive individualism, to the ideology of family privacy and the ideal of domesticity, forms a rich and complex integument around the developing mode of production. But, as capitalism moved, after the war, into its more technically-advanced, corporate, consumer stage, this cultural integument was eroded. Critical rifts began to appear in this superstructural complex. The post-war reorganisation of the technical and productive life of the society, and the unsuccessful attempt to stabilise the mode of production at this more 'advanced' level, had an equally unsettling and 'uneven' impact on middle-class culture.

Many habits of thought and feeling, many settled patterns of relationship in middle-class culture, were disturbed by the cultural upheaval which accompanied this 'unfinished revolution'. This was not simply because the middle-classes -'backbone of the nation' - were suddenly exposed to the controlled hedonism of

63

the 'ideology of affluence'.   It was, more fundamentally,
because the shift in the way the mode of production was organised
required and *provoked* a qualitative expansion in the forces of
'mental production', a revolution in the spheres of modern
consciousness.   The harnessing of Capital's productive power
needed, not only new social and technical skills, new political
structures, but a more repetitive cycle of consumption, and forms
of consciousness more attuned to the rhythms of consumption,
and to the new productive and distributive capacities of the
system.   "Advanced capitalism ... is impossible without ... a
parallel expansion of the social 'brain' and nerves of communication ..."   (Nairn, 1968: 159).   A greater share of productive wealth thus went to the formation of consciousness itself:
to the production of that type of social intelligence which Marx
once predicted would "regulate the reproduction and growth of
wealth", as well as that type of false consciousness which found
its apogee in the spectacular "fetishism of commodities".

     This was an altogether different – puzzling, contradictory –
world for the traditional middle classes, formed in and by an
older, more !protestant' ethic.   Advanced capitalism now required,
not thrift but consumption; not sobriety but style; not post-
poned gratifications but immediate satisfaction of needs; not
goods that last but things that are expendable: the 'swinging'
rather than the sober life-style.   The gospel of work was
hardly apposite to a life increasingly focussed on consumption,
pleasure and play.   The sexual repressiveness and ideals of
domesticity enshrined in the middle-class family could not easily
survive the growth of 'permissiveness'.   Naturally, the middle-
classes took fright at this erosion of their whole way of life:
and when the middle-classes take fright, they conjure demons
from the air.   Traditional middle-class life, they imagined,
was being undermined by a conspiracy between progressive intellectuals, soft liberals, the pornographers and the counter-culture.
The fact is that this traditional culture was first, and most
profoundly, *unhinged*, not by enemies of the class outside,
but by changes within and stemming directly from the needs of
the productive system *itself*.   Long before *OZ* began its campaign
against a repressive sexual morality, that morality had been
eroded and undermined by, for example, the language of mass
advertising with its aggressively exploitative pseudo-sexuality.
As 'modern woman' undertook her 'long march' from *Woman's Own* to
Nova and *Cosmopolitan* she passed from respectable homebody to
bejewelled good-time-girl, swinger of the ad-trade, without
pausing for so much as a nod at Mrs. Whitehouse on the way.
Naturally, the older ethic was challenged, not in the name of
a fuller liberation, but only in the name of those needs which
could be satisfied by commodities.   Marcuse, profoundly and
accurately located this controlled drift from the traditional
class ethic into a consumer-based permissiveness, as a *repressive*

desublimation (Marcuse, 1964). Since traditional middle-class
morality was hinged around repressive sublimation, this controlled
desublimation was profoundly disturbing.

Gradually, a struggle has emerged between the traditional
bourgeois - more accurately, 'petit-bourgeois' - strata and the
more 'progressive' modern middle classes. But, in the first
flush of affluence, the guardians of the middle-class ideal first
encountered the break in the shape of 'youth': first, working-
class, then its own. In the name of society, they resisted its
hedonism, its narcissism, its permissiveness, its search for
immediate gratifications, its anti-authoritarianism, its moral
pluralism, its materialism: all defined as 'threats' to societal
values springing from both aspirant working-class youth and
mal-formed, badly-socialised middle-class youth. They mis-
recognised the crisis *within* the dominant culture as a conspiracy
against the dominant culture. They failed (as many members of
the counter-cultures also failed) to see the cultural 'break' as,
in its own traumatic and disturbing way, *profoundly adaptive* to
the system's productive base.

"It may be true that the more advanced social systems of our
own era may well be caught up in unprecendented dialectical
conflicts of their own that threaten their internal stability"
(H. Aitken, quoted in Nairn, 1968: 158). The counter-cultures
were born within this qualitative break inside the dominant culture: in the *caesura* between the old and the new variants of the
dominant ethic. But for some time, youth appeared, phenomenally,
as both its most aggressive and its most visible bearers. The
response was, characteristically, two sided. Traditionalists
bewailed the 'crisis in authority', the loss in the stable reference points of older class cultures. The progressive strata,
however, boosted, incorporated and mercilessly exploited it,
commercially. Youth Culture was thus the first 'phenomenal form'
of the cultural crisis. Though the revolt of middle-class
youth was not contained by this adaptive framework, its subsequent
trajectory owes much to its ambivalent starting-position between
the two 'moral worlds' of the system: that is, to its paradoxical
position within capitalism's uneven and incomplete transition.

If we think of the 'middle class revolt' in its purest,
counter-cultural phase, though much of what it embodied was
overtly antagonistic to sacred, traditional middle-class values,
some of its goals were, objectively, profoundly adaptive for the
system in a transitional moment. "One of the main functions of
radical upheavals ... is to engender the new ideas, techniques,
attitudes and values which a developing society requires but
which the proprietors of its superstructure are unable to bring
into being themselves because their social position is inevitably
tied to the *status quo* (Silber, 1970: 11). Alternative values,
dysfunctional for the 'protestant ethic', may form the necessary,
contested, contradictory bridge between older structures and the

controlled de-sublimation of a post-protestant capitalism.

Hegemonic cultures, however, are never free to reproduce and amend themselves without contradiction and resistance. Modern capitalism may have 'required' a new cultural-ideological ethos for its survival: but the passage from old to new was traumatic - and incomplete. A crisis in the dominant culture is a crisis for the social formation as a whole. Of course, opposition and resistance will assume different forms (See Raymond Williams, 1973). Movements which seem 'oppositional' may be merely survivals, traces from the past. (Cf: some aspects of counter-cultural 'pastoralism'.) Some may be merely 'alternative' - the new lying alongside the old. Marcuse has observed that "the simple, elementary negation, the antithesis ... the immediate denial" often leaves "the traditional culture, the illusionist art, unmastered" (Marcuse, 1969: 47). Others are truly 'emergent'; though they, too, must struggle, against redefinition by the dominant culture, and incorporation. Movements which are simply 'alternative' can provoke a backlash response which develops them internally, and forces them to become more truly oppositional. They can *become* 'emergent'; or be *redefined* and absorbed, depending on the historical conjuncture in which they arise. The post-war middle-class counter-cultures present us with just such a confused and uneven picture.

Some aspects of this cultural upheaval were, clearly, adaptive and incorporable. The counter-cultures performed an important task on behalf of the system by pioneering and experimenting with new social forms which ultimately gave it greater flexibility. In many aspects, the revolutions in 'life-style' were a pure, simple, raging, commercial success. In clothes, and styles, the counter-culture explored, in its small scale 'artisan' and vanguard capitalist forms of production and distribution, shifts in taste which the mass consumption chain-stores were too cumbersome, inflexible and over-capitalised to exploit. When the trends settled down, the big commercial battalions moved in and mopped up. Much the same could be said of the music and leisure business, despite the efforts here to create real, alternative, networks of distribution. 'Planned permissiveness', and organised outrage, on which sections of the alternative press survived for years, though outrageous to the moral guardians, did not bring the system to its knees. Instead, over-ground publications and movies became more permissive - *Playgirl* moved in where *OZ* had feared to tread. The mystical-Utopian and quasi-religious revivals were more double edged: but the former tended to make the counter-culture anti-scientific in a mindless way, and over-ideological - the idea that 'revolution is in the mind', for example; or that 'youth is a class'; or that Woodstock is 'a nation': or, in Jerry Rubin's immortal words, that "people should do whatever the fuck they want" (Silber, 1970: 58) - and the quasi-religious revivals gave to religion a lease of life which nothing else seemed capable of doing. The new individualism of 'Do your Own thing', when taken to its logical extremes, seemed like nothing so much as a looney caricature of petit-bourgeois individualism of the most residual and traditional kind.

This does not, however, exhaust their oppositional content. At the simplest level their emergence marked the failure of the dominant culture to win over the attachment of a sector of its 'brightest and best'. The disaffiliation from the goals, structures and institutions of 'straight society' was far-reaching. Here, the counter-cultures provided, at the very least, that social and cultural breathing-space - a hiatus in the reproduction of cultural relations - in which a deeper disaffiliation was hatched. It cracked the mould of the dominant culture. 'Repressive desublimation' is a dangerous, two-sided phenomenon. When the codes of traditional culture are broken, and new social impulses are set free, they are impossible fully to contain. Open the door to 'permissiveness' and a more profound sexual liberation may follow. Raise the slogan of 'freedom', and some people will give it an unexpectedly revolutionary accent and content. Invest in the technical means for expanding consciousness, and consciousness may expand beyond predictable limits. Develop the means of communication, and people will gain access to print and audiences for which the web-offset litho press were never intended. "The ideologies cultivated in order to achieve ultimate control of the market ... are ones which can rebel *in their own terms* ... the cult of 'being true to your own feelings' becomes dangerous when those feelings are no longer ones that the society would like you to feel. Testing the quality of your world on your own pulse can bring about some pretty strange heart-beats" (Mitchell, 1971: 31). In fact, as soon as the counter-cultures began to take the new slogans at face value, the slogans were transformed into their opposite. Though the nature of this inversion remained, centrally, ideological and cultural - 'superstructural' in character - the systematic up-turning of the traditional ethic gave the counter-cultures an objective oppositional thrust which was not wholly absorbable - and was not wholly absorbed. A sustained assault on the ideological structure of a society is a moment of high contradiction; especially if it occurs in societies which increasingly depend precisely on the institutions of consciousness-formation both for the engineering of consent and the social control of the productive process. This represents a *break* in society's "higher nervous system" (Nairn, 1968: 156). This break not only "brings the contradictions out into the open", converting private alienation into 'trouble in the streets'. It tends to - and did - unleash the "powers of the coercive state violence that are always there as a background

support" (Mitchell, 1971: 32).   And repression - or rather,
"this relationship between the quietude of consensus and the
brutality of coercion" hardens the line between the 'permissive'
and the impermissible, creates solidarities, installs the
counter-cultures as a semi-permanent free-zone, and pushes
forwards the incipient tendency towards politicisation.   In
the period between 1968 and 1972, many sectors of the counter-
culture fell into 'alternative' paths and Utopian solutions.
But others went forwards into a harder, sharper, more intense and
prolonged politics of protest, activism, community action,
libertarian struggle and, finally, the search for a kind of
convergence with working-class politics.

    The subsequent evolution of middle class counter-cultures is
too complex a story to unravel here.   The Counter-culture, with
its flourishing alternative press and institutions has fragmented,
diffused, though it has not disappeared.   The interpenetration
of alternative life-styles and values with radical politics is
a continuing feature.   Certain counter-culture themes stimulated
an organised political 'backlash' (on drugs and pornography, for
example).   Other themes have led on to new kinds of politics:
women's liberation and gay liberation, for example.   The 'Utopian' experimentation with alternative ways of living - the commune
and the collective - continues among sectors of *both* the
political and 'post-political' segments.   Many individuals have
more or less permanently 'dropped out', or gone into 'uncareers'
around the fringes of the counter-culture *milieu*.   Many have
been recruited into the left groups and sects.   Others have
turned to community activism or to radical social work.   Some
have preserved the essence of the libertarian ideal, but redefined
it in more political terms - there is a 'libertarian', an
anarcho-syndicalist, as well as a 'marxist' oriented counter-
politics.   In general, this *partial convergence* between middle-
class counter-cultures and radical politics has been over-
determined by the general turn into a more authoritarian, 'law-
and-order' mood in the control culture, by the gathering political
and economic crisis, and above all by the resumption, especially
after 1972, of a more open and vigorous industrial and non-
industrial working class politics. (See Diagram).

    The overall trajectory of middle-class youth is thus difficult
to estimate.   Irwin Silber has argued that, "the working class
understands on some gut level that the 'cultural revolution' is
no revolution at all.   Far from freeing the worker from the reality of capitalist exploitation, it will only leave him defenceless
against the class enemy.   The worker recognises ... that this
'cultural revolution' is only a thinly-disguised middle class
elitism, a philosophy engendered by those elements in society
who can still find partial individual solutions to the realities

of class oppression. The worker's tenuous hold on economic security does not permit those individual acts of self-liberation which reflect themselves in 'groovy' life styles ..." (Silber, 1970: 26). But this account underestimates both the depth of the 'break' effected by the 'cultural revolution' and the economism of working class resistance. Marcuse has argued that "in the domain of corporate capitalism, the two historical factors of transformation, the subjective and the objective, do not coincide: they are prevalent in different and even antagonistic groups". (Marcuse, 1969: 56) But this both underestimates the depth of the economic crisis in capitalism, and posits a simple split between "the human base of the process of production" (workers) and "the political consciousness among the non-conformist young intelligentsia", which is untenable and undialectical (Marcuse, 1969: ibid). Nevertheless, it remains true that nowhere has this convergence been completed. Where authentic counter-cultural values and 'focal concerns' survive, they appear *divergent* with respect to *both* traditional middle-class *and* working-class values and strategies. In this discrepancy, middle-class sub-cultures continue to reveal their transitional class character and displaced position, and articulate the extremely uneven tempo of the post-1968 break in the traditional structures. (We have tried, below, to express this *double divergence* diagrammatically.)

At one level, middle class counter-cultures - like working-class sub-cultures - also attempted to work out or work through, but at an 'imaginary' level, a contradiction or problematic in their class situation. But, because they inhabit a dominant culture (albeit in a negative way) they are strategically placed (in ways which working-class sub-cultures are *not)* to generalise an internal contradiction for the society as a whole. The counter-cultures stemmed from changes in the 'real relations' of their class: they represented a rupture inside the dominant culture which then became linked with the crisis of hegemony, of civil society and ultimately of the state itself. It is in *this* sense that middle-class counter-cultures, beginning from a point *within* the dominant class culture, have become an emergent ruptural force for the whole society. Their thrust is no longer contained by their point of inception. Rather, by extending and developing their 'practical critique' of the dominant culture from a privileged position inside it, they have come to inhabit, embody and express many of the contradictions of the system itself. Naturally, society cannot be 'imaginarily' reconstructed from that point. But that does not exhaust their emergent potential. For they also prefigure, anticipate, foreshadow - though in truncated, diagrammatic and 'Utopian' forms - emergent social forms. These new forms are rooted in the productive base of the system itself, though when

Traditional Middle Class	Counter-Culture	Working Class
status	style	class
nuclear family	commune	extended family
career	'uncareer'/right not-to-work	job
pro-business	anti-business & union	pro-union
home	'pad'	home
residential area	'enclave'	neighbourhood
work/leisure	work-is-play	work/leisure
formal repres- entation	'participation'	formal democracy
elitism	'leaderlessness'	democracy
civic/private	personal-is-the -public	public/private
graded public education/ private school	'free school'/ de-schooling	mass public education
club	'scene'	pub
high culture	life-is-art	mass culture
high fashion	'boutique'	chain store
high consumption	anti-consump- tion	mass consumption
materialist	anti-material- ist	materialist
restraint	'freedom'	constraint
sober	libertarian	respectable
adapt to roles	transcend roles	negotiate roles
masculine/ (feminine)	break gender roles	masculine/(feminine)
possessive individualism	'fraternal' individualism	collective

they arise at the level of the 'counter-culture' *only*, we are
correct to estimate that their maturing within the womb of society
is, as yet, incomplete. They prefigure, among other things, the
increasingly *social* nature of modern production, and the outdated
social, cultural, political and ideological forms in which this
is confined. The counter-cultures come, at best, half-way
on the road to making manifest this base contradiction. Some
analysts suggest that this comes through clearest in what Marcuse
has called 'the new sensibility'. Nairn points, in the same
direction, to the prefiguring of a new kind of 'social individual'.
He speaks of the promise that "'youth' can for the first time
assume an other than biological meaning, a positive social meaning,
as the bearer of those pressures in the social body which prefigure a new society instead of the reproduction of the old one"
(Nairn: 1968: 172-3). These larger meanings of the rise of
the counter-cultures cannot be settled here - if only because,
historically, their trajectory is unfinished. What they did
was to put these questions on the political agenda. Answers
lie elsewhere.

I. The social reaction to youth

    As we have already hinted, the dominant society did not calmly
sit on the sidelines throughout the period and watch the sub-
cultures at play. What began as a response of confused perplex-
ity - caught in the pat phrase, 'the generation gap' -
became, over the years, an intense, and intensified struggle.
In the 1950's, 'youth' came to symbolise the most advanced point
of social change: youth was employed as a *metaphor* for social
change. The most extreme trends in a changing society were
identified by the society's taking its bearings from what youth
was 'up to': youth was the *vanguard party* - of the classless,
post-protestant, consumer society to come. This displacement
of the tensions provoked by social change on to 'youth' was an
ambiguous manoeuvre. Social change was seen as generally
beneficial ('you've never had it so good'); but also as
eroding the traditional landmarks and undermining the sacred
order and institutions of traditional society. It was therefore,
from the first, accompanied by feelings of diffused and dispersed
social anxiety. The boundaries of society were being redefined,
its moral contours redrawn, its fundamental relations (above all,
those class relations which for so long gave a hierarchical
stability to English life) transformed. As has been often
remarked (Cf: Erikson, 1966; Cohen, 1973, etc.), movements
which disturb a society's normative contours mark the inception
of troubling times - especially for those sections of the population who have made an overwhelming commitment to the continuation
of the *status quo*. 'Troubling times', when social anxiety is
widespread but fails to find an organised public or political
expression, give rise to the displacement of social anxiety

71

on to convenient scapegoat groups. This is the origin of the 'moral panic' - a spiral in which the social groups who perceive their world and position as threatened, identify a 'responsible enemy', and emerge as the vociferous guardians of traditional values: moral entrepreneurs. It is not surprising, then, that youth became the focus of this social anxiety - its displaced object. In the 1950's, and again in the early 1960's, the most visible and identifiable youth groups were involved in dramatic events which triggered off 'moral panics', focussing, in displaced form, society's 'quarrel with itself'. Events connected with the rise of the Teds, and later, the motor-bike boys and the Mods, precipitated classic moral panics. Each event was seen as signifying, in microcosm, a wider or deeper social problem - the problem of youth as a whole. In this crisis of authority, youth now played the role of *symptom* and *scapegoat*.

'Moral panics' of this order were principally focussed to begin with, around 'Working-class youth'. The tightly organised sub-cultures - Teds, Mods, etc. - represented only the most visible targets of this reaction. Alongside these, we must recall the way youth became connected, in the 1958 Notting Hill riots, with that other submerged and displaced theme of social anxiety - race; and the general anxiety about rising delinquency, the rising rate of juvenile involvement in crime, the panics about violence in the schools, vandalism, gang fights, and football hooliganism. Reaction to these and other manifestations of 'youth' took a variety of forms: from modifications to the Youth Service and the extension of the social work agencies, through the prolonged debate about the decline in the influence of the family, the clampdowns on truancy and indiscipline in the schools, to the Judge's remarks, in the Mods vs. Rockers trial, that they were nothing better than "Sawdust Caesars". The waves of moral panic reached new heights with the appearance of the territorial-based Skinheads, the football riots and destruction of railway property.

To this was added, in the mid-1960's, a set of 'moral panics' of a new kind, this time focussing around middle-class youth and 'permissiveness'. Working-class youth groups were seen as symptomatic of deeper civil unrest. But middle-class groups, with their public disaffiliation, their ideological attack on 'straight society', their relentless search for pleasure and gratification, etc., were interpreted as action, more consciously and deliberately, to undermine social and moral stability: youth, now, as the active *agents* of social breakdown. The first wave of social reaction in this area crystallised around social, moral and cultural issues: drugs, sexuality, libertinism, pornography, the corruption of the young - the key themes of the 'permissive revolution'. (This produced, in response, the first organised anti-permissive 'backlash' amongst the moral guardians -Mrs.

Whitehouse, the Longford Report, the Festival of Light, SPUC., etc.) The second wave crystallised around the 'politicisation' of this counter-culture - student protest, the new street politics, demonstrations, etc. Here 'youth' was cast, not simply as the conscious agents of change, but as deliberately pushing society into anarchy: youth as the *subversive minority*. And now The Law, which had been mobilised from time to time, in its 'normal' routine way, to deal with hooliganism and vandalism, was brought more formally and actively into play. This shift inside the control culture, from informal outrage and moral crusading to formal constraint and legal control, had wider origins (which we cannot enter into here: see the Law and Order Sections of the forthcoming study of Mugging, CCCS.). But it came to bear heavily and directly on youth: the succession of trials and legal actions (the trials of *OZ* and *IT*, the arrests of prominent counter-culture figures for drug possession, the Little Red School Book affair, the drug and pornography 'clean-ups' instituted by the police, etc.) were matched by equally dramatic legal controls against youth's more political wing (the Garden House trial, the trials of Peter Hain and the Springbok Tour protesters,the Angry Brigade Trial and the widespread use of conspiracy charges). When these are taken together with the much-augmented activity of the police and Special Branch, the extension of the law to industrial relations, strikes and picketing, the affairs of the five dockers and the Shrewsbury pickets, it makes sense, from about 1970 onwards (not surprisingly, in step with the return of the Heath government to power), to speak of a qualitative shift in the nature and activities of the control culture, a sharp movement towards 'closure' - the birth of a 'Law 'N Order' society. Though youth was, in this polarising climate, by no means the only object of attack and control, it continued to provide one of the pivots of more organised and orchestrated public campaigns. In these campaigns, politicians, chief constables, judges, the press and media joined hands and voices with the moral guardians in a general 'crack-down' on 'youth' and 'the permissive society'. The sharpening of control was nowhere so evident as in the activities of police and courts, local councillors and residents, against black youth - a moral panic which yielded, in 1972-3, the near conspiracy of the 'Mugging' scare. (But in fact, from about 1969 onwards, the black community, and especially black youth, is being constantly 'policed' in the ghetto areas.)

The contradictoriness of this 'control' response to youth must not be neglected. In the 1950's, the press publicised and patronised the 'Teds' in the very same moment that the fire hoses were brought up to control the crowds queuing to see 'Rock Around The Clock'. 'Mods' appeared, simultaneously, in court and on the front pages of the colour supplements. The date of the Mods vs. Rockers show-down coincided with the 'Mod' fashion

73

explosion, with the 'takeover' by 'mod' styles of the Kings Road
and the birth of 'Swinging London'. Hippies trailed their
flowered gear all the way across the television screen to the
addict centres.   Mick Jagger was flown by helicopter, virtually
straight from the Old Bailey to meet venerable figures of the
Establishment to discuss the state of the world. There is a
continuing, and characteristically twofaced musing in the high-brow
press over the fate and fortunes of pop music throughout the
period.   We cannot examine either the detail or the roots of
this ambivalence here, though we hope we have said enough to
indicate that the two faces of the social reaction to youth -
patronising publicity and imitation versus moral anxiety and
outrage - both had their roots in a deeper social and cultural
crisis in the society.   However, as the disaffiliation of
working-class youth became more pronounced, more traditionally
'delinquent' in form, as the counter-culture became organised and
politicised, and as other sources of political dissent (especially
from the organised working class movement) moved into greater
visibility, above all, as the first flush of economic 'affluence'
gave way to crisis and stagflation, the bloom faded.   Whenever
the 'Law and Order' society went campaigning - as it did with
increasing frequency in the late 1960's and 70's - some section
of youth was never very far from the centre of social concern,
and of social control.   Yet, looking across the whole span of
the period, it is difficult to estimate firmly whether the more
overt 'attack' on youth was of greater or lesser significance
than the tendency, throughout the period as a whole, of the
dominant culture to seek and find, in 'youth', the folk-devils
to people its nightmare: the nightmare of a society which, in
some fundamental way, had lost its sway and authority over its
young, which had failed to win their hearts, minds and consent,
a society teetering towards 'anarchy', secreting, at its heart,
what Mr. Powell so eloquently described as an unseen and nameless
"Enemy".   The whole collapse of hegemonic domination to which
this shift from the 1950's to the 1970's bears eloquent witness,
was written - etched - in 'youthful' lines.

FOOTNOTE

1.   But see also, for the original formulation of the important concept
      'homology', Willis (1972).   A shorter version of this study is
      shortly to be published in a revised form as *Profane Culture*,
      Chatto and Windus.

74

Some notes on the relationship between the societal control culture and the news media, and the construction of a law and order campaign

▌ The Media and the Control Culture: a symbiotic relationship

(1)   THE CONTROL CULTURE AS PRIMARY DEFINERS: MEDIA AS REPRODUCERS

deviant ────────⟶ control culture ────────⟶ media
event   as primary definers   as reproducers

>   (e.g. the press description of a killing on August 17th,
>   1972, as a "mugging gone wrong" was the direct reproduc-
>   tion of a police spokesman's statement.)

Notes: a.   The routine structures of news production -
          impartiality and objectivity - direct the media in the
          first instance to outside, accredited sources.   In
          the case of 'deviant' events, this, in practice, means
          the representatives of the Control Culture (e.g. police,
          judiciary, Home Office).   Thus, news items are based in
          the reproductions of primary definitions presented by
          the Control Culture.

          b.   The structure of 'balance' requires the admission
          of alternative definitions, but these almost always come
          later, and so are required to reply on terrain already
          marked out by the primary definitions;   and they, too,
          must come from accredited alternative sources (organisa-
          tions or 'experts'), and not from 'deviants' themselves.

(2)   THE MEDIA AS PRODUCERS: TRANSFORMATION, OBJECTIFICATION AND
       THE 'PUBLIC VOICE'

deviant ──────⟶ control culture ──────⟶ media as   (assumed
event   as primary definers   producers   audience)

>   (e.g. *Daily Mirror* headline, 14th June, 1973, AGGRO
>   BRITAIN was used to summarise the Chief Constables
>   Report for 1972, where the words were not used.)

Notes: a.   Once primary definitions are 'in play', the media
          can *transform* these by translating them into their own
          public language.   This language is based on the

particular paper's assumption about its audience and *their* language.

b.   This process of transformation is, like all news items, a process of *objectification*, i'.e. it makes an event a concrete, publicly knowable event.   In addition, the 'public' language makes it appear that the media is operating independently of the primary definers.

c.   Also, in a more active role still, the media can actually *campaign* on an issue, by claiming - through editorials - to speak with the 'voice of the public'.

(3)   THE CLOSURE OF THE CIRCLE

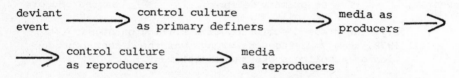

(e.g. "The newspapers have made it known that sentences for attacks on the open highway will no longer be light." Mr. Justice Caulfield, at Leicester Crown Court, quoted in the *Daily Express*, 21st March, 1973.)

Note: Once the media have spoken in their voice, on behalf of the inaudible public, the primary definers can then use the media's statements and claims as legitimations (magically, without any visible connection) for *their* actions and statements, by claiming press - and via the press, public - support.   In turn, the ever attentive media reproduce the Control Culture statements, thus completing the magical circle, with such effect that it is no longer possible to tell who first began the process;   each legitimates the other in turn.

2   The mechanics of a Law and Order campaign

(1)   MORAL PANICS: THREE HISTORICAL TYPES:

(i)   *Discrete Moral Panics*   (early 60's, e.g. Mods and Rockers)

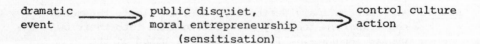

(ii) *'Crusading' - mapping together discrete moral panics to produce a 'speeded-up' sequence* (late 60's, e.g. pornography, drugs.)

sensitisation   →   dramatic   →   control culture
(moral entrepreneurship)   event   action

(iii) *Post-Law 'n' Order Campaign: an altered sequence* (early 70's, e.g., mugging).

sensitisation → control culture → dramatic →
                organisation and   event
                action

→ control culture
   intensified action

Note: In the final example, we must note the tendency of the Control Culture to act in *anticipation* of the public visibility of a particular 'scare'.

(2) THE 'SIGNIFICATION SPIRAL'

A way of publicly signifying issues and problems which is instrinsically *escalating*, i.e. it increases the perceived potential *threat* of an issue through the way it becomes signified.

Elements: (a)   The identification of a specific issue.
            (b)   The identification of a "subversive minority".
            (c)   'Convergence' or the linking by labelling of the specific issue to other problems.
            (d)   The notion of 'thresholds' which, once crossed, can lead to further escalation of the problem's "menace" to society.
            (e)   The element of explaining and prophesying which often involves making analagous references to the Unites States - *the* paradigm example.
            (f)   The call for firm steps.

Note: From 1968 onwards, this became *the* media paradigm for handling threatening issues across the *whole national daily press* (e.g., *Sunday Express* editorial, 27th October, 1968, and *Sunday Times* editorial, 27th April, 1969; both on students.)

77

(3)   CONVERGENCE

The linking of the specific issue to others by labelling,
either explicitly or implicitly.

three types:

	Real Movement	Example	Signification
i	Actual Convergence	Homosexuals— Gay Liberation Front (GLF)	Potentially accurate
ii	Some Convergence	GLF— Marxist Left— 'Red' conspiracy	increasingly contains a purely ideo- logical dimension
iii	No Convergence	Students—hooligans	purely ideo - logical

Note: As the period progresses there is a tendency to 'map'
together increasing numbers of problems as constituting
one single threat, and for this convergence to contain
an increasing purely ideological construction (see,
for example, the report of Powell's Northfield Speech,
Sunday Times, 14th June, 1970).

(4)   THRESHOLDS

Boundaries staking out progressively societal tolerance
limits

78

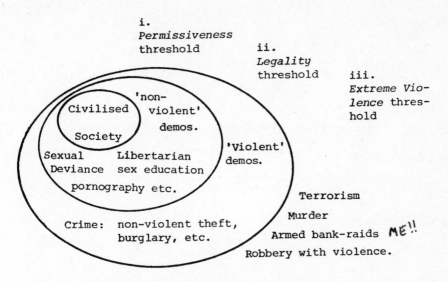

i.
Permissiveness
threshold

ii.
Legality
threshold

iii.
Extreme Violence threshold

'non-violent' demos.

Civilised Society

'Violent' demos.

Sexual Deviance   Libertarian sex education

pornography etc.

Crime: non-violent theft, burglary, etc.

Terrorism
Murder
Armed bank-raids ME!!
Robbery with violence.

i)   Crossing of Permissiveness threshold
      threatens to undermine social AUTHORITY   (moral standards)

ii)   Crossing of Legality threshold
      threatens to undermine social LEGITIMACY   (parliamentary
                                                  channels)

iii) Crossing of Extreme Violence threshold threatens to
      undermine social CONTROL   (the State itself)

Notes: a.   As period progresses there is an increasing tendency
             for events to be pushed beyond thresholds
             e.g.   1966-70: threshold of Permissiveness dominant

                    1970-on: threshold of Legality dominant

                    1972-on: threshold of Extreme Violence
                             dominant

        b.   Events are projected across thesholds by stressing
             the illegal or violent (or both) aspects of the
             permissive, or the violent aspects of the illegal.
             Thus, in our example (above) non-violent protest
             demonstrations, at most a 'permissive' flouting of
             social authority can be projected across the
             thresholds of Legality and Extreme Violence by
             being signified as violent.   In this way, by
             being signified as a threat to Social Control, firm
             control measures are legitimated.

These notes derive from the work of the CCCS Mugging Group.

79

ETHNOGRAPHY

CULTURAL RESPONSES OF THE TEDS

Tony Jefferson

Note: *In his review of Teddy Boy culture, Tony Jefferson deals with three related aspects: the way the "sense of group" of the Teds and their low or "near-lumpen" status made them extremely sensitive to insults, real or imagined; the way this over-sensitivity became attached, primarily to the distinctive dress and appearance of the group; and the elements which the Teds borrowed from the dominant culture and reworked into a distinctive style of their own. This "proletarianisation" of an upper-class style of dress was no mere stylistic flourish: it expressed, Jefferson argues, both the reality, and the aspirations of the group. A longer version of this paper is available* (Stencilled Paper No.22, CCCS).

In the light of growing structural inequalities /argued earlier in the paper/ how can we read the Teds' cultural responses as symbolic articulations of their social plight? If we look at the cultural responses adopted, in turn, what becomes apparent in decoding them is an attempt to defend, symbolically, a constantly threatened space and a declining status.

a)   Group-Mindedness: The group-mindedness of the Teds can be read partly as a response to the post-war upheaval and destruction of the socially cohesive force of the extended kinship network. Thus the group life and intense loyalty of the Teds can be seen as a reaffirmation of traditional slum working-class values and the "strong sense of territory" (Downes, 1966: 119), as an attempt to retain, if only imaginatively, a hold on the territory which was being expropriated from them, by developers, on two levels:

(1)   the actual expropriation of land;

(2)   the less tangible expropriation of the culture attached to the land, i.e. the kinship networks and the "articulations of communal space" mentioned by Cohen (1972: 16).

b)   Extreme Touchiness to Insults, Real or Imagined: If we look
at their extreme touchiness to insults, real or imagined, we find
that most of these incidents revolved around insults to themselves
personally, to their appearance generally, and their dress in
particular.   To illustrate this point, using one of the more
dramatic examples available; the first 'Teddy boy' killing, the
Clapham Common murder of 1953, was a result of a fight between
three youths and a group of Teds which had been started when one
of the Teds had been called 'a flash cunt' by one of the youths.
(For a full account of this incident, and the subsequent trial,
see Parker, 1969.)

My contention is that to lads traditionally lacking in status,
and *being further deprived of what little they possessed* /‾a
reference to the declining social situation of the Teds, argued
earlier in the fuller version of this paper‾/ there remained only
the self, the cultural extension of the self (dress, personal
appearance) and the social extension of the self (the group).
Once threats were perceived in these areas, the only 'reality'
or 'space' on which they had any hold, then the fights, *in
defence of this space* become explicable and *meaningful* phenomena.

If we look closely at the objects of Teddy boy fighting, this
notion of defending their space is, I believe, further amplified.
Group fights, i.e. fights with other groups of Teds, are explicable in terms of a defence of the social extension of the self-
the group (hence, the importance of 'group-mindedness').
Fights which ensued when individuals insulted Teds are explicable in terms of *a defence of the self and the cultural extension
of the self symbolised in their dress and general appearance.*
Especially important in this area is the touchiness to insults
about dress.   This I shall enlarge upon in the next section on
'Dress'.

Whilst many of their fights resulted from extreme sensitivity
to insults, even their attacks on the Cypriot proprietors of
Cypriot cafes, and Blacks, can be read in terms of defence: a
defence of status.   Their position as 'lumpen' youths was
worsening *independently* of the influx of Commonwealth immigrants
in the early 1950's, but in the absence of a coherent and
articulate grasp of their social reality, it was perhaps inevitable that they should perceive this influx as causal rather than
coincidental.   Thus, they rationalised their position as being,
in part anyway, due to the immigrants and displaced their
frustration onto them.   An additional irritant was the perception
many Teds had of immigrants as actually making it - the corollary
of this, of course, was that they were making it 'at the Teds'
expense'.   The cafe-owning Cypriots were one example of those
who had 'made it'.   Others were the coloured landlords and

racketeers.   Living, as many Teds did, in dilapidated inner urban
areas scheduled for re-development, they came into contact with
the minority of coloureds, who, because of the hopelessness of
their position, (being coloured and working class,) were forced
into positions of very limited options (small-time racketeering
and pimping were probably two of the more available and attrac-
tive).   And so the myth of the coloured immigrants being either
pimps, landlords or in on the rackets, very prevalent among Teds,
(and many white working class adults) started and spread.   The
repercussions of all this, the 1958 'race-riots' in Nottingham
and Notting Hill are known, sadly, only too well.   That it should
have been the Teds who started them lends weight to my thesis.
That large numbers of working class adults responded in the way
they did, by joining in, demonstrates that it was not only the
young 'lumpen' who were experiencing a worsening of their
socio-economic position.   But, in an age of 'affluence' the
real structural causes could not be admitted, and predictably,
were not.   Instead, the nine *unskilled working class adolescents*
who started the Notting Hill riots, were savagely sentenced to
four years' imprisonment apiece.   The obvious scape-goating
involved, as in all similar cases of scape-goat punishments, was,
and still is, a sure sign of mystification at work - the protective cloak of the ruling classes being drawn closer to prevent
its real interests becoming too visible.

The attacks on youth clubs are perhaps easiest to explain if
one remembers that many youth clubs banned all Teddy boys purely
on 'reputation'.   Simple revenge must then have constituted the
basis for some attacks.   Additionally, though, there was the
chronic lack of public provision of facilities to match the
increase in adolescent leisure (see, for example, Fyvel, 1963:
120-3).   Consequently, much was then expected of what was
provided - far too much.   When these failed to live up to the
expectations, as they invariably did, the disappointment was
invariably increased.   Thus, ironically, the youth clubs that
did exist, far from alleviating adolescent leisure problems
actually exacerbated them.   (For a fascinating account of the
trials and tribulations experienced in this area and of a valiant
but short-lived attempt to supply the kids with what they *wanted*
see Gosling, 1962).   Finally, the attacks on bus conductors.
Since these attacks were usually on conductors on late-night bus
routes, this suggests that the opportunity of anonymity, and
possibly alcohol, combined to increase the already high level of
sensitivity to imagined insults.

c)   *Dress and Appearance:* Despite periodic unemployment, despite
the unskilled jobs, Teds, in common with other teenagers at work
during this period, were relatively affluent.   Between 1945-1950,
the average real wage of teenagers increased at twice the adult
rate (see, for example, Abrams, 1959).   Teds thus certainly had

money to spend and, because it was practically all they had, it assumed a *crucial* importance. Much of the money went on clothes: the Teddy boy 'uniform'. But before decoding this particular cultural articulation, a sketch of the 'style' and its history is necessary.

Originally, the Edwardian suit was introduced in 1950 by a group of Savile Row tailors who were attempting to initiate a new style. It was addressed, primarily, to the young aristocratic men about town. Essentially the dress consisted of a long, narrow - lapelled, waisted jacket, narrow trousers (but without being 'drainpipes'), ordinary toe-capped shoes, and a fancy waistcoat. Shirts were white with cutaway collars and ties were tied with a 'windsor' knot. Headwear, if worn, was a trilby. The essential changes from conventional dress were the cut of the jacket and the dandy waistcoat. Additionally, barbers began offering individual styling, and hair length was generally longer than the conventional short back and sides. (This description is culled from a picture of the 'authentic' Edwardian dress which was put out by the *Tailor and Cutter* and printed in the *Daily Sketch,* 14th November, 1953, in order to dissociate the 'authentic' from the working-class adoption of the style.)

This dress began to be taken up by working class youths sometime in 1953 and, in those early days, was often taken over wholesale (The *Daily Mirror* of 23rd October, 1953, shows a picture of Michael Davies, who was convicted of what later became known as the first 'teddy boy' killing, which would bear this out. In fact the picture shows him in a three piece matching suit, i.e. without the fancy waistcoat.)

The later modifications to this style by the Teds were the bootlace tie; the thick-creped suede shoes (Eton clubman chukka type); skin-tight, drainpipe trousers (without turn-ups); straighter, less waisted jackets; moleskin or satin collars to the jackets; and the addition of vivid colours. The earlier sombre suit colours occasionally gave way to suits of vivid green, red or pink and other 'primitive' colours (see Sandilands, 1968). Blue-suede shoes, post-Elvis, were also worn. The hair-style also underwent a transformation: it was usually long, combed into a 'D-A' with a boston neck-line (straight cut), greasy, with side whiskers and a quiff. Variations on this were the 'elephant's trunk' or the more extreme 'apache' (short on top, long at sides).

I see this choice of uniform as, initially, an attempt to buy status (since the clothes chosen were originally worn by upper-class dandies) which, being quickly aborted by a harsh social reaction (in 1954 second-hand Edwardian suits were on sale in various markets - see Rock and Cohen, 1970 - as they became rapidly unwearable by the upper-class dandies once the Teds had taken them over as their own) was followed by an attempt to create their own style via the modifications just outlined.

This, then, was the Teds' one contribution to culture: their adoption and personal modification of Savile Row Edwardian suits. But more important than being a contribution to culture, since culture only has meaning when transposed into social terms, their dress represented a symbolic way of expressing and negotiating with their social reality; of giving cultural *meaning* to their social plight. And because of this, their touchiness to insults about dress becomes not only comprehensible but rational.

But what 'social reality' was their uniform both 'expressive of' and 'a negotiation with'? Unfortunately there is, as yet, no 'grammar' for decoding cultural symbols like dress and what follows is largely speculative. However, if one examines *the context from which the cultural symbol was probably extracted* - one possible way of formulating one aspect of such a grammar - then the adoption of, for example, the bootlace tie, begins to acquire social meaning. Probably picked up from the many American Western films viewed during this period where it was worn, most prevalently, as I remember them, by the slick city gambler whose social status was, grudgingly, high because of his ability to live *by his wits* and *outside* the traditional working class *mores* of society (which were basically rural and hardworking as opposed to urban and hedonistic), then I believe its symbolic cultural meaning for the Teds becomes explicable as both expression of their *social reality* (basically outsiders and forced to live by their wits) and their *social 'aspirations'* (basically an attempt to gain high, albeit grudging, status for an ability to live smartly, hedonistically and by their wits in an urban setting).

THE MEANING OF MOD
Dick Hebdige

Note: "The meaning of Mod" is the second extract from Dick
Hebdige's study of sub-cultural styles in the 1960's. Here,
in contrast with his piece on black culture (where the background
is less familiar), Hebdige spends less time on a description of
the 'Mod' style, and focusses instead on the modes of stylistic
generation in Mod sub-culture. He examines the way objects and
things were borrowed by the Mods from the world of consumer
commodities, and their meaning transformed by the way they were
reworked into a new stylistic ensemble. This involved expro-
priating the meanings given to things by the dominant consumer
culture, and incorporating them in ways which expressed sub-
cultural rather than dominant values. The study also suggests
how the Mods raised consumption, the commodity, style itself to
a new level - a sort of 'fetishising' of style, which produced the
effect commonly described as 'narcissistic'. This analysis gives
empirical substance to the argument that sub-cultures live their
relation to their real situation as an 'imaginary' relation.

ITS APPEARANCE

Like most primitive vocabularies, each word of Wolverine[1], the
universal Pop Newspeak, is a prime symbol and serves a dozen or
a hundred functions of communication. Thus 'mod' came to refer
to several distinct styles, being essentially an umbrella-term
used to cover everything which contributed to the recently
launched myth of 'swinging London'.

Thus groups of art-college students following in Mary Quant's
footsteps and developing a taste for the outrageous in clothing
were technically 'mods'[2], and Lord Snowdon earned the epithet
when he appeared in a polo necked sweater and was hastily grouped
with the 'new breed' of 'important people' like Bailey and
Terrence Stamp who showed a 'swinging' disregard for certain
dying conventions. But for our purposes, we must limit the
definition of the mods to working class teenagers who lived
mainly in London and the new towns of the South and who could be
readily identified by characteristic hairstyles, clothing etc.
According to Melly (1972), the progenitors of this style appear
to have been a group of working class dandies, possibly descended
from the devotees of the Italianate style; known throughout the
trad world as mods who were dedicated to clothes and lived in
London. Only gradually and with popularisation did this group
accumulate other distinctive identity symbols (the scooter, the
pills, the music). By 1963, the all night R and B clubs

held this group firmly to Soho and central London, whilst around
the ring roads the Ton up boys thundered on unperturbed, nostal-
gically clinging on to rock and roll and the tougher working
class values.

Whether the mod/rocker dichotomy was ever really essential to
the self-definition of either group remains doubtful.   The
evidence suggests that the totally disparate goals and life styles
of the two groups left very little room for interaction of any
kind.   After the disturbances of Whitsun 1964, at Clacton, in
which hostilities between mods and rockers played no important
part (the main targets for aggression being the pathetically
inadequate entertainment facilities and small shopkeepers) the
media accentuated and rigidified the opposition between the two
groups, setting the stage for the conflicts which occurred at
Margate and Brighton during the Easter weekend and at Hastings
during the August Bank holiday[3].   The fact that the mod clashed
before the camera with the rocker is, I suspect, more indicative
of the mod's vanity than of any really deeply felt antagonism
between the two groups.   The mods rejected the rocker's crude
conception of masculinity, the transparency of his motivations,
his clumsiness, and embraced a less obvious style, which in turn
was less easily ridiculed or dismissed by the parent culture.
What distinguished the Bank Holidays of 1964 from all previous
bank holidays was not the violence (this was a fairly regular
feature) but the public debut of this style at the coastal resorts.
The very visible presence at Margate, Brighton, and Hastings of
thousands of disturbingly ordinary, even smart teenagers from
London and its environs somehow seemed to constitute a threat to
the old order (the retired colonels, the tourist-oriented
tradesmen who dominated the councils of the south coast resorts).
The mods, according to Laing,"looked alright but there was
something in the way they moved which adults couldn't make out"
(1969).   They seemed to consciously invert the values associated
with smart dress, to deliberately challenge the assumptions, to
falsify the expectations derived from such sources.   As Stan
Cohen puts it, they were all the more disturbing by the impression
they gave of "actors who are not quite in their places" (1973).

I shall go on now to analyse the origins of this style in the
experience of the mods themselves by attempting to penetrate
and decipher the mythology of the mods.   Finally, I should like
to offer an explanation of why an overtly inoffensive style could
manage to project menace so effectively.

HALFWAY TO PARADISE ON THE PICCADILLY LINE

The mod's adoption of a sharp but neat and visually understated
style can be explained only partly by his reaction to the rocker's
grandiloquence.   It is partly explained by his desire to do

justice to the mysterious complexity of the metropolis in his
personal demeanour, to draw himself closer to the Negro whose
very metabolism seemed to have grown into, and kept pace with
that of the city.   It is partly explained by his unique and
subversive attitude toward the commodities he habitually consumed
(more of this second point later).

The life style to which the mod ideally aspired revolved
around night clubs and city centres which demanded a certain
exquisiteness of dress.   In order to cope with the unavoidable
minute by minute harassments, the minutiae of highspeed interactions encumbent upon an active night-life in the city, the mod
had to be on the ball at all times, functioning at an emotional
and intellectual frequency high enough to pick up the slightest
insult or joke or challenge or opportunity to make the most of
the precious night.   Thus speed[4] was needed to keep mind and
body synchronised perfectly.   His ideal model-mentor for this
ideal style would be the Italian mafiosi-type so frequently
depicted in crime films shot in New York (one step above London
in the mod hierarchy).   The Brooklyn sharp kid had been emulated
by the wartime black marketeer, the "wide boy" and the post war
"spiv" and the style was familiar, readily accessible and could
be easily worked up.   Alternatively, an equally acceptable,
perhaps even more desirable image was projected by the Jamaican
hustler (or later "rudie") whom the mod could see with increasing
regularity as the decade wore on operating with an enviable
"savoir-faire" from every available street-corner.   Thus the
pork-pie hat and dark glasses were at one time essential mod
accessories.   If the grey people (who oppressed and constricted
both mod and negro) held a monopoly on daytime business, the
blacks held more shares in the action of the night hours.[5]

Another and perhaps more pervasive influence can be traced
to that of the indigenous British gangster style, the evolution
of which coincides almost exactly with that of the mods[6].   With
the introduction of the Gaming Laws in 1963, London had become a
kind of European Las Vegas and offered rich rewards and a
previously unattainable status to Britain's more enterprising
criminals.   The famous protection gangs of the Krays and the
Richardsons (from East and South London respectively; both
major breeding grounds of mod) began converging on the west end,
and many working class teenagers followed their elders into the
previously inviolable citadels of Soho and Westminster to see what
fruits were offered.   The city centre, transfigured and updated
by the new nightlife, offered more opportunities for adventure and
excitement to the more affluent working class youth; and the
clandestine, intergang warfare, the ubiquitous, brooding menace,
provided a more suitable background to the mod's ideal life-style.
As the gangsters stuck faithfully to their classic Hollywood
scripts, dressing in sober suits, adopting classic Capone

poses, using sawn off shotguns on each other, petrol bombing each other's premises, being seen in whispered consultation with bespectacled "consiglieres", Soho became the perfect soil on which thriller fiction fantasies and subterranean intrigue could thrive; and this was the stuff for which the mod lived and in which his culture was steeped[7]. It was as if the whole submerged criminal underworld had surfaced, in 1965, in the middle of London, and had brought with it its own submarine world of popular fiction, sex and violence fantasy. As it acquired power it explored the possibilities for realising those fantasies - the results were often bizarre and frequently terrifying. The unprecedented marriage between East and South London criminal cultures and West End high life and the Chelsea jet sets bore some strange and exotic fruit, and one of its most exquisite creatures was the Soho mod.

A MUGSHOT OF THE IDEAL MOD

In a *Sunday Times* magazine of April, 1964, Denzil, the seventeen year old mod interviewee fulfils the ideal mod role, 'looking excruciatingly sharp in all the photographs and describing an average week in the life of the ideal London mod.'

> Monday night meant dancing at the Mecca, the Hammersmith Palais, the Purley Orchard, or the Streatham Locarno.
> Tuesday meant Soho and the Scene club.
> Wednesday was Marquee night.
> Thursday was reserved for the ritual washing of the hair.
> Friday meant the Scene again.
> Saturday afternoon usually meant shopping for clothes and records, Saturday night was spent dancing and rarely finished before 9.00 or 10.00 Sunday morning.
> Sunday evening meant the Flamingo or, perhaps, if one showed signs of weakening, could be spent sleeping.

Even allowing for exaggeration the number of mods who managed to even approximate this kind of life could not exceed a few hundred, perhaps at most a few thousand. In fact probably no one possesses the super-human stamina (even with a ready supply of pills), let alone the hard cash which would be required to get a mod through this kind of schedule but the fact remains that Denzil did not let the side down. He has pushed the group-fantasy, projected the image of the impossible good life that everybody needed, right down and onto the indelible printed page. And meanwhile, every mod was preparing himself psychologically so that if the opportunity should arise, if the money was there, if Welwyn Garden City should be metamorphosed into Piccadilly Circus, he would be ready. Every mod was existing in a ghost world of gangsterism, luxurious clubs, and beautiful women even if reality only amounted to a draughty Parker anorak, a beaten up Vespa, and fish and chips out of a greasy bag.

90

A SNAPSHOT OF THE STANDARD MOD

The reality of mod life was somewhat less glamorous. The average Mod, according to the survey of the 43 Margate offenders interviewed by Barker and Little (1964) earned about £11 a week, was either a semi-skilled or more typically an office worker who had left Secondary-modern school at fifteen. Another large section of mods were employed as department store clerks, messengers, and occupied menial positions in the various service industries of the West end. The mods are often described as exploring the upward option, but it seems probable that this has been deduced incorrectly from the mod's fanatical devotion to appearance, and the tendency to boast when in a blocked or amphetamine-induced state. As Denzil says: "There's a lot of lying when you're blocked about the number of girls you go out with in the week, how much your suit costs, etc. ..." The archetypal mod, would, I think, be more likely to be the eighteen year old interviewed in the Barker-Little sample whose only articulated ambition - to become the owner of a Mayfair drinking-club - towered so high above his present occupation as a meat porter that he no longer seriously entertained it; but had realistically if resentfully accepted society's appraisal of his worth ("more or less manual - that's all I am"), and existed purely for and through his leisure-time. The bell-boy hero in Pete Townshend's new rock opera about the mod experience - *Quadrophrenia* - is apparently, similarly resigned to an insignificant and servile role during the day, but is all the more determined to make up for it at night. Like the fifteen year old office boy in Wolfe's essay "The Noonday Underground" (Wolfe, 1969b) whose clothes are more exquisitely tailored than the bosses', the mod was determined to compensate for his relatively low position in the daytime status-stakes over which he had no control, by exercising complete dominion over his private estate - his appearance and choice of leisure pursuits.

The wide gap between the inner world where all was under control, contained and lit by self-love, and the outer world, where all was hostile, daunting, and loaded in "their" favour, was bridged by amphetamines[8]. Through the alchemy of "speed", the mod achieved a magical omnipotence, whereby the dynamics of his movements were magnified, the possibilities of action multiplied, their purposes illuminated. Amphetamine made life tolerable, "blocked" one's sensory channels so that action and risk and excitement were possible, kept one going on the endless round of consumption, and confined one's attention to the search, the ideal, the goal, rather than the attainment of the goal - relief rather than release. The Who's song *The Searcher* stresses the importance of the search-as-end-in-itself:

I ain't gonna get what I'm after
Till the day I die.

Speed suspended the disappointment when the search failed, inevitably, to turn up anything substantial and gave one the energy to pick up and start again. It also tended to retard mental and emotional development (by producing dependency, by working against communication stimulating incessant vocal at the expense of aural activity) whilst accelerating physical deterioration. The mod lived now and certainly paid later. As the mod was swept along the glossy surface of the sixties hopelessly attempting to extend himself through an endless succession of objects, he would realise at some point that his youth (perhaps the unstated and impossible goal) was by no means everlasting. Tommy, the pinball wizard would eventually, and with great reluctance, face up to the fact that the game was limited by time and that there were never any replays. Hence the mid sixties obsession with the processes of ageing apparent in the songs of The Who and the Rolling Stones (both Mod Heroes).

From The Who's *My Generation,* the theme song of the battlefields of 1964:

Things they do look awful cold
Hope I die 'fore I get old.

From the Rolling Stones record *Mother's Little Helper,* which deals with middle-aged amphetamine-addiction, an understandably predictable mod nightmare:

What a drag it is getting old.

And thus, finally we come to the elaborate consumer rituals of the mods, their apparently insatiable appetite for the products of the capitalist society in which they lived, their fundamental and inescapable confinement within that society.

Whilst not suggesting that the mod style had stumbled across any serious flaw in the monolith of capitalism, I shall now attempt to indicate how it did handle the commodities it took to itself in a unique and subversive manner. If it found no flaws it did at least come across a few hairline cracks. It did at least beat against the bars of its prison.

CONSPICUOUS CONSUMPTION AND THE TRANSFORMED COMMODITY

The mods are often charged by the self-styled commentators of pop with a debilitating tendency to multiple addiction. The argument goes something like this - being typically alienated consumers, the mods eagerly swallowed the latest brand of pills in order to borrow enough energy to enable them to spend the maximum amount of time consuming the maximum amount of commodities, which, in turn, could only be enjoyed whilst under the influence of speed. However, despite his overwhelming need to

92

consume, the mod was never a passive consumer, as his hedonistic middle-class descendant often was[9]. The importance of style to the mods can never be overstressed - Mod was pure, unadulterated STYLE, the essence of style. In order to project style it became necessary first to appropriate the commodity, then to redefine its use and value and finally to relocate its meaning within a totally different context. This pattern, which amounted to the semantic rearrangement of those components of the objective world which the mod style required, was repeated at every level of the mod experience and served to preserve a part at least of the mod's private dimension against the passive consumer role it seemed in its later phases ready to adopt .....

Thus the scooter, a formerly ultra-respectable means of transport was appropriated and converted into a weapon and a symbol of solidarity. Thus pills, medically diagnosed for the treatment of neuroses, were appropriated and used as an end-in-themselves, and the negative evaluations of their capabilities imposed by school and work were substituted by a positive assessment of their personal credentials in the world of play (i.e. the same qualities which were assessed negatively by their daytime controllers - e.g. laziness, arrogance, vanity etc. - were positively defined by themselves and their peers in leisure time).

Thus, the mods learned to make their criticisms obliquely, having learned by experience (at school and work) to avoid direct confrontations where age, experience, economic and civil power would inevitably have told against them. The style they created, therefore, constituted a parody of the consumer society in which they were situated. The mod dealt his blows by inverting and distorting the images (of neatness, of short hair) so cherished by his employers and parents, to create a style, which while being overtly close to the straight world was nonetheless incomprehensible to it.

The mod triumphed with symbolic victories and was the master of the theatrical but ultimately enigmatic gesture. The Bank Holiday incidents, and the November 5th, 1966, scooter-charge on Buckingham Palace (a scarcely remembered and largely unreported event of major importance to the mods involved) whilst holding a certain retrospective fascination for the social historian and calling forth an Agincourt-like pride in those who took part, fail to impress us as permanently significant events, and yet an eighteen year old mod could say at the time about Margate: "Yes, I was there ... It was like we were caking over the country" (quoted in Booker, 1969).

The basis of style is the appropriation and reorganisation by the subject of elements in the objective world which would

otherwise determine and constrict him.   The mod's cry of
triumph, quoted above, was for a romantic victory, a victory of
the imagination; ultimately for an imagined victory.   The
mod combined previously disparate elements to create himself into
a metaphor, the appropriateness of which was apparent only to
himself.   But the mods underestimated the ability of the
dominant culture to absorb the subversive image and sustain the
impact of the anarchic imagination.   The magical transformations
of commodities had been mysterious and were often invisible to
the neutral observer and no amount of stylistic incantation could
possibly affect the oppressive economic mode by which they had
been produced. The state continued to function perfectly no matter
how many of Her Majesty's colours were defiled and draped around
the   shoulders of skinny pill-heads in the form of sharply cut
jackets.

AUTOPSY REPORT ON ONE WHITE NEGRO NOW DECEASED:

   I have already emphasised the positive values of the mod's
relative exclusiveness, his creation of a whole supportive
universe which provided him not only with a distinctive dress,
music, etc. but also with a complete set of meanings.   I
should like to conclude by suggesting that it was this same
esotericism, this same retreatism which led to the eventual and
inevitable decline of mod as a movement.   For the mod was the
first all-British White Negro of Mailer's essay (1968), living
on the pulse of the present, resurrected after work only by a
fierce devotion to leisure, and creating through the dynamics of
his own personality (or more accurately through the dynamics
of the collective personality of the group), a total style
armed, albeit inadequately, against a patronising adult culture,
and which need look no further than itself for its justifications
and its ethics.   Ultimately it was this very self-sufficiency
which led to the Mod's self-betrayal.   Being determined to
cling to the womb of the Noonday Underground, the smokefilled
clubs and the good life without ever facing the implications of
its own alienation and to look merely to its own created and
increasingly commercialised (and therefore artificial and
stylised) image, mesmerised by music, stultified by speed, Mod
was bound eventually to succumb; to be cheated and exploited
at every level.   The consumer rituals were refined and multiplied
ad infinitum and came to involve the use of commodities directed
specifically at a mod market by a rapidly expanding pop industry.
Dress was no longer innovative - nobody "discovered" items like
levi jeans or hush puppies any more.   Style was manufactured
from above instead of being spontaneously created from within.
When a mod magazine could declare authoritatively that there was
a "NEW MOD WALK: feet out, head forward, hands in jacket
pockets", then one had to acknowledge, reluctantly, that this
particular white negro had, somewhere along the line, keeled over
and died.

1. A reference to the language of Tom Wolfe. See, for examples
    of his work: Wolfe (1966; 1969a; 1969b; 1971).

2. The current fashion for camp rock derives much of its creative
    impetus from the extreme narcissism and self-conscious urbanity of
    this group. Bowie and Bolan were among its more conspicuous
    members.

3. For a full account of the role of the media, and other elements in
    the 'societal reaction', in the creation of the mod/rocker dichotomy
    see: Cohen (1973).

4. I use the term to cover "blues", "purple hearts", "black bombers",
    dexedrine, benzedrine, ephedrine and methedrine which were easily
    available to the mods in the mid 60's.

5. The 'hard mods' especially emulated the negro and this emulation
    became explicit in the style of their direct descendants - the
    skinheads.

6. With the conviction of the Krays in 1969 and the introduction of
    new and more restrictive gambling legislation in the same year,
    this style took a crippling blow.

7. This is not so far fetched as it may at first appear. The mid-
    60's gangsterism was a game, a serious, highly dangerous and
    profitable game, but a game nevertheless, the rules of which had
    been fixed in a mythical Hollywood-Chicago years before. The
    effectiveness of an extortion racket depends primarily on its
    flair for publicity; on a consistent projection of mean psychopath
    (Richard Widmark-type) roles; on its convincing presentation of a
    real yet ultimately unspecifiable menace. It functions through
    the indulgence of all those who come into contact with it in a
    popular fantasy and adheres rigidly to the conventions of that
    fantasy. It is in a word, living cinema. Overstated and
    oversimplified, I know, but for a detailed elaboration of this
    point, see my *stencilled paper* No. 25., CCCS, University of
    Birmingham.

8. For confirmation of the centrality of speed in the mod's life-style
    one need look no further than to the cultural significance assigned
    to the scooter, the first innovative means of transport introduced
    by a British youth sub-culture (the **motor bike was borrowed from**
    the States). The verb 'to go' was included in both "Ready Steady
    Go" and "Whole Scene Going", the two mod programmes and testifies to
    the importance of movement.

9. The distinction between the two styles can best be illustrated by
    comparing the major symbolic exhibitions of the mod's solidarity -
    the Bank Holiday gathering, with its equivalent in Hippie
    Culture - the festival. At the coast the mods were impatiently
    reacting *against* the passivity of the crowd; each mod was a
    creative subject capable of entertaining an unimaginative adult
    audience arrogantly displaying the badge of his identity to a
    nation of featureless picture-watchers. The hippie's festivals,
    on the other hand, deliberately avoided contact with other
    cultures (when contact did occur, as at **Altamont, it was often**
    disastrous), were conducted in remote locations in a complacent
    atmosphere of mutual self-congratulation, and centred round the
    passive consumption of music produced by an elite of untouchable
    superstars (c.f. **Eisen, ed.,** 1970, for a collection of essays
    describing how several thousand spectators failed to do anything

about a few score outlaw bikers).   If this comparison seems
unfair we need only look to the mods' consumption of R and B and
Tamla Motown in their clubs.   The mods never consumed their
music statically (the hippies generally *sat* and watched) but would
use the music as a catalyst for their own creative efforts on the
dance floor, even dancing alone if need be.   Perhaps the distinction
can be formulated in two equations:

$$\text{WORKING-CLASS} + \text{MOD} + \text{SPEED} = \text{ACTION}$$

$$\text{MIDDLE-CLASS} + \text{HIPPIE} + \text{MARIJUANA} = \text{PASSIVITY}.$$

THE SKINHEADS & THE MAGICAL RECOVERY OF COMMUNITY
John Clarke

Note: *In this extract from his longer study of 'Skinhead culture'
John Clarke describes the way this sub-culture focuses around the
notions of 'community' and 'territory'. Skinhead culture selectively reaffirms certain core values of traditional working class
culture, and this affirmation is expressed both in dress, style
and appearance, and in activities. The reaffirmation is a
symbolic, rather than a 'real' attempt to recreate some aspects
of the 'parent' culture. The preoccupation in Skinhead culture
with territory, with football and 'fanship', and with a particular
kind of masculinity thus represents what Clarke calls their
'magical recovery of community'. See also the use of this
example in Clarke's MA Thesis, "Reconceptualising Youth Culture"
(CCCS. Birmingham) and in "Skinheads and Youth Culture" (CCCS
Stencilled Paper No. 23).*

Our basic thesis about the Skinheads centres around the notion
of community. We would argue that the Skinhead style represents
an attempt to re-create through the 'mob' the traditional working
class community, as a substitution for the *real* decline of the
latter. The underlying social dynamic for the style, in this
light, is the relative worsening of the situation of the working
class, through the second half of the sixties, and especially
the more rapidly worsening situation of the lower working class
(and of the young within that). This, allied to the young's
sense of exclusion from the existing 'youth sub-culture'
(dominated in the public arena by the music and styles derived
from the 'underground') produced a return to an intensified
"Us-Them" consciousness among the lower working class young,
a sense of being excluded and under attack from a variety of
points. The resources to deal with this sense of exclusion
were not to be found within either the emergent or incorporated
elements of youth sub-cultures, but only in those images and
behaviours which stressed a more traditional form of collective
solidarity. Material from *The Paint House* illustrates this
sense of oppression:

> Everywhere there are fucking bosses, they're always trying to tell
> you what to do ... don't matter what you do, where you go, they're
> always there. People in authority, the people who tell you what
> to do and make sure you do it. It's the system we live in, its
> the governor system.

Schools, you 'ave to go, doncha?   The teachers and the headmaster,
they're the authority, ain't they?   They're telling you what to
do and you're glad to get out and leave and that, aren't ya?
They think because you're young and they pay you and that, that
they can treat you how they like and say what they want.
Then there's the 'old bill' and courts ... they're all part of
authority.   Official and all kinds of people in uniforms.
Anyone with a badge on, traffic wardens and council and all that
... yeah, even the caretaker at the flats, they even 'as goes at
you.   Then when you finish at work or at school, you go to the
clubs and the youth leaders are all just a part of it.
(Daniel and McGuire, eds., 1972: 67).

But the skinheads felt oppressed by more than just the obvious
authority structure; they resented those who tried to get on
and "give themselves false airs", people from within the neighbourhood who had pretensions to social superiority; they resented
the "people on our backs":

All these dummoes at school, who always do what they're told ...
they're the ones who end up being coppers and that.
I hate them do-gooders who come to ' 'elp the poor in them slums
...'   They're all nice and sweet and kind, they pretend to be
on your side and by talking nicely find out about you but social
workers and people like that, they ain't on your side.   They
think they know how you should live.   They're really authority
pretending to be your friends.   They try to get you to do things
and if you don't do them, they've got the law on their side.
With all this lot against us, we've still got the yids, Pakis,
wogs, 'ippies on our backs.   (ibid: 68).

The sense of being "in the middle" of this variety of
oppressive and exploitative forces produces a need for group
solidarity, which though essentially defensive, in the Skinheads
was coupled with an aggressive content, the expression of
frustration and discontent through the attacking of scapegoated
outsiders.   The content of this solidarity, as we shall see in
our consideration of the elements of the skinhead style, derived
from the traditional content of the working class community - the
example, *par excellence*, of the defensively organised collective.

However, the skinhead style does not revive the community in
a real sense; the post-war decline of the bases of that community
had removed it as a real source of solidarity; the skinheads had
to use an *image* of what that community was as the basis of their
style.   They were the 'dispossessed inheritors'; they received
a tradition which had been deprived of its real social bases.
The themes and imagery still persisted, but the reality was in
a state of decline and disappearance.   We would suggest that
this dislocated relation to the traditional community accounts
for the exaggerated and intensified form which the values and
concerns of that community received in the form of the skinhead
style.   Daniel and McGuire claim that:

Rather than a community spirit, the Collinwood gang tends to have
an affinity with an image of the East Enders, as being tough,
humorous and a subculture of their own ... The gang sees itself
as a natural continuation of the working class tradition of the
area, with the same attitudes and behaviour as their parents and

grandparents before them.   They believe that they have the same
stereotyped prejudices against immigrants and aliens as they
believe their parents have and had, *but they play these roles
outside of the context of the community experienced by their
parents* .... (ibid: 21-22.   Our emphasis).

These observations are reinforced by comments from the
Skinheads themselves about the gang and its relation to the
locality:

> When people kept saying skinheads, when they're talking about
> the story of us coming up from the East End, this has happened
> for generations before, past ... I mean where does skinhead come
> into it?
> It's a community, a gang, isn't it, it's only another word for
> community, kids, thugs, whatever ... (ibid: 21; 31).

The kids inherit the oral tradition of the area from the parent
culture, especially that part which refers to the community's self
-image, its collective solidarity, its conception of masculinity,
its orientation to "outsiders" and so on.   It is perhaps not
surprising that the area with which the Skinheads are most
associated should be the East End, which from a sociological
standpoint has been seen as the archetypal working class community.
Its internal self-image has always been a particularly strong one,
and has been strengthened by its public reputation as a "hard'
area, a reputation which in the mid-sixties was further intensified by the glamorous careers of the Krays.

Finally, we would like to exemplify this relation between the
Skinheads and the image of the community through some of the
central elements of the skinhead style.   One of the most crucial
aspects is the emphasis on territorial connections for the
Skinheads - the "Mobs" were organised on a territorial basis,
identifying themselves with and through a particular locality
(e.g. the "Smethwick Mob", etc.).   This involved the Mobs in
the demarcation and defence of their particular 'patch', marking boundaries with painted slogans ("Quinton Mob rules here",
etc.), and maintaining those boundaries against infractions
by other groups.   This territoriality, like the community, has
its own focal points around which interaction articulates - the
street corner meeting place, the pub, and the football ground.
Although the football ground did not necessarily coincide with
the mobs' patches, its own local identification and the already
existent activities of the Ends provided a particular focal point
for the Mobs to organise around.

Football, and especially the violence articulated around it,
also provided one arena for the expression of the Skinheads'
concern with a particular, collective, masculine self conception,
involving an identification of masculinity with physical toughness, and an unwillingness to back down in the face of "trouble"[1].
The violence also involved the Mobs' stress on collective
solidarity and mutual support in times of 'need'.   This concern
with toughness was also involved in the two other most publicised

skinhead activities - "Paki-Bashing" and "Queer-Bashing".
Paki-bashing involved the ritual and aggressive defence of the
social and cultural homogeneity of the community against its
most obviously scapegoated outsiders - partly because of their
particular visibility within the neighbourhood (in terms of
shop ownership patterns, etc.) by comparison with West Indians,
and also because of their different cultural patterns (especially
in terms of their unwillingness to defend themselves and so on)
- again by comparison with West Indian youth.

   "Queer-Bashing" may be read as a reaction against the erosion
of traditionally available stereotypes of masculinity, especially
by the hippies.   The Skinhead operational definition of "queer"
seems to have extended to all those males who by their standards
looked "odd", as this statement from a Smethwick Skinhead may
indicate:

> Usually it'd be just a bunch of us who'd find somebody they
> thought looked odd - like this one night we were up by Warley
> Woods and we saw this bloke who looked odd - he'd got long hair
> and frills on his trousers.

We may see these three interrelated elements of territoriality,
collective solidarity and 'masculinity' as being the way in which
the Skinheads' attempted to recreate the inherited imagery of the
community in a period in which the experiences of increasing
oppression demanded forms of mutual organisation and defence.
And we might finally see the intensive violence connected with
the style as evidence of the 'recreation of the community' being
indeed a 'magical' or 'imaginary' one, in that it was created
without the material and organisational basis of that community
and consequently was less subject to the informal mechanisms of
social control characteristic of such communities.   In the
skinhead style we can see both the elements of continuity (in
terms of the style's content), and discontinuity (in terms of its
form), between parent culture and youth subculture.

FOOTNOTE

1.   For fuller accounts of the changes in football during the
     post-war period, which had some bearing on the Skinhead choice
     of this particular locale, see, for example, Taylor (1971a and
     1971b) and Critcher (1975).

DOING NOTHING
Paul Corrigan

Note: *Paul Corrigan's study of Sunderland street-corner culture,*
The Smash Street Kids, *is shortly to be published by Paladin.*
It testifies to the intense activity which is involved in the
common pursuit of 'doing nothing', and to the fact that what most
adults see as an endless waste of time, an absence of purpose, is,
from the viewpoint of the kids, full of incident, constantly
informed by 'weird ideas'.   Corrigan argues - and shows in this
extract - that much the most common and intense activity engaged
in by the majority of working class kids is the simple but absorb-
ing activity of 'passing the time'.

For most kids where it's at is the street; not the romantic
action packed streets of the ghetto but the wet pavements of
Wigan, Shepherds Bush and Sunderland.   The major activity in
this venue, the main action of British subculture is, in fact,
'doing nothing'.

> What sort of things do you do with your mates?
> DUNCAN: Just stand around talking about footy.   About things.
> Do you do anything else?
> DUNCAN: Joke, lark about, carry on.   Just what we feel like
> really.
> What's that?
> DUNCAN: Just doing things.   Last Saturday someone started
> throwing bottles and we all got in.
> What happened?
> DUNCAN: Nothing really.

All these activities come under the label of 'doing nothing'
and they represent the largest and most complex youth subculture.
The major element in doing nothing is talking.   Not the arcane
discussion of the T.V. talk show, but recounting, exchanging
stories which need never be true or real but which are as
interesting as possible.   About football, about each other,
talking not to communicate ideas, but to communicate the experience of talking.   It passes the time and it underlines the group
nature of the different ways that the boys have of passing the
time.   A great deal of joking goes on.   It was between the area
of talking, joking and carrying on that things emerged that the
boys called 'weird ideas'

> Do you ever go out and knock around with the lads?
> ALBERT: Sometimes when I feel like it.
> What do you do?
> ALBERT: Sometimes we get into mischief.
> Mischief?
> ALBERT: Well somebody gets a weird idea into their head,
> and they start to carry it out, and others join in.

Weird idea?
ALBERT: Things ... like going around smashing milk bottles.

It is the 'weird idea' that represents the major something
in 'doing nothing'. In fighting boredom the kids do not choose
the street as a wonderfully lively place, rather they look on it
as the place where there is the most chance that something will
happen. Doing nothing on the street must be compared with the
alternatives: for example, knowing that nothing will happen with
Mum and Dad in the front room; being almost certain that the youth
club will be full of boredom. This makes the street the place
where something might just happen, if not this Saturday, then
surely next.

The weird ideas then are born out of boredom and the
expectation of future and continuing boredom, and this affects
the sort of weird ideas that they are. A good idea must contain
the seeds of continuing change as well as excitement and involvement. Smashing milk bottles is a good example of this since
it typifies the way in which they are put into effect. To ask
the kids why they smash milk bottles is to ask a meaningless
question.

What do you do on street corners?
DICK: Police never saw us do anything wrong, so they shouldn't
pick on us. But we just used to play around, smashing things.
What sort of things?
DICK: Anything really - I dunno why - just ideas.

The answer to the last question, for example, is not really
possible within the boys' own terms, outside of the total
experience of the time. For we are not talking about boys
going out on a Saturday night looking for milk bottles to
smash, rather it is purely an interesting thing that occurs.

What do you do when you just knock around the streets?
RICHARD: Sometimes we get into fights, or trouble, but mostly
nothing much.
Just try and give us an example.
RICHARD: Er ... last Saturday we was hanging about and someone
kicked a bottle over and it smashed. Then we all started smashing bottles.

And lest someone should build a model of deviancy amplification around the smashing of milk bottles, other smashing
objects are included in the weird ideas.

EDWARD: I've been in trouble recently because my friends
smashed a shop window, but that's all.
STEVEN: Well you know the Grand Prix down there. Well, we
duff up the machines and get free goes on them. You know the
corporation buses, well, they go in for a cup of tea and we'll
go and open the doors and kick the buses in.

The other major component of 'doing nothing' is fighting.
Within this context fights are an important and exciting
occasion - they are easy to create and are interesting events;
they don't carry too many risks. For some of the boys it

104

represents a casual occurrence; for others it was the major
occurrence of every Saturday night - for them it was the biggest
element of nothing.

> What do you do on an average Saturday night?
> DAVE: Saturday night, why, er, we usually go down an off-licence
> and get something to drink, some cider or some beer. We usually
> go around me mate's place and play records, watch telly and then
> just knock around.
> What do you do when you are knocking about?
> DAVE: Just kick about, play football or something, cause a bit
> of mischief around the streets.
> Mischief?
> DAVE: Well, we just seem to get into it on the streets.
> Do you ever get into any fights?
> DAVE: No ... well not many.

It would be useless to try and explain why these fights occur.
Given nothing to do, something happens, even if it is a yawn; or
someone stumbling into someone else; someone remembering an
ancient insult; and it's this that brings about the fights.
Something pathetic and forgotten outside of 'nothing' becomes
vital within that set of behaviour.

There are some other kids though where fights are a bit
more likely to happen.

> What do you do on an average Saturday evening?
> FRED: I go down the station, you know in the Town Centre, and
> shoot through to Newcy, a whole gang of us. Then we walk around
> Newcy, ready for trouble. We find a few Maggie supporters and
> kick them in. Have a good scrap we do.
> What sort of fights?
> FRED: Well not real fights, as some of them might be quite
> matey, but still, when you put the boot in, you put the boot
> in, but we are friendly after like.

> What do you do on an average Saturday evening?
> PAUL: I knock around in a gang and we get into fights, scraps
> ... you know ...
> What sort of fights?
> PAUL: Well we meet up with another gang and start chucking
> milk bottles at them. Mainly the South Hylton Gang.
> Why do you do that?
> PAUL: So they can't get near us.
> What happens when they do?
> PAUL: We have a scrap. It's good fun.
> Do people get hurt?
> PAUL: No.

These fights are less spontaneous than the others, but they
still arise out of Saturday's 'Nothing' rather than any
territorial or group factor on its own. Their context defines
the nature of the fight. If those fights were *real*, the streets
of British cities would be littered with corpses. They are
merely something ... in nothing.

THE CULTURAL MEANING OF DRUG USE

Paul E. Willis

Note: Paul Willis's study of the role of drug use in the Hippy sub-culture of a large industrial city is part of a longer study, comparing the life-styles, outlooks and musical preferences of two sub-cultural groups - a group of Hippies and a group of Motorbike Boys. The thesis explored the 'fit' between the life and values of these groups, the things they did, the uses they made of objects, machines and drugs, and the musical preferences they expressed. Basically, Willis argues that there must be a 'homology' between the values and life-style of a group, its subjective experience, and the musical forms the group adopts. The preferred music must have the potential, at least, in its formal structure, to express meanings which resonate with other aspects of group life. Some of the things a sub-culture uses are in an even tighter 'fit' with the group, and this Willis calls, not a 'homological' but an integral relation. He suggests in his study, that the motorbike itself stood in an integral relation to motorbike culture, and that drugs were integral to Hippy culture: "Drugs importantly mediated many areas of the Hippies' life", including the group's relation to music. An extract from the study of Motorbike culture was published in WPCS 2. The full comparative treatment is available in his unpublished PhD, "Pop Music and Youth Groups" (CCCS, University of Birmingham, 1972).
All names have been changed in this piece.

Drugs were habitually used by the hippies; this is widely documented and supported. A local Vicar's survey showed that drug use was widely accepted, and another survey by a C. of E. worker written up, but unpublished, as "Spiritual Undercurrents on the Drug Scene", took the hippies without question as archetypal examples of the drug users. The drug squad saw the hippy scene as the main centre of drug use and trafficking within the whole city. The drug squad also reckoned that the numbers involved in the drug scene were 'doubling about every eighteen months'. Drugs also made their impact on every day social interaction: they were just about the central topic of conversation on the scene, and great stress was laid on knowledge of various types of drugs. There was widespread resentment at the police's and society's attitude to drugs, and one of the more

106

available ways of demonstrating cultural 'in-ness' was to make a tirade against the straights' 'paranoia' about drugs. However none of this catches the special nature of the hippy drug use. People from all the different group-shadings which I worked with talked about drugs, were in possession of the drugs, were opposed to the police, exhibited clear behavioural signs of being drug users. Ron had some of the most detailed knowledge about drugs of anyone in the groups, and yet he had no status on the 'head-scene? Any group of students experimenting on the drug scene shows similar characteristics, and it is not through this atom-istic cataloguing that we can discover the real importance of drugs to the hippy culture.

A comment Les made remained opaque to me for a long time, but it gives a lead towards understanding the special distinct-iveness of drug use by hippies . He said that it was "possible to take acid and not 'trip', and possible to 'trip' without taking acid; there were many 'heads' in 'straight' society." In fact, the importance of drugs did not lie in their direct physical effects, but in the way they facilitated passing through a great symbolic barrier erected over against 'straight' society. The 'head', a more recent title for hippy , derived from the more specific 'acid head', more exactly represents the elements of drug experience in the culture. He is defined not simply by drug use, but by his *existential presence* on the other side of this symbolic barrier. It *was symbolic* and *not actual,* so that individuals with a 'beyond the barrier consciousness' could be 'real' 'heads', even though they did not take drugs. On the other hand, those who took drugs, but without feeling their symbolic significance, were not 'heads': they were just experimenters. On the 'straight' side of the barrier was the world of personal responsibility, grey colours, gaucheness and lack of style, on the other side was the world of freedom, lack of responsibility and stylishness -'the hip'. The drugs did not intrinsically contain this second world: they should not be thought of as microfilms of experience surreptitiously slipped on to the deep projector of the mind. They were merely the tripswitch to bring about an entry into areas which were essentially self-created. It was explained to me many times that the experience of the previous period was a 'blue-print for the trip':-

> VAL: Well, you have to prepare yourself, I mean, you might only have to prepare yourself, say, for a week or a month, twelve months, maybe, but it takes yogas a whole life-time, ten years, twenty years, a whole life-time.
> NORMAN: Your 'trip' consists of what you've done weeks before, and the state of your mind at that particular moment.

In a way, drugs could be thought of as cultural placebos - keys to experience, rather than experience itself. But this is *not* to say that hash and acid in particular do not have marked

107

chemical effects.   They do, and the perceived change of consciousness in the subject is probably the basis for his existential passage - he feels *something* has happened, which he supp-
lies a content for.   The physiological basis of change could
equally well be interpreted in a thousand different *cultural*
forms, and the objective chemical basis of changed consciousness
does not contradict the possibility of reaching a similar state
of existential awareness in non-physical ways[1].   As Les said
in one discussion:-

> LES: (referring to experiences of heightened consciousness).
> Could be by itself or could be with acid, could be with any
> drug or without any drug, that's the whole point, you know,
> drugs give you the opportunity to change your consciousness,
> in other words, give you new insights.   They just provide the
> opportunity, different people use them in different ways for
> different reasons, and this is what a lot of the fuck-ups on
> the scene is about. 'Straights' use alcohol to blot out -
> NORMAN: - to lower -
> LES: to lower the level of consciousness, and they use smoking
> to lower the level of neurosis, caused by their own paranoia,
> and, you know, shit is used to increase one's perception of
> one's **surroundings** according to one's senses.   In other words,
> visual perception is heightened possibly and definitely
> audio-perception.

Though drugs were only keys, they were still accorded a kind
of sacred place in the head culture.   Their use was surrounded by
ritual and reverence.   These rituals often increased the amount
of the drug actually taken in, which provided a greater physiological response open to specific cultural interpretation.   This
is the **manner** of the dialectical relationship between the drugs
and the culture.   For the head, any drug, and especially acid,
was the symbolic key to experience that had always been *immanent*,
but which could only become fully manifest on the other side of
the symbolic barrier.   This symbolic key did not so much let
consciousness into strange lands, as *guilt* out of familiar lands:
the landscape was no less transformed.   The drug could be seen
to some extent as taking the blame for one's state of consciousness and therefore, paradoxically, as increasing the freedom of
consciousness.   The *belief* that "it's the drugs, not me" allowed
the individual, for a time, to see into the contradictions between, into the dialectic between freedom and determination.   In
a number of small ways, this kind of awareness is clear in the
tapes, from Les's "it's difficult when you're stoned", at a
complex point of the argument, to the joking and caricatured
recognition of the conventional stereotype concerning loss of
autonomy, in this exchange:-

> TONY: (referring to an earlier comment that he had been forced
> to withdraw after a long argument).
> You know it was just, it was just the first original smash in
> my mind, and it came out of my mouth, and -

LES: That's the trouble when you take drugs, man, I'm gonna
go out and rape somebody in a minute
/laughter/
TONY: Let's go and rape some old woman down the street.

More important than these localised examples was the
general symbolic insight that man was determined by the structures
around him.   Drugs symbolised a fundamental ontological change
from the sense of feeling oneself as an autonomous determining
agent, to feeling oneself, in part, as a determined variable
in the world.   And that sense for the *cultural* drug user was
not confined to drug experience only.   The economy, politics,
society, industry, pollution, the police, upbringing, all became
determining variables on the individual's consciousness.   This
produced a lessening of the responsibility felt for oneself, and
a corresponding lessening of guilt.   But for the head,
paradoxically, in existential terms, the dialectical counterpart
to these insights was a vastly increased sense of personal
freedom.   He could rest at long last from the ceaseless personal
struggle to hold the void back, to hold the common-sense world
together, he was released from the ever more restricting demands
of common sense.   He had seen through the precarious nature of
reality and its apparent freedoms, to its real social determinants.
In psychiatric terms, which the 'hippies' often used, there was
'ego-loss' and also the experience of a 'meta-egoic' state.
The head could ride the forces, experience the forces, that the
alert autonomous mind would have nervously blocked.   He was
free experientially because he was relieved of the personal task
of holding the world together.

Instead of resisting force, you could respond on a different
plane altogether.   You could relax and let it happen to you;
it was an experience.   All experiences would have their own
distinctive flavour which you could savour to the full.   Judged
in this way, even being busted was only a calamity for those who
tried so desperately to avoid it, for those whose sensibilites
had been irrevocably reduced by the compulsive urge to barricade
experience away.   In a sense, then, nothing could harm the head,
when 'high': he was beyond the reach of coercion in the public
world.   Because he had seen the ultimately coercive nature of
life, and had found it liberating, nothing could touch him again.
Of course, the head did not feel quite so safe when he 'came
down', but something of these feelings remained all the time; it
was even a brief understanding of this perspective which put him
on the 'hip' side of the symbolic barrier.

To the head, the 'straight' consciousness, the everyday
assumption of autonomy in the world, in fact, meant limiting
consciousness to a microdot in the full spectrum of potential
states of consciousness.   That dot which an accidental turn of
history - the discovery of ratio-technical analysis - had
magnified into the whole known world of thought.   If you could

trust yourself to leave that tight circle of apparent certainty,
then you would be free to enter vast new experiential areas.
Drugs were seen as the way *par excellence* of unwinding the
apparent tightness of reality, they seemed to begin to unravel
the real world, whether you liked it or not.   The head did like
it, and took it as the cue to go much further, he passed through
the symbolic barrier.   The 'straight' on drugs did not like it,
and waited until the threads took themselves up again.

   The ability of drugs, and especially acid, to open up
blocked experiential areas was commented on frequently by our
group:-

   LES: You can actually see, and I have seen, music.   I have
   seen it bubbling out of the speakers.
   VAL: You see, you are *trapped* by all your senses, you're trapped
   by touch and smell and taste and sight and sound, but you can
   take acid, the cross-over, so you are no longer trapped, you are
   no longer trapped in the way you see the world.
   LES.: With acid you tend towards a total experience of all the
   senses, particularly the visual ones.   You can see other senses,
   I haven't seen a smell, but I have seen a sound, and have heard
   a colour ... I have been, well, I did lay a 'chick' on acid once,
   and it was the most incredible experience I think I have ever
   had, because the whole orgasm becomes total, er'm, ... not
   only in the neurological centre of the brain that gives you a
   sensation of pleasure, not only in the tip of the penis, but
   over the whole of the body, man, in the tips of my fingers, I
   had orgasm after orgasm.   Now that was a state of as near bliss
   that I think I shall ever get to ... it was totally incredible and
   the only thing that stopped me having these orgasms was my own
   physical strength, energy had just drained away from my limbs.
   It was the most incredible experience, because I could just
   feel the energy draining away, I was aware my muscles were
   converting less oxygen ... most incredible thing.

   The head, as distinct from the drug user on the 'straight'
side of the symbolic barrier, was continually, if tangentially,
commenting on, and drawing attention to, the unusual in common
situations.   Although living in the shared world, they saw
more facets in it, and light refractions from it, even without
drugs, than ever a 'straight' could.   The head 'gazes at', the
'straight' 'manages' the real world.

   One crucial aspect of this yielding to experience and the
experiential riding of determination, was the total preoccupation
with the 'now'.   If experience was all, then presence was all,
and the main dimension of presence was 'nowness'.

   ROBIN: 'Dope' has meant a certain amount of freedom, as a
   result of, of ... being much more aware of what is, you know, ...
   what is rather than what was or will be.   You know ... er'm ...
   I believe that one must live in the present, you know, this instant, now, experiencing now for what it is, because it is, because
   it is for no other reason.   I suppose I could have gone into a
   monastery and meditated and, perhaps, found out the same thing

110

in about fifty years, I've just found out how to do it, acid
just speeded up the process of it, you know, well quite considerably.

This encapsulation by the 'now', and the feeling of freedom
to 'walk around and feel the moment', led to a total breakdown
of conventional notions of time.   Industrial and job-oriented
time is crucially concerned with order, i.e. what needs to be
done before something else can be done - a massive critical path
of consciousness.   Without a fairly well determined and commonly
accepted time structure of this kind, intricate linear tasks,
especially relying on the integration of different specialisms,
could not be completed.   External coercion of time experience in
this way is not always humanely relevant, as we can see from the
very common feelings of boredom and frustration on the shopfloor
- the deserts of distance workers feel between themselves and
the hooter, the strange randomness of the hooter when it does
come.   The heads felt the inappropriateness of conventional time
particularly powerfully in the course of a 'trip'.

> NORMAN: You realise that time is man-made, there is no such
> a thing as 'time', it's a load of cock, something that man has
> made to computerise himself by.

One of the commonest criticisms made by the church workers
in the field, was that the 'hippies' were 'so unreliable'.   By
the same token, though, if you met a head by accident, and he
became interested in something, he would simply stay talking
until the thing was thoroughly worked out.   There was no
"I must dash now" or "I can only stop a minute" to head off the
danger of a *real* meeting.   This subjective sense of time, the
maximal openness of the senses and the essential lack of autonomy
felt on the drug experience, could dispel normal senses of
revulsion: objectively distasteful situations became pleasurable
and even fascinating.

> ROBIN: Well, like I was with a 'chick' and she was sick all
> over the floor, man, we were both sort of really spaced out, the
> room was swirling and I couldn't tell where I began or anything
> else, but I got it together to clean up the sick.   I wasn't
> even revolted by it, and usually I am, you know, someone has
> only got to be sick in the same room as me normally, and I want
> to puke as well.   But I was in there with my bare hands
> scooping the sick up into a bowl.
> ....
> LES: They had this bog at Bath, and it must have been a football
> pitch long, and it was like corrugated iron bent double in V-
> sections, like on to the other all the way down.
> DEREK: You've got to be a tall guy standing at one end.
> LES: And everybody was sort of pissing, it was just people all
> down this thing, and I was at the small end, and it was like a
> fucking river, I was 'tripping' like fuck, and it was beautiful
> you know, I got really hung up on the piss.
> DEREK: All the dogends and matches floating down.
> LES: It was beautiful, the stink was fucking terrible.

111

The loss of ego, the loss of protective reflexes, and openness to the strange, cumulatively made another forbidden area open to the head - the psychotic in himself. The underside of experience, usually so well contained by our conventional consciousness, became as available as normal experience to the deeply 'tripping' head, and sometimes they could not differentiate between the two. Often a person 'tripping' will seem to be clinically psychotic, and, of course, LSD was first used in laboratory conditions in an attempt to recreate schizophrenic conditions. There is much less certainty now that the LSD experience is the same as the schizophrenic[2], but there is little doubt that for many the 'trip' is a journey into the 'darker sides of their nature'.

It was certainly true that there was a very clear association between drug use and conventionally understood psychiatric breakdown. In their sombre way the drug squad attest to the clarity of this relation.

> B: Very often we will talk to a kid on the drug scene, and he's talking about drugs, and we suddenly realise that it's not drugs that are affecting this kid. It's something much more deep-rooted, and we refer many of them to hospital. And this has been found at the hospital that, although they've been hiding behind drugs, they have had a psychiatric illness, not a severe one. You can get a kid who says "I'm addicted to 'pot', you know". Some doctors would think it a so-called cannabis psychosis, but I know that, er'm, the way certain doctors operate is this: if they get a person come into them, if he's been referred by, and from other referrals, they will forget drugs entirely and start examining as a psychiatric patient, and they will probably find somewhere along the line, that he has got some slight psychiatric disorder, you know, he would be a schizophrenic or ...

However, although at this point limited in our abilities to follow the heads, we should not dismiss the psychotic aspects of drug use as pathological. The knowledge and awareness of the shadowy and mysterious aspect of our normal consciousness has been crushingly cut short, and branded sick, by modern medical wisdom. I think it is in this sense of confrontation with the psychotic in oneself that Les most fully meant 'some people can 'trip' without acid'. It was possible to be on the 'hip' side of the barrier without contact with drugs if you had some degree of awareness of these nether regions.

There is a contact here with a development in the hippy scene away from drugs and towards religion[3]. Seen as a 'healthy' development from the outside, because of the apparent renunciation of drugs, it is in fact very close to drug experience in the symbolic sense. It is very much to do with the attempt to know oneself more fully. The use and sense of drugs, then, was not bounded by the immediate action of taking drugs, or by the behavioural correlates of taking drugs. The real meaning of drug use was in the entry into a large symbolic world. Once into this world, the actual presence of drugs was not of immediate concern.

112

One could be 'high' without the use of drugs, and the quality
of normal experience, apart from drug experience, was changed.
In certain respects, the passage through the symbolic barrier
separating the 'straight' from the 'hip' presents us with a classic faith paradox. Either you understand or you do not, and
there is no way of bridging the gap with logical argument.
Nor could the presence of this symbolic world be proved to a
disbeliever, especially a disbeliever who has already decided
that you are 'sick'. The kind of questions that might occur to
'straight' outsiders becomes irrelevant inside, and even to ask
certain things was already to show that the questioner could
never appreciate the answers. This 'Catch 22' aspect of the
drug culture was a source of particular annoyance to well-meaning
agencies and sympathetic groups. It is one of the biggest
barriers to an appreciation of the culture from outside.
A concern with 'causes', their isolation, and ultimately, their
modification, and the concern with escalation from soft to hard
drugs are the bases of the vast majority of attempts to understand
the drug culture. They all aim at making the drug user re-assert
his own autonomy within the causal chain. These approaches
simply never meet the real terms of the experience of the head
on drugs. For the head, when you understood the dialectical
nature of your own determinations, paradoxically when you were
most determined, you were most free to experience the full rich-
ness of consciousness. Your expanded consciousness, in its
enveloping omnipotence, could see *normal* consciousness as a
supremely unimportant, world-work-soiled-mean-little-affair.
Exhortations for a return to this world would simply confirm the
head's new mapping of experience. The exhorter is simply part
of that 'mean little affair', and the work/responsibility base of
his comments show that it remains as 'mean' as ever.

Within their respective terms, the drug user knows the social
worker much better than the social worker knows him. The point
of greatest divergence between the objective, causal understanding
of the drug phenomenon and the real experiential nature of involvement in it, is precisely this contradictory notion of freedom.
For the 'objective' group, freedom is self-responsibility, for
the 'subjective' group, you are only really free when you are not
responsible for yourself. The unwillingness of the head to make
a real attempt to contradict the outside definitions of his drug
use, compounds the complexity of the situation. The exhorter
feels the drug has taken an even deeper hold in some mysterious
way, and surpasses the user's normal powers of communication.
The exhorter redoubles his effort to speak to what is left of the
old autonomous self to get it to throw out the vile invader.
The head, in turn, is simply made more certain that the exhorter
can never see the 'truth'.

This sense of 'faith understanding', or understanding as

an immediate sense impression, spread noticeably to other aspects of their lives. They were very impatient with causal and outside explanations, they wanted the experience of a thing and were bored by the shell of experience-explanation. The consistency with which such feelings were lived out in the head culture, was remarkable: experience over against ratio-technical understanding was perhaps the main and most commonly shared tenet of the whole movement. This did not mean that language was made redundant, on the contrary, the hippy culture was highly verbal, but the use of language was not aimed at getting at 'truth', or objective, shared understanding of processes. Language was used as a way of encouraging feelings, and *states* of understanding, by graceful and intricate, sometimes mischievous, suggestion, counter-suggestion, contrast, paradox and surprise. A lot was left unsaid and to be assumed. Words, as it were, carved shapes in the material of this atmosphere, rather than tried to represent it objectively.

These feelings coupled with super-human concentration on the now and ability to transform everyday experience, and particularly the braving of the psychotic, made the heads fertile ground for mystical experience. This was likely to happen, especially on an acid 'trip', and once experienced, put the individual finally on the 'hip' side of the symbolic barrier. The actual nature of this experience is very hard to come at, and was for the heads, although they liked to talk *about* it, the most ineffable experience of them all; it could never be presented in terms other than itself. The mystical experience was the quintessential symbol and recognition of the central values in the head's drug world. It put the individual finally beyond the reach of the everyday world and its insistence on autonomy. If you were part of the cosmic consciousness, part of God, in fact you *were* God, then the notions of causation and personal autonomy were misunderstandings of only a very tiny subsection of life, which you totally transcended and engulfed. All aspects of life were part of you, so how could you war against yourself?

There was a point of contact here between the head drug scene and Eastern religion and culture. Very rarely was there a detailed knowledge of these religions, a knowing exterior usually covered deep ignorance below. The East was taken more as a *metaphor* for their position than as a literal counterpart. I would argue that the lack of objective knowledge about the East does not undermine *the genuineness of the experience leading* to the Eastern metaphor. Here are a few examples from the tapes of mystical experiences on acid being recounted in the natural group setting:-

114

LES: I believe there is a Godhead and I believe in the pure
energy of life which I've found out a lot about on acid, it was
a tremendously religious thing with me at one time.
DEREK: Yes, but do you believe there is a figurehead?
LES: Yeah, where my head is now I take it as my Bible, the
I-ching, or whatever you would like to call it, the Chinese
book of changes.
NORMAN: Do you think what you are doing now, or what you are
experiencing, what knowledge you gain, is going to be of any
benefit to you?
LES: Of course it is.
DEREK: Experience is life.
LES: It's going to be the most enormous benefit, not only
for myself, but I hope for my fellow man. I believe when I
go through the book of changes, and I see the Hexagram, the
changes shown to me. Not only do I try to live my life along
these lines at that particular moment, but I believe that what
I am doing according to the book of changes and according to
my own views of humanity and according to my concepts of the
Godhead, the pure energy life force, this is gonna make things
better for other people, the people that surround me immediately,
the people that I know. My debt to society, if you want to put
it that way, that the things I owe my fellow man, I owe myself.
. . . .
LES: Yeah, because the Eastern concepts of religion have a lot
in common with acid, or the acid concepts of religion.
VAL: The West takes the view that God is a transcendental being,
in other words he's separate from the world, and you enter into
the kingdom of heaven if you've been a good man in this life.
/laughter/
Any you know you may become one with God, but the East takes
the view that God is immanent and we are God in God, you know
God is in us, and this is what acid gives you.

The involvement of acid with their transcendental experience
does not invalidate it as some have argued. Firstly, there is
the central point of this whole paper, that the crucial importance
of drugs lies not in their pharmacological properties, but in
their appropriation in to a much greater symbolic system.
Although the drugs tripswitched entry in to this world, the
symbolic world itself was embodied and lived out, in common,
everyday human processes. The transcendental experience was
very much more a product of *inhabiting this world*, than a
product of certain chemicals acting on the brain. Secondly,
even assuming for a moment that the chemical determinant of
consciousness was a more powerful factor than the cultural one,
it still does not invalidate the experiential integrity of the
mystic episode. No matter what its causes, it is still experienced as real. Experience cannot be judged on the basis of its
causes; it can only be judged by its nature and effectiveness in
life.

A Sub-Cultural Pharmacology,

Although I have been describing the 'head' drug scene in terms
of one great symbolic divide, the heads themselves did make more
complex distinctions between different types of drugs.   *Hash* was
the common denominator of all drugs, and was the most commonly
used drug.   Used in the right manner, with the appropriate
symbolic ascriptions of meaning, it was a genuine part of the
head experience.   But it was also recognised that many other
groups used the drug in quite different ways, with quite different
meanings.   *Acid* was seen as much more powerful altogether, and
as a much more culturally positive drug.   It was possible to
take acid without tripping though, and this was the non-cultural
use, but it was felt that 'straights' were likely to take the
drug only once and then be 'frightened off'.   Many hippies
on the scene were themselves frightened of the drug, and there
was wide recognition that it had very great potential dangers.
Those hippies who were nervous of the drug were not out-group
figures; they were part of the wider symbolic world, and so
understood, *at some level,*what it was like to trip regularly.
But the fact that they did not use acid prevented them from ever
being seen as 'real' heads.   The 'real' heads did not use
acid indiscriminately, they were aware of the' danger of becoming
an 'acid freak'.   They used it regularly and carefully, preparing
themselves quite meticulously for the experience, or finely
spotting the mood in which acid would go well.

Heroin was as much beyond acid as acid was beyond hash, but
in a less culturally-appropriate manner.   The dangers of "H"
were well recognised, but there was no real pity for the person
totally hooked on heroin or cocaine; the attitude was still,
it's up to him, if he got in to it, it must be doing something
for him, it's his *trip*.   I did not work with any hard drug
addicts, and according to the drug squad the level of drug
addiction in the city had fallen right down to single figures
from the scores registered in the middle '60's.   Heroin was
a drug that was not talked about too much on the scene, if you
were using it, even occasionally, only your closest associates
would know.   One head I knew well did tell me that he had used
'H' occasionally and that as long as you kept a careful check on
the amount and frequency and kept to 'skin popping' rather than
'mainlining', you could avoid dependency and all the consequent
horrors.   It was certainly true that, although the dangers of
the drug were well known, there was not the same fear of the drug
that one meets in 'straight' society.   It was seen simply as a
powerfulagency rather than a powerful adversary, normally to be
avoided, but to be welcomed under extreme circumstances.   I think
there was much more controlled use of heroin, careful skin popping,
on the scene than most of the control agencies realised, although
I didn't have consistent evidence of this.

The cultural meaning of 'H' seemed mainly to be in a symbolic extension of its supposed physical irreversibility. To get on to heroin was not just to pass through the symbolic barrier dividing the 'straight' from the 'hip', it was the unanswerable closure of relations with the straight world. In some respects this passage on 'H' was culturally similar to the passage on acid, but on 'H' you had not only made the passage to that extreme degree, you had burnt your boats and could not return. In one way this made 'H' the supreme expression of drug culture meanings. It was an expression of loyalty to beyond-the-barrier meanings that the straight could never begin to understand, and which straight society could never bring you back from. On the other hand, in a kind of indirect admission of the supremacy of symbolic states over real and physical ones, 'H' was partly distrusted. Its meanings were bound to be the last ones before the void, you would die - what an unanswerable anti-straight-supremely-hip-way 'to go' - but you would still go, and that was an exceptionally high price to pay. In this sense the cultural meaning of 'H' was the closest to its pharmacological base of all the drugs used in the head scene; in this case *only* both the cultural and pharmacological approaches agree that the final cost of its use is death, although the meaning of the passage in each case is very different.

The role of *amphetamines and barbiturates* seemed to be rather outside of the main stream. They were not central to the head scene in the way that dope and acid were. They were usually associated more with other cultural groups. In the hippy scene they seemed to be used more on an *ad hoc* basis, to stay awake, or to allow the completion of some task or another. When they were taken in the appropriate symbolic mode, then their effects were culturally appropriate at about the strength of the hash experience, but it did not seem to me that there was wide use of pills in this way. A 'blow' would have been much more acceptable under most circumstances unless there was some particular reason to force oneself to remain active for long periods. There was the question of supply of course, and where nothing else was available pills would be taken. In a drug culture with strong symbolic structures, all drugs are seen as valuable, and any drug is capable of giving appropriate effects. Core members of the culture had tried just about all the drugs one could think of, and it is possible that crushed up barbiturates were occasionally used for mainlining as a substitute for 'H', but it was a practice that I personally didn't come across.

This description of the ranking of different drugs as the heads saw them, should not be taken as evidence of 'escalation', in the sense of the conventional theory that soft drug use inexorably leads to hard drug use. Although there were cognitive differ-

117

ences between the various drugs used on the scene, the move from
one to another was determined by states of consciousness that
can much better be understood from the point of view of cultural
meaning, than from the point of view of the intrinsic properties
of the drugs.   It is really only in the case of heroin that
there is a decisive link between the cultural meaning ascribed to
the drug and the drug's 'objective' pharmacological effects.
The cultural move from one drug to another then is relatively
independent of their pharmacological nature; it is possible to
escalate to another consciousness without drugs, and it is also
possible to take drugs without such escalation.   The drug
user more intimately knows the nature of the move from hash to
acid, and especially the move from acid to heroin, than those
concerned on the outside.   Once an individual or group has
entered the symbolic world of drugs, mere withdrawal of drugs
would do very little, the head would soon find another way to
put himself beyond the straights, perhaps at much greater cost
to conventional society.   The greater correspondence of
the cultural and the pharmacological at the heroin level means
that there would be some truth in the conventional notion of
escalation at this point.

FOOTNOTES.

1.   See Young (1972) who argues that drug use must be understood
      socially as well as pharmacologically, which is an advance on
      much of the theorising in the area.   But he seems to imply
      that both are about equal in importance, whereas my argument
      is that the socio-cultural factors *far* outweigh the pharmacol-
      ogical.
2.   See the minutes of the 'Drug Dependency Discussion Unit', King
      Edward's Hospital, London (1972: 3)
3.   The Jesus-Freak movement in California, now spreading to England
      is the most obvious example of this development.

ETHNOGRAPHY THROUGH THE LOOKING-GLASS

Geoffrey Pearson and John Twohig

Note: *Paul Willis' study of drug use in the Hippy sub-culture
(extracted below) stands squarely in the interactionist and
ethnographic traditions associated with Howard Becker, David Matza
and other writers who share their orientation in the sociology of
deviance (for further elaboration, see the critiques by Brian
Roberts and Steve Butters, below).   That is, following, say,
Becker's marijuana essays in Outsiders (Becker, 1963), Willis
places greater emphasis on the way drug experiences are socially
constructed, culturally defined and learned in the context of
sub-cultural use, than on the physiological or pharmacological
properties of different kinds of drugs.   Thus, in constructing
his typology of drug use, Willis relies heavily on how his
'actors' defined their experience, supported by his own ethnographic observation.   Strictly speaking, Willis acknowledges that
different drugs do have physiological effects, so that cultural
definitions must be seen as 'making these effects socially
meaningful'.   This is close to Jock Young's position in The
Drugtakers (Young, 1972), where Young speaks of "the fit
between pharmacology and culture" and of the "cultural
structuring of drug effects".   Pearson and Twohig, in their
study of drug use (extracted below) put the emphasis the other
way: sub-cultural contexts of use, they argue, influence drug
experiences less than the properties of different drugs and the
means of taking them - what they call "technologies of ingestion".
On the basis of this more 'materialist' - some would say, more
biologically determinist - reading, Pearson and Twohig develop
a critique of the whole Becker 'social-construction-of-meaning'
approach and its roots in ethnographic studies which, they argue,
has tended to become received sociological dogma - a sociology of
meanings without a material or practical base.*

The ethnography of deviant subcultures runs along the inside
codes of the culture and 'tells it like it is'.   Or so it says.
What then happens when we show the ethnographer's texts to the
members of the deviant subculture?   Will they recognise themselves in what he says about their experience?   Is what they
think (about what he thinks they think) the acid test of
ethnography?   Or does ethnography have some other hidden

function (something which makes it plausible, also fashionable and compelling) other than mirroring *verstehen,* warts and all.

Ours was a clumsy and rather too obvious approach to an interrogation of what ethnography offers (Pearson and Twohig, undated). We asked drug users what they thought of Howard Becker's 'phenomenology' of how marijuana smoking is experienced from the inside, and we also tried to match their comments against differentiations which we found within the deviant subculture. We would not go about the problem in this way now. Nevertheless, our clumsy approach raises serious questions against Howard Becker's ethnography and the way in which it is handed down as a catechism by sociologists.

First, we will rehearse Becker's arguments. Then, a brief presentation of some of our own ethnographic data follows, including how Becker's ethnography is mirrored back by the deviant group. Finally, some conclusions.

THE SOCIAL CONSTRUCTION OF DRUG-INDUCED EXPERIENCES

Howard Becker's essays "Becoming a Marijuana User" and "Marijuana Use and Social Control" are fundamental contributions to the sociology of deviant conduct (in Becker,1963). Together with his excursion into the origins of LSD psychoses - "History, Culture and Subjective Experience" (in Becker, 1971) - they have passed into the folk wisdom of sociology. The experienced effects of drugs, Becker argues, are not direct chemical effects. Instead they are mediated by the cultural meanings attached to drug use. Crucially, "how a person experiences the effects of a drug depends greatly on the way others define those effects for him" (ibid: 311). Becker maintains that the effect of expectations, setting, cultural definitions, etc. (in sum the social construction of drug-induced experiences) is so important that a person who has taken a drug "may be totally unaware of some of the drug's effects, even when they are physically gross" (ibid: 310). A person who is 'under the influence', in short. is in Becker's view under the influence of something other than the drug itself. Becker's phenomenology of drug use is thus operating at the intersection of biology (or pharmacology) and culture.

Becker traces out the career of the marijuana user from rookie to being someone who is experienced in the use of the drug for pleasure (or "fun", as Becker puts it). He argues that "successful" marijuana use is not guaranteed by the pharmacological properties of the drug, but that it must be *learned*. Learning takes place in three stages.
1. *Learning the technique:* "The novice does not ordinarily get high the first time he smokes marijuana, and several attempts

120

are usually necessary to induce this state.   One explanation of
this may be that the drug is not smoked 'properly', that is, in
a way that insures sufficient dosage to produce real symptoms
of intoxication" (Becker, 1963: 46).   In the absence of such
technical know-how, Becker argues, the drug could not be seen as
potentially pleasurable and "marijuana use was considered
meaningless and did not continue" (ibid: 48).

   2.   _Learning to perceive the effects_: "Even after he learns
the proper smoking technique, the new user may not get high and
thus not form a conception of the drug as something which can be
used for pleasure" (ibid).
   The problem, Becker argues, is that the novice needs to learn
to identify the drug effects.   They are not self-evident, nor are
they self-evidently connected with the intake of the drug.   The
perception of the effects, therefore, must be pointed out by, and
learned through, participation in the drug culture;   that is, the
novice learns what it is to be "under the influence" from learned
and influential members of the subculture.   We can note here
that the importance of pharmacology is beginning to recede in
Becker's sociology.

   3.   _Learning to enjoy the effects_: "One more step is necessary if the user who has now learned to get high is to continue use.
He must learn to enjoy the effects he has just learned to
experience" (ibid: 53).   The chemically induced effects, Becker
is saying, are ambiguous: the symptoms of being 'high' are not
self-evidently pleasurable and, therefore, the marijuana user
must literally learn the motivation for pleasure-seeking drug
use in the course of using the drug (and not before).   Learning
what is "fun", and how it is "fun", is once again, according to
Becker, mediated by the subculture of experienced drug users.

   In summary, Becker is saying that pharmacology must take a
back seat in the understanding of the subjective experience of
drug-induced effects.   Subjective experience will depend on
expectations, setting, culturally prescribed meanings, etc. -
drug effects are not immediate; they are mediated (and determined) by culture.

"HOWARD BECKER, CHANGE YOUR DEALER!"

   To repeat: Becker's essays have been adopted by phenomenological sociology as gospel.   David Matza lends his own authority
to the position, arguing that:

> In 'Becoming a Marijuana User' the sociological conception of
> man became thoroughly human ... /The essay7 may be regarded as
> a 'recipe', a faithful summary of how to do what people have
> somewhat unwittingly been doing all along ... it could well have
> been titled 'How to Smoke Pot'. (1969: 109-110)

121

Matza develops this powerful recommendation at great length;
it becomes enshrined as a new sociological orthodoxy.   More
recently, for example, a British writer echoes the Becker-Matza
formula:

> The process of becoming a /cannabis7 user ... involves acquiring
> the ability to both *identify* and learn to enjoy its effects.
> These are neither self-evident nor intrinsically pleasurable.
> Indeed, there is a growing body of opinion which regards the
> drug as being pharmacologically little more than a placebo.
> (Auld, 1973: 569)

What follows is a brief summary of some evidence which challenges
this orthodoxy.

We wish to ask the questions: What kind of 'phenomenology' of
drug use is it which forgets (or erases) pharmacology?   How does
it come about that sociologists swallow such a de-toxified account
of the toxic effects of drugs?   But first we ask: how do drug
users (as opposed to sociologists) respond to this 'recipe' for
acquiring their habit?

One man, an experienced drug user, summarised for us one
of the key issues.   Becker had suggested that novices need to
learn to perceive the effects.   What was his own experience?
"Perceive the effects???   Wow!   (prolonged laughter)   The
effects were just ... WHAAM!!! ... like a hammer at the back
of the head ... that guy Becker should change his dealer!"
He had smoked for the first time with his brother and a group
of friends.   From what he said, he had smoked rather a lot of
cannabis resin rolled into large tobacco 'joints'.   He was
"blocked", he said, for what seemed like a very long time and
eventually fell asleep listening to music.   His dramatically
phrased experience that the pharmacological effects of cannabis
pressed themselves upon him (without subcultural mediation) is
representative of a large group of drug users who did not
recognise themselves in Becker's phenomenology.   There were many
rude comments about the stupidity and wrongheadedness of this
sociological account;   several joked that if Becker's subjects
needed to learn to spot the effects, then they had been given a
"bum deal".

We will call this first technique *heavy technology*.   The
experience was not universal and a second man can speak for
another sub-group who had a different route to cannabis use,
involving a different technology of smoking and apparently
different effects.   He first smoked cannabis (in Britain in
1967-68) when he was passed a joint by a friend at a party.   He
anticipated 'pretty colours ... like I thought LSD might be ...
sort of psychedelic effects", but what he got was a fit of the
giggles.   "A few of us cracked a lot of stupid jokes ... I'd
had a lot of booze, wine, beer and I was probably already a bit
pissed".   He smoked occasionally over a period of years for

fun at parties.   The drug, he said, did not always seem to work.

In many ways this second group of users - using the drug for
kicks at parties and gatherings, its effects usually seen through
the haze of alcohol - conformed most closely to Becker's version
of a drug using career.   The drug effects were reported to be
more ambiguous.   It often did not seem to work on the first
occasion, and some people gave up at that point.   What it meant
to be 'high' was less recognisable.   This second form of drug
use we call *party technology*.

Our impression is that the crucial distinction between these
two sub-groups is *technology (how the drug is ingested)* and that
different technologies produce different drug effects.
Expectations, culture, setting seemed unimportant.   Ritual
sometimes surround drug use, but it varied widely and with no
significant pattern.   In all cases, the thing which linked the
patterning of different effects, different subcultural life-
styles, and different patterns of drug use was technology.   We
have only mentioned two technologies here, for the sake of brevity.

Some users moved freely between the different technologies, and
experienced different effects.   For example, one woman had
occasionally smoked (and enjoyed) cannabis at parties - again
after drinking alcohol.   She later became friendly with a
group of 'heads' of the heavy technology type: "It was so
different.   Sort of more vivid and it slowed you down, or
seemed to, and you could really enjoy music without wanting to
giggle and talk all the time ... there was hardly any talking".
It is important that our subject here is not describing the
influence of 'setting', but the effects of a different technology.
And although we would not wish to deny the possibility of
'setting' influences, this kind of evidence stands as a correction
to the one-sided sociological emphasis on 'setting' alone.

Equally, to say that technology (and therefore pharmacology)
was the principal determinant of the subjective experience of
drug effects is not to deny individual drug users either
intentionality (what might attract them to drug use, or what
ideologies might surround drug use) or choice (either to give
up cannabis use, or prefer one technology as more pleasurable).
For example, the same woman said of the 'heads': "They sit
around, smoke a lot, get really stoned and sit around listening
to music - Soft Machine or Pink Floyd or something like that ...
really stoned ... but just sitting around.   That's not my scene
at all, it's just too passive, too boring."   And we must emphasise again that it is not merely life-style (that is, culture)
which she is rejecting here; but technology.

123

SOCIOLOGICAL IMPERIALISM, BLIND-SPOTS AND ECSTASIES

As a contribution to the understanding of drug-induced experience and drug subcultures our evidence is trite. But that was not our question: our intention was, and is, to interrogate the recently fashionable 'interactionist', 'phenomenological' and 'insider' sociologies. To return to our questions: first, how to account for the discrepancy between the ethnographer's text on drug use and drug users' experiences?

In one sense, there is no surprise. Becker takes his sample (we guess) from a 1950's American subculture surrounding jazz music, jazz clubs and the growth of the *avant-garde* style of be-bop. (In fact, he does not tell us much about the other cultural aspects of the scene he is setting, and this is a major weakness in his ethnography of drug use.) We take our subjects from an early 1970's, post-flower-power and hippie generation of white, largely middle class, British youths. These two subcultures (and their macro-cultural contexts) are worlds apart, and the experiences are different: perhaps Becker is vindicated and our work only shows how cultural values and 'setting' do influence perceived drug effects.

But our purpose is not to verify or falsify Becker's work (just how would you verify ideographic observations?) but to understand how his ethnography is passed down by sociologists as gospel. How, to put that another way, a particular piece of research which contains some puzzling assumptions becomes reified (and deified) by the professional practice of sociologists. We are concerned with the ideological content of ethnography, its background assumptions. Elsewhere, one of us has developed at length the ideological themes buried in modern sociologies of deviance - the 'smell of theory' as we call it (Pearson, 1975: Part 1). Here we present only a few, brief, concluding observations.

1. Drug users tell us that the drugs in Howard Becker's studies must have been weak; we are saying that pharmacology has a weak hand in his theory. The background assumptions of his theory say: biology is not really that important.

This is a convenient assumption for professional sociologists, in that it demonstrates that the world has a need for professional sociology: sociology is said, literally, to over-determine biology and pharmacology. And it thus encourages sociological imperialism (where the important thing to do is not to engage in critical research, but to defend the methods and principles of sociology) and the blind-spots of abstract sociological whimsy: just as drugs get forgotten in this ethnography of drug use, so in the ethnographic studies which surround the sociology of medicine (for example) there is a total forgetfulness that the object of study is *health care* and *service to people*. We are dropped, instead, into a de-politicised and de-moralised phenomenological never-never land.

2.   The under-emphasis of the toxicity of drugs also fits neatly with the left-liberal intellectual bandwagon to legalise 'soft' drugs. Again, this ideological background assumption simply short-cuts the difficult moral-political issues in drug control. The theory's phoney radicalism acts as an excuse for confronting human-practical dilemmas.

3.   The thesis of the social construction of even the most intimate aspects of personal experience reflects the fear (persistent among bourgeois intellectuals) that advanced industrial society overwhelms every nook and cranny of private life; and that modernity and the 'massification' of society invade (and threaten) the very possibility of human subjectivity.

At the same time, ethnographic study provides intellectuals with a source of hopeful entertainment in the subjectless mass society. For, its own invasions of privacy (which it calls research) seem to re-construct and celebrate the microscopic detail of everyday life. In this way the popularity of ethnography does not only register a fear; it also offers a magical solution to the problem which is feared.

Ethnography thus joins the mad scramble to rescue our threatened subjectivity (c.f. Jacoby, 1973: 37-49). It is ecstatic over the possibility that even the hidden depths of our lives are well-normed and in good working order. But, if subjectivity and privacy are threatened, is ethnographic study the way to combat the threat? An apt remark by Colin Fletcher sums up the frail aesthetics of ethnography: "Qualitative research is ... practised and developed in the interludes between wars ..." (1974: 140).

COMMUNES
Colin Webster

*Note: The search for some kind of collective or group social
arrangement for living, alternative to the nuclear family, has
been a central theme for the middle class 'counter-cultures'.
The commune 'movement' - though, as Colin Webster shows here,
focussed around very different themes - represents the active
search among young people for such an alternative: and many
others not actively committed to the 'commune' as an ideal have
nevertheless, along with other activities, spent some time in
or experimented with a commune-style of life.   Communes thus
provide one of the core 'alternative institutions' of the
Counter-culture.   In this piece, Colin Webster (on placement
at the Centre for a year from Birmingham Polytechnic) offers
a rough 'thematic typology' of the main variants in the commune
movement.*

> Sir Thomas More was an inveterate punster, and Utopia is a mock
> name for either Outopia, which means no-place, or Eutopia -
> the good place.
> (Mumford, 1922)

It has been estimated that in 1970 there were over 2000
rural communes along with several thousand urban groups in the
United States, and approximately 50 serious communal ventures
of differing types in Britain[1].   In the rest of Europe too,
communes exist in most major cities, inspired to some extent
by the highly publicised Kommunes 1 and 2 founded in Berlin
during 1967.

We wish merely to briefly examine this social movement among
some disenchanted youth between the years 1965-75 by drawing
up a thematic typology.   This typology is substantiated
primarily by empirical fieldwork conducted by sociologists,
accounts published by Communards, and personal experience.

RURAL THEME

This theme finds its practical embodiment in the American
'back-to-the-land' communes constituted during the 1960's.
It contains within it sets of contradictory tensions between
the different idealised or anticipatory visions of Nature (as
wilderness or Paradise, desert or garden, source of terror or
source of salvation) which underpinned the movement, and between
these idealisations and the practical experiences of living

them out. It is possible to see ways in which these sets of contradictions found symbolic form in the various ritualised, expressive activities which attended the movement. Thus, to use the examples of perhaps the most publicised rural communes, the highly involved, active, even frenetic dancing and drug taking style epitomised by Kesey and the Pranksters (see Wolfe, 1969a) existed uneasily alongside, but within the same overall trajectory, as the meditative, reflective, passive, 'cool', white-robed, transcendental style of Leary and his acolytes at Millbrook (See Leary, 1970).

The legitimations of the commune movement, whose composition is that of *urban* middle class youth, function through nature, metaphors, expectancies, and a nostalgia for an experience of nature which neither they, nor their forbears, actually underwent. The return to origins is legitimated historically and practised contemporaneously inasmuch as archetypes are sought in American history and are acted out *'now'* as primitivism, voluntary poverty, an anti-technological bias, and a relaxation of sexual norms. These sometimes find extreme expression as 'eschatological nudism' and sexual freedom, and these serve as ritual anticipations of 'Paradise'. The eschatological basis of the rural theme also takes the form of the 'end-of-the-world', both *experientially* (the dropout experiences *his* or *her* urban, middle-class world ending) and through the *imagery* of environmental pollution, ecological catastrophe, racial strife, war and the 'demonic' technocratic system that supports it. The commune becomes here a 'saving remnant' and ritually and practically anticipates the paradise that will come after the old 'demonic reality' has passed away - here the messianic aspects of chiliasm become dominant. Closely related to this is the coming-to-awareness of the re-territorialising and holistic possibilities of men mediated through the widespread use of hallucinogenics (although also mediated in other ways). These 'visits to the inner landscape' are contrasted to the open-ended spatial exploration in nature metaphors, where natural space is experienced as a frontier/barrier, the overcoming of which opens up a series of options, anticipating experimental possibilities (in the *country*); and where *urbanism* is understood as the loss of access to experimental space.

These legitimations are sufficient, often enough, to warrant serious choices, realised in the rural commune, since it is built on the basis of post-agrarian experience: the resulting isolation, radical change in the structure of daily life, learning of new skills, and the deep challenge to identity, contribute to making the rural venture *the purer form of the movement*[2].

128

EUTOPIAN THEME

A recurring *transitional* moment among the life-histories of 'dropouts' is utopian, or, more accurately, 'outopian'. But having no place to go, the dropout becomes, a 'mendicant' who exists parasitically in the interstices of the welfare state. Drug use (among other mediators), within the deviant sub-culture occupied by disenchanted middle-class youth, contributes to the breakdown of the contemporary protestant ethic. This loosening of ties to the dominant ideology (will, calculation, instrumentalism, deferred gratification) may result in a striving for 'Eutopia', which takes the form of joining and or building a commune, according to the availability of resources. Alternatively, the transitional phase may seek other 'solutions', one of which is the return to the 'straight' job (the drop-out is incorporated). Whatever solution is taken during this transitional moment, priorities are reassessed, and this is often the period cited by the drop-out as one of 'becoming aware'[3].

MONOGAMOUS THEME

The essence of commune relationships is their *fragility* and relative absence of structural underpinnings to sustain them, when, and *if*, they become problematic. There are relatively few legal marriages or binding jobs, and little investment in the environmental locality. The 'present orientation' of intense relationships are supported by a reluctance to believe in the future or serial monogamy, and a diffuse desire to remain "polymorphously childlike". The compensatory support for fragility is a romantic *image* (which is not expected to be realised), and communal *solidarity*.

Paradoxically, monogamous, heterosexual couples constitute the norm in most communes. In this respect expressive communes differ from instrumental communes, the latter often constituted by middle class 'swingers', holding promiscuity as the norm. In expressive communes there is often a *drift* towards group marriage *because of the fragility,* and this functions to decrease the tension that ensues from living moment by moment. A typical sequence illustrating this tension is thus: communard (male) picks up woman, with or without child, takes her home, where an ambiguous status of 'his woman' is conferred. He may leave again and not return, or return alone, or with another woman. This is more pronounced in urban communes where the 'splitting' phenomenon is supported by the greater availability of significant-others-to-be. Moreover, no norm takes priority over the individual's (especially male) search-for-self. The frequency of woman-with-child receiving a series of men is seen as less disruptive (and more dependable since she provides welfare income). Thus a common situation is that of what we

call *the strong woman* in communes who stabilises for her child
('domesticity' norm), counterposed to the man's metaphysical
'voyage of discovery' (realisation of the individual norm).
This is undermined in urban communes which often emphasise their
concern over the status of women, and where self-support is
more manifest[4].

CHILDREARING THEME

The apparent commitment to *equality* is most noticeable in
the area of communal social life where the granting of adult-
like autonomy to children is a major tendency. But here again
we witness contradictions, inasmuch as the solidarity affirming
nature of child-birth ceremonies (which symbolize the collective
property as home and individuals as members of a single family)
is in tension with the distinctive communal 'theory of children'
in which they tend to be viewed as independent, self-contained
persons. Though the extent of child 'ownership' seems to
diminish sequentially as the child gets older, the dominant mode
is still mothers-with-children, and communal childrearing, as
yet, is usually considered too radical. A further development
takes the form of status allocations of 'women' and 'children'
being collapsed into the egalitarian notion of *'people'*, who,
to be sure, participate in the higher cosmic unities ('we are
all one'). Problematic developments within interpersonal
adult-child relations are often understood astrologically, and
children in particular are susceptible to being labelled as
"cosmic Wards" with their own *karmas* (or fates) which must be
worked out by the children themselves. The socialisation of
the child is thus very different from middle class norms; but
how *significant* this is has yet to be ascertained[5].

RELIGIOUS THEME

Under this theme we include *explicitly* religious communes,
other than those considered in the Rural theme which evolve
less consciously from religous metaphors embedded in the culture,
and are not overtly creedal. Creedal and highly intentional
communes often exist on the basis of an *absence,* symbolised by
an external divine or sacred force and actualised by an authoritarian, charismatic guru or 'divine leader', who may or may
not be present at the commune or 'ashran'. Examples of these
are the 'Temples' of The International Society for Krishna
Consciousness, the 'ashrans' of the Divine Light Mission, and
the 'communities' of the Children of God. We can call such
projects 'ascetic-religious' communes. Alternatively, the
'religious-mystic' commune has a belief in an *immanent* divine
force and a desire to attain oneness with the whole (again,
'we are all one'). This is closely related to the rural
theme in that there is little concern to change the world as

an externality, but much concern with self-liberational
techniques, practised more or less reflectively[6].

URBAN-ACTIVIST THEME

   Relative to rural communes, urban communes generally
emphasise theoretical self-understanding, concretised in both a
life-style politics, revolving around the theme of 'individuation
as Praxis', and in *political* practices, of which the commune is
a part.   But they seem less able to sustain communal life-
style.   Kommunes 1 and 2 provide an ideal-type of the commune
with urban-activist interests, focussing on sexual-emancipatory
and child-rearing themes, as well as on more overtly political
questions.   Typical of the anti-authoritarian movements which
have been strong in Germany since 1968, the Kommunes combine a
concern (following Reiche, 1968) with the processes of
character formation, and a concern (following Marcuse, 1970)
with combatting the effects of 'repressive desublimation'.
The internal character, they argue, is structured and shaped
by the needs of the much-expanded consumption function in modern
capitalism: and the family is seen both as the genesis of
consumption and the means by which the "culture industry"
(advertising, the media, etc) penetrates the character-structure
of children.   This consumption-function requires that the sexual
instincts be repressed and manipulated, but it is the family
which carries through this repressive 'work' on behalf of the
system, principally through its dominant child-rearing practices.
The family, which was seen as defensive of its members in the
liberal era, today, under monopoly capitalism, provides both a
retreat from community (*privatisation* of the individual and the
dissolution of the individual is achieved at the same time)
and reproduction of the socio-economic requirements of the
status quo.   It directs instinctual needs into conformity
with the dominant norms.   The commune's objectives are tne
rational liberation of the instincts and potentialities 'here
and now' as a prior condition of revolutionary transformation
via liberatory child rearing and a 'working through' of
relationships.   This defence against repressive desublimation
avoids both promiscuous object-relationships and the pseudo-
gratifications of consumerism.   Less reflectively, urban communes are often seen as *'nodal points'*, as sources of affection,
and as destructuring the rush of city life.

   Other types of urban commune, although having some relationship to the above, take the form of political-economic struggle,
such as that of the squatting movement instigated in London by
libertarians such as Ron Bailey.   This involved the setting up
of communes in empty buildings in the context of housing shortag-
es created by misallocation of resources through the property
market.   Groups such as the *Provos* in Amsterdam and the *Diggers*

in California set up community self-help projects, taking an
overtly political form within the life-style politics movement.
Generally, we can conclude that urban communes are invariably
created as centres of urban-activism and often have revolutionary
-style politics of a 'grass roots' nature[7].

INFRASTRUCTURAL THEME

There is evidence of a more scientific knowledge of man's
place in the eco-system, within the 'alternative technology'
movement.   Widely distributed journals such as *Undercurrents,
Science for People*, and *The Whole Earth Catalog* promote a
unique mixture of traditional and futuristic technologies,
derived from Buckminster Fuller and others, in which there is
a new science and a new knowledge being generated, embodied
practico-technically in what we call *infrastructural communes*.
This theme is evidenced in a sophistication of theoretical and
technical rules and the e application at communal centres of
alternative technology (in Scotland and Wales in particular).
This theme has a series of complex homologies to the irrationalist
trends discussed in the rural theme.   Productive communes/
communities are seen as forming the economic infrastructure
upon which the new social organisation will rest, thus overcoming
the traditional dichotomies between the productive process and
social relations, work and play.   Within the utopian/practical
debates an assumption of a symbiotic relationship between man
and nature is counterposed to the eco-catastrophe created by the
'mystification' of this relationship.   Vegetarianism and mysticism (man is at one with the eco-system and the cosmos) is
counterposed to the exploitative treatment of nature.   Human social organisation is seen to have identity with ecological organisation, thus throwing forth the themes of Buddhist Economics, the
use of non-fossil fuels, diversification and decentralisation of
production, anti-urbanism, and self-sufficiency.   The irrationalist moments of these interests are often contained in contradictory homologies between futurist technologies, cybernation
and science fiction fantasies and primitivism.   These are
embodied in the homologies between Pessimism - Eschatology -
Apocalypse[8].

THERAPEUTIC THEME

A 'therapy' may be derived from a physical and cultural
environment within which particular types of people, conventionally labelled sick or deviant by the dominant culture, can be
cared for, encouraged to be autonomous, and helped to grow, in
the sense of becoming able to live a 'more meaningful life'.
Therapeutic communes range from communes-as-encounter-groups
to spaces in which 'journeys through madness' are embarked
upon, such as at the Kingsway Community in London.   The influence

132

of the existential psychoanalysts R.D. Laing and David Cooper, upon this type of commune, particularly in Britain, has been noted by Juliet Mitchell:

> By the 1960's the post-war baby, once nurtured by its home-bound mother had become a teenager ... As the cult of mother and child went its relentless way, the child, who had become adolescent, escaped either in day dreams of rebels without a cause, or increasingly with a cause - a cause against their parents. The late 50's or early 60's marked the rise of youth politics - C.N.D., the New Left, Committee of 100, were dominated by young people. Schizophrenia was prevalent in adolescents - was it, too, a symptom of the revolt against the claustrophobic family? *Laing caught and helped create the moment with this question* (1975: 230, our emphasis).

It should not surprise us, in the light of the above, that Doris Lessing, in *The Four-Gated City* (1972), suggested an homology between *Madness* (as 'Regeneration?'; c.f. Laing, 1967), *Science Fiction* (c.f. Heineman, undated) and *Mysticism* (c.f. Laing, *op. cit.*).[9]

CONCLUSION

In conclusion, we draw attention to the tensions and contradictions which pervade the commune movement: between rationalist and irrationalist themes and practices; between nature mysticism and nature-as-eco-system; between religious end-of-the-world philosophies and notions of eco-catastrophe; between mystical, occultist and astrological legitimations and technical ones; between woman-with-child as 'Mother Earth' and woman and child as autonomous; between madness and rebirth, personal and political, community and society, individual and collective, urbanism and ruralism; and, finally, between Outopia and Eutopia.

FOOTNOTES

1. For a comparison of estimates see Rigby (1974a) and Melville (1972).

2. For references to the rural theme specifically within the counter-culture, see McDermott (1971) and Kaufman (1971). For more general references to nature mysticism/chiliasm see Cohn (1971) and Roszak (1972).

3. The Eutopian theme is a thread running through all the literature on the Commune movement, but, more generally the 'Utopian mentality' in history is analysed by Mannheim (1972) and most adequately and radically (in the sense of going to the roots) by Bloch (1970 and 1971).

4. Specifically. in terms of what is happening in Communes, see R. and Della Roy (1972) and J.and H. Ogilvy (1971). Sexual struggle and discussion of monogamy generally is found in all Womens Liberation movement literature, but in relation to urban-communes, see R. Reiche (1968).

5. The child-rearing theme is discussed in Berger, Hackett and Millar (1972), Bookhagen et. al. (1973) and Zicklin (1973).

6. See Rigby (1974a and b) and the journal *Resurgence*. Otherwise there is very little published research on this theme. For the religious-utopian tradition see Cohn (1971), Roszak (1972), and, again for sheer depth of understanding, Bloch (1970 and 1971). For a survey of contemporary influences on youthful/counter-cultural mysticism and religion, see Needleman (1971). Also look at the movement publications of the various sects.

7. On Kommunes 1 and 2 see Bookhagen et. al. (1973) and Reiche (1968). On squatting see, for example, Bailey (1973), and on the related European student movement see Statera (1975).

8. See the journals and magazines cited in the text. Here there is little published research apart from the eschatological - chiliast influences already cited, but see Schumacher (1974), Harper (ed., forthcoming), and Bookchin (1971).

9. See Rigby (1974a and b), Cooper (1967, 1972 and 1974) and Laing (1967). Also the magazine of the Encounter movement: *Self and Society*.

REGGAE, RASTAS & RUDIES
Dick Hebdige

Note: *This is an extract from a longer study of "Reggae, Rastas and Rudies: Style and the Subversion of Form", by Dick Hebdige, and forms part of his MA Thesis, "Aspects of Style in the Deviant. Sub-Cultures of the 1960's".* The full-length chapter and other papers from this thesis are available among the CCCS *Stencilled Papers, Nos. 20, 21, 24 and 25.* The extract deals mainly with the Jamaican cultural context: the structure of Ras Tafarian beliefs: its envelopment in musical form, especially ska and reggae: the social and cultural meaning of the music: its transplantation to Britain; its partial incorporation by white Skinheads, and its use by black 'rude boys' to subvert and resist incorporation. The extract omits a fuller analysis of Ras Tafarian beliefs and its recent history as a movement; a discussion of the importance and use by 'rude boy culture' of elements from the Hollywood gangster film; an analysis of the inter-relationships between 'black' and East End culture in Britain; and a section on method - all included in the longer version of the Chapter.

I Babylon on Beeston Street

> The bars they could not hold me,
> Walls could not control me.
>> from The Wailer's *Duppy Conqueror*

> I was born with the English language and it proved
> to be my enemy.
>> James Baldwin (in interview).

> Revolution soon - come.
>> Bulldog quoted in Thomas (1973)

The experience of slavery recapitulates itself perpetually in the everyday interactions of the Jamaican black. It is principally responsible for the unstable, familial structure (disrupting the traditionally strong kinship networks which even now survive among the peoples of West Africa) and obviously goes on determining patterns of work and relations with authority. It remains an invisible shaping presence which haunts the slums of Ghost Town and even now defies exorcism. In fact it is interpolated into every verbal exchange which takes place on the teeming streets of every Jamaican slum.   As Hiro (1973) points out: "the evolution of the creole language was related directly to the mechanics of slavery".   Communication was systematically blocked by the white overseer who banded slaves of different tribes together on the plantations so that cultural links with Africa were effectively severed.   The laws which forbade the teaching of English to slaves meant that the new language was secretly appropriated (by rough approximation, by lip reading, etc.) and transmitted orally.   The 17th century English spoken by the master class was refracted through the illicit channels of communication available to the black and used to embody the subterranean semantics of a nascent culture which developed in direct defiance of the master's wishes.   Distortion was inevitable, perhaps even deliberate.

Subsequently, the language developed its own vocabulary, syntax and grammar; but it remains essentially a shadow-language fulfilling in a more exaggerated and dramatic way those require-ments, which, under normal circumstances, are satisfied by region-al working-class accents and group *argot*.   Form implicitly dictates content, and poles of meaning, fixed immutably in a bitter and irreversible experience, silently reconstruct that experience in everyday exchange.   As we shall see later, this fact is intuitively grasped by the members of certain West Indian subcultures, and language is used as a particularly effective means of resisting assimilation and preventing infiltration by members of the dominant groups.   As a screening device it has proved to be invaluable; and the "Bongo talk" and patois of the Rude Boy deliberately emphasise its subversive rhythms so that it becomes an aggressive assertion of racial and class identities. As a living index to the extent of the black's alienation from the cultural norms and goals of those who occupy higher positions in the social structure, the creole language is unique.

The expulsion of the black from the wider linguistic community meant that a whole culture evolved by a secret and forbidden osmosis.   Deprived of any legitimate cultural exchange, the slave developed an excessive individualism and a set of cultural artefacts which together represent the vital symbolic transactions which had to be made between slavery and freedom, between his material condition and his spiritual life, between his experience of Jamaica and his memories of Africa.   In a sense, the trans-ition was never satisfactorily accomplished, and the black Jamaican remains suspended uneasily between two worlds neither of which commands a total commitment.   Unable to repair this cultural and psychological breach, he tends to oscillate violently from one world to the other and ultimately he idealises both.   Ultimately, indeed, he is exiled from Jamaica, from Afri-ca, from Britain and from Brixton, and sacrifices his place in

the real world to occupy an exalted position in some imaginative
inner dimension where action dissolves into being, where
movement is invalidated and difficult at the best of times,
where solutions are religious rather than revolutionary.

In fact, the initial rationalisations of slavery took an
explicitly religious form. Barred from the white man's churches,
the slave learnt the Christian doctrine obliquely and grafted it,
with varying degrees of success, onto the body of pagan beliefs
which he had carried over from Africa. The residual supersti-
tions (voodoo, witchcraft, etc.) persist even now beneath the
surface of the Christian faith and periodically reassert themselves in their original forms in the hills and rural areas of
Jamaica, and are resurrected in the music of the more esoteric
city-based bands[1]. The schools of Christian worship native to
Jamaica still retain the ancient practices of the trance,
spirit-possession, and "speaking in tongues", and these Churches
(the Pentecostal Church, the Church of God in Christ, etc.)
continue to attract enormous congregations. As a means of
consolidating group ties and of articulating a group response to
slavery, these nonconformist churches were to prove very valuable
indeed. By appealing at once to the individual (by subscribing
to the doctrine of personal "grace") and to the group (by
promising collective redemption), they provided an irresistible
solution - a means not of closing the gulf but of transcending
it completely. The Bible offered limitless scope for improvisation and interpretation. The story of Moses leading the
suffering Israelites out of captivity was immediately applicable
and won a permanent place in the mythology of the Jamaican black.
The various cults pursued the ambiguous apocalypse along exactly
those paths traced out elsewhere by Norman Cohn, (1970), proclaim-
ing at different times divine revolutions, *postmortem* revelations.
Whenever God seemed to be procrastinating, there were always the
chiliastic cults of the rural areas ready to hurry things up.
Even now, on occasion "Pocomania" (literally "a little madness")
spreads with brief but devastating effect through the townships
of the hills, and the Revival is, of course, always there to be
revived. A million millennia counted out in days and months
and minutes have come and gone and still God speaks to wild-eyed
men in dreams. Judgment Day, the Day of Turnabout is never
remote: it is always the day after tomorrow. And Judgement
Day is dear to the heart of every Rasta and every Rudie; and
for these it means the redistribution of an exclusively secular
power.

The displacement of material problems onto a spiritual plane
is of course by no means peculiar to the black Jamaican. The
ways in which this essentially religious perspective is trans-
muted into a utopian-existentialist one are, perhaps, more
extraordinary and certainly more pertinent to the phenomenon

137

under consideration here. Christianity still permeates the
West Indian imagination, and a Biblical mythology continues to
dominate, but at certain given points in the social structure
(namely, among the unemployed young and the deviant adult population) this mythology has been turned back upon itself so that
the declared ascendancy of Judaeo-Christian culture (with its
emphasis on work and repression) can be seriously scrutinised
and ultimately rejected. Instrumental in this symbolic reversal
were the Rastafarians.

The Rastafarians believe that the exiled Emperor Haile
Selassie of Ethopia was God and that his accession to the
Ethiopian throne fulfils the prophecy made by Marcus Garvey,
"Look to Africa, when a black king shall be crowned, for the day
of deliverance is near." But the religious milieu in which
Rastafarianism was evolved demanded a specifically Biblical
mythology and this mythology had to be re-appropriated and made
to serve a different set of cultural needs, just as the
"Protestant Ethic" in Western Europe had performed its own
re-appropriation of the original Judaic form. By a dialectical
process of redefinition, the Scriptures, which had constantly
absorbed and deflected the revolutionary potential of the
Jamaican black, were used to locate that potential, to negate the
Judaeo-Christian culture. Or, in the more concise idiom of the
Jamaican street-boys, the Bible was taken, read and "flung back
rude".

Thus, Haile Selassie was not only the Ras Tafari, the Negus,
the King of Kings, and the Living God, but also specifically the
Conquering Lion of the Tribe of Judah. (More recently, the simple appellation "Jah" has been used.) In these formulations the
racial and religious problems which had preoccupied the Jamaican
black for centuries converged and found immediate and simultaneous
resolution. Predictably, the cult drew its support chiefly from
the slums of Kingston. The U.C.W.I. research paper of 1960, *The
Ras Tafari Movement in Kingston, Jamaica*, reporting a first-hand
study of the movement, managed to set out a broad base of beliefs
common to all Rastafarians (M. G. Smith et al. 1960). The four
point manifesto went as follows:

1. Ras Tafari is the Living God
2. Ethiopia is the black man's home.
3. Repatriation is the way of redemption for
   black men. It has been foretold and will
   occur shortly.
4. The ways of the white man are evil, especially
   for the black.

The most striking feature is how the Biblical metaphors have
been elaborated into a total system - a code of seeing - at once

supple and holistic, universal in application, and lateral in direction. The black races are interpreted as the true Israelites and Solomon and Sheba are the black ancestors of Haile Selassie, the black god. Babylon really covers the western world (though many locksmen exclude Russia which has been identified as the Bear with three ribs which "will come to stamp up the residue thereof so that Babylon shall be a desolation among the nations" - *Revelation* XVIII). The police, the Church, and the Government (particularly old political leaders like Bustamante and the elder Manley) are the agents of imperialism and will share the terrible fate of the white oppressors. Ethiopia is the true name for all Africa. Since 1655, the white man and his brown ally have held the black man in slavery; and although physical slavery was abolished in 1838, it continues in a disguised form. All black men are Ethiopians and the Jamaican Government is not their government. It subordinates itself to Great Britain which still regards Jamaica as a colony. The only true government is the theocracy of the Emperor Haile Selassie, though Communism is much more desirable than capitalism - which is the system of Babylon. Marriage in church is sinful and the true Ethiopian should merely live with a black "Queen" whom he should treat with the utmost respect. (She, for her part, must never straighten her hair.) Alcohol is forbidden, as is gambling. Jamaican beliefs in obeah, magic and witchcraft are superstitious nonsense and have no empirical validity. Revivalism compounds mental slavery. Ganja is sacred. Worldly possessions are not necessary in Jamaica and the individual ownership of property is frowned upon. Work is good but alienated labour is quite simply a perpetuation of slavery All brethren are reincarnations of ancestral slaves; reincarnation is the reaffirmation of a lost culture and tradition. All brethren who regard Ras Tafari as God, regard man as God. 'Men' are mortal sinners and oppressors. 'Man' are those who know the Living God, the brethren and are immortal and One, living eternally in the flesh of all brethren - (One Locksman will address another as "bra" (brother) and will double up the first person singular "I and I" - instead of using the "you and I" construction).

Beyond these "certainties" which remain relatively static, the locksman habitually resorts to the rhetorical modes of the Bible - the riddle, the paradox, the parable - to demonstrate that he is in possession of the "true word". Michael Thomas (1973) quotes a hermetic locksman called Cunchyman who tells how he has conquered the tyranny of work by "capturing" an axe (which can kill thirteen men who use it for chopping wood all their lives) and hanging it on the wall. In an interview with *Rolling Stone*, in 1973, Bob Marley, the Rasta Leader of the "Wailers" (perhaps the first reggae band with a truly international following) shows how "destruction come outta material things" by using his guitar as a reified metaphor (the guitar plays beautiful music but it

can kill if there is a short circuit). Such syncretic and
associative patterns of thought make all knowledge immediately
(i.e. magically) accessible. Thus, when sufficiently stoned,
the locksman will, as Michael Thomas (1973) asserts, discuss
literally anything (e.g. which is more powerful - lightning
or electricity; which is faster - the shark or the porpoise)
with all the casuistry and conviction of a Jesuit priest.
Ultimately, technology capitulates to belief; belief succumbs
to knowledge; and thought is really felt. At this point, a
harmonious relationship between the inner and outer dimensions
is made possible and the "bra" is said to "head rest (or "in-
dwell") with Jah." This explicit identification with the Godhead
automatically demands a denial of linear systems; an end to all
distinctions, and invites an extreme subjectivism. Mysticism,
of course, means stasis, and the movement suffered ultimately
from the quietist position towards which it naturally inclined[2].
The conversion of science into poetry did not lead to the expected
redistribution of real power (even though this power was merely
"apparent"; in Rastafarian mythology, a "figment" of Babylonian
"vanity")[3]. But the crucial act of faith constitutes an
archetypal technique of appropriation which escaped the traditional religious displacement by grounding God; it entailed a
radical reappraisal of the black Jamaican's potential and enabled
the locksman to reassess his position in society. And if all
this seems a little too esoteric, we need only turn to the Rude
Boy to confirm the validity of the Rasta perspective. For the
secularisation of the Rasta Godhead coincided with the politicisation of the dispossed Rude Boy, and the new aesthetic which
directed and organised the locksman's perceptions, found a perfect
form in reggae.

2   Music and the overthrow of form

> A hungry man becomes an angry man.
> A rude boy quoted in White (1967)

> Preacher man say Great God come down from the sky
> Make every body feel happy, make everybody feel high.
> But if you know what life is worth
> You will look for yours on earth,
> So now I seen the light
> I'm gonna stand up for me rights.
> From the Wailer's *Get up, Stand up for Your Rights*

Reggae itself is polymorphous - and to concentrate upon one
component at the expense of all others involves a reduction of
what are complex cultural processes. Thus, reggae is trans-
mogrified American 'soul' music, with an overlay of salvaged
African rhythms, and an undercurrent of pure Jamaican rebellion.
Reggae is transplanted Pentecostal. Reggae is the Rasta hymnal,

140

the heart cry of the Kingston Rude Boy, as well as the nativised national anthem of the new Jamaican government. The music is all these things and more - a mosaic which incorporates all the strands that make up black Jamaican culture; the call and response patterns of the Pentecostal Church, the devious scansion of Jamaican street talk, the sex and the cool of U.S. R. and B., the insistent percussion of the locksmen's jam-sessions, all find representation in reggae.

Even the etymology of the word "reggae" invites controversy. In Michael Thomas (1973), Bulldog, a rude boy who has made the grade in West Kingston, claims that it was derived from "ragga" which was an "uptown" way of saying "raggamuffin" and that the implied disapproval was welcomed by those who had liked the music. Alternatively, there have been readings which stress the similarity with the word *raga* (the Indian form) and still others which claim that reggae is simply a distortion of Reco (who, with Don Drummond, was one of the original "ska" musicians). The emergence of the music itself has provoked even fiercer debate, and one's response to the music depends upon whether one believes the music evolved spontaneously out of a group experience or as part of a conscious policy of "nativisation" dictated from above. Patterson (1964) tends to play down the folk-aspects of reggae and gives a correspondingly unsympathetic account of Rastafarianism (which he interprets as mystification through "group fantasy"). Kallyndyr and Dalrymple (undated) mention only those folk-aspects, and tend to be somewhat uncritical. In McGlashan (1973), the King (a leading sound-system man amongst the black British community) offers a characteristically unempirical and metaphorical explanation which provides another prime example of Rasta 'logic'.

> Reggae is protest, formed out of suffering ... You got to have that hard strong feeling ... That feeling come from mothers' breast, man, the breast milk. It's true! ... the natural milk comes from the mother's breast, man. It give you that ... that ... stickiness in your body man, an' that feelings, man, to create things that supposed to been created.

Whilst acknowledging the fallibility of such rhetorical excesses, I would support the King against Patterson, simply because the commercial interests of the entrepreneurs who controlled the new record industry militated against any kind of intervention by the central government. Moreover, the impetus toward Africanisation required no encouragement from above - it was already showing itself in the development of the Ras Tafari movement and in the disillusioned withdrawal of the unemployed youth. The locksmen were not only the militant core of the Rasta movement; they also provided a nucleus around which less coherent forms of protest could gather, and the dialogue which ensued found operatic expression in reggae.

Before 'ska' (the forerunner of reggae) Jamaica had little
distinctive music of its own.   Jamaican 'mento' was a rather
emasculated musical form, combining local dialect 'folk songs'
with a respectable version of African rhythm - a derivation
from what had originally been very potent stuff indeed.   Beyond
this and Harry Belafonte, the North Coast did the samba to the
strains of Willy Lopez and his swish Latin orchestra.   But in
the 1950's, in West Kingston, R. and B., imported from America,
began to attract attention.   Men like Duke Reid were quick to
recognise the potential for profit and launched themselves as
disc-jockeys forming the flamboyant aristocracy of the shantytown
slums;   the era of the sound system began.   Survival in the
highly competitive world of the backyard discos, where rival
disc-jockeys vied for the title of the "boss-sound", demanded
alertness, ingenuity and enterprise;   and, as American R. and B.
began to lose its original impetus in the late fifties, a new
expedient was tried by the more ambitious d-j's, who branched out
into record production themselves.   Usually, an instrumental
recording was all that was necessary, and the d-j would improvise
the lyrics (usually simple and formulaic: "work-it-out,
work-it-out" etc.) during "live" performances.   Certain important
precedents were set by these early recordings.   Firstly, the
musicians were generally selected from the vast bank of unemployed
labour;   used for one session, paid a pittance, and returned to
the streets.   The ruthless exploitation of young talent
continues unabated in certain sections of the local record industry.   Secondly, the music remains, even now, essentially tied
to the discos and is designed principally for dancing.   Thirdly,
the tradition of "scatting" across a simple repetitive backing
with impromptu lyrics, continues to produce some of the more
interesting and exciting reggae.   Lastly, and most importantly,
the "ska" beat made its debut on these early unlabelled discs.
Ska is a kind of jerky shuffle played on an electric guitar with
the treble turned right up.   The emphasis falls on the upbeat
rather than on the offbeat as in R. and B., and is accentuated
by the bass, drums and brass sections (trombones were an indispensable part of early ska).   Ska is structurally a back-to-front
version of R. and B.

Once again, as with language and religion, distortion of
the original form appears to be deliberate, as well as inevitable;
and inversion seems to denote appropriation, signifying that a
cultural transaction has taken place.   However, the alchemy
which turned soul into ska was by no means simple.   The imported
music interacted with the established subterranean forms of
Jamaica.   The Cumina, Big Drum, and burra dances had long since
resurrected the rhythms of Africa, and the context in which these
forms were evolved directly determined their shape and content.
They left an indelible mark on the semantics of ska.
The burra dance was particularly significant;   played on the bass,

142

funde and repeater drums, the burra constituted an open celebration of criminality. Since the early 30's, it had been the custom for the inhabitants of the West Kingston slums to welcome discharged prisoners back into the communities with the "burra". The music consolidated local allegiances and criminal affiliations at the expense of commitments to the larger society beyond the slums. As the locksmen began to clash regularly with the police in the late 40's, a liaison developed between locksmen and hardened criminals. The dreadlocks of the Rastamen were absorbed into the arcane iconography of the outcast and many Rastas openly embraced the outlaw status which the authorities seemed determined to thrust upon them. Still more made permanent contacts in the Jamaican underworld whilst serving prison terms for ganja offences. This drift toward a consciously anti-social and anarchist position was assisted by the police who attempted to discredit the movement by labelling all locksmen as potentially dangerous criminals who were merely using mysticism as a front for their subversive activities. As has been observed so often elsewhere, predictions such as these have a tendency to find fulfilment, and criminals like Woppy King, who was later executed for murder and rape, joined the Rastafarian fraternity and affected the extravagant style of the dreadlocks In time, the locksmen took over the burra dance completely, calling the burra drums "akete drums". Inevitably, the criminal ambience which surrounded the music survived the transference and the Niyabingi dance which replaced the burra translated the original identification with criminal values into an open commitment to terrorist violence. The crime and music of West Kingston were thus linked in a subtle and enduring symbiosis; and they remained yoked together even after the infiltration of soul. Moreover, the locksmen continued to direct the new music, and to involve themselves creatively in its production. Meanwhile, a survey in 1957 had revealed that 18% of the labour force was without work, and, as the Doxey Report was to state twelve years later, it had now become conceivable that: "many young persons will pass through the greater part of their lives having never been regularly employed " (Doxey, 1969). The embittered youth of West Kingston, abandoned by the society which claimed to serve them, were ready to look to the locksman for explanations, to listen to his music, and to emulate his posture of withdrawal. Thus, it should hardly surprise us to find that, behind the swagger and the sex, the violence and the cool of the Rude Boy music of the sixties stands the visionary Rastaman with his commodious rhetoric, his all-embracing metaphors.

And so, ska was resilient, armoured music; "rough and tough" in more ways than one. Its inception guaranteed it against serious interference from above or manipulation at the level of meaning. The stigma which was originally attached to ska by the official arbiters of good taste in Jamaica relates directly

to the criminal connotations of the "burra" dance, and the early
attempts on the part of the government at manufacturing a national
sound were frankly unsuccessful.   Eddie Seaga, who set up one of
the first record companies in Jamaica (*West Indies Records*) was
one of those middle-class 'nationalist' entrepreneurs who tried
to promote ska to the world as a representative (and therefore
respectable) "native" form.   His admission to the Labour Cabinet
encouraged him in this project and alongside his attempt to
organise West Kingston as a political constituency he recruited
Byron Lee and the Dragonaires, a "class act" which was currently
playing the North Coast, and sent them first to West Kingston to
study the new music, and then to New York to present the finished
product.   The music suffered somewhat in the translation.
Byron Lee was too polished to play ska properly, and raw
ska was too "rude" to interest a world market at that time.

So, ska was left, more or less to its own devices.   In the
early sixties, the record industry developed under the auspices
of Seaga at *West Indian Records*, Ken Khouri at Federal Studios
and Chris Blackwell, a white man and son of a plantation owner,
at *Island* records.   But Blackwell did not confine himself to
the West Indies; he soon went on to exploit the market in
England, where more records were being sold to the homesick
rudies than to the native Jamaicans[4].   Blackwell bought
premises in the Kilburn Road and began to challenge the
monopoly which the *Bluebeat* label had managed to acquire over
the West Indian record market in Britain.

His triumph over Bluebeat was publicly acknowledged in 1964,
when he launched the first nationally popular ska record, *My
Boy Lollipop*, sung with an endearing nasal urgency by the sixteen
year old Millie Small.   Blackwell set up another label, *Trojan*,
which dealt with most of the British releases and left Lee Gopthal
to supervise the distribution from South London.   Then, sometime
in the summer of 1966, the music altered recognisably and ska
modulated into 'rocksteady'.   The horns were given less emphasis
or were dropped altogether, and the sound became somewhat slower,
more somnambulant and erotic.   The bass began to dominate and,
as rocksteady, in its turn, became heavier, it became known as
reggae.   Over the years, reggae attracted such a huge following
that Michael Manley (the present Prime-Minister) used a reggae
song *Better Must Come* in his 1972 election campaign.[5]   His
People's National Party won by an overwhelming majority.

But this does not mean that the music was defused; for
simultaneously, during this period, the Rude Boys were evolving
a visual style which did justice to the tesselated structure of
ska.   The American soul-element was reflected most clearly in
the self-assured demeanour; the sharp flashy clothes, the "jive-
ass" walk which the street boys affected.   The politics of

144

ghetto pimpery found their way into the street-talk of shantytown Jamaica, and every Rude Boy, fresh from some poor rural
outback, soon began to wheel and deal with the best of them in
the ubiquitous bars of Ghost Town and Back O' Wall.[6] The rude
boy lived for the luminous moment, playing dominoes as though
his life depended on the outcome - a big-city hustler with nothing
to do, and, all the time rocksteady, ska and reggae gave him the
means with which to move effortlessly - without even thinking.
Cool, that distant and indefinable quality, became almost abstract, almost metaphysical, intimating a stylish kind of stoicism -
survival and something more.

And, of course, there were the clashes with the police.
The ganja, and the guns, and the "pressure" produced a steady
stream of rude boys desperate to test their strength against
the law, and the judges replied with longer and longer sentences.
In the words of Michael Thomas (1973), every rudie was "dancing
in the dark" with ambitions to be "the coolest Johnny-Too-Bad on
Beeston Street". This was the chaotic period of ska, and
Prince Buster lampooned the Bench and sang of "Judge Dread", who
on side one, sentences weeping Rude Boys ("Order! Order! Rude
Boys don't cry!") to 500 years and 10,000 lashes, and on side
two, grants them a pardon, and throws a party to celebrate their
release. The dreary mechanics of crime and punishment, of
stigmatisation and incorporation, are reproduced endlessly in
tragi-comic form on these early records, and the ska classics,
like the music of the "burra" which preceded them, were often a
simple celebration of deviant and violent behaviour[8] Sound
system rivalries, street fights[7], sexual encounters, boxing
matches[9], horse races[10], and experiences in prison[11], were
immediately converted into folk-song and stamped with the ska
beat. The disinherited Dukes and Earls, the Popes and Princes
of early ska came across as music-hall gangsters and Prince
Buster warned in deadly earnest, with a half-smile that
"Al Capone's guns don't argue"[12].

But in the world of "007"[13] where the rude boys "loot" and
"shoot" and "wail" while "out on probation", "the policemen
get taller", and "the soldiers get longer" by the hour; and in
the final confrontation, the authorities must always triumph.
So there is always one more confrontation on the cards, and there
is always a higher authority still, and that is where Judgement
Day works itself back into Reggae, and the Rastas sing of an
end to "sufferation" on the day when Judge Dread will be consumed
in his own fire. The Rastafarian influence on reggae had been
strong since the earliest days - ever since Don Drummond and
Reco Rodriguez had played tunes like *Father East, Addis Ababa,
Tribute to Marcus Garvey* and *Reincarnation* to a receptive
audience. And even Prince Buster, the "Boss," the Main Man,
the individualist par excellence, at the height of the

anarchic Rude Boy period, could exhort his followers in *Free Love*, to "act true", to "speak true", to "learn to love each other," advising the dissident rudies that "truth is our best weapon" and that "our unity will conquer." In the burlesque *Ten Commandments*, Prince Buster is typically ambivalent, proselytising, and preaching, and poking fun all at the same time; but the internalisation of God which marks the Rasta Creed is there nonetheless behind all the blustering Chauvinism:

> These are the ten commandments of man given to woman by me,
> Prince Buster, through the inspiration of I.

As the decade wore on, the music shifted away from America towards Ethiopia, and the rude boys moved with the music. Racial and class loyalties were intensified, and, as the music matured, it made certain crucial breaks with the R. and B. which had provided the original catalyst. It became more 'ethnic', less frenzied[14], more thoughtful, and the political metaphors and dense mythology of the locksmen began to insinuate themselves more obtrusively into the lyrics. Groups like the Wailers, the Upsetters, the Melodians and the Lionaires emerged with new material which was often revolutionary, and always intrinsically Jamaican. Some rude boys began to grow the dreadlocks, and many took to wearing woollen stocking caps, often in the green, gold and red of the Ethiopian flag to proclaim their alienation from the West. This transformation (if such a subtle change of gear deserves such apocalyptic terminology), went beyond style to modify and channel the rude boys' consciousness of class and colour. Without overstressing the point there was a trend away from the undirected violence, bravado and competitive individualism of the early sixties, towards a more articulate and informed anger; and if crime continued to offer the only solution available, then there were new distinctions to be made. A Rude Boy quoted in Nettleford (1970) exhibits a "higher consciousness" in his comments on violence:

> It's not the suffering brother you should really stick up
> it is these big merchants that have all these twelve places ...
> with the whole heap of different luxurious facilities ....,what
> we really want is this equal rights and justice. Everyman have
> a good living condition, good schooling, and then I feels things
> will be much better."

I would suggest that, as the Rastas themselves began to turn away from violent solutions to direct the new aesthetic, the rude boys, steeped in ska, soon acquired the locksmen's term of reference, and became the militant arm of the Rasta movement. Thus, as the music evolved and passed into the hands of the locksmen there was an accompanying expansion of class and

146

colour consciousness through the West Indian community. Of course, I would not isolate the emergence of a "higher conscious-ness" from larger developments in the ghettoes and on the campuses of the United States. Nor would I dismiss the stimulative effect of the Jamaican Black Power movement which, by the late sixties, was being led by middle-class students and was clustered around the University of the West Indies[15]. But I would stress the unique way in which these external develop-ments were mediated to the Rude Boy (in Brixton as well as Back O' Wall), how they were digested, interpreted and reassembled by the omniscient Rasta Logos situated at the heart of reggae music. In spite of Manley and Seaga, reggae remained intact. It was never dirigible, protected, as it was, by language, by colour, and by a culture which had been forced, in its very inception, to cultivate secrecy and to elaborate defences against the intrusions of the Master Class.

Moreover, the form of reggae itself militated against outside interference and guaranteed a certain amount of autonomy. Reggae reversed the established pattern of pop music[16] by dictating a strong repetitive bassline which communicated directly to the body and allowed the singer to "scat" across the undulating surface of the rhythm. The music and the words are synchronised in good reggae and co-ordinated at a level which eludes a fixed interpretation. Linguistic patterns become musical patterns; both merge with the metabolism until sound becomes abstract, meaning non-specific. Thus, on the "heavy" fringes of reggae, beyond the lucid but literal denunciations of the Wailers, Count Ossie and the Mystic Revelation of Ras-Tafari condemn the ways of Babylon implicitly, taking reggae right back to Africa, and the rudie dee-jays (like Big Youth, Niney, I-Roy and U-Roy) threaten to undermine language itself with syncopated creole scansion and an eye for the inexpressible. Language abdicates to body-talk, belief and intuition; in form and by definition, reggae resists definition[17]. The form, then, is inherently subversive; and it was in the area of form that the Jamaican street boys made their most important innovations.

3 The Skinhead Interlude - when the stomping had to stop

At the moment we're hero-worshipping the Spades - they can dance and sing .....
We do the shake and the hitchhiker to fast numbers, but we're going back to dancing close - because the Spades do it.
    19 year old mod quoted in Hamblett and Deverson, eds. (1964:22)

I turn now to the formation of an equivalent culture inside the West Indian community in Britain, and the context in which reggae was received in South London. I shall try to show

how it was used by the young blacks to transmute a situation of extreme cultural dependence into one of virtual autonomy.

There is no need to reiterate the early history of reggae in this country. I have already mentioned the important role played by Chris Blackwell and Lee Gopthal in the importation of the new music. Gradually, as *Trojan* began to flood the market, ska took over from bluebeat as the steady pulse which set the pace of the black Britons' nightlife. The era of the African "waterfront boys" which Colin MacInnes (1957) describes was definitely on the wane and the days of Billy Whispers were numbered at last as the Jamaican hustler, pimp and dealer began to come into his own. The music was transmitted through an underground network of shebeens (house parties), black clubs, and the record shops in Brixton and Peckham, and Ladbroke Grove, which catered almost exclusively to a West Indian clientele. Almost but not quite. As the early music mobilised an undefined aggressiveness and generated a cult of extreme individualism, its appeal was not confined to the members of the black community only. It soon became also the theme music of the "hard mods", who often lived in the same depressed areas of South London where the immigrants congregated, and who soon started emulating the style of the Rude Boy contingent. Thus, they wore the "stingy-brim" (pork pie) hats and the shades of the Jamaican hustler and even went out of their way to embrace the emblems of poverty which the immigrant often found unavoidable and most probably undesirable. Thus, the ill-fitting ankle-swinger trousers, which usually suggest that the wearer has been forced to accept hand-me-downs, were 'echoed' in the excessively short levis for which the "hard mod" showed a marked predilection. Even in 1964, at Margate and Brighton, mods were seen in boots and braces, sporting the close crop which artificially reproduces the texture and appearance of the short negro hair styles, favoured at the time by the West Indian blacks. In 1965, Prince Buster's *Madness* became something of a craze in some mod circles and was regularly requested at the big dance halls frequented by the South London mods. That liaison between black and white rude boy cultures which was to last until the end of the decade and was to provoke such a puzzled reaction from the commentators of youth culture had begun in earnest.

Ska obviously fulfilled the needs which mainstream pop music could no longer supply. It was a subterranean sound which had escaped commercial exploitation at a national level and was still 'owned' by the subcultures which had originally championed it. It also hit below the belt in the pleasantest way possible and spoke of the simplicities of sex and violence in a language which was immediately intelligible to the quasi-delinquent adolescent fringe of working-class culture. The developing white "progressive" music was becoming far too cerebral and drug-orientated to have any relevance for the "hard mods" whose lives remained totally insulated from the articulate and educated milieu in which the new hippy culture was germinating. And of course, the B.B.C. was hardly the ideal medium - ska became scratchy and lost all its punch when played on a transistor - there was simply not enough bass. Moreover, the lyrics of records like Prince Buster's *Ten Commandments* and Max Romeo's *Wet Dream* were rarely acceptable, and most new releases were immediately classified as unsuitable. Thus, the music remained secret and was disseminated in the Masonic atmosphere of close communal and subcultural interactions. The *Ram Jam* in Brixton was one of the first clubs in London where white and black youths mixed in numbers; but already the disreputable and violent associations began to accumulate round the new music. There were tales of knives, and ganja at the *Ram Jam*, and there were more than enough risks for any white rudie prepared to take his life into his hands to step into Brixton, and prove his pilled-up manhood.

By 1967, the skinhead had emerged from this larval stage and was immediately consigned by the press to the "violent menace" category which the mainstream pop culture of the time appeared increasingly reluctant to occupy. As the startling flora and fauna of San Francisco were making their spectacular debut along the King's Road in the summer, Dandy Livingstone, the first British reggae star to gain national recognition, sang *Rudy a Message to You* to audiences in the less opulent boroughs of South London, and rallied his followers around a different standard altogether. The links which bound the hard mod to the rude boy subculture were drawn even tighter in the case of the skinhead. The long open coats worn by some West Indians were translated by the skinheads into the "crombie" which became a popular article of dress amongst the more reggae-oriented groups (i.e. amongst those who defined themselves more as midnight ramblers than as afternoon Arsenal supporters). Even the erect carriage and the loose limbed walk which characterize the West Indian street-boy were (rather imperfectly) simulated by the aspiring 'white negroes'. In clubs like the *A-Train*, *Sloopy's* and *Mr. B's*, the skinheads mingled with young West Indians, called each other "rass" and "pussy clot"[18], cracked their fingers like thoroughbred Jamaicans with as much panache and as little wincing as possible, talked "'orses" and "pum-pum"[19] and moved with as much studied cool as they could muster.

This spontaneous movement towards cultural integration (with the West Indians only; *not*, needless to say, with the Pakistani and Indian immigrants) was unprecedented but it was not to have any permanent salutary effect on race relations within South London's working-class communities. For, despite the fact that the skinhead might dance the "shuffle" or the "reggay" with a certain amount of style, despite the fact that he might speak a

few random phrases of patois with the necessary disregard for
English syntax, it was all a little artificial - just a bit too
contrived to be convincing.   Despite everything, he could never
quite make that cultural transition.   And when he found himself
unable to follow the thick dialect and densely packed Biblical
allusions which mark the later reggae he must have felt even more
hopelessly alienated.   Excluded even from the ranks of the
excluded, he was left out in the cold, condemned to spend his
life in Babylon because the concept of Zion just didn't make
sense.   And even if he could make that sympathetic passage from
Notting Hill to Addis Ababa, from a whiteness which wasn't worth
much anyway, to a blackness which just might mean something more,
he only found himself trapped further in an irresolvable contra--
diction.   For the rude boys had come of age and the skins were
sentenced to perpetual adolescence, and although Desmond Dekker
topped the British charts in 1969 with *Israelite* (a cry to
Ethiopia) the brief miscegenation of the sixties was at an end[20].

    The "Africanisation" (or "Rastification") of reggae which I
have already emphasised in the sections on Jamaica, militated
against any permanently close contact between black and white
youth cultures.   Once again, the precise "moment" at which the
search for racial identity produced a significant rupture with
earlier patterns of behaviour can be expressed mythically.
In an article by Gillman (1973) on the Harambee project in the
Holloway Road, a young West Indian disc jockey based in South
London, describes the impact of the record *Young, Gifted and
Black* on an audience which comprised both black and white rudies:

> There was that song *Young Gifted and Black* by Mike and Marcia,
> and when we played it all the skinheads used to sing 'young
> gifted and white' and they used to cut the wires to the speakers
> and we had some fights and less white people used to come up
> after that[21].

    This parting of the ways had been preparing for years outside
the dance-halls, in the daytime world of school and work.
Firstly, as Dilip Hiro points out, the close proximity **into** which
black and white children were thrown at school tended to break
down the cruder racial myths.   The illusion of white superiority,
fostered in the black parents by an Anglicised education in the
West Indies, could hardly be supported by their children who were
growing up next to their supposed superiors without noticing any
appreciable difference either in performance or potential.
On leaving school, nonetheless, the black youth was often
confronted with open discrimination on the part of prospective
employers.   As the demand for unskilled labour diminished, the
black and white school leavers were thrown into fierce competition
for what work was available, and the white youth, more often than
not, was given preference.   If the black school leaver was more
ambitious and sought skilled work, he was likely to be even more

bitterly disappointed. A correspondent of the *Observer* (July 14, 1968) showed that white youths in "deprived" areas of black settlement like Paddington and Notting Hill were almost five times more likely to get skilled jobs than coloured youngsters. Michael Banton (1967) estimated that by 1974, one in six of the school leavers in the inner London area would be coloured and the rivalry has obviously escalated accordingly. The predicament facing the black youth on leaving school, then, made him review his position with a more critical eye than his parents. To the first generation of immigrants from the West Indies, England had promised a golden future, and if that promise had not been fulfilled, there seemed little point in looking elsewhere. In fact, to do so would be to admit defeat and failure and so the older immigrant went on working on the buses or queueing up for the dole and kept his bitterness stashed away under his insouciant smile. But the young black Briton was less inclined to shrug and forbear, and the reassessment of the African heritage currently underway in Jamaica and the U.S.A. was bound to provide channels through which his anger could be directed and his dignity retrieved. Thus the cry of the Rastas for African redemption was welcomed by the disappointed diaspora of South London. Exiled first from Africa, and then from the West Indies to the cold and inhospitable British Isles, the longing for the Healing of the Breach was felt with an even greater poignancy by the dispossessed Rude Boys of Shepherds Bush and Brixton.

Hiro contrasts the new black consciousness of the coloured youth in Britain against the more sober attitude of the West Indian parents in the example of Noel Green, born in London in 1958, whose father Anthony complains:

> As a young child he wanted to be called an Englishman. But now /in 1969/ he considers himself a West Indian and a black person   (1973).

These developments were translated into specifically Jamaican terms and the men of the dreadlocks began to make an incongruous and sinister appearance once more on the grey streets of the metropolis. By 1973, McGlashan could report the bizzare conjunction of Africa and Ealing at the West London Grand Rastafarian Ball, where Rastas, twice removed from the mythical homeland, yearned in unison for an end to "sufferation" as giggling white girls danced to the reggae. The cult of Ras Tafari appealed at least as strongly to the black youth of Great Britain as it did to their cousins in Jamaica. If anything it proved even more irresistible, giving the stranded Community at once a name and a future, promising the Lost Tribes of Israel just retribution for the centuries of slavery, cultivating the art of withdrawal so that rejection could be met by rejection. All this was reflected in and communicated through the music which had found in Britain an even larger and more avid audience than in its

country of origin.   Of course, the skinheads turned away in
disbelief as they heard the Rastas sing of the "have-nots"
seeking "harmony" and the scatting d-j's exhorting their black
brothers to "be good in (their) neighbourhood".   More odious
still to the skinheads was the Rasta greeting of "Peace and Love"
which many young rudies adopted (along with the Rasta handclasp).
The wheel had come full circle and the skinhead, who had sought
refuge from the posturing beatitudes of the pot-smoking hippie
in the introverted coterie of the black delinquent young, was
confronted with what appeared to be the very attitudes which had
originally dictated his withdrawal.   It must have seemed, as
the rudies closed their ranks, that they had also changed their
sides, and the doors were doubly locked against the bewildered
skinhead.

We need only turn back to the mythology of Rastafarianism
which I have already attempted to decipher, to see that such
an outcome was, in fact, inevitable sooner or later.   The
transposed religion, the language, the rhythm, and the style of
the West Indian immigrant guaranteed his culture against any
deep penetration by equivalent white groups.   Simultaneously,
the apotheosis of alienation into exile enabled him to maintain
his position on the fringes of society without feeling any sense
of cultural loss, and distanced him sufficiently so that he could
undertake a highly critical analysis of the society to which he
owed a nominal allegiance.   For the rest, the Biblical terms,
the fire, the locks, and Haile Selassie et al served to resurrect
politics, providing the mythical wrappings in which the bones of
the economic structure could be clothed so that exploitation
could be revealed and countered in the ways traditionally
recommended by the Rastafarian.   The metasystem thus created
was constructed around precise and yet ambiguous terms of
reference and whilst remaining rooted in the material world of
suffering, of Babylon and oppression, it could escape, literally
at a "moment's" notice, into an ideal dimension which transcended
the time-scale of the dominant ideology.   There were practical
advantages to be gained by adopting this indirect form of
communication, for if a more straightforward language of rebellion
had been chosen, it would have been more easily dealt with and
assimilated by the dominant class against which it was directed.
Paradoxically, "dread" only communicates so long as it remains
incomprehensible to its intended victims, suggesting the
unspeakable rites of an insatiable vengeance.   And the exotica
of Rastafarianism provided distractive screens behind which the
rude boy culture could pursue its own devious devices unhindered
and unseen.

1. Exuma, for example, sing of the Obeahman, duppies (ghosts) and zombies.
2. Nettleford (1970) claims this drift towards quietism was accelerated by the excesses of the Red Hills and Coral Gardens affrays which turned many locksmen away from violent solutions.
3. This was perhaps the great disappointment of the Sixties (cf. the demise of the hippies, and the Paris students of 1968, also the failure of Laing's "meta-journey" to really get him anywhere - see Juliet Mitchell, 1974: 225-292). Nettleford (1970) criticises the emergent Black consciousness in Jamaica for failing to adopt a more rigorous and analytic approach to African Studies.
4. In Brixton, for instance, 80% of the black population came from Jamaica, and record shops in the area soon began to specialise in bluebeat and ska.
5. Manley also won support in the rural areas where a Holy Roller type of religion still lingers on, by appearing in public carrying a stick which he called "The Rod of Correction", with which he promised to beat out all 'duppies' (ghosts), and to drive injustice away.
6. A popular game amongst the Jamaican working class.
7. See *Earthquake* in which Prince Buster challenges a rival to do battle on Orange Street.
8. See every other record of this period.
9. See Niney's *Fiery Foreman meets Smokey Joe Frazier*.
10. See The Pioneers' *Long Shot Kick the Bucket*, about a horse which dies with everybody's money on it.
11. See *54-46* by the Maytals again (this is the number Toots was given when imprisoned on a ganja charge).
12. Lyrics from *Al Capone* by Prince Buster.
13. From *Shanty Town* by Desmond Dekker.
14. Cunchyman said that the Americans "don't know how to move slow" - see Thomas (1973).
15. *Abeng*, the official organ of the Black Power movement in Jamaica, translated Rastafarian "metaphorics" straight into Marxian dialectics. Economic analysis jostled uneasily against the intensely personal testimonies of individual 'sufferers' in the columns of the paper. Among other events the banning of the Black Power historian, Walter Rodney, by the University helped to crystallise the movement in a political direction. See Rodney (1969).
16. Though 'heavy rock' also has an emphatic and hypnotic bass line, there is nothing equivalent to the 'scat' in rock. Some modern jazz plays with language at this level, but this jazz is produced principally by black musicians (Albert Ayler, Roland Kirk, Pharoah Saunders, John Coltrane, etc.)
17. In a similar way, the syntax of "heavy" soul obviates the need for lexical meaning. James Brown looks at the relationship between "the pronunciation and the realisation" in *Stoned to the Bone* and gives a catalogue of the various words used to denote "mind-power": ("vibes E.S.P.," "positive thinking" etc.) but discards them all by discarding language itself: "But I call it What it is what it is".

This tautologous equation is repeated again and again until
it synchronises with the strong, repetitive backing and is
eventually absorbed.

18. Jamaican swear words that don't really bear translating!
19. i.e. gambling and women.
20. The skinhead style, of course, survived into the 70's particularly
    in the Midlands and the Northern industrial towns but it did not
    maintain its early strong links with black culture. Skinheads
    in Birmingham (where race relations have always left a lot to be
    desired) were often openly hostile to West Indians, and football
    tended to take over from reggae as the central preoccupation of
    the skinhead group.
21. Later, in the same article, two boys who live at the hostel are
    reported discussing the finer points of "mugging". Their comm-
    ents show that they are prepared to make racial distinctions and
    they refer frequently to "suffering", a key concept in
    Rastafarianism which seems to be used as an index to the believ-
    er's eligibility for salvation by trial: First boy: We don't
    touch our own people. I never thought of doing it to a black
    man. Second Boy: A black man know that we all suffering the
    same.

Appendix: Unemployment, the Context of Street-Boy Culture

Rachel Powell

   In 1943, the unemployment rate in Jamaica had stood at
25.6%; by 1945 it was exacerbated by the return of Jamaican
ex-Servicemen and those employed in the U.K. for the war period
(Richmond, 1954: 140).   Simey (1946: 136) analysed reports
of previous commissions, and noted the contradiction between
the necessity for greater national productivity in order to
finance improved social services (required with quite exceptional
urgency in West Kingston), and the probability that greater
individual productivity, motivated by desire for higher standards
of living, would yet further aggravate the shortage of jobs.
During the 1950's and 60's, Jamaica attained the world's
highest *per capita* productivity increase (Lowenthal, 1972: 297),
and industrial development, mainly in mining and tourism, was
considerably expanded.   Bauxite mining, developed largely by
Canadian interests, provided relatively very well-paid jobs
for some - at a median of £415 p.a., nearly four times the
median wage for men - but those "some" comprised less than 2% of
the total labour force, and included an unknown proportion of
expatriate employees (Francis, 1963).   Similarly, figures for
1958 (from the Institute for Social and Economic Research,
Kingston) showed the distribution of benefit from tourist-trade
expansion - £1 million, about 6% of total expenditure, paid in
taxes; approximately 27% in tourism-related wage earnings; and
39% forthwith remitted to organisations and individuals outside
Jamaica.   Internally, such development meant that Jamaica also

registered the world's current record for inequality of income
distribution, the best-off 5% of the population commanding 30%
of national income, the poorest 20% sharing a mere 2% (Ahiram,
1966).   External concern at this potentially explosive
situation may be reflected in a *Jamaica Weekly Gleaner* report
(10.11.1971) that agreement had been concluded, between the
Canadian and Jamaican Governments, for insurance cover "against
certain risks not normally insurable with commercial insurers ..
including expropriation /i.e. nationalisation/ inability to
repatriate earnings or capital, loss due to insurrection,
revolution or war".

Individually, also, post-war development meant change.   In
1955, in the rural areas, M. G. Smith found that - of a sample of
men aged under twenty-five - only 16% had worked full-time for
the week preceding survey;   44% had worked half-time or less;
15% had got no work at all (Smith, M. G., 1965:   197).   The
average rural family in the sample, there including all age-groups,
had about five members and could dispose of approximately £2 per
week total expenditure (Smith, M. G., 1956).   Comparisons of
"necessary" and "choice" expenditure suggest that contemporaneously, *in both Jamaica and the U.K.,* an effective degree of real
choice in expenditure was attained only at incomes around £14
per family per week (Powell, 1972).   Perhaps unsurprisingly,
the 1960 Jamaican Census recorded a very heavy drain of population
from rural areas to the Metropolitan district, where almost 40%
of those then resident had been born elsewhere in Jamaica
(Francis, 1963).

The same source revealed that 46% of men resident in the
Metropolitan area earned less than £4 per week, and nearly 8%
less than £1.   Employment tabulations gave a city unemployment
rate of 11.9%, and a rather remarkable 6% for Jamaica overall.
Critics observed that the week selected for Census, April 1st-
7th coincided with crop season, and said rather little about the
situation of those only employed for half the year.   13% of
city workers were recorded as underemployed, and the rural
parishes, even in crop time, showed a median of 30%.   Ruscoe
(1963:   67) quoted a *Daily Gleaner* (2.7.62) estimate of a
steady 100,000 unemployed, 15% of available labour force, plus
an unknown percentage of the half-employed, and concluded that
the Government regarded employment figures as classified information.   By April 1972, however, the incoming *People's National
Party* Government was frank enough, in a B.B.C. interview, to
include among its inherited problems unemployment rates, in
Kingston, running at 15%-20% for adults, and as much as 30%
for young people then seeking their first jobs.

A STRATEGY FOR LIVING
Iain Chambers

Note: *Iain Chambers is working on a critique of the more formal-
ist and a-historical aspects of the semiotic approach to the analysis of culture and ideology. His assessment of the work of
Roland Barthes was published in WPCS 6. So far, his work has
been mainly applied to the area of film and visual texts. Here,
he poses the question of how political and historical analysis
might be combined with formal analysis in the study of black
music. The historical experience and structural position of
black Americans, their subordination to the cultural hegemony
of white America, is used to explain both the characteristic
forms of black music, and what happens when that music is adopted
and adapted to express the quite different experience of white
American (and British) youth.*

> Liberation for blacks will come out of the
> revolutionary culture, consciousness, and
> ,experience of Afro-America.
>
> Earl Ofari.

> At lilac evening I walked with every muscle
> aching amongst the lights of 27th and Welton in
> the Denver coloured section, wishing I were a
> Negro, feeling that the best the white world
> had offered was not enough ecstasy for me, not
> enough life, joy, kicks, darkness, music,
> not enough night.
>
> Jack Kerouac (1958)

The roots of rock 'n' roll lie deep within the historical
experience of the black men and women of the United States, and
essential to that history is the passage of black peoples into
the New World. This passage was produced by the West European
expansion beginning in the late fifteenth century and was carried
westward across the Atlantic by colonialism and the slave trade.
Thus, the forced emigration of black men and women from their
West African homeland cannot be divorced from the development
of capitalism and its concomitant ideology of racism: the justi-
fication of the exploitation and dehumanisation of sections of
society in the interests of profit. Black music is inextricably
bound into the Afro-American consciousness of this history in an
alien world where social divisions of class were complicated by
the added dimension of the cultural division of race.

157

In this situation black men and women have worked up their experiences of the past and the present into a music which, whilst reflecting the interpenetration of black and white, of Africa and Europe, crucially revolves around the black experience, black consciousness of economic and social deprivation, and the continuing enslavement in a racist ideology. To describe the resultant music as 'autonomous' is to stress the political substratum of black music: its relative independence from white hegemony, despite the attempts of white culture - from Stephen Foster's minstrels and 'black-face', through rag-time and the big swing bands, to 'white' blues singers - to appropriate and neutralise it. In the history of black expression in the U.S.A. it is music, above all, which has retained its roots in the black experience. One has only to think of the more successful incorporation of blacks in other forms of expression such as literature, entertainment and sport where their blackness is either conveniently ignored or else reified, making them 'invisible men'. Attempts to use these channels for black ends are heavily censured, as the career of Muhammad Ali, or the howl of rage over the Black Power salute at the Mexico Olympics in 1972, clearly exemplify.

> **The tradition of all dead generations weighs**
>
> **like a nightmare on the brain of the living.**
>
> **K. Marx (1951)**

Produced by the descendants of former slaves, black music, in the hybrid form of rock 'n' roll, was reproduced by another section of the American working class: the white, rural, southern poor. The empirical evidence of this appropriation in the history of the early days of rock 'n' roll is quite clear, but the profound implications of this connection need to be spelt out, since most commentators reduce it to the level of stylistic appropriation, and in the process depoliticise and undercut its profundity.

Ever since the bargain of 1877 between the northern bourgeoisie and the southern aristocracy which ended Reconstruction, class issues in America have consistently been turned into race issues. This had the effect of keeping the working class divided against itself and labour weak in its relation to capital. The first major attempts to organise American labour - the Knights of Labour - refused to have any truck with black workers. The early years of the twentieth century were marked by sharp interracial tension, with whites seeing blacks as a potential threat to their job security; and these divisions were aggravated by the severe economic recessions that the U.S.A. experienced in the three decades leading up to the First World War.

By the 1920's the first tentative attempts by black intellectuals to establish some basic rights for black people (National Association for the Advancement of Coloured People) were super-

seded by Marcus Garvey's movement that stressed the African
origins of American blacks.   In the wave of revolutionary
upsurge running throughout the First World War years and
continuing into the 1920's, the Garvey Movement created a mass
base amongst American blacks.

> **Well they call it stormy Monday**
>
> **But Tuesday's just as bad ....**
>
> **A traditional blues.**

The immediate post war black migration up the
Mississippi valley to such northern industrial cities as Detroit,
Gary and Pittsburgh created a clash between expectations and
harsh realities that was to explode in the 1930's.   In that
explosive decade, although many blacks were unemployed and on
relief, they also played an important part in the extremely
militant rank and file movement which peaked in 1937 with half
a million involved in sit down strikes.   One of the products
of this militancy was the formation of the C.I.O.   But it was
really the ending of the decade and the shift into a war economy
which provided blacks (at least, black men) with the opportunity
to advance and win more economic power.   This set the terrain
not only for an incipient black bourgeoisie, but for the call for
advancement of black social and political rights as well.

Although some blacks were able to exploit the contradictions
of imperialism, American capital had learnt the lesson of 1929.
Just as in the '30's it proceeded through neo-Keynsian measures
and the New Deal to institutionalise the class struggle in the
white industrial sector so, in the post World War II period, with
black riots in army camps and northern cities, it sought to
contain the black upsurge politically.   The principal forum for
this containment was the Democratic Party.   In 1948, Truman ran
on a civil rights ticket in the presidential elections and won.
In 1954 came the famous Supreme Court ruling against Segregation
in schools, coupled with tough white Southern resistance: blacks
still await the full implementation of this legislation over
twenty years later.   But even this limited progress was frozen
in the red-baiting Cold War days of the '50's.   Since the thaw,
most developments - until the ghetto rebellions of the 1960's -
have continued to reflect the successful integration of racism,
into all parts of society, by capital.

The successful expansion of American capital after the 1930's
has maintained divisions within the working class - divisions
which divide the class by race as well as by sex, nationality and
skill.   It is an expansion that has moved out from the factory
to the whole of society (the 'Social Factory') and has ensured
capital's continuation and relative stability.   These divisions
are played out in the day to day antagonisms that split the
working class: in the struggle between blacks and whites for
jobs, housing, education and social and political power.   These

159

divisions continued to plague the American scene in the 60's and with specific 'effects' on the political level. The rise of the black nationalist, black power and separatist black political movements from the mid 1960's was a response to this double exploitation by class and race.

The black national liberation struggles in Africa were a major inspiration to the increasing black militancy of the decade as expressed in lunch counter sit-ins, civil rights marches, the riots in Watts etc., the Black Muslims and the formation of the Black Panthers. But the brutal and successful suppression of the latter by the Nixon administration demonstrates the weakness of a politically immature sectional politics which fails to forge a mass base. The working class struggles continue to be sectional: blacks, women, students, anti-war. This has led to a 'radical' sectoral politics but not to a socialist politics: a whole series of 'anti' movements - 'anti-racism', 'anti-sexism', 'anti-imperialist' - which were often also anti-working class!

> It was if a driverless vehicle were speeding
> through the American night down an unlighted
> street toward a stone wall and was boarded on the
> fly by a stealthy ghost with a drooling leer on
> his face, who, at the last detour before chaos,
> careened the vehicle down a smooth highway that
> leads to the future and life; and to ask these
> Americans to understand that they were the
> passengers on this driverless vehicle and that
> the lascivious ghost was the Saturday night
> crotchfunk of the Twist, or the 'Yeah, Yeah,
> Yeah' which the Beatles hijacked from Ray Charles,
> to ask these Calvinistic profligates to see the
> logical and reciprocal links is more cruel than
> asking a hope to die Okie Music buff to cop the
> sounds of John Coltrane.
>
> Eldridge Cleaver (1970)

Let us now return to the music and examine why black music, in particular the blues and rhythm-and-blues, were taken up, and in the process transformed by another section of the working class that was visibly antagonistic to it. The sketch above has pointed to the common class interests of these two sections, but also to their division through capital's exploitation of racism. The result is that the white working class stands over and above the black working class economically and culturally. This allows whites the power to re-define the music produced by those who are objectively of the same class but who are culturally subordinate to white hegemony.

160

The other side is that these 'outsiders', the black working
class, were thus in a better position than the white members of
their class to produce a positive and coherent expression of their
oppression. From plantation to ghetto, black culture, and especially black music, has provided one of the strongest means of
survival - a secret language of solidarity, a way of articulating
oppression, a means of cultural resistance, a cry of hope. Not
surprisingly, the black politics of the 1960's was heralded by a
massive upsurge of black culture and black consciousness. The
fact that the reaction to oppression often took a cultural rather
than an overt political form was also due to the cultural power
of white society to determine what aspects of black experience
were 'acceptable' and what were not. While black 'entertainment' and black 'art' became acceptable, black politics most
certainly never did. And black culture itself came under fire
as soon as blacks made its political meanings manifest.

In the 1950's the music was taken up largely by young, southern
working class whites, seeking to mark their difference from the
generations of the Depression in a period when even the most
backward sector of the American economy - southern agriculture -
was being regenerated by the boom stimulated by Eisenhower
Republicanism and the economics of the Cold War. This establishment of difference, of a new identity, by white American
youth in the early '50's was strengthened by the outcry of white
southerners against, for example, the young Elvis Presley for
singing "nigger music". And this was prior to the big live
performances which followed, when the whole assemblage of hair,
clothes, dancing, music and mannerisms - the *style* of Presley - made
him the rallying point of parental wrath, north *and* south of the
Mason-Dixon line.

> She bought me a silk suit
>
> She put some luggage in my hand
>
> And I was high over Albuquerque
>
> Heading for the promised land.
>
> Chuck Berry, *The Promised Land*

This contradictory relationship between white youth sub-
culture and black music was given the Madison Avenue seal of
approval. The morganatic marriage was legitimised, the commodity
label minted; from this unholy alliance the 'American teenager'
stepped forth. Some of these 'poor country boys' - Presley,
Johnny Cash, Roy Orbison, Jerry Lee Lewis - did make it to the
'big time', alienating, in the process, the last vestiges of
their rural or class origins. Through that process everything
was sucked in which could be drawn to feed and expand the dream
of teenage success. The itinerant bluesman met the cowboy on
the streets of the city and black expression was incorporated
into the existential shell of white, urban romanticism. The
black stud becomes a midnight cowboy; Mississippi John Hurt's
"Candyman" becomes the Rolling Stones' "Midnight Rambler".

161

Outside this process of incorporation and emasculation stood black music itself: an affective expression produced and located concretely in the Afro-American experience. The dimensions of that experience remained intact and unchanged: slavery; economic, social and political deprivation; racism; life in the ghetto. The music continues to have a largely underground 'invisible' existence. Throughout the 1950's and 1960's, black music gives white rock and pop successive transfusions of life and energy - it is the unwritten and unsung source of a thousand variations and imitations. But it is the white imitators who reap the glamour and the publicity - and the money. Black musicians are confined to the ghetto party, the small night-club, the studio sessions, the endless travelling to one night stands at the bottom of the bill. Yet, despite this merciless exploitation, black music continues to thrive, develop and change, in tune with its own autonomous roots and forms.

Like all folk music, black music is an *affective* music as opposed to the increasing rationality and 'mathematical' logic (and illogic) of contemporary Western classical music. As with most European folk music, West African music, from which most black music derives, is based upon the pentachord, the five note scale. (In fact, European pipe music - e.g. Scottish, Sicilian, etc. - is closer to the blues than it is to European 'classical' music.) When taken up by white audiences and reproduced by white musicians, black music undergoes a transformation in the process of being recast into a fresh *context*. Important in this respect is the simplicity and yet the amazing potential for development and improvisation contained in the basic twelve bar blues pattern. It was a music whose rudiments were easy to master and yet capable of providing the basis for the musical explorations of either a Jimi Hendrix or a John Coltrane. (When, in 1955, Charlie Parker, one of the most complex and advanced of jazz musicians, lay dying, he wondered aloud to Art Blakey "when the young people would come back to playing the blues". See Hall and Whannel, 1964: 89). In Britain it was the twelve bar pattern in the form of 'skiffle' that formed the link between the difficulties of playing revivalist jazz and the democratisation of music-making heralded by the hundreds of skiffle groups that emerged in the late 50's and early 60's. But skiffle was itself a borrowing from black music - the 'spasm bands' of New Orleans in the 1890's and the 'jump' bands of Harlem in the 1940's.

Black music was a product of the cultural determinacies operating upon the black working class but it was also a form arising directly from the material conditions of that particular existence: the call and response patterns and the field hollers developed while working the land are still to be found deeply inscribed in black music today, whether in R. and B., Soul or

162

Jazz.   It is generally accepted that the slurred notes so
characteristic of the blues resulted from fitting music composed
on a five note scale on to instruments designed for the equal
tempered eight note scale.   But what is important about all
these stylistic features is not only how they represent a
response to a specific cultural context but also how that context
serves to underpin the music as a *shared experience between
performer and audience*.   A situation held together by a culture
which resists and survives, by a particular situation, as well
as by class forces cemented by racism.   This complex led to
a heightened self-consciousness that could not fail to be
articulated in the music.
    Black music survived by its capacity to reflect and adapt to
the differing experiences and conditions of black people - as
slave, field-hand, cotton-picker, bar-room entertainer, prosti-
tute, maid and waitress.   A further line of development was
opened - one which greatly facilitated its appropriation by
white youth subculture - with the black migration to the northern
cities.   In the heartlands of the working class, black music
was further refined to catch the experiences of inner city life.
The guitar was electrified and rhythm sections added to set the
noises of the ghetto into the blues.   The blues became R and B.
By the 1960's in the U.S.A. "the city is the black man's land"·
(James Boggs), and the music produced there reverberates throughout the Harlems of the world.   The blues, as Jimmy Rushing
prophesied, had become "everybody's business".

                    Get out in that kitchen and

                    rattle those pots and pans

                    from *Shake, Rattle 'n' Roll*

    I would like to make this argument, about the way black music
is transformed in the course of white appropriation, by examining
two versions of *Shake, Rattle 'n' Roll,* which appeared during the
very beginnings of rock 'n' roll in the early 50's.   The hit
parade version by Bill Haley and the Comets (the exception that
proves the rule: Haley was one of the few early rock 'n'
rollers *not* to be southern and young) was a cover version of
Big Joe Turner's R. and B. hit.   Haley's removal of the
explicit sexual references in the lyrics has been noticed by
several writers, but what is of equal significance is the different dynamics between the vocals and the instruments in the two
versions.
    In the Haley version the voice is up front with the music
as a backcloth.   This stems from several strands in the history
of white music making in the States.   Before becoming a rock 'n'
roll act, Bill Haley and the Comets had been a Country and Western band for several years.   Although it's a complex relationship, C. and W. is basically an amalgam between the blues and
European folk music.   In C. and W. music there was a heavy
emphasis placed upon it as a dance music, as there also was with

much of the blues and R. and B., with someone shouting out the dance steps.   In Haley's *Shake, Rattle 'n' Roll* this heritage is not lost: the lyrics are not so much sung as shouted.   This emphasis on the vocal also meshes with the Tin Pan Alley practice, where it was the singer - Crosby, Sinatra, Como - not the song that was important - and the main vehicle of commercial exploitation.

Here, we must take account of the further series of mediations involved in the manufacture of music with the gigantic expansion of the record industry after the Second World War.   With this expansion the emphasis shifted from the *recorded performance* to the *performance recording,* which in turn was associated with the move from the vocalist to the recording star.   Rock 'n' roll marks another first for capitalism!   It was the first music to gain popularity primarily through records.   It went through a productive process of arrangers, songwriters, producers and session musicians and was then 'serviced' by D.J.'s, radio stations and live performances.   It was basically only in the black popular music of the 1950's that the *recorded performance* still remained important.   (It would be unfair to suggest that some of the early Presley and Jerry Lee Lewis records were not in a similar category; but these were soon swallowed up by mass assembly line musical and - in Presley's case - film production.)

In the original *Shake, Rattle 'n' Roll* version by Joe Turner we find a close integration between the vocals and the instruments with the voice participating as an equal not a privileged instrument.   Where Haley's shouted lyric is the product of white music making, so in the Turner version, with its close integration of vocals and instruments, we find the product of another cultural tradition: a tradition in which the blues guitarist or pianist usually composed the music, wrote the lyrics and then performed it.   Similarly in jazz, the 'standard' songs which were used formed only the chordal base-sequence for the real music making: the improvisation.   (The 'be-bop' period associated with Charlie Parker and, after him, 'progressive jazz', took this practice of improvisation across a 'standard' chord progression to extreme limits.)   The resulting music was an expression held together and concretised in the shared cultural and social context of audience. and performer, for reasons that I hope the preceding sections have. made quite manifest.   In other words this music is worked up in a living social and cultural context that may later be 'captured' on record.   This relation between 'lead' and participants, pioneered in the early field holler, was retained and reproduced in the live jam-session so characteristic of more advanced 'performed' jazz.

Even when there was a conscious attempt by white musicians, under the direct influence of black music, to capture this

integration of voice and instrument - the Stones; electric
Dylan; the Beatles, the latter on their first L.P. attempting
to achieve a 'live' feel in the studio - the importance of the
vocal was rarely subverted, except sometimes by the Stones in
their heavy handed way: *Tumbling Dice* is probably the best
example.   Just to stress the point of how musical stylistics can
be located in social and cultural determinacies, the different
emphasis between the vocals and the instruments is again clearly
demonstrated if one compares Chuck Berry's 1957 recording of his
own song *Route 66* with the Stones' version recorded in 1963.
Again, we find in the latter, Jagger singing 'up front' with the
rest of the Stones laying down a 'backing', whereas in the Berry
version the voice and the guitar are interchangeable.

> I really did like the way you started off this
>
> meeting with song.   It reminded me that when I
>
> was a youngster working in the logging camps of
>
> Western Washington, I'd come to Seattle occasion-
>
> ally and go down Skid Road to the Wobbly Hall, and
>
> our meetings there were started with a song.
>
> Song was the great thing that cemented the I.W.W.
>
> together.
>
> Harvey O'Connor, C.I.O. militant

I have tried to locate black music as a music produced by a
particular section of the working class, whose expressions have
been viewed as largely peripheral in the dominant social definitions.   I have suggested that this gives the music a *tension*;
it opens up cracks which reveal the dialectic between its history
and its signification, and this in turn enables us to posit
social and cultural meaning both in its production and then in
various appropriations.   It points to the profundity of the
position of music in the culture of the black American working
class.   As one writer has put it, for the black person the
ideology of Soul "is a powerful weapon in his strategy for
living."   On the other side it suggests why white
appropriation of black music always appears to be more superficial.   Once cut loose from its original context, the music is
recast as a stylistic facet.   Thus, in Britain in the 1960's,
we find Skinheads rewriting 'black pride' lyrics as 'white pride'
This apparent superficiality is no doubt strengthened by the
tensions which arise when white youth groups try to ride out
the contradictions of appropriating a music that struggles in
its very forms against white hegemony.

In this piece I have not attempted to set up some crude
analogy between black and youth on one side, white and parent
on the other.   Obviously the mediated appropriation of black

music by youth in Britain, and working class youth in particular, met and expressed very different concrete needs.   Nevertheless, embedded in black culture, in black music, are oppositional values which in a fresh context served to symbolise and symptom-atise the contradictions and tensions played out in British working class youth sub-culture.

STRUCTURES, CULTURES, AND BIOGRAPHIES
Chas Critcher

Note: *This is an extract from a pamphlet on 'Mugging'
written by members of the 'Centre, and published by the Paul,
Jimmy and Mustafa Support Committee. The pamphlet, 20 Years,
dealt with the Handsworth case where three youths were given long,
deterrent sentences for 'mugging' an Irish labourer. Though
'mugging' was not exclusively a black crime, it was closely
associated, in the media and in the public mind, with black youth.
During 1972-3, there was a major 'moral panic' about the growth
of 'mugging': the pamphlet argues that this phenomenon cannot
be understood outside of an appreciation of the situation of
black youth and the 'logic' which might make 'mugging' a
rational option for black kids trapped by a racist society.
In filling out this notion of how social situations lead
certain individuals to what the control culture defines as a
'criminal' solution, the extract makes use of three related
concepts: structures, cultures and biographies. Though
the particular application here is to black youth and crime,
the scheme has a far wider reference for the position of youth
groups in general. 20 Years is available from the Action
Centre, 134, Villa Road, Handsworth, or from the Centre.
Fuller accounts of the Centre's work on 'mugging' are available
in Tony Jefferson's MA, "For a Social Theory of Deviance: The
Case of Mugging, 1972-3", in Jefferson and Clarke, 1974, CCCS
Stencilled Paper No. 17, and in the forthcoming Centre study of
the 1972-3 Mugging Panic.*

The sentences passed on Paul Storey, James Duignan and
Mustafa Fuat were the climaxes of a process of 'moral panic',
which found its need for vengeance fulfilled in the victimisation
of three juveniles. The sentences bore no relation to the
nature of the crime committed as we understand it, nor did they
reflect the relatively limited and wholly non-violent previous
records of the three boys. Even without the 'mugging' panic,
it is doubtful whether existing ways of thinking about
explaining or treating crime would have produced a very different
outcome. There would have been a difference of degree but not
of kind in the sentencing. The extreme rigidity of the
judicial and penal systems means that the more difficult a crime
is to understand, the easier it is to revert to ideas of basic
savagery as the easiest explanation, and this justifies
savage sentences. It is not only the inflexibility in understanding an individual or a set of crimes which leads to such

sentences, but a failure to understand the nature of all criminal activity, the failure to relate criminal acts in the life of the criminal as a member of society.

Thus, we wish to offer a framework for understanding crime, which if used for this particular case demonstrates that the traditional ways of interpreting and punishing crime cannot begin to understand or 'treat' a crime as complex as this one. We wish to distinguish three elements in the life-situation of any individual which bear upon the likelihood of him or her becoming involved in criminal activity. These are the factors of structures, cultures and biography. *Structures* we define as those 'objective' aspects of anyone's life-situation which appear beyond the individual's control, having their sources in the distribution of power and wealth in the society. Taken together, such structural factors place the individual or family in relation to other individuals or families. Work, income, housing and education act perennially as the basic structures in this society, but in certain places at certain times other structural factors may assume a crucial importance, as does the factor of race in many of the inner rings of our large cities, where it becomes the final link in a chain of discrimination. Firstly, then, a person or close social grouping is situated in relation to the basic structures of society: they circumscribe present experience, and are the limits of any foreseeable future. We are not saying that being at the wrong end of these structures - in poor housing, with little educational opportunity, the most soul-destroying jobs, and a low income - gives rise on every occasion to crime, or that if these structural contraints were removed, then crime would largely cease. People do not respond to their environment in such a crude way. They create, and have created for them, ways of thinking and acting which embody ideas, beliefs, values, notions of right and wrong. These we call *cultures*.

> I just take it for now because I can't do nothing about it. I just got to take it until some chance come along. Then I can f--- somebody up. Get back what's owing to me. But that chance hasn't come up yet. It might take a long time. I'll see it when it comes though. The older generation of black people in this country still turn the other cheek and we can't get it together as long as there's people like that around. We've all got to think in our mind that we've got to f--- these people up and get back **everything that's owing to us.**
>> (18 year old black Briton, quoted in Gillman, 1973)

> Then I had to do some more stealing because I was broke. I broke into a Baker Street flat ... but I didn't get any money. I was tired - like an old man, because I was on the streets. I had that kind of attitude of not caring what became of me. I was taking drugs now. I was taking pills.
>> (22 year old black Briton quoted in Hines, 1973: 39)

I've got five convictions.   Two of them is stupidness - sus,
receiving ice-cream.   The other three were robbery and I didn't
do any of them.   On one I spend six months on remand and I went
to the Old Bailey and the jury find me guilty and the judge fine
me 10 shillings.   Ten shillings and I spend six months inside
and the judge have the cheek to ask me if I had the ten bob on
me now .... I never used to hate white people.   I still don't
hate all of them.   But it's them who teach me how to hate ...
I've done 15 months inside altogether, locked away for things
I never done.   How can I like people who locked me away?
                    (an 18 year old Jamaican youth, quoted in
                    Gillman, 1973)

When you do it, most of the time you do it for some money ...
When you ain't got nothing at all and you get a pound it's
a lot of money ..... You want to go out tonight and you ain't
got no way of getting any money and you're just walking down
a road thinking of a way to get some money and all of a sudden
you see this guy and you say well .....
                    (Unidentified black youth, quoted in Gillman,
                    1973)

There is not just one culture in society, any more than
there is one idea of right and wrong.   There may be a minimum
agreed definition of what conduct people are not willing to
accept as allowable, and this may be contained in some parts of
the law, but much law in its definition of serious crime
reproduces the values of the culture subscribed to by those in
authority.   What is normal in one culture, may be deviant in
another.   This may include family patterns, ideas of property,
and even the acceptability of violence.   Often, the person who
appears in court accused of criminal activity has done no more
than what the cultures available to him have defined as the
natural and normal thing to do.

Crucial here are the cultural options open to the
individual through the cultures to which he has access.   Such
cultures may stem from youth, class, ethnic or simple geographi-
cal groupings: an individual may have just one or several
cultures available, and each culture may present clear or
ambiguous moral values.   Again, we are not trying to say that
every criminal act is simply explained by the cultural situation
of the individual, only that this factor needs to be taken into
account, particularly where the individual has little access
to cultures which are law-abiding.

Structures and cultures rarely receive much attention
in sentencing policy, except as vague references to "keeping
bad company" or "having a bad environment".   Much more stress
is placed on the individual's private life: school record,
psychiatric state, and, especially, family circumstances.
There is some attempt here to explain "what has gone wrong",
but the overall perspective is one which sees the individual
in a very limited social situation, tenuously tied to society

by a few basic transmitters of moral values, which can easily
fail through some malfunctioning or lack of response from the
individual.   There is thus in vogue a common-sense about the
"broken-family" as a cause of crime.   This common-sense is
limited and uneasy.   It is limited, because it is never allowed
to *wholly* explain an extreme form of crime, such as violence.
There are still some acts which are "beyond the pale", and the
tendency is to revert to ideas of savagery and moral turpitude.
It is uneasy because not all "broken" families lead to crime,
and it can never thus be a sufficient explanation in itself.

   This vacillation results from a miscomprehension about the
role of *biography* in an individual's total life-situation.   It
has no conception of structure or culture, and thus has no
context in which to situate a particular biography.   It implies,
indeed, a rather curious image of how society works: we are all,
it would appear, more or less alone, struggling with the devil
within us, and saved only by the strictures and warmth of
family, friend and teachers.   The whole social context of crime
can never be grasped from such a standpoint.

   For us, biography is the network of personal circumstances,
decisions, and (mis)fortunes which occur within a situation
already highly structured and with a limited number of available
cultural options.

> One night when we came out of the club in Bayswater it was
> raining heavily.   We were hoping to go on the tube (to sleep);
> but it was closed.   So we walked up the road a bit and came to
> an entrance to a block of really luxurious flats.   When you
> enter the foyer, carpets were on the floor and all that.
> We sat on the couch and closed the front door, but it was still
> a bit drafty.   So we thought we should get the lift and go to
> the top, and then we came back down.   We sat down in the foyer
> where we were before.   We sat there for about half an hour and
> two policemen walked by and saw us.   They came in.
> They said they would like to search us.   We asked them why,
> since we hadn't done anything.   They said we were loitering with
> intent to steal.   They searched us and found nothing.
> So we got in the police car, which the first policeman phoned
> for.   While we were sitting in the car, two other policemen
> went upstairs and investigated.   They stayed for a while and
> came back and said that they saw a telephone box with scratches
> on it.   They said that that was what we were trying to break
> into.   We told them that we didn't even know that there was
> a telephone box.   So they took us to Paddington Green Police
> Station and charged us.
> The next morning we went to court and they remanded us.   We
> went to Ashford Remand Centre.   Two weeks later they remanded us
> again, so we kept going back to court.   Finally the case came
> up and it was dismissed because of lack of evidence.   So we
> spent over a month 'inside' for nothing.
> My friend's parents were in court and they knew then what was
> happening (i.e. that their son had been 'sleeping rough')
> and he went back to live with them.   I was not represented

in court.   I mean, I had legal aid and all that, but my parents
were not there.
So when the case was dismissed, I was on my own, and my
welfare officer found me a place.   She told me that it was a
hostel, and I said 'not another hostel'.   She said that there
was nothing else she could do.
She and I went to this hostel.   I stayed there for a couple of
hours and went out.   I didn't go out with the intention of not
coming back.   I went up to the West End.   I saw a friend and
he gave me some money and I went up to a club and stayed all
night.   After that I didn't bother to go back to the hostel
for about four days.   I returned to the hostel, but I didn't
fancy staying there any more.
I was on my own.   I thought - 'What am I going to do?'
I didn't really want to steal.   As I saw it, only two
alternatives were open to me: go back to the hostel; or
stay and get myself some money.
I decided to stay out.   I started to steal all over the place.
I used to snatch hand-bags.   I used to go down to Ladbroke
Grove, East London and watch what they were doing.   When they
snatched handbags, I snatched handbags.

(from the biography of a - now - 22 year old London-born black
of Nigerian parents, quoted in Hines, 1973: 33-35.)

It may ultimately be that biographical factors (including
some conscious choice) are crucial in the final thrust towards
criminal activity, but the problems which the crime "acts out"
have been set by the interaction of structural and cultural
factors over and above the individual actor.

How, then, can this framework help us to understand one
criminal act or a series of such acts, like a "wave" of muggings?
First, we need to see whether distinctive social groupings are
involved in such activity.   It is no coincidence that many
so-called muggings are committed by youths from the twilight or
inner-ring city areas, or the barrenness of new council estates.
The structural constraints acting on the inhabitants of such
areas are severe indeed: to those with little visible stake in
society it may seem absurd to behave according to the prescrip-
tions of the status quo.   And even more so, if there are
available cultures which offer realisable definitions of identity,
like that of professional criminals, or a gang.   In some cultural
situations, 'solutions' may be available, which reject a place
in 'normal' society, without *immediately* breaking basic laws.
Hippies, for example, could present the model of such an option.
This is not to say hippies are virtually criminals, or that a
criminal can offer such an articulate critique of society as
that proffered by the hippies.   It is simply to recognise
that becoming a hippy or a criminal is to act out problems set
by the individual's life-situation.   Which 'solution' is
adopted depends on having friends, relatives or other sources
of knowledge about the availability and viability of such cultures.   This is not to say that such choices are always consciou-

171

sly made. Nobody sits down and decides "all my troubles will
be solved if I become a mugger". But for an unemployed
statusless youth in an inner-ring area 'mugging' may be an available means of both making some material gain and gaining some
status. And such status may be sought not only from friends,
but in a back-hand way, from some important social institutions.
If the press were to decide that stuffing potatoes in cats' ears
was to be the new juvenile perversion, and could find an example
of it being done, then undoubtedly it would occur to some extent,
since for some juveniles in some situations any model of deviant
behaviour would be taken up. In that way, activities like
'mugging' can be precipitated by certain kinds of media treatment: it becomes the most available model of behaviour for
those excluded from conventional models.

Of course, the predisposition to such behaviour has to be
present, and there is no doubt that some purely biographical
factors, such as the absence of a stable father-figure *can* in
certain situations be crucial, although in *others* where
different structural and cultural conditions apply, it may not
be so important in shaping the child's future life. (The
absence of a father is always problematic in our society, because
of an obsession with the nuclear family.) Precisely what we
have been insisting here is that crime can only be understood
as a social activity with the actor placed in a total situation:
not just where he lives or how he got on at school or whether
he had a job or how he related to his father, but all of these
and more, together in a total life situation. Of course, to
ask that is to ask for a totally new way of thinking about
crime, which present ruling groups are nowhere near, and likely
to resist. We can see this more clearly if we look at the
kinds of penal policies which would follow from the framework
of understanding we have been outlining.

People who support the Handsworth sentences have often
asked those in opposition what they think should have been
done with the three boys who committed such a vicious crime.
The question seems a fair one, but we would suggest that its
basic premise makes it a loaded question. It still begins
from a solitary act, isolated from similar acts committed by
different individuals, and from other acts committed on
different occasions by these individuals. Violent crimes do
not drop out of the sky or well up from the satan deep in the
breast of every man. They are generally (with the important
exception of "crimes of passion") committed by people who have
already given fair warning of criminal intent. If a society
maintains a basically retributive penal policy with a thin
veneer of naive case-work ideology, it runs the risk of failing
to identify the crucial factors in someone's life-situation which
lead them to criminal behaviour. Without an attempt to

identify and deal with underlying causes, criminal conduct is
likely to escalate, until finally society's patience is exhausted, and the guilty party is incarcerated.   By this time, things
have often been allowed to go too far, and the individual is
firmly wedded to crime as a way of life.   This is not just a
plea for an early warning system, because this would remain
ineffective as long as there was no attempt to understand
crime comprehensively.   Such an effort is unlikely to be made,
since consideration of structural and cultural factors brings
into question some fundamental aspects of the existing social
order, such as the distribution of wealth and power, and
unequal access to housing and employment markets.

So, the reply to that question - what should have been
done - has to be that lots of different things should have been
done earlier, and that anything short of an attempt to change an
individual's whole life situation is likely to fail.   The
charge that such a reply is utopian and fails to deal with the
here and now, misses the point.   The quarrel here is not just
with one particular sentence, or an illiberal penal policy;
it is with the whole way crime is being set up as a problem,
and the ideas of social stability, human motivation, and
legitimate retribution, which underly social response to crime.
We cannot offer a 'right' sentence in the framework of a penal
system which is based on a wholly erroneous conception of crime.
We might be able to offer a complicated strategy of structural
and cultural change aimed to open, rather than close, biographical choices, which might reduce the resort to crime as a cultural solution, but such a revolutionary blueprint would be out
of place here, and we trust its content would be obvious from
what has been said.   What we can say is that in this case
the continuous failure of the dominant modes of thought
to even begin to try to understand the nature of this crime,
has resulted in sentences which solve nothing, either for the
individuals concerned, or for those wishing to prevent the
repetition of such activity.   The "detention" sentence is
indeed a paradigm of social response to crime: hedging,
hypocritical, and, in the last analysis, savage.

THEORY II

STYLE

John Clarke

The Creation of Style

1.   LEISURE AND THE WORKING CLASS

The subcultural styles with which we have been primarily
concerned in this volume are not limited to the sphere of
leisure, but it is centrally in this domain that they have become
most visible.   This may seem obvious, but in fact it requires
explanation.   Leisure is often represented as 'free time', an
area of 'free choice'.   In fact working class leisure time is
neither free nor unconstrained by structural and cultural determinants.   Yet there is a sense in which leisure represents
(and has historically represented, at least since modern working
class culture took shape in the latter half of the nineteenth
century) an area of *relative* freedom.   We would argue that this
is primarily because the tight discipline of work, maintained
through technical organisation and managerial supervision, as
well as by the physical structure of tasks and co-ordination
between tasks, cannot be maintained in the same way outside the
workplace.   It also derives from the fact that the relation of
the working class to leisure is 'disciplined' by a cash relation.
Working class leisure is limited by the amount of the weekly
budget which can be devoted to recreation: but working class
consumers have the power to withhold what cash they have from
the providers of leisure services, and consequently have a
relative freedom to choose between a variety of alternatives.
This is particularly so in relation to those who provide
services exclusively to a working class clientele (small
shopkeepers, pub landlords, etc.).   Foster (1974), in his study
of mid-nineteenth century Oldham, calls this the power of
"exclusive dealing": the threat to withdraw custom was actually
used to persuade shopkeepers who failed to vote for Radical
candidates in the 1837 election.   In addition to these 'customary rights' of a working class clientele over services mainly
provided by someone else, there are the leisure facilities
provided *by* the working class community itself - societies,
clubs, associations, most particularly the Working Men's Clubs
(taken over by the clientele from industrial finance in 1884).
An instance somewhere between the two is the case of football
which, despite its non-working class financial and management
structure, has, since the 1880's, been massively shaped by its
supporters.

175

This 'relative freedom' in leisure has been contested throughout: there has, indeed, been an unending struggle about control
in the area of working class leisure. The activities aimed
to control, discipline and "improve" the working class have often
been exerted most forcefully in this area. This imposition has
taken different forms: the attempt to suppress popular football
in the early 1800's[1]; or the highly successful modern efforts to
'upclass' and 'consumerise' the working class pub[2]; right through
to the extensive statutory and voluntary ways (e.g., the
contemporary youth service or the quasi-military 'youth brigades')
of giving working class youth "something constructive to do".
These have been limited by the manpower required to monitor
'illegitimate' leisure activities and the necessarily voluntary
nature of the more constructive leisure pursuits.

Much of working class culture has thus, since the mid nineteenth century, taken shape around the sphere of leisure - football, the pub, working men's clubs, activities in the street, and
so on. These are not only simply institutions or even values
expressed in particular activities, but forms of expression of
the whole experience of the class. The rigours of work are not
forgotten when the indulgences of leisure begin. But the
'relative freedom' of leisure has allowed a *displacement* of
central class concerns and values, developed in work,
to the symbolic activities of the leisure sphere. The ethos
of 'masculinity' in football culture, for example, cannot be
understood outside the homologous relation it bears to the
masculine focus and organisation of much of industrial production:
a 'man', like a footballer, has to be able to "take some stick
and keep coming back for more" ... One of the most complex things
in working class leisure and sport is to understand fully this
combination of both release from, and reproduction of, the rhythms
of work in the apparently free activities of leisure.

The focus of working class youth on leisure becomes fully
comprehensible when placed in this framework. As we argued
earlier, this is intensified by working class attitudes to youth,
especially boys, where adolescence itself **is** seen as a time of
relative indulgence and freedom before adult responsibilities
set in - and, thus, a time, pre-eminently, of leisure.
This, in turn, was greatly intensified and reshaped by the
expansion and investment, post war, in the 'youth market'.

The privileged position of leisure as a sphere for the post
war young is clear. But we must now consider a qualititative
difference: the point where not only does youth structure
much of its activities and concerns around leisure, but actively
employs this area for the construction of very distinctive sub-
cultural *styles*. Style, we argued, cannot be seen in isolation
from the group's structure, position, relations, practices and

176

self-consciousness. Nevertheless, here, we give privileged attention to the 'moment' of stylistic creation. This is the moment when activities, practices, outlooks *crystallise around* certain very limited and coherent expressive forms. In what follows, therefore, we take the existence of a subculture for granted, and look instead at how this directs the group to the selective appropriation of symbolic objects from the "field of possibles" and how the relations and practices of the group then become fixed in terms of the way these 'bits' are organised into a stylistic cluster.

2. GENERATING STYLE

In describing the process of stylistic generation, we have made partial and somewhat eclectic use of Levi-Strauss' concept of *bricolage* - the re-ordering and re-contextualisation of objects to communicate fresh meanings, within a total system of significances, which already includes prior and sedimented meanings attached to the objects used (Levi-Strauss 1966; 1969). Together, object and meaning constitute a sign, and, within any one culture, such signs are assembled, repeatedly, into characteristic forms of discourse. However, when the *bricoleur* re-locates the significant object in a different position within that discourse, using the same overall repertoire of signs, or when the object is placed within a different total ensemble, a new discourse is constituted, a different message conveyed.

Levi-Strauss' formulation of the precise nature of the original sign, and the relationship between that original and the new, is adapted, of course, to the analytic demands of his primary material - mainly that derived from small-scale societies where 'ideological' communication has been institutionalised in the form of myth or totemic systems. There, myth is the characteristic discourse, and it exists *as* myth because it has been traditionalised and accepted by the whole society: however numerous the variants, the basic form has become myths-of-the-X-people. We, however, are considering recently-current 'unofficial' styles, where the stylistic core (if there is one) can be located in the expression of a partly-negotiated *opposition* to the values of the wider society[3].

Yet there does remain a basic form of discourse, to which the subcultural *bricoleur* must refer if the message is to be communicated. In this case, the discourse is that of *fashion*. Like Levi-Strauss' myth-*bricoleur*, the practitioner of subcultural *bricolage* is also constrained by the existing meanings of signs within a discourse - the objects, the 'gear' used to assemble a new subcultural style must not only already exist, but must also carry meanings organised into a system coherent enough for their relocation and transformation to be understood *as a transformation*.

There's no point in it, if the new assemblage looks exactly like, carries exactly the same message as, that previously existing.

Secondly, where the elements of myth-*bricolage* are mainly natural objects, naturally available for contemplation, those objects adopted by the subcultural *bricoleur* are physically appropriated - worn and used - and they are *commodities*, produced originally for specific markets. That is, their pre-transformation existence was posited on the existence also of *other* groups, most frequently subsections of the dominant class, who would originally have bought, used and expressed their own life-style through these object-signs.

The oppositional significance of much subcultural *bricolage* - as distinct from the traditional significance perceived by Levi-Strauss - need not, therefore, confuse us. Given that capitalism and class-conflict are characteristic of our society - as in tribal societies they are usually not - oppositional meanings may be arrived at via two routes of transformation, neither excluding the other. Meanings alternative to those preferred by the dominant culture, generated within the experience and consciousness of a suppressed social group, may be brought to the surface, and so transform the original discourse. That transformation depends on the existence of opposed classes. Or the form of the commodities themselves may generate new, opposi-tional meanings. Those commodities must exist in the market. They must be financially within reach of the style creators before they can be used. Since they have been produced (else-where) for specific markets, they already carry meanings, messages, concerning unequal access to commodities, and about differentially -valued life-styles. Transformation and re-signification, to re-value life-styles previously disqualified, or to express class-conflict, can take place because messages of that order were already 'written-in' there, in those commodities: the original object-signs were posited upon a divided society, however much their preferred meanings attempted to mask that reality.

The generation of subcultural styles, then, involves differen-tial selection from within the matrix of the existent. What happens is not the creation of objects and meanings from nothing, but rather the *transformation and rearrangement* of what is given (and 'borrowed') into a pattern which carries a new meaning, its *translation* to a new context, and its *adaption*. For example, the "Edwardian Look" (an upper class and student revival), borro-wed by the Teddy Boys, re-combined with extraneous items, the bootlace tie and the brothel-creepers, emerged with a new and previously uncharacteristic meaning. Dick Hebdige's piece on the Mod style (in the Ethnographic section) describes a transfor-mation apparently less attuned to the resonances of class-oppo-sition within the original mode, but wherein a subtle rearrange-

178

ment of objects profoundly altered the significance of the
resulting symbolic ensemble.

3.   THE SEMANTICS OF SELECTION

    Having said this about the creation of style in general, we
need now to raise the question of why a particular group adopts
a particular set of symbolic objects and not others.   The
important point here is that the group must be able to *recognise
itself* in the more or less repressed potential meanings of
particular symbolic objects.   This requires that the object in
question must have the "objective possibility" of reflecting the
particular values and concerns of the group in question as one
among the range of potential meanings that it could hold.   It
also requires that the group self-consciousness is sufficiently
developed for its members to be concerned to recognise themselves
in the range of symbolic objects available.   This developed
self-consciousness both in terms of its content (their own self-
image, etc.) and in terms of its orientation towards symbolic
objects is the means through which the style is generated.
The selection of the objects through which the style is generated
is then a matter of the *homologies* between the group's self-
consciousness and the possible meanings of the available objects.
The neatest description of such a homological relation between
object and group is perhaps George Melly's famous description of
Rock 'n' Roll as "screw and smash" music for the Teds (1972:   36).

    Paul Willis (1972) has argued that, though in a formal sense
early Rock 'n' Roll and 'West Coast Rock' have the potential to
carry and express different meanings, there is a clear homology
or *fit* between the intense activism, physicality, externalisation
of attitudes in behaviour, taboo on introspection, and love of
speed and machines of his "Motor-bike Boys" and the early Rock
'n' Roll music to which they were exclusively attached;   just
as there is a homology between the 'structurelessness',
introspection and loose group affiliation of his "Hippie"   group
and their preferred music.   It is the objective potential of
the cultural form (i.e., in this case, music) and its fit with
the subjective orientation of the group which facilitates the
appropriation of the former by the latter, leading (sometimes) to
a sort of stylistic fusion between object and group.   However,
the eventually produced style is more than the simple amalgam of
all the separate elements - it derives its specific symbolic
quality from the arrangement of all the elements together in
one whole *ensemble*, embodying and expressing the group's self-
consciousness.

4.   THE BASIS OF STYLISTIC DIFFERENCES

    What must also be stressed is the specificity of each style.

179

This means sensitivity not merely to the objective variations in each style, in the sense of the differences between the objects of which each is visibly composed, but also to the different material and cultural conditions under which the styles are generated. Thus the symbolic aspects of the particular style are constructed out of a specific matrix of group concerns, centring around a particular set of activities, which take place within a characteristic set of institutions. This specific group nexus is generated out of the wider network of the material and cultural context of the working class community, which, as we saw in the theoretical overview, is constructed and reconstructed both by, and in response to, the broader social movements of the society as a whole through their particular local consequences. Thus the symbolic aspects of dress of the Ted style are only one part of the particular group's response to their complexly mediated social position. To give a *fuller* account of the style we would firstly have to analyse the material and cultural position of the group in relation to the local experiences of post-war social reorganisation in South London. Then we would have to examine the general nature of the group's relations and consciousness, before finally considering how these are embodied in the objects used by the group in the formation of the visible aspects of a *style*. This analysis must also account for the relations between the particular objects chosen and the group, and for how those particular objects function to *objectify* the group's self-image. (A commentary on the latter stages of this sort of analysis for the Teds can be found in Tony Jefferson's contribution to the Ethnography section.)

5.   STYLE AND GROUP IDENTITY

So far, we have dealt with the internal processes involved in the selection and appropriation of various symbolic objects in the generation of a style. Now we must broaden that focus to consider the functions of the style for the group in relation to other groupings. We have said that the style objectifies the group's self-image. We must now stress that their self-identity is generated not simply through the internal processes of the group, but by the development of the group in relation to its situation - a situation which includes significant groups of others. The process of forming the group's identity is as much due to "negative" reactions to *other* groups, events, ideas, etc., as it is to positive reactions towards particular directions. One of the main functions of a distinctive sub-cultural style is to define the boundaries of group membership as against other groups. This is usually thought of as being a reaction to other groups within the youth, sub-cultural arena (e.g., Mods vs. Rockers; Skinheads vs. Hippies and Greasers; etc.). While there is much of importance to be said about this particular dimension, the range of groups involved is, potentially

180

at least, much wider than just other "opposing" youth subcultures.
Possible the best example of the range of groups against which
the subculture defines itself is in the chart taken from *The Paint
House* where a range of groups is classified as belonging to one
of: "The governor System", "People on our Backs" or "traitors";
each position carries a conception of that particular group's
relation to the image of local community which was one of the
primary organising concerns of the skinhead subculture.   This
gives a *concrete dimension* to both that sense of community -
of 'territory'-and the sense of 'oppression" felt by the Skinheads.
It identifies *sources* of attack and oppression which the Skinheads
experienced, and also *targets* for the Skinheads' symbolic-collective
"defence" of that image of community.   This example raises a
further point about the subculture's relation to different
outgroups - their reaction against certain groups does not necess--
arily manifest itself *primarily* in the *symbolic* aspects of the
style (clothing, music, etc.), but must be looked for in the
whole range of activities, contexts, and objects which together
constitute the stylistic ensemble.   Thus, the Skinhead reaction
against Hippies is not solely manifested in their opposed dress
and hair styles, but in the physical assaults on Hippies (often
under the guise of "queer bashing" or their "invasions" of the
Free Concerts in Hyde Park).   Similarly, their 'defence of
community' appears not simply in a variety of symbolic phenomena
("working" clothes, painted slogans, etc), but again in physical
and violent *action* (Paki-bashing; "gang" battles, etc.), as well
as in their "reoccupation" of the traditional institutions of
working class leisure - pubs and football grounds.

6   CONSEQUENCES OF STYLISTIC DIFFERENTIATION

    However, it is also true that a significant part of the
development of particular styles seem to have evolved in relation
to *one* other particular subcultural "outgroup".   The Mods and
Rockers are the best instance of this directly oppositional
development.   The Barker-Little survey of the Margate offenders
gives examples of how the two groups defined their own image, in
part, by reference to their differences from the other group:

> The Mods and Rockers had a positive and negative image of
> themselves: the positive revealed how they saw themselves,
> the negative by how they saw their rivals.   Both saw them-
> selves mainly in terms of dress, either the well-known
> smooth get-up of the Mods, or the leather jacket and faded
> blue jeans of the Rockers.
> The negative images are different.   Rockers see Mods as
> effeminate.   'They can wear skirts if they like, so long as
> I don't pick one up as a girl': that was a tolerant opinion.
> Mods see Rockers as slovenly and dirty: 'Long greasy hair -
> they use axle grease.   They stink of petrol fumes'.
> (1964: 121)

Similar points recur throughout commentary on the Mods and Rockers episodes: Mods ridiculing the crude, traditionally masculine, self-image of the Rockers, and counterposing their own "cool" and sophistication to that crudity; Rockers focussing on the "effeminacy" of the Mod style. However, Stan Cohen's analysis of the social reaction to the Mods and Rockers (1973) warns us against taking too simple a view of this 'oppositional' form of image creation. Cohen argues that the original seafront "battles" were based around divisions, not between Mod vs. Rocker, but between locals and those down from London (although it seems possible that membership of Mods and Rockers may well have itself been distributed to some extent along these divisions). However the subsequent news coverage handled the "battles" in terms of a *West Side Story* scenario of confrontations between two "Supergangs", thereby fixing the division as essentially a 'battle between styles'. Murdock notes the consequences of this:

> ... Not surprisingly, this imagery of polarisation penetrated the self-image of group members, with the result that elements of style which had previously been neutral became focii of inter-group antagonism and conflict. This conflict in turn served to confirm and further amplify the original (media) image. (1974: 217)

Cohen's analysis offers us two general warnings: firstly, not to collapse the lengthy and complex process of stylistic development into too narrow a moment of analysis, and thus neglect how certain aspects are taken up or become imbued with an especial significance at particular moments and in relation to particular events. Secondly, it warns us against seeing the development of the style as a process largely internal to the group once it has been set in motion. The external relations and structuring principles which place the group in a specific situation do not simply disappear from the scene once the group-style exists, but continue as part of the determinate environment in which the group moves and acts.

Finally in this section, we must pay some attention to the consequences of the existence of the style for the group. The creation of a distinctive style is not simply a matter of embodying the subculture's own identity and self-image. It also performs the function of defining the group's boundaries more sharply in relation both to its **members** and all outsiders, a function which has particular consequences for the group's continued existence. For example, Jefferson's analysis shows how the creation of a distintive Teddy-Boy style represented for the group one of the few means through which they could attain a particular status and exercise some control. The consequence of this was to make *appearance* a topic of especial sensitivity to group members. Jefferson argues that this accounts for their sensitivity and "over reaction" to insults

182

REAL RELATIONS – behind everybody's backs

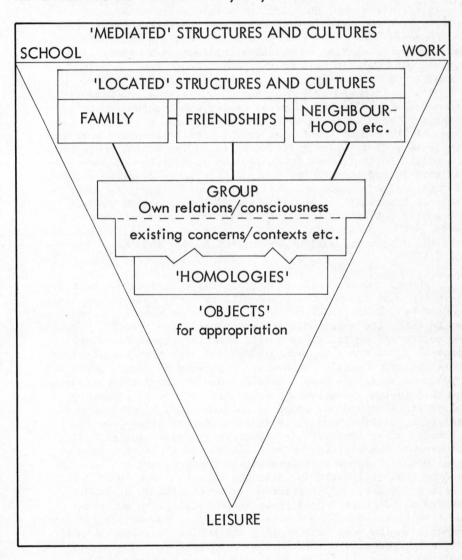

(real or imagined) from others.   In a different way, Fletcher's
account of the development of a Merseyside gang around "beat"
music (1966), illustrates how the changing concerns of the group,
and its increasing commitment to the music as a central concern
of group life, shifted the relations of the group (leading to some
members leaving), changed its recurrent activities and altered
the sorts of contexts around which group activities regularly
took place.   Not least, the genesis of a distinctive style
identifies the group, but also makes them more vulnerable to the
intervention of various forms of social reaction.   Thus, Rock
and Cohen (1970) give examples of dancehalls and cinemas
banning anyone wearing Edwardian suits from using their facilities; and Cohen's work on the Mods illustrates how police
turned "Mods" (i.e. anyone who looked like the public image of
a Mod) away from the seaside resorts, while local shopkeepers
and amusement halls barred young people who looked like Mods and
Rockers.   When police action against football hooliganism was
taken at the end of the '60's, youths wearing skinhead gear were
likely to suffer police harassment, including having their boots,
braces and belts removed by the police outside the ground;
all this in addition to the routine policing - ejection and arrest
of fans inside the ground, and escorts on their way to and from
football "specials".   We also have some evidence to suggest that
the police put pressure on some disco organisers not to admit
black youths dressed in certain distinctive 'Rudie' styles, even
when the discos are well known for the Reggae and 'Soul' repertoire.

   In short, the evolution of a style has consequences, both for
the group, and for how the group will be seen, defined and 'reac-
ted to' by others.   Sub-cultural styles have become the principal
way in which the mass media report or visualise 'youth'.   Judges,
the police and social workers will use stereotypes based on
appearance and dress to label groups and link them with certain
characteristic kinds of behaviour.   Aspects of dress, style and
appearance therefore play a crucial role in group stigmatisation,
and thus in the operation and escalation of social reaction.
Though it is beyond our scope in this section, we must observe
that such reactions generated among different groups, by the
existence of an identifiable style, must have consequences for
the group's own position in relation to the style they have
developed.   Whether this intensifies their commitment towards
greater group solidarity or develops that to a new level, or
whether, finally, social reaction is successful in dissuading
members so identified from their intentions, is an empirical
question to be established more precisely.   However, Jefferson's
comments on the Teds suggest that the public reaction to their
original appropriation of the Edwardian Suit was instrumental in
their developing their own distinctive accentuations and adapt-
ions of the basic suit.   He argues that the choice of uniform

was initially, "an attempt to buy status (since the clothes were originally worn by upper-class dandies) which, being quickly aborted by a harsh social reaction .... was followed by an attempt to create their own style ..."

The Diffusion and Defusion of Style

1.   DIFFUSION

Discussion of stylistic diffusion is beset with various traps; images too easily to hand, all-purpose accounts of how it all works - the 'explanation' in terms solely of media-advertisement, or of commercial manipulation, or in terms of natural epidemic contagion.   What we wish to stress is, first, the relative *openness* of the processes of stylistic appropriation, and, secondly, the significant part played by the *contradictions* inherent in attempts, made within the dominant culture, to exploit indigenous sub-cultural styles.   Contradiction at one level is evident in the commercial development, between the demands of marketing - novelty, rapid turnover of fashion, trendiness and discontinuity - and the demands of production, for standardisation, the ease and economy of continuity and scale of production.   At another level, exploitation of subcultural style, by the dominant culture, has itself two opposed aspects;   on the positive side a heavy commercial investment in the youth world of fashion and trends, and on the negative side a persistent use of style-characterisations as convenient stereotypes to identify and, hopefully, isolate groups dominantly regarded as "anti-social".   In this latter manoeuvre, the 'openness' of the processes is particularly critical, since the selective characterisations used (e.g. Mods=violence/drugs; Hippies=drugs/immorality; Skinheads= uncouth violence) are themselves symbolisations, and thus subject to potential discontinuity between the dominant 'encoding' of the message and the 'decoding' practised by the recipient[4].

As one example of the complex processes at work, then, we may consider the diffusion of the Skinhead style, which can, first, illustrate the mechanism of diffusion by face-to-face contact. Because the 'ends' at football grounds were already well 'organised' before the Skinhead style appeared, and because the Skinheads fixed on football as one of their major social theatres, frequent and geographically wide-ranging meetings of different groups occurred within a structured framework.   Even though these meetings were brief and of relatively violent nature, the style could be transmitted, from its progenitors to other groups who could identify within it at least some common significance. But we must note again here, how such contact produces a *selective* 'appreciation' of the original style, in those who borrow and adapt it.

185

Secondly, the news media select those aspects of the style which are to be made public, according to the dominant culture's perception of its significance. In the Skinhead case, as in others, the image is presented to the audience with wholly negative connotations. For those who share the dominant culture's perceptions, that 'encoding' may be 'decoded' without serious deformation. But 'deviant' readings may be made by groups of adolescents *already* involved in 'hooliganism' at football matches. There, media reports of groups similarly engaged, but distinguished by the clothes they wear and the haircuts they adopt, may provide for the 'unstyled' football supporters a means of entry into the full sub-cultural style. Their own structures of relevance (football/violence/group-membership) allow them to interpret news-items about gangs of Skinheads in a positive way, and read potential connections between the style and their own activities. But still they are *potential* connections, and if we allow a kind of 'cultural space', in which the previously-unstyled may re-work the already double-layered symbolic presentation ("original' Skinhead group's + media-relay) into their own group life-style, we can better explain the variations appearing between different geographically-located versions of the style.

In that example, we have considered news-oriented media presentation, and the negative side of the dominant culture's exploitation of sub-cultural style. But one point at least in that analysis is equally relevant to the discussion of positive, commercial and 'entertainment' forms of exploitation. Where the news-media strip down and dis-locate the indigenous style, in order to make their own symbolic (and derogatory) communication, they may actually widen the 'cultural space' which permits the selective re-working and re-appropriation of the style by geographically-dispersed groups. Similarly, the motivations of marketing prompt a generalisation and stripping-down of the original sub-cultural style; symbolic elements lose their first, integral relation to a specific life-context, and become thus more open to variation in the precise structuring of their re-appropriation by other groups, whose activities, self-images and focal concerns are not precisely the same.

It is necessary to stress that degree of 'spontaneous' re-structuring, *outside* the commercial mechanisms themselves, since it is easily obscured by parallel manifestations arising from the contradictions between the demands of production and of marketing. For large-scale commercial concerns, the contrary pull of economical product standardisation and saleable novelty can be partially eased by the practice of evolving a "formula" for a particular trend, and exploiting it to the last sale - as, for instance, in the hectic search, following the success of the Beatles, for as many groups as possible bearing Liverpool connections.[5] But that answer remains dominated by production demands, and the standardisation of a trend runs counter to the marketing necessity for the production of *new* trends to replace the old. Despite valiant (and, financially at least, not unprofitable) efforts in this direction, the music and fashion industries have generally been limited to working 'variations on a theme', and it has been rather too easy for actual subcultural variants of a style, attuned to a specific local complex of activities, and interpretations, to be subsumed under this commercially-expedient process.

Moreover, the major developments in commercial Youth Culture have been derived from innovations originating *outside* the commercial world, at a 'grass-roots' level. To be successful, an impetus of this kind must develop from local contexts and interactions, and satisfy local 'needs', before attracting large-scale commercial involvement (c.f. Herman's analysis of the 'Mersey Sound', 1971). Again, there is a complex series of parallelisms and interpenetrations. As far as the Youth Industry's concerns go, the styles exist as a potential exchange value in the youth market only if they can be sufficiently generalised to meet similar 'needs' of their consumers on a broader scale. But the role of the young themselves, in this process of diffusion, must not be overlooked. At one time the record companies regularly employed young musicians from groups that had broken up, to help them define, pre-test and, if possible, anticipate new musical trends - and even at times to try, unsuccessfully, to create them. In clothes, fashion and cosmetics, as well as in the 'manufacture' and marketing of specific 'Youth Looks', young entrepreneurs, in touch with their markets, have played a key role. Such fashion enterprises, and developments such as minor record labels, have anticipated trends and explored markets, often on a small scale and on the basis of relatively low investment, before the mass-production companies moved in.

The diffusion of youth styles from the subcultures to the fashion market, then, is not simply a 'cultural process', but a real network or infrastructure of new kinds of commercial and economic institutions. The small-scale record shops, recording companies, the boutiques and one or two-woman manufacturing companies - these versions of artisan capitalism, rather than more generalised and unspecific phenomena, situate the dialectic of commercial 'manipulation'. The whole mid-1960's explosion of 'Swinging London' was based on the massive commercial diffusion of what were originally essentially Mod styles, mediated through such networks, and finally into a 'mass' cultural and commercial phenomenon. The Beatles era is one of the most dramatic examples of the way what was in origin a sub-cultural style became transformed, through increasingly commercial organisation and fashionable expropriation, into a pure 'market' or 'consumer' style.

187

2. DEFUSION

Apart, then, from the continuing possibility of subcultural
re-definition and re-appropriation, two 'mass' processes are
identifiable. One is the contrary to genuine grass-roots
reappropriation: the commercial *defusing* of a particular style
in order to make it widely marketable. The other is the allied
emergence of the idea of a generationally-specific Youth Culture.
Both processes manage to evade the concrete realities of class.

By 'defusion' we mean that a particular style is dislocated
from the context and group which generated it, and taken up with
a stress on those elements which make it "a commercial proposition", especially their novelty. From the standpoint of the
subculture which generated it, the style exists as a *total life-
style;* via the commercial nexus, it is transformed into a *novel
consumption style.* Typically, the more 'acceptable' elements
are stressed, and others de-stressed. Herman's commentary on
Ready, Steady, Go and the Mod style is a perfect example of this
process:

> *Ready, Steady, GO!* was an enormously popular pop programme, on
> the lines of the earlier *6.5 Special,* with a live studio audience
> and groups miming to their records. It was part of the vast
> publicity machine that ensured a profit for the producers of
> mod-style goods. Each member of the audience received a
> politely worded letter reminding him or her to dress stylishly,
> to dance his or her best, not to smoke and generally to behave
> like a credit to British youth while on the show ... more than
> anything, it publicised already existing trends ... In fact,
> *RSG* more than once came out in favour of a kind of castrated
> mod, with no pills, no punch-ups, just the prettiness. *RSG*
> was one of the many places in which 'Mod' was 'restricted by
> partial incorporation'; the more unpleasant aspects had to be
> ignored if the mods were to be allowed to dance in front of
> the cameras. (1971: 54)

The symbolic elements, characteristically dress and music,
are separated out from the context of social relations, as the
elements most amenable to 'promotion' for the broader base of the
youth market. And that commercial formulation is precisely
the major dimension on which the existence of a unique generational culture has been posited. The market to which the
consumption style is directed is conceived of as a *generational*
one - the identity of the objects being sold is defined by their
'youthfulness'; it is not regarded as having any *class* basis.
This process is not so much a conspiracy on the part of the
manufacturers and salesmen, but rather a "natural" function of
the processes of bourgeois commodity and ideological production.
The production for a specifically youthful market was posited on
the image of a society moving towards 'classlessness'; this
definition was specifically embodied in the idea of a 'generation
gap' and the increasing affluence of the young. These market

definitions supported a whole range of processes of 'youthful production', intensified by the 'generalising' nature of bourgeois commodity production as a whole. This, in turn, reinforced the 'evidence' for the existence of a generic and generational Youth Culture, by *providing* the very artefacts which were seen to mark out its differences from Adult Culture. The commercial styles, however arrived at, served to define the changing content of the "Youth Culture" independently of the stylistic modes of differently-located groups.

The Limits of Style

Phil Cohen has suggested that subcultures attempt a "magical resolution" of class contradictions (1972). We want to fill out that idea of "magical resolution" by considering the limits of style in the context of the relation between a hegemonic culture and a subordinated one. By "magical resolution" we understand not only an attempt to engage the problems arising from class contradictions, but also attempts to *solve* them which, crucially, do not mount their solutions on the *real* terrain where the contradictions themselves arise, and which thus fail to pose an alternative, potentially counter-hegemonic solution. Hegemony means precisely the domination of major aspects of society through the control of the major social institutions, and the shaping of the society's culture in the image of that of the dominant class. To the extent that challenges which are offered to this domination are only partial or sectional they remain immanently what Gramsci calls "corporate".

In the case of working-class subcultures, one general source of their limitations is the intensified adoption of that part of their parent culture's problematic which sees leisure as a significant arena of 'relative class freedom'. By posing their "solutions" within this arena alone, the subcultural movements make a "magical" attempt at resolving the contradictions which face them, for the displacement to leisure involves the *suppression* rather than the transcendence of those other key areas where the contradictions are generated. This suppression takes the form of a purely magical transcendence of the areas of work and family.

In the case of the Mods, their attempted solution to the oppression and routinisation experienced at work was to dissolve it in their intensified exploitation of leisure time and their 'subversion' of the commodities used in leisure. The failure of the style to generate an alternative must, as Hebdige insists, be partly understood in terms of its own inherent contradictions, as well as in terms of the forces opposed to it. For example, the Mods' preoccupation with expressing themselves as "Style", as "Image", made them susceptible to incorporation by the commercial

sector and the media in precisely those terms, an incorporation
from the standpoint of the dominant culture. Similarly, their
subversion of commodities took place purely at the point of
consumption; the suppression of their work experiences in the
pursuit of subversive leisure-time left the productive mode, on
which, "in the last analysis", the commodity-form depends,
completely untouched.

The Skinheads' reconstruction of an image of working class
community in their own practice was essentially a defensive
response; but, more importantly, the symbolic affirmation of
"territory" concealed the decline in the real material basis of
the traditional community they were attempting to recreate.
That 'reworking' of community was undertaken solely within the
arena of leisure and lacked the relations, which, in its real
form, connected the world of community with the world of work.
The limits imposed by a purely leisure-based solution can lead
to the subculture's own dissolution.   Phil Cohen comments that:

> Subculture invests the weak points in the chain of socialisation,
> between the family/school nexus, and integration into the work
> process which marks the resumption of the patterns of the parent
> culture for the next generation.   (1972: 25-26)

It is precisely these "weak points" which we have argued allow
leisure to be experienced by working class youth as the dominant
life area, and which allow the 'space' for the form in which that
leisure is experienced - the subculture - to develop.   To
illustrate this transitory nature of these weak points, we have
chosen one particular aspect of the Skinheads' style.   One
of the aspects of the subculture's life style was a stress on
traditional images of "masculine" behaviour, and one of the forms
which this image took was a 'collective chauvinism' towards girls
around the subculture.   These girls, belonging to the collective
world of the group, were "available" for collective or individual
sexual experimentation, and were known as "slags" or "scrubbers"
 - distinguishing them from the "good girls"[6].   It is only while
the leisure arena, and the subcultural form in which it is
lived out, **remains** the dominant focus of the members' lives that
this collective chauvinism can be maintained.   "Steady" dating,
with one of the "good girls", necessitated a break with the
collective routines of group life, and a move to a more individualised form of sexuality.   The two processes are mutually
exclusive - demanding the commitment of scarce resources (time
and money) in different directions.   Consequently, with the
onset of individualised "courtship" patterns, the group life
and involvement declines, the subcultural alternative "dissolves"
through its failure to mount a viable alternative to the dominant
patterns of long term sexuality.

The subculture which fetishises leisure is viable only so
long as the collective pattern of leisure can be maintained as

predominant against other areas.   When work or family demands
come to assume greater significance, the style of collective
leisure, precisely because it provides no solutions or alternatives to those areas, dissolves as a continuing part of the
biography ... "in subcultures .. there are no career prospects
as such .." (Cohen, 1972: 26.)

These limits of working class subcultures can perhaps best
be shown by comparison with the relatively long careers in the
middle class subculture of the Hippies.   These stem from the fact
that although there, too, leisure appeared as the main focus of
attention of the subculture, there were also attempts (however
limited) to generate alternative strategies for work, production
and sexuality.   This is not to say that the Hippie subculture
did not have its own contradictions and limitations[7]: only
that its attempt to create alternatives over a wider range of
life-areas gave it greater viability as an alternative
cultural form.

FOOTNOTES

1.   See Walvin (1975).
2.   See Hutt (1973).
3.   The contrast is particularly sharp in regard to totemic systems,
     which offer a dominant and coherent framework of classification,
     through signs, for both natural and social worlds, overriding
     and stratification into Age-Grades, where these may be formalised
     within a tribal society.
4.   Though we cannot go into all the complexity of media processes
     here, see, among others, Hall (1973).
5.   Compare also Laing's (1969) commentary on attempts to reproduce
     the Presley image.
6.   On Skinheads' slags and scrubbers see Daniel and McGuire, eds.
     (1972: 35-36; 52-53).   The division is, however, not one
     peculiar to the Skinheads, see, for example, Willmott (1969)
     and Parker (1974).
7.   For an analysis of the Hippies in these terms, see Young (1973).

written in collaboration with SH, TJ, RP, BR.

CONSCIOUSNESS OF CLASS AND CONSCIOUSNESS OF GENERATION

Graham Murdock and Robin McCron

Youth against Class: The spectre of socialism

Our modern images of youth and adolescence were essentially
the creations of the Victorian middle class.   Although most of
the essential elements had been in existence well before then,
it was not until the 1850's that they began to coalesce around
the familiar themes of separation and dependence.   In common
with several other strands of Victorian ideology, the emerging
ethos of youth was forged in the 'new' public schools and publicised in the flood of magazines and novels which followed the
successful launching of *Boys' Own Magazine* in 1855, and the
appearance of *Tom Brown's Schooldays* a year later.   At first
this new definition of youth was confined to the offspring of
the middle classes.   In successive decades however, it was
increasingly detached from this original social base and generalised into a description of a universal stage of individual
maturation, so that by the turn of the century the social norms
of the middle class had become enshrined as the 'natural' attributes of youth *per se*[1].   From the outset, this image of youth
carried a peculiarly powerful cultural charge and was intimately
bound up with the hopes and fears of a middle class struggling to
hold its own against threats both at home and abroad.

The growth of German naval power was widely seen as a serious
threat to Britain's imperial possessions and to the sea routes on
which their security depended, but the disastrous South African
war which had revealed both the poor physical condition of the
troops and the inefficiency of the military command, had done
little to bolster confidence in Britain's ability to hold onto
the Empire.   In this situation, patriotism and the elevation
of the 'National Interest' above the claims of class were at a
premium.   At the same time, the increasing influence of
socialism and the growing strength of organised labour in both
the industrial and political spheres promised an intensification
rather than a dampening-down of class conflict at home.   The
British bourgeoisie therefore felt themselves to be threatened on

two sides; by the German enemy without and the socialist enemy within. Consequently, the question of cementing national unity was seen as more or less synonymous with the problem of containing working class militancy.

With the extensions of the franchise in 1867 and 1884, the pivot of containment had shifted away from coercion and towards ideology. In order to preserve the image of the State as a liberal democracy, governed by freedom of choice, strategies of incorporation were obliged to proceed primarily through inducement and persuasion rather than through coercion and force. Repression was not ruled out completely however. During the 1893 strikes for example, miners were shot at Featherstone and gunboats appeared off the Hull docks; a pattern that was to be repeated in 1911, with shootings at Ton-y-pandy and gunboats moored in the Mersey. These periodic shows of state force were the exceptions rather than the rule however. More important was the pervasive and continuous struggle to establish the hegemony of the dominant ideology, a struggle in which attempts to capture the hearts and minds of the rising generation played a key role. From the beginning then, the question of youth and its consciousness was inextricably tied to the issue of class consciousness and class conflict.

The struggle for hegemony over youth centred on the state-sponsored school system established in the wake of the 1870 Act. But for some considerable time the reach of schooling was decidedly limited. Until 1918, when the leaving age was fixed at fourteen, a sizeable section of working class adolescents left before then, thereby evading the schools' influence at what commentators had come to regard as a decisive stage in their mental and moral development. It was largely in an effort to reach these 'escapees' that agencies developed to penetrate and organise the leisure of working class adolescents. They included the Boys' Brigade, the Church Lads' Brigade, the YMCA, and most influential of all, Baden Powell's Boy Scouts.

Behind the preoccupations with health, cleanliness and abstinence, with which scouting is usually associated, lay an over-riding concern with the need to foster class unity in the interests of national and imperial defence. As Baden Powell put it in his best selling handbook of 1908, *Scouting For Boys:*

> If a strong enemy wants our rich commerce and Dominions, and sees us in Britain divided against each other, he will pounce in and capture them. For this you begin, as boys, not to think of other classes of boys to be your enemies. Remember, whether rich or poor, from castle or from slum, you are all Britons in the first place, and you've got to keep Britain up against outside enemies. (1930: 280).

These exhortations to patriotism and national unity were accompanied by attacks on socialism. "Many people", argued

193

BP, "get led away by some new politician with some extreme idea ...
Extreme ideas are seldom much good ... More thrift rather than
a change of government will bring money to all.   And a strong
united Empire will bring us power, peace and prosperity such as
no socialist dream could do" (quoted in Wilkinson, 1969:11).
Although the Scouts were easily the largest of the Edwardian
Youth organisations, the movement drew most of its members from
the middle and lower middle classes, and never managed to
capture a broad base of support among working class youth.
Nevertheless, there is little doubt that the ethos embodied in
scouting and publicised in the magazines and comics for youth
permeated popular thinking and helped to create "that mood of
sustained patriotism among youth that led to mass volunteering
on the outbreak of war in August 1914" (Springhall, 1971: 151).
After the armistice however, there was an upsurge of anti-militar-
ism which Baden Powell was quick to accommodate to.   Hence in
his *Scouting Towards Reconstruction* of 1918, the earlier stress on
imperial defence was replaced by calls for international co-opera-
tion and brotherhood.   At the same time however, the success of
the Russian revolution revived the twin spectres of socialism
and class war and led BP to renew his appeal for youth to unite
against the overtures of Bolshevism:

> There are men who, through their orators and their literature,
> preach class hatred and down with everything ... It is simple
> mad Bolshevism such as might bring about not merely the downfall
> of capitalists but the ruin of the great mass of quiet steady-
> going citizens and wage earners.
> (quoted in Wilkinson, 1969: 16)

   If the emerging images of youth were permeated with fears of
socialism and class conflict, they also carried the middle classes'
own doubts about the present state of capitalism.   These
insecurities were codified and invested with the seal of science
in Stanley Hall's seminal text book of 1904, *Adolescence*.
According to Hall, individual maturation recapitulated the
development of the race and the transition from childhood to
maturity corresponded to the leap from barbarism to civilisation.
Hence, the future of civilisation hinged on what happened during
the crucial intermediate stage of adolescence.   The condition
of youth therefore provided a yardstick against which the
progress or decay of capitalist society could be measured.   "Only
here," argued Hall "can we hope to find true norms against the
tendencies of civilisation generally." (1905: viii)   Where Hall
led, others quickly followed and built up an image of youth as a
force for regeneration and renewal, bearing the torch of idealism
and spirituality amidst the encircling gloom of rampant materialism.   Here for example is the eminent social reformer, Jane
Addams, in full lyrical flight in 1909:

> ... are we so under the influence of the Zeitgeist that we can
> detect only commercial values in the young as well as in the old?
> It is as if our eyes were holden to the mystic beauty, the redemp-

tive joy which young people might supply to our dingy towns.

We may listen to the young voices rising clear above the roar of industrialism and the prudent councils of commerce, or we may become hypnotised by the sudden new emphasis placed upon wealth and power, and forget the supremacy of spiritual forces in men's affairs.

(1972: 9; 161)

This image of youth as a regenerative force gained renewed power from the enthusiasm for reconstruction which followed the armistice of 1918. Youth, it was felt, would bring about a bloodless revolution which would abolish class inequalities and exploitation without class warfare and without socialism. As a newspaper editorial of 1919 put it:

This social revolution that we are launching is not an affair of classes. It has deeper roots. It is the revolt of the Young against the Old ... The victims will be those who have not seen the vision ... rich men who hold on to broad acres, haughty women who distil exotic perfumes from the sweat and toil of the masses they scorn, vulgar profiteers with swollen pockets and swollen bellies ... the half educated, intoxicated agitators who presume to organise and drive the manual workers ...[2]

This current of popular rhetoric found its academic expression in a conservative theory of history of which Ortega y Gasset was the principal exponent.

If the Russian revolution had succeeded, the attempt in Germany had failed; a failure which in Ortega's view marked the "sunset of revolution" in Europe and the death of historical materialism as a plausible theory of social change. "Changes of an industrial or political nature are superficial", he argued, and depend essentially on the complex of ideas embedded in the "vital sensibility" of the age. Moreover, he argued, these "changes in vital sensibility which are decisive in history", appear under the form of a generation, with the result that "The Generation" is "the most important conception in history" and "the pivot responsible for the movement of historical evolution" (1931: 15). In Ortega's schema then, youth replaced the proletariat as the primary subject of history and generational succession superseded the class struggle as the principal engine of change. Apart from vague assertions of "organic capacity" however, Ortega never addressed himself to the vital question of how exactly age groups developed a common consciousness and began to act as a coherent historical force, and it was left to Karl Mannheim to take up this question in his celebrated paper of 1927, "The Problem of Generations".

Generations, Classes and the Sociologists: the hidden debate

For Mannheim, generational consciousness had its origins in the attitudes and responses developed by particular close-knit "concrete groups" in the course of responding to their shared

social situation.   Once formed however, "these attitudes and
formative tendencies are", he argues, "capable of being detached
from the concrete groups of their origin and of exercising an
appeal and binding force "over generation members in similar
social situations who "find in them the satisfying expression of
their location" (1952: 307).   As a result, argues Mannheim, there
develops among these 'generation units' of similarly located contemporaries, "an identity of responses, a certain affinity in the
way in which all move with and are formed by their common experiences" - in short a shared consciousness (ibid: 306).   Once
crystallised, this 'generation unit' consciousness may broaden its
base still further and form the core of a new 'generation style'
separate from, and perhaps opposed to, the dominant style of the
adult generation.   The model Mannheim had in mind here was the
Wandervogel movement which originated in 1901 among a small group
of Berlin adolescents and rapidly gained the support of large
numbers of middle class German youths in the years before 1914.
But if the Wandervogelen illustrated Mannheim's thesis, they also
indicated its limitations.   In particular, the fact that the
movement had made little impact on working class youth raised the
crucial question of the relationship between generational consciousness and consciousness of class.   Mannheim tacitly acknowledged this as a problem and qualified his thesis by pointing out
that, "within each generation there can exist a number of differentiated, antagonistic generation-units". (ibid)   At the same
time however, the basis of these differentiations and antagonisms
was never made explicit and the relationship between age and class
was consequently left unexplored.   Nevertheless, Mannheim's
formulation did at least go beyond the very loose sense in which
'generation' had been employed till then, and began to specify
the necessary levels of analysis.   Unfortunately these careful
distinctions were mostly ignored by subsequent writers.

   Mannheim's essay was not translated until the early 'fifties,
and so for over twenty years it remained virtually unknown among
British and American sociologists, and even when it was finally
published it went largely unnoticed.   The problem it raised
however, was not neglected.   On the contrary, from the mid-
twenties onwards, sociologists on both sides of the Atlantic
became increasingly preoccupied with the question of generational
consciousness and its relation to social change.   This emerging
sociological literature tended to work within rather than against
the definitions of the situation established by popular comment-
aries on youth.   But there was a significant difference.
Whereas most earlier writers had made no secret of the fact that
they saw the question of youth and its consciousness as tied to
the wider issue of class stratification and class struggle, the
sociologists' increasing attachment to notions of 'scientific'
methodology and value-freedom led them to conceal or devalue the
political dimension of their work.   The debate with Marx's ghost,
and with the more substantial spectre of organised socialism,

continued of course, but it was conducted surreptitiously.   Hence,
in much of the mainstream sociological work on youth, until compar-
atively recently, class has either been evacuated altogether or
treated as relatively unimportant[3].

   In the same year that Mannheim's essay came out in Germany,
America saw the publication of Frederic Thrasher's influential
book *The Gang* (1927), in which he argued that adolescents in
downtown Chicago had responded to the social disorganisation
of the slum by creating a separate and self contained social
network of gangs, sustained by a distinctive culture.   The gangs
therefore operated in a sort of social no-man's-land which began
at the point where conventional institutions had broken down.
When Wall Street crashed and the Depression began two years later,
there was a general feeling that social disorganisation had broken
out of the inner city and become both widespread and endemic.
Hence it was scarcely surprising that sociologists should begin to
see the breakdown of generational relations and the development of
autonomous peer group cultures as features not simply of slum life
but of the general state of the nation.   But it was left to
Parsons in 1942 to suggest that these developing peer group cultures were in fact localised expressions of a more broadly based
generational consciousness which was crystalling around a distinctive 'youth culture' centred on hedonistic consumption.
Parsons' 'youth culture' was the culture of a generation who
consumed without producing - a generation whose lengthening
confinement in age-specific educational institutions was seen as
removing them, not only from the productive system, but also from
the class relations rooted in that system.   This emphasis on the
increasing centrality of age divisions and the corresponding
irrelevance of class inequalities, coupled with stress on consumption and leisure as the pivots of youth consciousness, was destin-
ed to dominate the sociology of youth for the next three decades.
   After 1945 these themes were amplified and recharged by the
widespread assumption that in the post war period the axis of
advanced capitalist societies was shifting from work to leisure
and that new relations of consumption were rapidly replacing the
old relations of production at the centre of social life.
The well publicised rise of the 'youth culture' rooted in the
leisure styles sponsored by the burgeoning youth-oriented
entertainment industry epitomised this shift perfectly.   Where
the boys' clubs and the Scouts had failed, the Beatles and Mary
Quant appeared to be succeeding.   The rising generation were in
the process of transcending class while preserving capitalism.
Nominal equality of access to the new leisure styles seemed to
be cancelling out the last remaining vestiges of class inequalities in life chances.   Post war youth, the inheritors of affluence,
therefore appeared as the vanguard of the coming 'society of leisure', in whose wake marched the 'new' working class with their
television sets and bottles of Beaujolais.   It was the old vision
of renewal without revolution, decked out in the imagery of

197

advertising.

Although downgraded, class did not disappear completely from the analysis of youth. On the contrary, studies both of the school system and of deviant behaviour repeatedly demonstrated the ways in which the life chances and life styles of working class adolescents were structured by their class location. At the same time however, the issues of educational inequality and juvenile delinquency were increasingly defined as self-contained 'problems' that could be quite adequately understood and dealt with by specialised research and remedial reforms. Consequently, the broader implications of these studies were left largely unexplored, and mainstream writing on youth remained securely wedded to the myth of classlessness.

The vision of youth as the vanguard of social change reached its zenith with the emergence of the 'counter culture' in the late 'sixties. This development took most commentators almost completely by surprise, and in the absence of a coherent class analysis the majority turned towards idealist theories. Charles Reich's, *The Greening of America,* a best-seller on both sides of the Atlantic, typified the dominant train of argument:

> Always before, young people felt themselves tied more to their immediate situations than to a 'generation'. But now an entire culture, including music, clothes and drugs, began to distinguish youth. As it did, the message of consciousness went with it.
>
> Consciousness is capable of changing and of destroying the Corporate State, without violence, without seizure of political power, without overthrow of any existing group of people .....
> (1972: 189; 253).

Youth it seemed, was in the process of becoming a generation 'for itself' with a distinctive consciousness and style, and the Hippies appeared as an advanced guard, "rehearsing *in vivo* possible cultural solutions to central life problems posed by the emerging society of the future" - a society of affluence and leisure. (Davis, 1970: 330).

The late 'sixties did mark a turning point, but the significant movement was not an advance towards abundance but a return to austerity. As the economic situation of the advanced capitalist societies worsened, it became increasingly apparent that the key conflicts of the future would not be contestations between generations over modes of consciousness and cultural style, but struggles between classes and class factions over economic resources and basic life chances But it was not simply a question of dusting off old theories. The complex of social changes that had taken place since the war may not have dissolved the class structure, but they had certainly altered many ways in

which people experienced and coped with it.   Consequently,
sociologists who acknowledged the centrality of class were presented with the problem of developing an analysis sensitive enough
to cope with the complexities of the contemporary situation.
This remains our basic task.

Youth presents a particularly difficult problem for analysis.
The post war period has seen the final institutionalisation of
adolescence through the establishment of universal secondary
schooling and the emergence of a whole complex of leisure and
entertainment facilities aimed specifically at youth.   These
agencies have not removed adolescents from the class system as
the 'youth culture' theorists maintained, but they have placed
youth in a special relationship to that system.   Age has
therefore become an increasingly important *mediation* of class
(especially for women), structuring both the forms of class experience and the ways in which these experiences are worked through.
At the same time, the ideologies which underpin the new institutions of youth - ideologies of equal opportunity, of consumer
sovereignty, and above all, of adolescence as a special and
uniquely important period - continue to conceal the centrality
of class inequalities and to emphasise the primacy of age divisions.
Hence the rhetoric of generational separation and youth equality
remains very much available, offering an insistent framework for
common sense understandings of social structure and social change.
As a result, age is important, not only as a mediation of class
experience, but also as a mediation of class consciousness.

The relationship between consciousness of generation and
consciousness of class therefore constitutes an important topic
for investigation.   It is important not only because it is
indispensable to a reconstituted sociology of youth, but also
because it is central to an adequate analysis of how class
consciousness comes to be formed, and of how this formation may
be blocked or forestalled.   At the present time explorations of
this relationship have developed in two main directions; the
first springs from a revival of interest in Mannheim's schema,
and the second from advances in subcultural analysis.

Mapping consciousness: Mannheim and beyond

The initial flurry of sociological speculation which greeted
the emergence of the 'counter culture' was very quickly followed
by a spate of empirical inquiries into the social origins and
ideologies of the hippies and communards.   These studies confirmed what the more perceptive commentators had realised all along -
that the 'counter culture' was essentially a movement of educated
middle class youth.   This led in turn to a revival of interest in
Mannheim's schema, and more particularly in his concept of the
'generation unit'.   Hence the 'counter culture' was increasingly

characterised, not as the crystallised consciousness of youth, but as the distinctive 'style' of a particular 'generation unit'.

Not only was Mannheim's schema revived however, it was also extended, as researchers recognised that contemporary youth not only contained "a number of differentiated, antagonistic generation units", but that these divisions were rooted in the wider structure of class inequalities. As two of the 'new' American sociologists of youth recently put it:

> A crucial but underdeveloped aspect of generational analysis concerns the importance of class groupings in the development of generation-based issues, and the necessity of examining the way in which superordinate and subordinate class groupings *mediate the experience of age-cohort membership.*
>
> (Laufer and Bengtson, 1974: 181, our emphasis)

Although these commentators acknowledge the importance of class, they continue to treat age as the primary focus of analysis. Class therefore appears as a secondary variable which is relevant primarily as a mediation of generational experience. Not surprisingly therefore, the empirical work generated by this formulation has by-passed the question of class consciousness and concentrated instead on the extent to which youth in various class locations share the consciousness and style embodied in the 'counter culture'[4]. Even so, this research marks a distinct advance over the recent work of Frank Musgrove, who continues to devalue the importance of class and to insist that the "counter culture is the pervasive spirit of a new generation" (1974a: 35)[5]. Recent studies of class consciousness among adolescents are equally lopsided however, in that they ignore the question of generational consciousness completely[6].

The next step is to move towards a more comprehensive analysis which explores the relationship between consciousness of class and of generation, and the relation of both to adolescents' overall conceptions of social stratification. As a beginning we need detailed mappings of the common sense categories and theories through which adolescents in different class locations describe and explain the stratification system. So far the most consistent and well worked out attempts at mapping everyday understandings of stratification have come from sociologists interested in class consciousness. Consequently, recent work in this area provides a convenient starting point for a critical examination of available methodologies.

In a recent work, Michael Mann has usefully distinguished four levels of class consciousness: *identity* - the definition of oneself as sharing a particular class location; the perception of the class structure as centred on the permanent *opposition* between capital and labour; *totality* - the acceptance of the first two levels as the defining characteristic both of one's own social situation and of the society as a whole; and finally, the vision

200

of an *alternative* social order towards which one moves through class struggle (1973: 13).   By and large, recent British work on class consciousness has concentrated on the first two levels focussing on people's class identifications and overall images of the class structure.

Nearly all these studies are based on a more or less standard battery of questions asked on a questionnaire or in the course of an interview.   At first sight these questions appear to be perfectly straightforward, e.g. "A lot of people talk about the different social classes in Britain.   What do you think is meant by the term 'social class'?   How many social classes are there?" (Stradling and Zuriek, 1973: 298).   Questions like these however, rest on the crucial but untested assumption that respondents have a clear definition of 'class' which forms the basis of a coherent image of the overall class structure.   This assumption is highly problematic.

Recent studies, including our own ongoing research, have indicated that conceptions of class are tangential or irrelevant to a number of people's understanding of stratification.   This does not mean that they are not aware of deep-seated social divisions and antagonisms, but simply that this awareness has not crystallised around the notion of class.   For, as two British sociologists have recently reminded us the "feelings of subordination, discrimination, unfairness and hostility which are the essence of class opposition ... can arise in a number of sectors of social life and be expressed in terms in which the word 'class' is never used" (Moorhouse and Chamberlain, 1974: 390).   This is not a particularly startling or new perception.   It has been grasped by countless social workers and teachers confronted with the hostility of their working class charges.   As one harassed master at a ragged school in Victorian London put it:

> ... here the very appearance of one's coat is to them the badge
> of class - for although they may not know the meaning of the word,
> they know very well, or at least feel, that we are the represent-
> atives of beings with whom they have ever considered themselves
> at war.
> (quoted in Carpenter, 1968: 60)

The ethnomethodologists may be correct in claiming that everyone in their own way is a sociologist, but this does not mean that everyone thinks and speaks like a sociologist.   Consequently, we cannot take it for granted that class constitutes a central category in people's everyday vocabulary.   On the contrary, how far this is the case is a matter for empirical investigation, and we must pay particular attention to cases where class situations are described in other terms.   We need in fact to restore the category of "false consciousness" to the centre of analysis.

Even where the term 'class' is used however, it may take on resonances which evade the standard sociological classifications.

A recent Australian study for example found that a sizeable number of respondents saw class primarily in terms of a division between people who were snobbish and kept themselves aloof, and people who mixed in easily with a wide range of social groups (Hillier, 1975). Now it may be, as the author himself suggests, that snobbishness is a particularly resonant concept among Australians, but it also crops up quite frequently in the British context, as in this extract from *The Paint House*:

> ... when I was at school I thought I was middle class ya know. So I said to me mum 'we're middle class' and she said 'You fucking ain't ya know; middle class is snobs.' And I didn't know. I thought because you wasn't a tramp you was middle class. I thought this because there was always people at school poorer than you ... so you might be 'igher.
> (Daniel and McGuire, eds. 1972: 73)

These sorts of localised conceptions of class are in fact the rule rather than the exception, for as David Lockwood has so eloquently pointed out:

> For the most part men visualise the class structure ... of their society from the vantage points of their own particular milieux, and their perceptions of the larger society will vary according to their experiences of social inequality in the smaller societies in which they live out their daily lives.
> (1966: 249)

A detailed awareness of concrete social contexts is therefore essential to an adequate analysis of social consciousness. This means going well beyond crude indicators of class location and examining the ways in which the class structure is actually experienced and understood at the level of everyday life.

At the same time however, it is important not to lose sight of the fact that localised conceptions of class are developed within the overall framework provided by the hegemonic ideology. They are consequently the products not only of people's persistent efforts to impose meaning on their own immediate experience of inequality and subordination, but also of their attempts to appropriate and rework the definitions of the situation offered by mass communications and education systems. The characteristic outcome is an uneasy amalgam of extrapolations from personal experience and elements derived from the dominant ideology[7]. In fact, "a social situation which gives rise to a coherent image of society may well be the exception rather than the rule" (Cousins and Brown, 1972: 3). Consequently, studies which gloss over these inconsistencies inevitably conceal the complexity of social consciousness.

Disjunctions and contradictions in class consciousness are likely to be particularly characteristic of adolescents, precisely because they are enmeshed in institutions which explicitly devalue and disguise the centrality of class inequalities, and offer an alternative conception which emphasises the importance of age differences. What impact this insistent celebration of youth has on adolescents' consciousness of class, remains a key topic for future investigation. The recent work of people like Richard Brown, Jim Cousins, and Theo Nichols suggests that, sensitively handled, interviews and eavesdropping still have a great deal to offer. But even at their best these techniques have a major drawback. Because they concentrate exclusively on verbalisations of consciousness, they ignore the ways in which social consciousness is objectified and expressed through other forms of social and cultural action[8]. Eventually then, it is necessary for analysis to "go beyond particular everyday conceptions ... and to show the consequences of these formulations and their application in action" (Hillier, 1975: 22). The attempt to develop such an analysis has formed one of the main trajectories of recent research on youth subcultures, including the work of the Birmingham Centre.

Reading Style: directions in subcultural analysis

The particular version of subcultural analysis we are concerned with here focusses on the way in which the shared social experiences of adolescents in particular class locations are collectively expressed and negotiated through the construction of distinctive leisure styles. Subcultural styles are made up of an amalgam of elements drawn from two main sources - the 'situated' class cultures embedded in the family and the local neighbourhood, and the 'mediated' symbol systems sponsored by the youth orientated sectors of the entertainment industry. These elements are not taken over raw, however. On the contrary, subcultural styles are the product of a cumulative process of *selection* and *transformation* through which available objects, symbols and activities, are removed from their normal social context, stripped of some or all of their conventional connotations and reworked "by members of the group into a new and coherent whole with its own special significance" (Clarke and Jefferson, 1974: 15). A central part of this process involves appropriating the ostensibly classless artefacts and commodities of the 'teenage culture' industry and investing them with class-based meanings and resonances. Subcultural styles can therefore be seen as coded expressions of class consciousness transposed into the specific context of youth and reflective of the complex way in which age acts as a mediation both of class experience and of class consciousness.

Since subcultural styles are coded expressions of consciousness, the primary act of analysis is an act of decoding. Hence, "reading" the style, in the sense of uncovering the meanings attached to its constituent elements and to the relations between them is seen as providing a method for mapping the class consciousness of youth as a complex and contextualised whole. Through his sensitive and elaborate "reading" of the style supported by a group of working class boys in north Paris for example, Jean Monod (1967) is able to present a finely textured account of their underlying conceptions of social stratification. But to date, the most comprehensive attempts at "reading" style have come from English research on working class youth, most notably Phil Cohen's pioneering account of East End subcultures (1972) and the subsequent work conducted at the Birmingham Centre on the style of the Teds, Mods, and Skinheads[9]. Taken together, these studies offer an original approach to the relations between class, age and consciousness, which no-one seriously interested in the possibilities of developing a more adequate sociology of contemporary youth can afford to ignore. At the same time however, the approach presented in these studies is subject to several important limitations.

Contemporary subcultural analysis has its roots in delinquency research and still reflects the preoccupations of that area. Hence, recent research continues to follow earlier work in focussing on the deviant rather than the conventional, on working class adolescents rather than those from the intermediate and middle classes, and most crucial of all, on boys rather than girls. As a result of these imbalances and lacunae, the range of recent studies remains relatively restricted. The neglect of adults is another significant gap in the available literature.

In contrast to the 'youth culture' theorists' simplistic insistence on the growing 'gap' between the generations, the proponents of subcultural analysis follow David Matza (1961 and Matza and Sykes, 1961) in stressing the complex patterns of continuity and disjunction between youth subcultures and the adults' cultures in which they are embedded. Phil Cohen for example, argues that "the latent function of subculture is ... to express and resolve, albeit 'magically', the contradictions which remain hidden or unresolved in the parent culture" (1972: 23). Similarly, John Clarke and his collaborators suggest "that the skinheads may be 'read' as an attempt to revive a culture which was changing and entering into new negotiations of its own with the dominant culture as a response to its changed structural position" (1974: 155). Despite the theoretical importance assigned to parental cultures in these studies, they do not examine them empirically, and consequently the crucial cultural relations between the generations are left largely at the level of assertion. The next step therefore, is to move towards a more *symmetrical* analysis, that takes adolescents *and* adults in the same basic class locations and examines in detail the correspondences and variations in their respective patterns of class experience, class consciousness and cultural action. Such an analysis is indispensable if we are to arrive at a more adequate and 'grounded' understanding of the way in which age position acts as a mediation of class location.

Subcultural studies are based on the very reasonable assumption that since adolescents' options for action are likely to be fairly restricted within the work situation, their responses to their class location will be most fully articulated in the spheres of consumption and leisure. By and large, this assumption is borne out by the available evidence. At the same time however, this emphasis on the importance of leisure has led researchers to concentrate almost all their effort in this area and to pay relatively little attention to adolescents' work experiences. This has produced the paradoxical situation in which an approach, which explicitly sets out to trace the links between class location and social consciousness, lacks an adequate analysis of the most powerful and insistent mediation of class position - the work situation. Without a detailed grasp of the ways in which class inequalities are experienced and negotiated at the point of production however, any attempt to relate particular forms of consciousness and cultural response to particular class locations must necessarily remain partial.

Clearly, filling these gaps is an obvious priority for future research, but it is not just a matter of adding more studies. There are also important problems of method to be confronted and worked through.

Subcultural studies start by taking distinctive subcultural styles and the groups who are involved in them, and then working backwards to uncover their class base. The result is an elegant and eminently plausible account of the homologous relation between cultural styles and structural situations. If this procedure is reversed however, and the analysis starts from the class location rather than from the cultural response, a serious problem presents itself, as it soon becomes apparent that the same structural location can generate and sustain a variety of responses and modes of accommodation.

Recent studies of working class areas for example, suggest that several distinct youth subcultures can coexist within the same locality, each drawing its bearers and supporters from boys in essentially the same class situation. Stephen Buff's Chicago research (1970), for instance, showed that while most of the boys in the area supported the dominant 'greaser' style, a significant minority had gravitated towards the 'hippie' style generated from within the middle class. Peter Willmott (1969) found a similar group of class 'defectors' among his Bethnal Green boys in the mid-sixties. The problem therefore, is not only to explain why styles like the Teds, Greasers, and Skinheads develop among particular groups of working class youth at particular points in time, but also to explain why adolescents sharing the same class location should be attracted to styles developed by other class factions. To explain these subtle variations in subcultural affiliations and underlying consciousness, we need to go some way beyond the relatively crude indicators of class position

205

that are often used - parental occupation, school position etc.
- and examine the concrete mediations through which class
inequalities are actually experienced and comprehended at the
level of everyday life.

The Willmott and Buff studies also raise another problem for
subcultural analysis, and one which we have become increasingly
aware of in the course of our own recent research in Leicester.
This is the question of 'conventional' youth.

Subcultural theory originally provided one of the main
theoretical planks of the study. Consequently, we started out
expecting subcultural styles to provide the dominant channel
through which adolescents articulated their definitions of
themselves and their social situation, an expectation which
seemed to be supported by the results of an early pilot study
(Murdock and McCron, 1973). As the main fieldwork phase got
under way however, it became increasingly clear that a number
of respondents were not involved in any of the available
subcultures in the town. Instead they tended to orientate
themselves around the styles sponsored by official youth agencies
or by the mainstream teenage entertainment industry. In contrast
to subcultural formations, these styles were not re-made or adapted to any great extent, but were taken over more or less intact.
Far from challenging or opposing the dominant meaning system they
were in fact expressions and extensions of it. A comprehensive
analysis of youth however, must necessarily be capable of
accommodating and explaining not only deviancy and refusal but
also convention and compliance By definition however, subcultures can only exist underneath the dominant culture; they cannot
exist within it, and consequently subcultural analysis cannot
cope with 'conventional' youth styles. This is not an argument
for jettisoning subcultural analysis, but it is an argument for
recognising its limitations.

Conclusion

At the present time then, the complex and subtle interplay between class location, age position and social consciousness has
begun to attract the attention of sociologists on both sides of
the Atlantic, and has so far generated several distinct and
largely self contained lines of analysis. But if the available
studies have not yet resulted in a coherent and unified approach
to the area, they have at least indicated, if only by default,
what such an approach entails.

Firstly, it must be *comprehensive* and include those youth
groups which have been ignored or relegated to the periphery of
available accounts. Secondly, it must be *symmetrical* and deal
not simply with adolescents but also with adults, and with the
relations between the two. Thirdly, it must be rooted in a
detailed empirical examination of the concrete work and non-work

contexts through which class inequalities are actually mediated into everyday experience. At the same time however, it must also be able to show how the forms of consciousness and action generated within these contexts are embedded in, and shaped by, more general structural and ideological formations. This requires a *structural* and *historical* analysis of the relations between shifts in the social and cultural position of youth and changes in the structure of class relations and class-based meaning systems. Without this more macro level of analysis, the approach's explanatory power will be severely curtailed. Consequently, developing conceptual and empirical linkages between specific instances and general social and cultural processes presents a central problem. But it is a problem that must be confronted and coped with, for ultimately the adequacy of the approach sketched here hinges on its capacity to illuminate the relations between biography and history. Clearly such an approach cannot be erected on the basis of any single methodology. Indeed, making a fetish of particular procedures and empirical techniques is just about the quickest way to bankrupt a promising line of analysis. Providing their limitations are recognised and allowed for, subcultural analysis, sensitive interviewing, and the 'new' social history, all have something distinctive to contribute.

Reconstructing the sociology of youth along the lines outlined here is not going to be easy, but we would argue that it is worth the effort. It is important not only because it holds out the promise of a more comprehensive analysis of present-day youth, but also because it is indispensable to a more adequate understanding of the formation of class consciousness and the dynamics of "false" consciousness in modern Britain. Just as earlier images of youth were haunted by the spectre of socialism, so contemporary socialism is haunted by the dominant mythology of generations. Demystification is therefore a necessary step towards exorcism.

FOOTNOTES
1. The 'democratisation' of adolescence is illuminatingly analysed in Chapter 3 of John R. Gillis (1974).
2. 'Collum', "The New England: Social Transformation to be led by Young Men Back from the War", *Daily Chronicle* (Monday, June 16th 1919: 4).
3. The problematic place of class in mainstream American and British work on youth is discussed more fully in: Graham Murdock, forthcoming.
4. See, for example: Patricia Kasschau, Edward Ransford and Vern Bengtson (1974).
5. See also: Frank Musgrove (1974b).
6. See, for example: Robert Stradling and Elia Zuriek (1973).
7. This point is illuminatingly discussed in: Theo Nichols (1974).
8. For a perceptive discussion of the limitations of techniques which rely on verbalisations, see: Paul Willis (1974).
9. See, for example: John Clarke, Dick Hebdige and Tony Jefferson (1974).

GIRLS AND SUBCULTURES

Angela McRobbie and
Jenny Garber

Earlier in this issue it was pointed out that sub-cultures "provided for a section of working class youth, *mainly boys*, one kind of strategy for negotiating their concrete collective existence" (our emphasis). The absence of girls from the whole of the literature in this area is quite striking, and demands explanation. Very little seems to have been written about the role of girls in youth cultural groupings in general. They are absent from the classic sub-cultural ethnographic studies, the 'pop' histories (like Nuttall, 1970), personal accounts (like Daniel and McGuire, eds., 1972), or journalistic surveys (like Fyvel, 1963). When they *do* appear, it is either in ways which uncritically reinforce the stereotypical image of women with which we are now so familiar - for example, Fyvel's reference, in his study of Teddy Boys, to "dumb, passive teenage girls, crudely painted" (1963): or they are fleetingly and marginally presented:

> It is as if everything that relates only to us comes out in
> footnotes to the main text, as worthy of the odd reference.
> We come on the agenda somewhere between 'Youth' and 'Any Other
> Business'. We encounter ourselves in men's cultures as 'by
> the way' and peripheral. According to all the reflections we
> are not really there.
>
> (Rowbotham, 1973: 35)

The difficulty is, how to understand this invisibility. Are girls, in fact, for reasons which we could discover, *really* not active or present in youth sub-cultures? Or has something in the way this kind of research is done rendered them invisible?

When girls are acknowledged in the literature, it tends to be in terms of their degree of, or lack of, sexual attractiveness. But this, too, is difficult to interpret. Take, for instance, Paul Willis' comment on the unattached girls in the motor bike sub-culture he studied:

> What seemed to unite them was a common desire for an attachment
> to a male and a common inability to attract a man to a long
> term relationship. They tended to be scruffier and less
> attractive than the attached girls. (1972)

Is this, simply, a typical and dismissive treatment of girls reflecting the natural rapport between a masculine researcher and his male respondents? Or is it that the researcher, who is actually studying motor-bike boys, finds it difficult not to take the boys' attitudes to and evaluation of the girls seriously, reflect it in his descriptive language and even adopt it as a perspective himself, within the context of the research situation? Willis does comment on some of the girls' responses to questions - giggling, reluctance to talk, retreat into cliquishness, etc. Once again, these responses are complex and difficult to interpret. Are they typical responses to a male researcher, influenced by the fact that he is a man, by his personal appearance, attractiveness, etc? Or are the responses influenced by the fact that he is identified by the girls as 'with the boys', studying them and in some way siding with them in their evaluation of the girls? Or are these responses characteristic of the ways girls customarily negotiate the spaces provided for them in a male dominated and defined culture? We must be able to locate and interpret these responses, which are extraordinarily complex, before we can understand the experiences and positions which are being mediated through them. For example, girls - especially young girls - may *retreat* from situations which are male-defined (where they are labelled and judged sexually) into a 'groupiness' or cliquishness of which "giggling" is one overt sign. In other situations (for example, in the classroom) group solidarity between girls may push them into a more aggressive response, where they use their sexuality to open avenues of approach to the young male teacher, or to embarrass him or undermine his authority. The important point is that both the defensive and the aggressive responses are structured in reaction against a situation where masculine definitions (and thus sexual labelling, etc.) are in dominance. We therefore have to interpret these responses before we can define properly the territory in which girls really operate, the spaces in which they are, sexually as well as socially located.

What follows is simply a first, tentative attempt to sketch some of the ways we might think about and research the relationship between girls and the sub-cultures. In doing so, we adopt some of the perspectives sketched out for boys in other parts of the journal: for example, the centrality of class; the importance of the spheres of school, work, leisure and the family; the general social context within which the sub-cultures emerge; the structural changes in post-war British society which partially define the different sub-cultures. We must, however, add the crucial dimension of sex and gender structuring. The question is then, how does this dimension reshape the analysis as a whole? It has been argued that class is a critical variable in defining the different sub-cultural options available to middle and working -class boys. Middle class male sub-cultures, for example, offer

more full-time 'careers', whereas working-class sub-cultures
tend to be restricted to the leisure sphere.   This structuring of
needs and options by class must also work for girls.   Thus it
is probably easier for girls to find alternative careers in, say,
the hippie or drop-out (i.e. middle class) sub-cultures than in,
say, Skinhead culture.   But then, in general, boys are more
likely to take up sub-cultural options than girls.   Such an
analysis suggests that what is true for boys' subcultures -
e.g. the structuring effect of class - is similarly true for
girls, *only more so*.   This assumes that the sub-cultural
patterns are, roughly, the same for boys and girls, only girls
are necessarily, *more marginal* on every dimension.

   It may be, however, that the *marginality* of girls is not the
best way of representing their position in the sub-cultures.
The position of the girls may be, not marginally, but *structurally*
different.   They may be marginal to the sub-cultures, not simply
because girls are pushed by the dominance of males to the margin
of each social activity, but because they are centrally into a
different, necessarily subordinate set or range of activities.
Such an analysis would depend, not on their marginality but on
their structured *secondariness*.   If women are 'marginal' to the
male cultures of work (middle and working class), it is because
they are central and pivotal to a subordinate area, which mirrors,
but in a complementary and subordinate way, the 'dominant'
masculine arenas.   They are 'marginal' to work *because* they are
central to the subordinate, complementary sphere of the *family*.
Similarly, 'marginality' of girls in the active, male-focussed
leisure sub-cultures of working class youth may tell us less than
the strongly present position of girls in the 'complementary' but
more passive sub-cultures of the fan and the fan-club.   (We
attempt, in the note following,   to represent this complementary
and subordinate kind of analysis in rough diagrammatic form.)

   Bearing this general argument in mind, we can now try to
identify a number of key questions to which subsequent work can
be addressed.   (1) Are girls really absent from the main post-war
sub-cultures?   Or are they present but invisible?   (2) Where
present and visible, were their roles the same, but more marginal,
than boys; or were they different?   (3) Whether marginal or
different, is the position of girls specific to the sub-cultural
option; or do their roles reflect the more general social-
subordination of women in the central areas of mainstream culture
- home, work, school, leisure?   (4) If sub-cultural options are
not readily available to girls, what are the different but
complementary ways in which girls organise their cultural life?
And are these, in their own terms, sub-cultural in form?
(Girls sub-cultures may have become invisible because the very
term 'sub-culture' has acquired such strong masculine overtones.)

211

Are girls really absent from sub-cultures?

The most obvious factor which makes this question difficult to answer is the domination of 'sociological' work (as in most areas of scholarly academic work) by men.   Paradoxically, the exclusion of women was as characteristic of the new 'radical' or sceptical theories of deviance as it had been of traditional criminology. The editors of *Critical Criminology* argue that the 'new deviancy theory' often amounted to "a celebration rather than an analysis of the deviant form with which the deviant theorist could vicariously identify - an identification by powerless intellectuals with deviants who appeared more successful in controlling events" (Taylor, Walton and Young, 1975).   With the possible exception of sexual deviance, women constituted an uncelebrated social category, for radical and critical theorists.   This general invisibility was of course cemented by the social reaction to the more extreme manifestations of youth sub-cultures.   The popular press and media concentrated on the sensational incidents associated with each subculture (e.g. the Teddy Boy killings, the Margate clashes between Mods and Rockers).   One direct consequence of the fact that it is always the violent aspects of a phenomenon which qualify as newsworthy is that these are precisely the areas of subcultural activity from which women have tended to be excluded.   The objective and popular image of a subculture as encoded and defined by the media is likely to be one which emphasises the male mambership, male 'focal concerns' and masculine values.   Or, as is the case with hippy subculture, when women do appear as part of the moral panic generated, it is usually in the relatively more innocuous roles - e.g. as sexually permissive.

Female invisibility in youth subcultures then becomes a self-fulfilling prophecy, a vicious circle, for a variety of reasons.   It may well be that girls/women have not played a vital role in these groupings.   On the other hand the emphases in the documentation of these phenomena, on the male and masculine, reinforce and amplify our conception of the subcultures as predominantly male.   Our 'way in' to the relationship between girls and subcultures is not an easy one.   Secondary evidence suggests, for example, that there *were* small groups of girls who saw themselves as Teddy Girls, and who identified with Teddy Boy culture, dancing with the Teds at the Elephant and Castle, going to the cinema with them and apparently getting some vicarious pleasure from relating the violent nature of the incidents instigated by the Teddy Boys[1]. - But there are good reasons why this could not have been an option open to many working-class girls.

Though girls participated in the general rise in the disposable income available to youth in the 1950's, girls' wages were, relatively, not as high as boys'.   More important, patterns of spending would have been powerfully structured in a different

direction for girls from that of boys.   The working class girl,
though temporarily at work, remained more focussed on home, Mum
and marriage than her brother or his male peers.   More time was
spent in the home.   Teddy boy culture was an escape from the
family into the street and the cafe, as well as evening and week-
end trips 'into town'.   Girls would certainly dress up and go out,
either with boy-friends or, as a group of girls, with a group of
boys.   But there would be much less 'hanging about' and street-
corner involvement.   In the working-class parental value system,
boys were expected to 'have fun while they could' (though many
working class parents regarded Teddy boy kinds of 'fun' as
pretty peculiar): but girls suffered the double injunction of
'having fun' while not 'getting yourself into trouble'.   The
sexual taboo, and the moral framework and 'rules' in which it was
embodied continued to work more heavily against girls than
against boys.   While boys could spend a lot of time 'hanging
about' in the territory, the pattern for girls was probably more
firmly structured between being at home, preparing (often with
other girls) to go out on a date, and going out.   Boys who
had, sexually and socially, 'sown their wild oats' could 'turn
over a new leaf' and settle down: for girls, the consequences
of getting known in the neighbourhood as one of the 'wild oats'
to be 'sown' was drastic and irreversible.

   There was certainly more attention than, say, in pre-war
youth culture to the teenage leisure market and its accompanying
manifestations (concerts, records, pin-ups, magazines), and girls
as well as boys would have shared in this.   But many of these
activities would have been easily appropriated into the
traditionally defined cultural space of a home or peer-centred
girls' 'culture' -operated mainly within the home, or visiting
a girl-friend's home, or at parties, without involving the
riskier and more frowned-on path of hanging about the streets
or cafes.   There was room for a good deal of the new teenage
consumer culture *within* the 'culture of the bedroom' -- experimenting with make-up, listening to records, reading the mags,
sizing up the boyfriends, chatting, jiving: it depended, rather,
on some access by girls to room and space within (rather than
outside) *the home* - even if the room was uneasily shared with an
older sister.

   This would lead us to suggest that girls were present, but in
marginal or at least highly patterned ways, in Teddy boy sub-
culture: but that - following the position outlined above - their
'involvement' was sustained by a complementary, but different
sub-cultural pattern.   The point can be made more concretely
by saying that, whereas the response of many boys to the rise of
rock-and-roll in this period was themselves to become active if
highly amateur performers (the rise of the skiffle groups),
girl participants in this culture became either fans or record

213

collectors and readers of the 'teenage-hero' magazines and love-comics. There were no teenage rock-star oriented 'love comics', such as emerged in the 1950's, for *boys* (though some boys may have covertly read their sister's!) Equally, there is no single record of a *girls'* skiffle group.

The picture is compounded if we take an equally 'hard' male-oriented working-class sub-culture of two decades later - the Skinhead groups of the 1970's. To judge from the popular sensationalism of the media, commented on above, the media image of Skinhead culture is primarily masculine. Actually there *are* small groups of 'Skinhead girls'; and, though their numbers are not large compared with the boys, their presence at football matches in an active role - traditionally, a massively male-oriented sport and occasion - may be significant. Moreover, whereas the 'girl-friends' of the Teds looked and dressed quite differently from the boys they were going out with, *some* Skinhead girls *do* look, dress and act in rather similar and supportive ways to their Skinhead boyfriends. There is some slight evidence to suggest a greater direct participation by a few groups of girls in this male-defined and focussed working-class sub-culture in the 1970's than, perhaps, would have been the case in the 1950's. But it is not sufficiently documented to build much of a hypothesis on. Certainly, there is more press coverage asking questions about the involvement of girls in gang and group activities (including violence) now than there was in the period of the Teddy Boys. But this may merely reflect the general increased visibility of women, and the greater attention to the question of the position of women generally in the culture now than was the case then. Again, it is difficult to decide whether the role of girls in the sub-cultures has actually changed, or whether their role has simply become more publicly visible. Certainly, a paragraph like the following, with its implicit attribution of a causal connection between violence and the rise of the women's movement, could not have appeared in the 1950's:

> Why are women, traditionally the gentler sex, so ready to resort to force? Is it simply that society itself is becoming more violent, or is it part of the fight for equality, a sort of 'anything a man can do I can do better'?
>
> (Berry, 1974)

If we wanted to begin, tentatively, to sketch in some of the things which form a sort of bridge between the relative absence of girls from Teddy Boy culture (except 'secondarily') and the small indication of a 'presence' of girls in Skinhead culture, we would need to touch on at least four inter-mediate features. First, there is the emergence of a 'softer' working-class sub-culture, in the mid-1960's, in which girls *did* much more openly and directly participate (though they remained, of course, subordinate to the boys). This is the Mod sub-culture (discussed

214

more fully below) in which (a) there were, clearly, Mod girls as well as boys; and (b) the boys and the girls in the Mod styles seemed to look more like each other, based partly on the fact that (c) Mod styles, and the Mod preoccupation with style and appearance made even Mod boys, in the eyes of their Rocker competitors as well as their own, more 'feminine'. Secondly, is the appearance, in the later 1960's of a middle class sub-culture - the Hippies - in which some girls and women played an active and visible role (though, again, we would argue, remaining in a subordinate position). Thirdly, there is the growth - no doubt related to the Mod and Hippy styles, as these came to be diffused and defused through the fashion trade and image-business - of 'Unisex' styles, with clothes designed to be worn equally by girls or boys, and the accompanying blurring of the sexually-distinct fashion images. Fourthly, there is the rise, within the pop industry itself, of the deliberately 'feminine', camp, or bi- and trans-sexual singer and star. These form certain important inter-mediary positions in the path which girls have taken from total invisibility to a 'relative' visibility in the sub-cultures between the 1950's and the 1970's. Again, this is extremely difficult and complex cultural material either properly to document or to interpret. It would be important, in any more substantive interpretation, to note *both* the relative shift in the visibility of girls in relation to the sub-cultural trends, *and* the fact that, no matter how visible and active a small group of girls become, or how much the sex-based images are blurred, the relative subordination of girls in the sub-cultures remains. As any study of the iconography of Mick Jagger, Garry Glitter or Dave Bowie would soon reveal, it is possible for male pop stars to be both 'more feminine' and 'aggressively male chauvinist' at one and the same time, within the same image. The feminising of the male image may in no way signal the complementary liberation of the female from the constraints of the feminine image.

The fact that, despite these surface shifts in the provided culture, the root attitudes towards the position of girls in the sub-cultures may not have changed all that much in two decades, is evidenced in the sexual attitudes of the Skinhead boys quoted in *The Paint House* (Daniel and McGuire, eds., 1972). There is nothing new about the kinds of crude typing in use in, say, the boys quoted in the "Jilly Crown, the Certified Whore" chapter. What we don't know is how the girls themselves respond to this kind of labelling - again, typically, no Skinhead girls contribute to *The Paint House*.

In short, the evidence about how active and present girls are in the main post-war sub-cultures is difficult to interpret finally, one way or the other, on what is presently known. Certainly, the weight of the evidence we have suggests that the

majority of girls organise their social life almost as an alternative to the kind of 'qualifications' and risks which direct
entrance into the boy culture (sub or mainstream) involves.
Though the girls know that where sex is concerned boys 'have
it easy', they don't have a sense of solidarity with girls who
are ranked among the boys as having 'cheapened themselves',
as the following quotation illustrates:

> It's always like that you know -it's not fair - but you have
> to watch who you're going around with.   Yeh - there's one up
> the club, I'm not saying her name but she's a proper one;   she
> walks past and says, 'alright Tina'? - But she's one person
> I wouldn't go around with 'cause you'd get a name for yourself.
> ('Tina', teenage girl[2])

It may, then, be a matter, not of the absence or presence of
girls in the sub-cultures, but of a whole alternative network of
responses and activities through which girls negotiate their
relation to the sub-cultures or even make positive moves away from
the sub-cultural option.

Where girls are visible, what are their roles?   And do these reflect the general sub-ordination of women in the culture?

   Three selected images will have to do duty here - where girls
clearly are present, but where the way they are present suggests
the way their cultural subordination is retained and reproduced.
The first is the image of the Motorbike girl, leather-clad, a
sort of sub-cultural pin-up heralding - as it appeared in the
press, certainly - a new and threatening sort of aggressive
sexuality.   This image was often used to herald the new sexual
permissiveness in press and media.   But it is important to note
how this presence was encoded in a purely sexual (albeit new,
modern and bold) way: the pan stick lips, the blackened eyes,
the numb expressionless look and the slightly unzipped leather
jacket.   This sub-cultural image was only a hair's breadth
away from, on the one hand, the new sexuality of advertising and
the modern fashion trade, on the other hand, the classic fetishism
of the pornography trade.   Within this apparently new sexual
permissiveness the real sexual subordination of the Motorbike
sub-culture was mystified.   In the general Motorbike culture,
a girl remained excluded from the central core of the culture:
she depended on the offer of a pillion seat by a boy rider, to
enable her to share in the particular sub-cultural highs - the
'ton-up' or the week-end away.   Few girls penetrated to the
symbolic core of the sub-culture - the motorbike itself, a
technical knowledge of the machines, their limitations and
capacities.   A girl's membership of the group was dependent on
the boy she was with - it was always tentative, easily resulting
in her expulsion from the group, depending on the state of her
relationship with the boys.   In the tighter versions of the
motorbike culture - in Hell's Angels groups, for example - the
whole focus of the group was overwhelmingly masculine: a _machismo_

culture of hard men.   Only the few women who could be as hard
as one of the boys could gain entry - and then only if she were
the leader's woman or a sort of 'Mama' to the chapter as a whole.
Hunter Thompson **suggests**, in *Hell's Angels* (1967),that Angels
frequently treated most women as sexual objects: they were either
'Mamas' or objects of the gang-bang.   The content and images
of relationships in this sub-culture may have been new and highly
deviant: but the way Hell's Angels tended to divide the female
world,into women-with-hearts-of-gold-who-looked-after-them and
prostitutes,is a binary opposition as old and traditional as the
hills.

    As we suggested above, Mod culture and the high visibility
of girls within it is probably more relevant to our argument.
Girls have always gone out to some kind of work in the brief
space between school and marriage; but, in the early sixties,
there may have been more late-teenage girls at work, and there
were certainly new kinds of occupations opening up, especially
'glamorous' jobs in the boutique, cosmetic and clothes trades,
and secretarial jobs, which, though in fact ultimately routine
and dead-end, had a touch of dressing-up and going to work 'in
town' about them, at least in the big cities.   In the boutique
trade, glamour and status often compensated for poor wages.   The
changing economic and occupational structure may have helped
girls in these kinds of jobs to take a more active part in the
consumerism of Mod culture.   But this greater involvement was
also structured culturally.   The mod ethos of individual 'cool'
could be more easily sustained, by girls, at home, in school or
at work, without provoking direct parental or adult reaction,
than a more aggressive and abrasive sub-cultural style.
Parents and teachers knew that girls looked 'rather odd, these
days', with their white, drawn faces and cropped hair, but, as
Dave Laing remarked of the Mods, "there was something in the way
they moved which adults couldn't make out" (Laing, 1969).
This relative fluidity and ambiguity of the culture meant that
a girl   could be 'around',without necessarily being directly
coupled with any one Mod boy: she could 'be a Mod', in a Mod
couple, in a crowd of other Mod girls, or even alone.   Participation had much to do with clothes, appearance and the stylised
look - like her male counterpart the Mod girl demonstrated the
same fussiness for detail in clothes, the same over-attention to
appearance.   Mod girls may have become more visible because boys
and girls in the sub-cultures looked more alike - it was probably
the diffusion of Mod styles which led the fashion trade to the
Unisex device.   But, as we have suggested, it may also have been
because the sub-culture, as a whole, as compared with either Teddy
boy or motor-bike culture, looked, as a whole, rather 'feminine'
- and this image was reinforced by the smartness of the Mod and
his proccupation with style and consumption and looks, his
general stylishness.   It is impossible to tell at this stage

217

why harshly chauvinistic attitudes, common elsewhere, seemed not to be so prevalent in Mod groups: but this is certainly the prevailing general impression. The position of Mod culture at the more feminine end of the sub-cultural spectrum may reflect simply their opposition to the other, 'harder', more masculine sub-cultures around them (the source of much Mod/Rocker competition). It may reflect the upwardly-mobile character and orientation of the sub-culture as a whole. It may have something to do with the greater relative confidence of the girls involved - a confidence which can't have been unaffected by the emergence, at about this point in time, of the Brooke clinics and the increase in the availability of the Pill for unmarried girls over sixteen. Of course, we can't say precisely what groups first took advantage of these facilities, but their availability must have enhanced the sexual confidence, at least of those who made use of them: and, as we've suggested, for girls in and around a male-focussed sub-culture sexual confidence is calculated to have an impact on social and cultural confidence.

The general tendency for girls to become more visible and relatively autonomous in Mod sub-cultures must be taken together with the continuing hold of the basic material and social structures pre-determining the lives of the girls and constraining and limiting this relative visibility/autonomy/space. As has been suggested, mod sub-culture may have enabled some participants to live out certain 'imaginary relations' to those constraining conditions, but not to transcend them. The 'relative autonomy' of Mod girls reflected their short-term affluence, but the jobs which provided the extra cash afforded short-term satisfactions, few career prospects, no opportunities of overtime bonuses nor wage-scales increasing much beyond the age of twenty. Longer, if not better educated, she had probably, none the less, been exposed mainly to the sort of Newsom thinking designed to 'interest the girls' as part of the 'early leavers' curricula: domestic or feminine subjects, child care, training in personal relationships, commercial and clerical practice ... (see Newsom, 1948; 1963). There is nothing to suggest that participation in Mod sub-culture sharply loosened the bonds between mothers and daughters, or significantly undermined the girls' self-conception and orientation towards marriage and the family.

The term 'Hippy' is, of course, an umbrella term, covering a variety of diverse groupings and tendencies. The aspect which is of most direct relevance here, is the point through which most girls would have entered or been drawn into one or other part of this amorphous culture - that is, through the middle-class student culture. There is available, for middle-class girls, a more obvious amount of unstructured, yet legitimate, space, lying somewhere between the confines of the actual Hippy sub-culture and the mainstream middle-class culture (sixth-form or student culture).

218

Thus for the middle-class schoolgirl, or first year university student, the flat, whether to live in or to visit, symbolises this gain in negotiated territory which cannot be penetrated by parents, and which because of the relatively unstructured nature of student life likewise cannot be forbidden. The middle-class girl student has more time, a more flexible timetable, three or four years during which marriage is positively discouraged, and finally, a softer environment, a more total experience not so strictly demarcated into work and leisure, which allows for the development of *personal* style.

On the other hand, given this flexibility, it would seem fair to say that there was remarkably little shift, both within this peripheral culture and within the main body of Hippy subculture, away from those roles which are traditionally female. The stereotypical images we associate most with Hippy culture tend to be those of the Earth Mother, baby at breast, or the fragile pre-raphaelite lady. Again, of course, we must be aware of the dangers of accepting uncritically the images which emerge via press coverage, as part of a moral panic, though the chances are that this panic itself represents the double bind - sexual permissiveness linked with motherhood may be more palatable than aggressive feminism. Certainly, as in more conventional areas of music, it is almost always as singers that "hippy" women have managed to exist and that, presumably, thanks to the uniqueness of the female voice. Given this, the types of images generally available seem to be very limited; the few women who have made it in this sphere usually fit either the gentle/lyrical/introspective image of, say, Joni Mitchell or the agressive/butch/whisky-sodden type associated with Janis Joplin or Maggie Bell.

However, it would be misleading not to acknowledge the space which the underground provided for alternative occupations/life-styles in which women have figured quite highly. *Spare Rib* as an 'alternative' publication can be firmly placed within this context and Caroline Coon of *Release* was one of many women working in the information/aid/relationship centres which sprang up as part of the counter-culture.

Do girls have alternative ways of organising their cultural life?

Some of what has been conjectured above may lead us to the conclusion that the majority of girls find alternative strategies to that of the boys' sub-cultures. The important question , then, may not be the absence or presence of girls in the male sub-cultures, but the complementary ways in which girls interact among themselves and with each other to form a distinctive culture of their own. One of the most significant forms of an alternative 'sub-culture' among girls is the culture of the Teeny Bopper. While this is in no way a new phenomenon (the girl/pop idol relationship has been in existence for the last twenty years), it is one of the most highly manufactured forms of available youth culture - it is almost totally packaged. Evidence of this can be cited throughout the entire pop trajectory, but what is significant about the Teeny Bopper syndrome of the 70's is that it was directed expressly at an even younger market i.e. ten - fifteen year old girls, too young even to have heard the Beatles, and who were certainly not turned on by the new heavy rock (E.L.P., Yes, Led Zeppelin or Deep Purple) which their elder brothers and sisters listened to so avidly. The attractiveness of this market with its quick turnover potential (Mark Bolan this week, David Cassidy the next) offered ailing American film and broadcasting companies a chance to boost their profits too, Screengems and M.G.M. in particular.

Even in relation to so manufactured a network we can locate a variety of negotiative processes at work amongst the girls themselves.

a) Teeny Bopper culture can easily be accommodated, for ten to fifteen year old girls, in the home, requiring only a bedroom and a record player and permission to invite friends; but in this capacity it might offer an opportunity for girls to take part in a quasi-sexual ritual (it is important to remember that girls have no access to the masturbatory rituals common amongst boys). The culture also offers a chance for both private and public manifestations - the postered bedroom or the rock concert.

b) Teeny Bopper culture is sufficiently flexible to allow anybody to join; it does not operate any exclusion rules or qualification on entry - thus differing greatly from the girls' school environment, where participation in certain activities demands a fair degree of competence and money.

c) There are no risks involving personal humiliation or degrada-
tion, no chance of being stood up or bombed out. Some Teeny Bopper girls we have talked to show a remarkable awareness of the fact that boys are all out for 'the one thing', and that girls lose all the way along in that game. Involvement in Teeny Bopper culture, then, can be seen as a kind of defensive retreat away from the possibility of being sexually labelled, but also as displaying a high degree of self-sufficiency within the various small female groupings; "we have a great laugh with the girls".

d) The obsession with particular stars, Donny Osmond etc., can be viewed as a meaningful reaction against the selective and authoritarian structures which control the girls' lives at school. That is, "obsessions" can be a means of alienating the teacher, and, if shared, can offer a defensive solidarity, especially for those who are conscious of themselves as being academic failures.

While there may certainly be elements in Teeny Bopper culture which enable girls to negotiate a space of their own, it has also to be said that the relationship between the girls and the idols conjured up, and, as far as one can tell, reciprocated, is suffused with fantasy elements - the displacement- and to some degree de-sexualising of what are patently commercial and sexually -manipulative icons of the Teeny Bopper market. Here the element of fantasisation and fetishisation which is present, at all times, to some degree in the heavy involvement - boys and girls - with the 'presentational images of commercial pop culture, is raised to a peculiarly high and powerfully charged pitch. There seems little doubt that the fantasy relationships which characterise this resistance depend for their very existence on the subordinate, adoring female in awe of the male on a pedestal. The culture also tends to anticipate the form of future 'real' relationships, and in so far as these are articulated in the magazine articles and stories, directs the girls hopefully towards romance and eventually an idealised version of marriage. All the way through the teenybopper spectrum then, the dialectic is, as it were, tighter. The small, structured and highly manufactured space that is available for ten to fifteen year old girls to create a personal and autonomous area seems to be offered only on the understanding that these strategies also symbolise a future general subordination - as well as a present one.

CONCLUSION

Our focus in this piece, then, has been one which tends to move away from the Subcultural group phenomena simply because, in our view, the sub-cultural group may not be the most likely place where those equivalent rituals, responses and negotiations will be located. We feel that when the dimension of sexuality is included in the study of youth subcultures, girls can be seen to be negotiating a different space, offering a different type of resistance to what can at least in part be viewed as their sexual subordination. So, although it could be the case that female youth culture corresponds, in form if not in activities to non-sub-cultural male groupings, comprising of anything from five to ten boys who "hang around together", we would tend to agree with Jules Henry who, describing the American teenage experience, points out that:

> As they grow towards adolescence, girls do not need groups, as a matter of fact for many of the things they do, more than two would be an obstacle. Boys flock; girls seldom get together in groups above four whereas for boys a group of four is almost useless. Boys are dependent on masculine solidarity

221

within a relatively large group. In boys' groups the emphasis is on masculine unity; in girls cliques the purpose is to shut out other girls. (1963)

We would add that girl culture, from our preliminary investigations, is so well insulated as to operate to effectively exclude not only other 'undesirable' girls - but also boys, adults, teachers and researchers[3].

FOOTNOTES

1. See also the role played by girl 'gang' members - described by Patrick (1972) - in carrying weapons for male members to dance halls, etc., and in providing support for them against the police after incidents.

2. This quotation is taken from a series of interviews currently being carried out among fourteen year old girls in a Birmingham Youth Centre.

3. The girls we have spoken to at the Birmingham Youth Centre constantly make jokes among themselves for the sole purpose of confusing or misleading the researcher who may well be infringing on their territory by asking personal questions, or whose presence at the weekly disco they resent. For example, one group of three fourteen year olds explained to us that the fourth member of their 'gang' had male genitals. The 'joke' lasted for about ten minutes with such seriousness that we were quite convinced until one of the girls said 'Dickie' came from Middlesex. The girls shrieked with laughter and the interview came to a halt.

A NOTE ON MARGINALITY
Rachel Powell and John Clarke

It is clear from everything said in the previous article that the analysis of the forms of girls' involvement (or non-involvement) in subcultures poses certain important theoretical questions which have not yet been fully answered. In this note we want to focus on a concept which we believe is employed by even those analysts who are concerned to give a symmetrical account of the situation of young girls. That concept - used implicitly and in an unarticulated way - we would tentatively describe as *marginality*. Marginality applies both to the theoretical constructions employed, in a quasi-analytical form, and to the perceptions of "reality". In the former mode, it is as if the social totality, and subcultural activity within it, can be explained in terms of what men do, and *then* the activity of girls can be explained through a further, more subtle subdivision of categories. In the perceptual mode, women's *real* activities are seen to take place in the same structural-cultural nexus as those of men, but in every instance women's participation is perceived as peripheral to the major tensions, conflicts and negotiations that compose a specific class situation. We believe this model (if, indeed, it is substantial enough to be called a model) is inadequate.

Diagrammatically, it suggests a series of concentric circles: the further out the circle, the more marginal its inhabitants are to the hub of the dominant culture - the world of the middle class male adult. Thus:

Diagram A

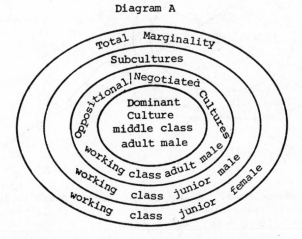

The diagram is schematised and selected in accord with one theoretical focus - the activity of potentially deviant girls. It is rather like attempting to elaborate a model of the whole society from a study of Skinheads, and its deficiencies become more apparent if we ask where *other* women should go. Are adult, middle class women nearer the middle, less marginal than adult working class men, for instance? A question of that sort has no single satisfactory answer, but it does undercut the validity of such a model. The model does have some descriptive power which derives from assumptions about both the *centrality* and the *private nature* of the family, and the family conceived of as the *proper sphere* of women.

From these assumptions, there is no problem about where to place the "other women" - we know where they are, they are *not there*, they are tucked away in the privatised and socially-invisible family life. They stand outside the world of power, contest and conflict, and consequently only girls who stand *outside* the family (and, more recently, "violent" girls and women) enter into that arena of challenge and control. That ideological placing of women can be diagrammed rather like this:

Diagram B

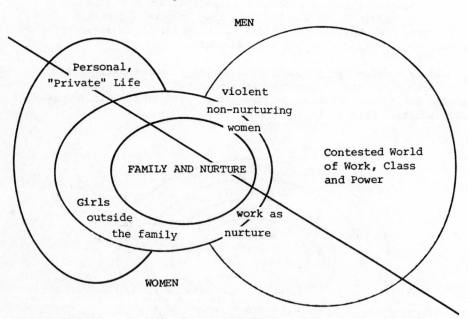

From the standpoint of the dominant culture, there is indeed a kind of marginality-problem represented here; it is the specific problematic of a particular formation of ideology and

224

control.   From that standpoint, the "problem of women" can be formulated as *How to manage the "dangerous passage" of young girls, from parental care - out from one family - and into a maternal role - back into a new family?*

We would argue that such a conception of a control problem directs us to thinking the problem of marginality in a very different way; by looking at the problem as identifying a potential "weak link" in the reproduction of the social relations of the society, it directs us to looking at girls' relations to the major institutional structures designed to effect that transition.   This allows the *real* possibility of a symmetrical analysis, by analysing the *differential* relation of boys and girls to the *same* set of major institutions.   By differential we mean an awareness of the relative salience and power of each institution in relation to boys or girls through that passage.   We have argued earlier in this volume that (male) subcultures inhabit the weak points between home/school and work.   A symmetrical analysis for girls directs us to the nature of that transition (to the question of whether girls stand in the same relation of marginality as boys to those institutions), and to available forms in which they can inhabit that passage.   As a starting point we would (over-) schematise the two passages as follows:

Diagram C

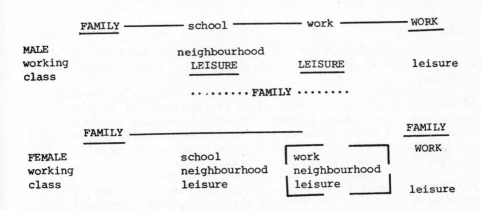

Notes. 1. The family of origin exerts a tighter and more permanent hold over girls than it does for boys, both in terms of their functions for its internal economy, and as practical training for their passage to the next.

2. The reproduction of the girl as "wife/mother" is reinforced in the other institutional spheres (school - depression of opportunity, feminine "vocational" training, etc.; leisure - consumable feminity, Romance, etc.).

3. Work exists as a potential source of relative freedom (economically, etc.) but it is counterbalanced by: (a) the dominant conception of it as an *interruption* in the family based dominant career; and (b) patterns of home residence among working girls - in part enforced by female wage levels.

Our argument is then, that women do not inhabit a separated and invisible part of the social formation, but are engaged in exactly the *same* institutional structures as men, but in different relations. It is the dominant ideological division between Home and Work which structures the invisibility of women, and not their *real* absence from the world of work. Their identification solely with the "privatised" world of the family has masked, firstly, the historical (not natural - and for a long time very uneven) removal of work from the home, and secondly, the continuing presence of working women. (It also masks the man's presence in the home.) Men and Women do not inhabit two empirically separated worlds, but pass through the same institutions in different relations and on different trajectories. We would, roughly, diagram the interlocking structure as in Diagram D.

Notes to Diagram D

1. As the diagram attempts to suggest, for both male and female, youth and adult, "social space" is heavily structured by class.

2. Given that basic division, however, social barriers of age, sex and to some extent class itself, manifest varying degrees of permeability according to actual location within the structure. Relative permeability is defined by the basic economic and ideological forms, but is experienced mainly as a *biographical* circumstance (see Critcher, above).

3. Dimensions of possible activity for both sexes are constructed around certain oppositions, but where, for men, the dominant oppositions are those of work/not-work, management/labour and work/leisure, women's experience of those *same oppositions* is heavily overlaid by the emphasis opposing family/not-family.

4. For girls, then, the actual "space" for subcultural activity is not marginal but *more tightly structured* than that available to boys. It is delimited by a doubly-structured subordination, and the elements available for subcultural *bricolage* (see article on Style, above) carry an even heavier load of prior-established meaning.

226

Diagram D

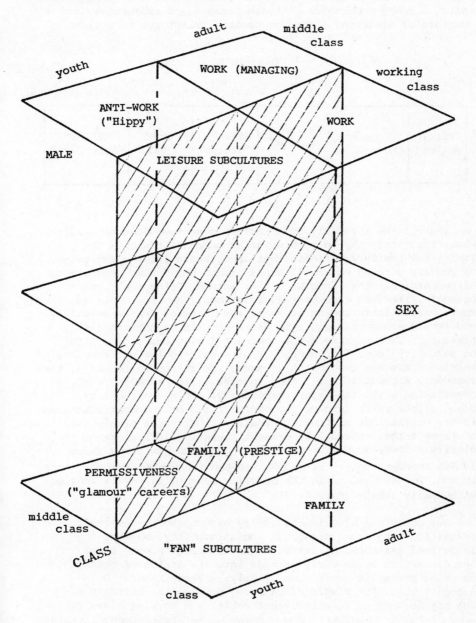

Finally, then, we would like to make a tentative sketch of some of the forms in which girls can inhabit the transition to "maturity", together with some observations about their consequences for the reproduction of female roles. For the working-class girl, a rough repertoire of these forms - not exhaustive, and not matters of discrete, either/or choice - might run as follows:

Diagram E

"Little Mother"	"Bedroom Culture"	"steadies"	disco "groups"	"Career Girl"	"Slags" "Scrubbers"

These forms (probably even including that of "Career Girl", whose trajectory may be seen as an accommodation within the Family/Not-Family antithesis, but about whose leisure activity we can say nothing here) all hinge around particular definitions of *femininity* - they involve either actual ("steadies") or potential/imagined cross-sexual relations, they reproduce in their varied forms one or other of the forms of female sexuality and female subordination, even where no male is empirically present. They may break the dominant family based conception of sexuality (e.g. "scrubbers"), but even in doing so, they reinforce another conception of sexual relations to the male, they reproduce subordination. They involve either acceptance of, or negotiation with, the major component of their own identity. Negotiations which involve the explorations of the contradictions in the definitions of female sexuality. The more highly-publicised of these forms, especially, present these ideological tensions clearly - Teeny-Bopper as Sex-in-tension-with-juniority (*when is Sex appropriate?*); Fan as Sex-in-tension-with-distance (*where is sex, in the head or in the body?*); Groupie as Sex-in-tension-with-family (*what-for is Sex?*).

But girls are *also* ideologically encouraged to see their sexual identity as an avenue of social mobility, whether that is defined (as normally for boys) as a passage across class boundaries, or as an early passage into the status of maturity, becoming Mother in one's "own" family. Where Diagram D suggests that, for *middle class* young people, the boundary of age may be seen as relatively permeable, for working class *girls* other forms of permeability may occur - semi-fantasised, certainly,

228

but also to some degree really possible. That is, in contrast to the experience of working class boys, girls' leisure activity may itself offer a "career" element. Some forms of passage, across the interlocking boundaries, clearly minimise this element - transitions into *male* young working-class occupied zones, as with some tough Skinhead girls, some Hard Mod girls. Others, however, involving transitions into young *middle-class* territory, as with some working-class Hippy girls, some highly successful Incorporated Mod "stars", may offer a considerably larger "career" prospect. And playing it straight and "steady" - crossing the age boundary into early marriage and motherhood, working class *adult* territory - offers the most recognisable "career" of all.

These notes, of course, remain schematic. What we now need is detailed ethnographic studies, to see whether our model works.

THE POLITICS OF YOUTH CULTURE
Paul Corrigan & Simon Frith

As our concern is with the *political* implications of youth
culture, we must begin by stressing that our remarks are tentative
and, in a sense, negative - they spring initially from a criticism
of the assumptions and conclusions of most existing accounts of
British youth.   Our own analysis follows Phil Cohen's (1972)
in placing the youth subculture in its class context - our
interest is in the politics of *working class youth*[1] but our
strategy is rather different from his: what we want to suggest
is that the mistakes made by analysts of youth in particular
are related to the mistakes made by the analysts of British
working class culture in general;   in other words, an understanding of the political implications of working class youth
culture must be based on an understanding of working class
culture as a whole.

The existing literature on British working class culture -
whether the literature of academic sociology or that of active
Marxists - is bound by a common thread, the notion of ideological incorporation.   Whatever the differences in their language,
the logic of right and left theorists is remarkably similar:
problem - the British working class is politically non-revolut-
ionary/quiet/passive;   *reason* - working class culture is rooted
in non-revolutionary/quiet/passive values;   *explanation* - the
working class has been ideologically incorporated, its values
reflect a profound acceptance of bourgeois culture.   This sort
of argument can be found in a variety of sociologists (Marshall,
1963, Runciman, 1966, Goldthorpe et al., 1969) and Marxists
(especially the *New Left Review* writers, following Gramsci, 1971).
And even those theorists who have partially criticised this
approach (Frank Parkin, 1971, and John Westergaard, e.g. 1974,
on the one hand, Edward Thompson, e.g. '1965, on the other) have
failed to make explicit its crucial oversimplifications.   We
would point to two in particular: firstly, the argument equates
culture with ideology but fails to place that ideology in its
structured, *institutional* context;   secondly, the argument
treats the working class as the passive recipients of their culture and fails to trace the active process by which a culture is
created from *material experience*.   In short, working class
politics is explained by reference to an intellectual and
ideational process, a process which, moreover, involves no
conflicts.

The analysis of working class youth culture rests on exactly

231

the same sort of oversimplifications, if not, perhaps, so
obviously. The sociology of youth culture has mostly been the
prerogative of deviance theorists and superficially it has, then,
focussed on those young people who appear to act *against* bourgeois
values. Paradoxically though, the explanations for this behaviour depend on an argument which stresses deviant groups' *acceptance* of bourgeois values - deviance is a result of a contradiction
(for the *individual* deviant) between these values and the material
possibility of living up to them; the subcultural approach to
delinquency, from A. K. Cohen (1955), through Cloward and Ohlin
(1960) to David Downes (1966), is a theory of ideological
incorporation gone slightly wrong. Even Stan Cohen's (1973)
change of emphasis (to the process by which deviancy is
created by the onlooker) leaves the basic point untouched -
deviant youth can only be understood by reference to *bourgeois*
values. For sociologists, youth culture has only negative
political implications: delinquents are incorporated kids with
problems, normal kids are, presumably, incorporated kids without
problems[2]. There is little disagreement with this conclusion
from Marxists who, almost without exception, interpret the
daily experience of the working class teenager as the total
(and totally successful) manipulation of a potential proletariat
into the very model of the capitalist consumer. The same
assumptions are made about youth as are made about working class
culture as a whole: there is no account of the *institutional*
context in which young people confront bourgeois ideology; there
is no account of the way in which teenagers *create* their culture
from their experience.

   The conclusion we draw from the existing literature on
youth culture is that *nothing* can be said about its political
implications because politics hasn't been allowed into the
discussion. If institutions are excluded from the analysis,
if no attention is paid to the active role of young people in
their culture, then *nothing* can be said about the concrete
struggles in which young people may (or may not) be engaged;
youth culture is non-political because it has been defined
that way. From our own work on youth culture[3] a description
emerges of behaviour and ideas which certainly aren't bourgeois
(even in the sense of being a 'reaction formation' to bourgeois
values); the problem is how to assess this reality politically,
how to develop an approach to youth culture in which politics
is the *centre* of the analysis.

   Again we take our lead from the broader problem of how to
analyse working class culture as a whole. If we look at this
culture historically it is clear that what we are looking at is
the history of a class struggling to survive and cope with a
variety of bourgeois institutions (the market, the work place,
education, the political system, the law, etc). Working class

232

culture can't be understood without reference to these institutions but neither can it be understood without reference to
the *struggles* involved - the working class has not been (and
could not be, given its material base) incorporated docilely,
simply at the level of ideas. Taking our own lead from
Gramsci (1971), we argue that the history of working class
culture can't be understood without reference to the history of
the State, to the history of those institutions which function
to reproduce and maintain the social relations of capitalism,
in part precisely by seeking to incorporate the working class
ideologically *and institutionally*. The State has material as
well as ideological force, incorporation has meant the destruction of institutions as well as their creation, it has involved
a variety of struggles besides the ideational one. The *politics*
of working class culture can only be understood by reference to
all the struggles in which the working class has been engaged.
We can best illustrate this by reference to the history of
education.

EDUCATION: THE WORKING CLASS IN A BOURGEOIS INSTITUTION

> *"What is the nature and height of the fence with which
> the playground is enclosed?"* (question on the report
> form of Her Majesty's Inspectors of Schools, 1840-1).

A cursory glance at the Minutes of the Committee of
Council on Education (and subsequent Department of Education)
for 1840-1870 reveals the way in which the State produced a
complex machinery to regulate working class education. Through
the Inspectorate, the training and certification of teachers,
the withholding of school grants, and so on, a particular
definition of education gained ascendancy. This process is
outlined in a number of studies, all of which show the success
of the bourgeoisie in establishing their domination of educational
structures. (See, for example, Johnson, 1970; Hurt, 1972;
Frith, forthcoming - b.) This process can be (and has been) seen
in isolation, simply as a *growth* of state education; but what
was involved was not just an imposition of education from above,
there was, equally, a struggle *against* forms of education; against, in particular, those educational institutions organised by
the working class for themselves.

> National education was not simply a matter of providing an
> elementary education to a class that was otherwise intellectually
> and morally destitute; it was, rather a matter of providing
> a particular *form* of education to a class which had (however
> unsystematically) alternative forms of learning available.
> (Frith, forthcoming - b).

The growth of state education was not simply the growth
of *intervention* in working class lives; it was a complex process
which involved the *destruction* of institutions as well. Altern-

ative means of education were seen as antithetical to the needs of a developing capitalist society.   For example:

> The education at Zion school differed in significant ways from the national process that was being developed contemporaneously in Leeds National Schools.   It was not age-specific - children and adults attended the Sunday and evening schools, the library and reading room together.   It did not require full-time attendance - it was an education designed for people in full-time occupation.   There was no obligatory curriculum, but a variety of educational activities and contents (three R's teaching, mutual improvement, religious instruction, newspaper reading, etc.)   And, anyway, the education provided by Zion school was not only teacher-related - the stress on mutual improvement, the natural progression from older pupil to younger teacher, blurred such distinctions .....
>
> (ibid).

Such a community based curriculum, organisation (and, indeed, educational *experience)* was one that the State's Schools Inspectors came across frequently:

> The colliers tend, in general, to prefer sending their children to the old kind of day schools kept by men of their own class ... A few of the masters seemed fairly well qualified to teach, in their own way, all they pretended to, reading, writing, arithmetic; but the majority of them are, as might be expected, men of very humble requirements.   The books that they use are those that the parents choose to send.   There can consequently be no regular courses of instruction in anything.   The Bible or Testament is read, but very little explanation is attempted. Each child is taught whatever Catechism is brought with him.
>
> (Tremenheere, 1844).

One can catch the horror in this Inspector's description: such education was anarchy - the books *they* wanted to read! No proper teacher!   No organisation!   No moral structure!

> In all that related to a knowledge of the world around him, of the workings of society, of the many social and economic problems which must force themselves daily upon the attention of the working man, the mind of the growing youth was left to his own direction, and therefore liable to take up the facts and principles as chance might dictate.   They are generally led into error and persevere with it as they want the knowledge to enable them to see where they went wrong.
>
> (ibid).

Despite such criticisms, these institutions undoubtedly provided an 'education', just as the National and State financed schools provided an 'education'.   The point is that two forms of *institution* were opposed, and the one had the power of the State behind it, the other only particularised, local, community pressures.   From the mid-nineteenth century onwards the *power* of the State was used to create the structures which provided the bourgeois definition of education and to discredit and destroy alternatives;   *this* was the process through which the hearts and the minds of the working class were 'captured by' bourgeois ideology;   through which the class was *'incorporated'*

234

Many Marxists read this story with a sigh: bourgeois domination is established, the working class does not have the power to resist, or to re-create its own institutions; given the lack of those institutions workers become, inevitably, participants in the bourgeois version of education - they go to bourgeois schools, learn bourgeois facts and theories, accept bourgeois values. But there is an unwarranted assumption in this argument - what the history of education describes is a process of *institutional* incorporation. Obviously this process involved an ideological struggle, but it was one fought out in terms of institutions; one sort of educational *experience* was replaced by another. Certainly the working class became enmeshed in bourgeois education - the localised, self-education of the 19th Century can be seen as a final futile gesture in the struggle of the British working class against their incorporation[4]; certainly working class culture now has to take account of this bourgeois-determined experience; but 'to take account' of an institution is not necessarily to *accept* it. To make the point a different way: institutional incorporation (which has been the experience of the British working class over the last 150 years) is not *necessarily* ideological incorporation and our objection to analysts of working class culture (both left and right) is that they confuse this distinction. They read the history of institutions as *direct* evidence of the history of culture; they conceal the real complexity of this relationship; their political conclusions are therefore suspect.

The difficulties of a correct analysis, in this respect, become sharply apparent at the point where educational experience becomes part of youth culture. How can we make *political* sense of working class school kids? They *do* go to bourgeois schools; their ideas about what education is and what it is for and how it should be organised *are* the ideas embodied in their schools; there are no alternative, working class, 'educational' institutions; no notion of resisting education *as education*. And yet the evidence is that working class kids, do, to a greater or lesser extent resist something in the school system - how else explain the overwhelming evidence (that any teacher would confirm) that a school is a battleground, the pupils' weapons ranging from apathy through indiscipline to straight absence. And in this battle the school always is (precisely in terms of ideology) the loser. Every use of formal, repressive power reinforces working class experience of education as *imposition* (and not as a good-thing-that-will-extend-my-horizons-and-make-me-a-good-person); every (regular) experience of failure confirms the reality that "this place has *nuthin'* for me" (Corrigan, forthcoming).

The irony of this situation (something which most analysts miss) is that the kids' ideological resistance to bourgeois

235

education (i.e. their rejection of a set of norms and values) takes place in the context of and as *a result of* their incorporation in bourgeois institutions[5]. The point is actually an obvious one: working class *experience*, even of bourgeois institutions, is not bourgeois experience; the working class situation, even within bourgeois institutions, is not a bourgeois situation - this is the reality of class conflict (in *every* sphere of life) that seems to have vanished from functionalist analyses. To summarise this discussion with reference to youth culture (there are many other questions raised about education which we can't discuss here): youth culture must be understood as a response to the problems posed by a framework of *bourgeois* institutions but that response is the response from a *working class* experience of those institutions. The problem is to decide in what sense that response equals resistance and under what circumstances that resistance has *political* implications.

At present we just don't have the sort of knowledge on which clear answers to these questions can be based and we want to conclude, instead, by suggesting guidelines for the research that must now be done. Firstly, then, the political analysis of youth culture must focus on the culture's 'working classness' rather than on its youthfulness (just as the politics of education must focus on class and not just classroom relations). This is not to deny that young people are in a 'special' situation (largely because of their relative - and only relative - freedom from family and occupational ties) but *emphasising* this makes political analysis impossible. For a start it means exaggerating the differences between youth culture and its class context at the expense of the continuities. The concept of 'generation gap' (derived from theories of middle class youth) is inappropriate and incorrect for working class teenagers; even if they are involved with different *institutions* from their parents (schools etc.) all the evidence is that their response to them is based on similar *values*: if teenagers do act in 'non-adult' ways the adult response is still tolerance and encouragement - "boys will be boys", "have a good time while you can", "I wish I had your chances"[6]. And a focus on the youthfulness of youth culture means a focus on the psychological characteristics of young people - their adolescence, budding sexuality, individual uncertainties, and so on - at the expense of their sociological characteristics, their situation in the structure of the social relations of capitalism.

Working class young people are, in sociological terms, an actual and potential *labour force* and it is this (not their youth) which determines their social situation and structures their institutional relationships (and it is this which unifies their diverse experiences, links them to their elders and gives their culture its political potential). Our second rule for researchers is that all the relevant institutions must be *connected*

236

in sociological analysis, just as they are in working class experience. The reality of the teenage world is the *combination* of family and school and apprenticeship and job and police and courts and youth clubs and social workers and commerce and mass media, and it is this *combination* to which youth culture is a response - we should stop trying to isolate youth culture with respect only to commercial leisure *or* to the school *or* to the law. It is no accident that the institutional components of youth culture match the Althusserian list of State apparatuses (Althusser, 1971). Young people's experience is precisely the experience of the State's attempt (more strident than for their elders because their position is as yet less secure) to ensure their contribution to the reproduction of capitalism. It is in this context that the notion of resistance becomes possible: the question is not whether working class kids can remain independent of bourgeois institutions (they can't) but what is the nature of their 'dependence', what are its effects on the work of particular institutions on the one hand, and on the general process of reproduction on the other. The point we are stressing here is that it is the very 'overdetermination' of youth culture (the very intensity and variety of State battering that young people receive) that also determines the possibilities of resistance - we are thinking, for example, of the ways in which kids can use the symbols of pop culture as a source of collective power in their struggle with schools or police.

And that brings us to our final point (which we could make particularly for left theorists). There is no doubt that the symbols of commercial leisure (pop music, fashion) have a crucial role within youth culture[7] and the left have responded to this with a number of variations on the theme of "the corruption of the innocent". We have already suggested that young people are not, in this sense, innocent - they are already embedded in the institutional structure of capitalism - and we now want to query the notion of corruption. Certainly the agencies of pop culture (record companies and teenage magazine and clothes shops and so on) *exploit* young people (hardly a surprising aspect of capitalism); the question is to what extent they *manipulate* them. The picture the left offers is of teenagers as entirely passive consumers, buying, playing, acting just as commerce dictates, accepting the values that the media embody, stripped of any autonomous source of joy or creation or rebellion - by the time they are grown up these pop-corrupted teenagers are little more than sullen sheep[8]. This picture, vivid enough in the pages of *Marxism Today*[9] fades somewhat before the reality of West Ham's North End or a Slade concert. Are these exuberant, proud, belligerent, *solid* kids really best understood as pure consumers? The mindless creatures of commerce? Once again the distinction must be made between institutional and ideological incorporation - the fact that young people are heavily involved in commercial institutions does not mean that their response is simply a determined one; we need to know a lot more about the youthful audience's reaction to and use of the media, we cannot base our arguments simply on the intentions of the exploiters.

To summarise our argument: any political judgment of youth culture must be based on treating it first as a *working class* culture, secondly as a cultural response to a *combination* of institutions, and thirdly as a response which is as creative as it is determined. Our own, unsystematic, judgement is that even if youth culture is not political in the sense of being part of a class-conscious struggle for State power, it nevertheless, *does provide* a necessary pre-condition of such a struggle. Given the structural powerlessness of working class kids and given the amount of state pressure they have to absorb, we can only marvel at the fun and the strength of the culture that supports their survival as any sort of group at all. If the final question is how to build on that culture, how to organise it, transform resistance into rebellion, then that is the question which takes us out of youth culture and into the analysis of working class politics generally [10].

FOOTNOTES

1. The political analysis of youth culture has been horribly confused by the development since the mid-sixties of the 'counter-culture' of bourgeois youth. Both students and hippies are the objects of a sort of analysis which is inappropriate for working class teenagers (even if the distinction between the two groups is not as absolute as some writers - e.g., Graham Murdock - have suggested) and in this piece we therefore pay no attention to, for example, Blackburn and Cockburn (eds.), 1969, or Neville (1971). Work remains to be done on the relationship between the various youth groups.

2. The sociological literature on non-delinquent working class kids is sparse and tends to focus on particular aspects of their life only (e.g. in school *or* the transition from school to work *or* at play). The only attempt at a general analysis that we can think of is in Willmott (1969), an important book if only for its straightforward point that 'ordinary' working class youth culture is not bourgeois.

3. See Corrigan (forthcoming) or Frith (forthcoming-a).

4. This rather cryptic comment is a reference to a point that emerges in the Thompson/Anderson debate. A lot of the evidence that Thompson uses in his account of the *making* of the English working class is actually evidence of a work force struggling *not* to become a proletariat (i.e. disciplined, market-bound, labour power). This (heroic) struggle certainly fed into the culture that the English proletariat subsequently developed but it is important to stress that this working class didn't *create itself*, it was "made" (to use Thompson's important word) by the *struggle* between capitalist demands and workers' responses to these demands. In the Thompson/*NLR* debate the protagonists often take up positions which represent only one side of the dialectic (Thompson emphasising the workers' self-creation,

238

Anderson and Nairn emphasising their dependence on the bourgeoisie). The historian of education would make a similar mistake if he were simply to move from an over-emphasis on the bourgeois role in education to an over-emphasis on workers' self-help. It was part of the logic of capitalism that a work force be properly educated, but, the fact that resistance was therefore (and in that respect) futile is not to say that the struggle wasn't vitally important for the subsequent development of working class culture.

/ The main references for the Thompson/NLR debate are:- Thompson,E.P., 1963; Anderson, 1964; Nairn, 1964 a, b and c; Anderson, 1965a; Thompson, E.P., 1965; Anderson, 1965b; Poulantzas, 1966. /

5. The apparent contradiction of this situation is reflected in the very muddled state of left political thinking about education. On the one hand we have the organised working class political parties, Marxist and non-Marxist alike, *leading* the movements over the last hundred years to increase the State education that their children are daily resisting; on the other hand we have the less well organised, child-centred and 'libertarian' left treating schools as straightforwardly repressive, truants as revolutionary heroes and seeking to 'free' working class children from their education (c.f. the deschooling debate).

6. In a questionnaire survey of fifteen and sixteen year olds in Keighley (Yorks) in 1972 I discovered that most of the working class kids (unlike their middle class contemporaries) couldn't understand the notions of youth culture or generation gap, didn't think of themselves as being, in any significant sense, different from their parents. (SF)

7. The importance of pop music, in particular, has been confirmed (and never analysed) by every sociological study of young people since the late fifties and Mark Abrams's classic description of the teenage consumer has never been revised (1959).

8. This view of youth as passive participants in an imposed culture even underlies the more sophisticated theory of "deviancy amplification" - c.f., Stan Cohen's account of the Mods (1973).

9. For the most graphic example of this approach see John Boyd's contribution to *Marxism Today's* current debate on youth culture (1973).

10. In this piece we have (in common with almost every other writer on youth culture) ignored women - our notion of "the working class kid" is a male one. We have no excuse except ignorance - we know very little about the culture of teenage girls - but we don't want to conceal the serious political problems of working class sexism, adult and young.

Education: a chronology

Government policy and secondary school re-organisation

extension of tripartite system

limited comprehensive experiments: grammar schools safeguarded

push towards comprehensive schools – national policy (circular 10/65)

('57) Leics. plan established

CSE examinations begun ('65)

Major reports

('54) 'early leaving'

('59) Crowther: '15-18'

('63) Robbins: ' higher education'

('63) Newsom: 'half our future'

('67) Plowden: 'primary schools'

Public Scho Commission ('68-'70)

→ 570 EPA schools funded

→ action research on EPA's

'Liberal' thought and education policy

major concern with equality of access

much work in sociology of education on equality of opportunity and the social nature of selection

Pupil Action

('68) strike of pupils at Miles Platting

('69) national pupils meeting SAU formed

Playground violence reported

('68) knifing at Holloway school

Alternatives

and

under-ground education press

'libertarian ____ teacher'

Action by teachers and parents

'STOPP' ____

'WHERE' _____

'ACE' _____   education shops

left-wing teachers call for action on pay

govt pay offer

'Rank and File' formed

½ day strike ('69) by ILTA teachers

national campaign

Reaction

Risinghill closed ('65)

concern with 'standards'

'save our grammar schools' campaign

'Black Papers' ('69)

Haringey banding dispute

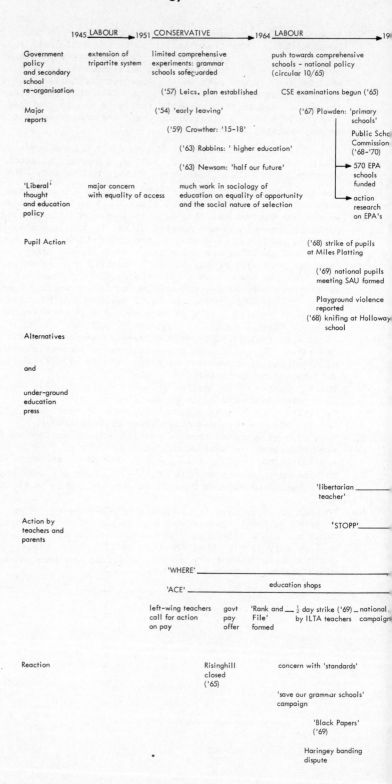

70 CONSERVATIVE ➤ 1974 LABOUR ➤

ove to comprehensivisation slows –
vernment policy change
ircular 10/70)

government policy again
pro-comprehensive
(circular 4/74)

Open University begins

E Mode III exams begun

('72) James: 'teacher
education'

('74) bullock:
'literacy

ROSLA

tion research ➤ ('72) Halsey reports on ➤ Midwinter sets ➤ community
educational priority up 'priority' schools
(liberal policies in education movement
have failed)

widespread strikes ('72)
NUSS formed

Childrens Rights
Conference ('71)

strike for Searle ('71)
over 'Stepney Words'

schooling literature ➤ Penguin Education Specials ➤ series ceases

ee schools started ➤ 30 free schools
hite Lion established by 1972
cotland Road ('71)

ternative educational experiments
school without walls': 'learning exchange':
un with learning')

'radical ➤
education'

'childrens' rights ➤
workshop

'Y-Front' ➤

'Hard Cheese' ➤

➤ 'libertarian education' ➤

'childrens rights'/'kids' 'teachers action ➤
ceases 1972 collective'

STOPP' ➤

port by ➤ 'teachers against ➤
Coard racism'

WHERE' ➤

ACE' ➤

ational campaign ➤ teachers strikes ➤ Scots teachers
n teachers pay strike ('74)
Oct–Dec

Chris Searle ➤ wins court
dismissed action ('72)

'Little Red School Book' Mackenzie suspended
seized

'black paper
Thatcher's 'cuts' three'

growing concern with ➤
violence

NAS report on LEA enquiry
violence ('72) into violence ('73)

race/intelligence truancy centres
debate set up

METHOD

NATURALISTIC RESEARCH INTO SUBCULTURES AND DEVIANCE

Brian Roberts

Apart from journalistic accounts, the study of sub-cultures has been, mainly, pursued within the framework of sociological inquiry rather than, say, within social history. But, for good and comprehensible reasons, the sociological study of 'deviant sub-cultures' has (like its subject-matter) been itself 'deviant' with respect to mainstream sociology. The 'mainstream' tradition in sociology is positivistic. It aims for an object-ive scientific completeness - 'science' here meaning not, as in the German, the serious, rigorous and systematic study of an area or phenomenon, but, more narrowly, a mode of inquiry as close as possible to what rather ill-informed social scientists believe are the methods of 'natural science'. The fact that this view of how natural science works is outdated, a nineteenth rather than a twentieth century conception, has not prevented sociology from pursuing what it has taken to be its true, if elusive, 'ultimate goal'. The reliance on quantification, the use of the analytic method, the adoption of an a-historical standpoint, the search for 'objective causality', are all part of this deeper philosophic quest - not for truth, but for a particular kind of certainty. The idea that societies are structurally-functioning 'wholes', integrated around a 'central value system' with a single social and moral order has also been part of that quest, though it has come to the fore with an overwhelming ideological force especially in the more recent period. Positivistic methods of inquiry, into societies concei-ved as functionally-integrated wholes, naturally find conflict and 'deviance' from the dominant norms and social order particularly perplexing, though Merton's attempts to harness the field to structural-functionalism must not be forgotten (Merton, 1968: 175-248).

The study of 'deviance' has, therefore, been associated with a rather different sociological tradition and perspective - one closer in some ways to the methods of investigation of ethnogra-phic anthropology than those of positivistic sociology. In America, where the great bulk of the work on subcultures has been done, the perspective adopted has been defined as Naturalism (see Matza, 1969); and the research practice employed has been, principally, that associated with the various forms and strategies of 'participant observation.' 'Naturalism' was pioneered by the Chicago School in the 1920's and 30's (see Faris, 1967); though less prominent in the 1940's and early 1950's, when Parsons and Merton dictated the field, it was considerably revived, with special reference to the areas of deviance, crime and delinquency, in the later 1950's and the 1960's.

In the simplest terms, and as its name implies, Participant Observation is carried out when the sociologist enters 'the field' to observe at close hand 'how it works'. He withdraws periodically to his research base, to set down his observations and conversations and draw from them conclusions about the nature of the phenomenon he has been studying. As George McCall and J. L. Simmons recognise (1969: 1), PO is a practice similar in many ways to that of a sophisticated newspaper reporter; and indeed, Chicago sociology owed much to the journalistic and 'muckraking' traditions, for several early Chicagoans - such as Robert Park - had been journalists (see Faris, 1967). This practice differs in certain crucial respects from the dominant forms of the sociological enterprise, and its practitioners have usually been aware of the differences. Much PO work has derived inspiration from a lineage of writers which includes George Simmel, Wilhelm Dilthey, John Dewey and George Herbert Mead[1]. All were liberal humanists with wide interests in 'the human sciences': they thus provide an alternative, less respectable tradition to that inaugurated by Auguste Comte, Frederic le Play, Emile Durkheim, Beatrice and Sidney Webb, and by behaviourist social psychology, which provided the positivist methodology of established social science[2]. But PO has never become a complete alternative to positivism in sociology. It has often been on the defensive, vis-a-vis the mainstream sociological enterprise; and it has sometimes, and in some respects, turned out to be standing rather awkwardly on some of the same ground. Good observation can lead to explanatory hypotheses: but it is not subject to the full discipline of 'control of variables' and 'replicability of design', the logic of hypothesis-testing, the quantitative tracing of 'objective' causal chains, which is demanded by the positive method. PO has never fully confronted the positive method on its own terms. Instead, it has formed a sort of sociological 'subculture' of its own: a more humanistic and 'empathic' enclave within the mainstream.

In the naturalistic perspective, research becomes not an objective study but an interchange through a shared language (not the 'scientific' variable-language: see Blumer 1956) between the observer and the people with whom he participates ('the hosts'). It is based on a Symbolic Interactionist social psychology, derived primarily from Mead (1934). It understands action as always informed by the giving and taking

of meaning.   Action is not behaviour, but 'meaningful action',
a meaning-loaded exchange between actors.   Naturalistic PO
research is also close to the approach of the social anthropologist who goes into a strange world and tries - by exploration,
observation and participation - to figure out how this world
works.   But whereas the anthropologist often really is a
stranger in the world of native culture, the 'field' into which
the modern PO ethnographer voyages may be as close at hand and
'familiar' - or unfamiliar - as another district of his own city.
The assimilation of PO to 'ethnography' changes the focus from
objectivity and quantification to 'empathic understanding'
(understanding from the inside, taking the perspective of the
native) and to qualitative work.   But the actual practice of
PO reflects a continuing lack of nerve before the demands of
positivism.   Thus PO has rarely been pursued in a rigorously
ethnographic and qualitative way.   In practice, it is, not a
single method, but a repertoire of methods, even including survey
techniques and statistics[3].   Most participant observers back up
observation with other, somewhat more 'objective' techniques.
PO is, then, a "blend or combination of methods and techniques"
(McCall and Simmons, eds., 1969:1) defined as much by the scale
and character of its subject-matter (primitive societies, deviant
sub-cultures, complex organisations, social movements, communities, informal small groups) as by its methods.

    Positive methods distance the researcher from the object of
inquiry and serve to neutralise his impact on the field.   PO
exploits the interchange between researcher and his field: in
some ways, the closer the better.   The observer must not only
get familiar enough to be able to reconstruct the field as the
'native' sees and experiences it: he must to some degree
'experience' it himself.   (In this sense, PO is by definition
closer in outlook to Weber's criterion of 'subjective meaning'
than to Durkheim's injunction to "treat social facts as things":
Its stress on 'experiencing' and sympathetic identification makes
it, fundamentally if not philosophically, phenomenological .)
But closeness has its costs.   How can one describe and define a
field without taking into account the impact of the researcher's
'participation' on it (his 'Hawthorne effect', so to speak)?
What are the ethical rules which allow him to distinguish between
observation and intervention?   What are the dangers of the
researcher 'going native'?   And can the results of his closeness
- a qualitatively full description - get beyond description, to
the level of 'science'?   PO lays a heavy burden of tact and
tactics on the researcher: empathy without identification,
understanding without 'being taken for a ride', rapport without
compromise.   In an odd way, the participant researcher, like
his positivistic colleague, also has problems about 'neutrality'
(though they are not the same as the problems positivism has
with 'scientific neutrality').   The Naturalist has assimilated

himself to Simmel's 'Stranger': he is *in* but not entirely *of* the culture. (See Wolff, ed., 1964: 127).

The advantages of PO lie in the quality of knowledge about the field which it yields. The researcher gets to know both the intimate surface of his 'field' and also how the real world runs under the surface. He picks up the 'informal' as well as the formal culture. He is sensitised to the experiential nuances of the native members. His approach is shaped by a *humanistic* affirmation of the reality and validity of lives and experiences other than his own - a humane belief in social *contact*. A less charitable view is that he is seduced into a vicarious, romantic attachment to 'other cultures'. This romantic trap is often tactically off-set by the adoption of a certain hard-boiled surface-style: the participant researcher is the man (and the image *is* characteristically male) who has looked 'real life' in the eye, the 'guy who's done the leg-work', the person who's 'seen it all'. Perhaps the fact that so much PO work has been done in Chicago has contributed to this 'private eye' image. But, as readers of Raymond Chandler will know, every private eye conceals, beneath his shoulder holster, a warm, romantic heart.

Chicago may also partly account for the fact that so much of the work of the Participant Observer has been done in the 'under-side' of city life - among outsiders (criminals, bohemians, drop-outs, hobos, delinquents, deviants and criminals). Something of the romance of the 'outsider' has undoubtedly rubbed off on him. And vice-versa. Becker's insight into the 'world' of the jazz musician owes much to the fact that he started life as a jazz pianist (Becker, 1963). Polsky was a veteran shooter of pool before he wrote his study of 'the pool-room hustler'. (Polsky, 1971). And so on. But the Chicago setting is really too simple and environmental an explanation. The fact is that, in requiring the researcher to situate himself, empathically, in the place of 'the other' and see life from that position, the method and perspective of PO optimally equip him to deliver to over-ground society the 'good news' about subterranean logic, the life and world-view of people and groups who view the over-ground society from 'under-ground'. The *appreciative* nature of his approach has made him the natural scientific ally of the Outsider - a sort of Inside Outsider.

The subject matter of Naturalistic inquiry is often exotic: but the treatment is often 'common-sensical'. What the scientific researcher sees as odd and deviant (from the point of view of the 'common value system') does not amaze and shock the 'Naturalists'. Not only is their practice 'naturalistic' (i.e. going into the natural environments of the city much neglected by other researchers), but their practice *naturalises*

246

the strange, the bizarre.   The best books in the tradition are so faithful to the life they describe that they seem to be mere naturalistic 'recreations' of it - sometimes provoking the response, 'what you've found out is what we've always known - why bother to write a book about it?'   Of course, pure Naturalism, in sociology as in art, is an illusion.   What the researcher sees and understands is a product of who he is, what assumptions he brings to his study, what bits he selects as important enough to describe, how he enters the field, what happens to him in his 'first days', whether he is lucky enough to meet a particularly sensitive and acute respondent or not, etc., etc.   But the ideal of Naturalism remains - to depict and describe faithfully, without distortion or preconception: to arrive at a faithful reflection of a social world.

More recently there has been an attempt to formulate the PO process more formally, to lay out protocols for the practice, to define the rules of the 'research act', or to show how 'grounded theory' can be squeezed out of a comparative treatment of ethnographies (see, for example, Glaser and Strauss, 1968; Denzin, 1970).   But these 'higher level' thematisations have not fully achieved the necessary task of making the researcher's framework and assumptions explicit, or of locating descriptions and ethnographies within the context of wider explanatory theories (not all of which, after all, need be positivistic). There are, of course theoretical difficulties about making a bridge between descriptively-full ethnography and more structural or functional or historical theories;   as social anthropology, which has been in this game much longer, knows only too well.   But there is also a sense that, being unwilling either to accept the framework offered by mainstream sociology, or to elaborate any alternative framework, Naturalism has side-stepped some of these larger questions.   This side-stepping, this strategic bracketing, is obvious even from some of the terms most commonly used in PO: for example, 'the field' (see Geer, 1969) with its implicit notion of a terrain with 'natural' boundaries, a well-defined setting (but how does 'the field' intersect with the other areas, say, of the city?).   Or 'world', with its implicit notion of an existential self-enclosed space (but what when the 'world' of the police intersects the 'world' of the hobo or the addict?).   Naturalism, of course, also owed its name to the Chicago School idea that the city was divided and organised into these rather distinct, ecological, areas, each with its own 'world' - almost natural social spaces, distinct from one another (see Faris, 1967, Park and Mackenzie, eds., 1967). Whatever are the reasons - and they are certainly complex - it is true that Naturalism has been better at investigating sympathetically the distinct 'worlds' of particular kinds of social outgroups than it has in defining what happens when 'worlds' with different resources and power at their disposal connect and

collide.   Of course, the typical subject-matter of Naturalism -
deviance, crime, delinquency - forced the key question of social
control on to the Naturalist's agenda.   But this has principally
been studied in terms of immediate and localised 'interactions'
with the control culture: the delinquent on the street-corner
and the social worker; the addict and the local cop; the hobo
and the welfare agency.   Only rarely, and recently, has Naturalism gone further up the scale of institutional power and the
hierarchy of credibility; or looked at the relation between the
poor and the powerful in structural as well as (or rather than)
inter-actional terms.   This has come to provide one of the
key turning points in the whole field (Cf: the Nicolaus (1969)
critique and the Becker (1967) - Gouldner (1968) exchange).   It
produced some crucial modifications in the field of Naturalism
itself (for example, the shift from an inter-actional to a
transactional approach, discussed below), as well as some more
personal conversions (e.g. Matza, 1969).   These have not stemmed
from certain internal contradictions in the logic of PO alone.
They were placed on the PO agenda by the shattering political
events in the US in the mid-1960's and one of the things these
events shattered most effectively was the *innocence* and *naivety*
of the early naturalistic perspective.

The last ten years has seen the emergence and growth, from
within the perspective of Naturalism, of a new sociology of
deviance, distinguished by the importance it places on one
particular kind of 'social interaction': that which is involved
in the exercise of social control.   Social groups don't simply
interact - they interact to some end.   And one of the most
salient 'ends' is the exercise of control by one group over
another, and through it, the maintenance and defence of the
social order.   This reintroduces the dimension of *power* into
what had sometimes appeared a power-less world of reciprocal
interactions.   Deviance or delinquency are now seen, not as
arising naturally from the world of the 'outsider', but as part
of an ascribed social identity, arising in the interaction
between groups which are unequal in the distribution of power.
The 'deviance' of a group is not 'natural' but the result of a
specific kind of social construction: and one of the key
mechanisms of this process is the power to define situations *for*
others, and the power to label others - and make those labels
stick.   The work *inter alia,* of Becker (1963; **ed., 1964),** **Goffman**
(1961; 1968), Erikson (1962), Kitsuse (1962) and Lemert (1967),
belong to this 'transactional' phase in the evolution of
Naturalism.   Labelling is understood as part of a process or
sequence of events.   Groups as well as individuals undergo
'careers'.   In these careers, the identities, self-conceptions
and commitments of groups and individuals are altered.
Depending on their dealings and transactions with other groups,
deviants can become more or less confirmed in their commitment

248

to a deviant career. A distinction is made between the original act (primary deviation) and the acts which follow once a deviant identity has been crystallised and stabilised through the ascription of a label (secondary deviation).

Labelling or transactional theory, while developing out of and preserving much of the spirit of earlier 'ethnographic' Naturalism, centres attention no longer on the internal world and processes of the group or field, but on the transactions (real and symbolic) between groups. It remains interactionist in the sense that the label and control by the powerful of the deviant is not treated as a 'structural' or behavioural input, but as a meaningful act or set of acts which is meaningfully interpreted and responded to by the deviant (e.g. fuller commitment to the deviance which has been ascribed to him). Control is understood as working by the making of 'rules': deviance, then, is action which breaks the rules defined and maintained by others. This does undermine the absolute authenticity of the 'field' common to earlier PO, since the field is now clearly structured by, and responding to, rules made for rather than by itself. Indeed, some critics have argued that this now locates deviance *too* much in terms of rule-breaking, too much in terms of the 'reaction' of social control agencies, and gives too little to the way the controlled subject or group sees the world from its point of view. Other critics argue that the 'labelling' perspective does not go far enough in terms of how transactions are themselves *framed* by history and by structures. Milton Mankoff has stated very clearly some of the deficiencies in the 'social reaction' perspective:

> Among the theoretical problems are the ... failure to consider the *continuing* effects of the social structural and psychological sources of initial rule-breaking in the development of career deviance, the lack of concern with the vulnerability of certain rule-breakers to self-labelling processes which may reduce the significance of *objective* labelling practices in determining deviant careers, and the related omission of any serious analysis of the types and severity of actual social sanction which facilitate 'successful' labelling. (1971: 216)

Others have gone further in trying to spell out how interactionism can be made compatible with a much wider social, structural and historical framework, thereby gaining explanatory power at the 'wider' as well as the more 'immediate' levels (e.g. Taylor, Walton and Young, 1973; 1975; see also the earlier critiques from various standpoints, by Akers, 1967 and Gibbs, 1966).

These developments in the American practice of sociological Naturalism have been reflected in Britain, above all (though by no means exclusively) in the work of the National Deviancy Conference (see Cohen, ed., 1971; Taylor and Taylor, eds., 1973; Rock and McIntosh, eds., 1974). This is the closest British sociologists came to setting up an institutional base

comparable to the American Society for the Study of Social
Problems, which has given American Naturalism a powerful presence.
Here, the attempt was made to develop this 'sceptical revolution'
theoretically, as well as to make empirical application of PO and
transactionalism to British cases. The American inspiration
was fairly direct and openly acknowledged within the NDC, though
its appearance in Britain at that time no doubt had other, more
deeply structural causes (the massive expansion in British
sociology in the 1950's, the need for people with a sociological
and social work 'background' in the expanded welfare-state,
administrative and managerial structures, the growth of social
protest movements - often related to social problems and deviancy
- in the 1960's, the rise of the student movements and the
'counter-culture'). The NDC was shaped by a group of sociologists
and criminologists fully committed to the 'sceptical' perspective;
it attracted not only young graduates and researchers, many of
whom were active in the student movement or in the counter-
culture, but also the various 'radical social work' organisations
and alternatives which sprang up in the wake of the birth of the
'Underground' (Case Con for radical social workers, Red Rat for
radical psychologists, Ass for radical lawyers; movements like
the new prisoners union, PROP, and the old but much reactivated
National Council for Civil Liberties). It provided a focus for
many diverse 'alternative sociologies' - neo-marxist, libertarian
as well as naturalistic and transactional in perspective. In
the NDC (as previously in the Chicago School days) the line
was once again blurred between sociological work and the worlds
of the deviant being studied. Jock Young, whose studies of
drug subcultures are a testimony to the fruitfulness of this
inside-outside relationship, has himself, ironically, called the
'deviancy/deviant sociologists' the "Zoo-Keepers of Deviance"
(1970). The main practitioners of the NDC certainly combined
several aims: the development of a critique of positivistic
sociology and criminology; good empirical research using PO and
transactional approaches; direct contact with and involvement in
the radical causes and constituencies closest to their concerns.
In his overview of the history of the NDC, Stan Cohen (1974) has
spoken of the problems posed for the radical sociologist in
finding "a way of staying in without selling out".   In its
earlier days the NDC was immensely productive and catalytic.
It conferences were well attended - forums for a whole range of
radical causes and groups rather than in any strict sense meetings
for professional sociologists - even radical ones.   In this
period, too, a number of key studies of an 'ethnographic' or
'transactionalist' kind were published as well as, from some
strands within the NDC milieu, attempts to shape up a fuller,
'alternative' criminological or sociological theory.   Inevitably,
however, the tensions and contradictions have become more obvious, and there has been some fragmentation, much separating out
into different strands, and a loss of direction and impetus.

It is worth looking at these further, since so much of the work of importance in deviance and subcultural theory was originated within the NDC 'umbrella'; but also because the contradictions are ones which are theoretical and methodological, as well as personal or social or political, and relate to questions of how most effectively further work in this area can be usefully pursued. Options for radical scholarship and political intervention do not simply *emerge*. The alternative strategies must be confronted and fought over, if that pioneer outpost which the NDC established is to provide a new base for solid advance, rather than mere field-commissions for its original troopers.

There seem to us, basically, three things at issue here. The first is a question of theory. Is a general theory - a theory of the whole social formation - generalisable or workable-up from its 'regional' development in the area of deviance, or from its earlier Naturalistic interactionist or transactional beginnings? What was won, what lost, what needs to be retained but modified, in what ways, as this shift from the ethnographies of deviance or the social control culture to the level of the social formation as a whole is made? Some work - by no means at any conclusive stage - has been done along these lines, and the 'critical criminologists' clearly hope that a 'political economy' of society can be developed out of some of the key points in the Naturalistic perspective. Their critics would argue that this is not possible without a *break* with the fundamental tenets of 'symbolic interactionism'. This debate - which seems to us absolutely pivotal for any further theoretical development of the field - has, unfortunately so far, remained at an implicit, largely 'personal' and *unorganised* level. The NDC owes it to itself, as well as to the promise it stimulated among those who have been influenced by its work, to take up again this quite central argument. It clearly has everything to do with the interface between symbolic interactionism, transactional theory and varieties of marxism.

The second issue is, then, the question of methods, which is more fully discussed by Steve Butters below. But methods cannot, ultimately, be divorced, either from theoretical perspectives, or, indeed, from the third issue, the question of interventions. What kinds of social and political intervention follow from, and are consistent with, the intellectual and theoretical practice? In some ways, while 'radical sociology' remained closely tied to the Naturalistic perspective, it inevitably followed that its strategies of intervention were most closely linked with the constituencies being studied - the politicisation and support of deviant, delinquent, criminal sub-cultures. There is a close 'fit' between a radical Naturalism and a certain kind of radical-libertarian intervention. But both the theoretical perspective and the historical climate

251

is changing.   What changes in the forms of intervention follow from these?   There is also the argument that an interventionist strategy cannot be 'attached' to an intellectual practice, so to speak, afterwards and from the outside, in this way.   Rather, the theoretical perspective must flow out of an active 'politics'.

FOOTNOTES

1.   For Simmel see Wolff (ed), 1964; for Dilthey see Rickman (ed), 1961, and Habermas, 1972 (chapters 7 and 8); for Dewey see Mills, 1966 (Part Four); and for Mead see Strauss (ed), 1965.

2.   For Comte see Andreski (ed), 1974: 137-198.   References and comments on the other contributors to the 'positivist tradition' may be found in Easthope, 1974 which provides a very useful bibliography.   Easthope has considerable sympathy with the 'positivists', which gives a restrictive slant to his chapter on Participant Observation and Life Histories.

3.   Following Herbert Blumer's attack on survey methodology (Blumer 1954 and 1956) Howard S. Becker and Blanche Geer sang the praises of participant observation as the method which yielded the most complete accounts of social events for any sociological study, (Becker and Geer, 1957).   They were slapped down in a reasoned reply by Martin Trow, co-author of big surveys on trade unionism, fascist-minded voters, and college students, - ("Every cobbler thinks leather is the only thing."   Trow, 1957); and they partially withdrew, allowing a place to survey methods. Subsequently, Becker developed a procedure for counting the weight of evidence in support of a PO hypothesis within field observational notes in a rule-of-thumb form which he called 'quasi'statistics': see Becker et al, 1961: 43-45 (reprinted in McCall and Simmons, 1969: 252-254).

written in collaboration with SH.

THE LOGIC-OF-ENQUIRY OF PARTICIPANT OBSERVATION
Steve Butters

INTRODUCTION

Work on subcultures at CCCS did not arise from any formal
investment in a sociological 'methodology'.   Paul Willis's study
of motorbike boys (1971), Dick Hebdige's account of subcultural
currents in Fulham (1974), represent an original working-through
of substantive issues, not the putting-on of a professional style
of research.   But, as the Subcultures Group developed its work
on delinquency, youth styles and 'the culture industry', questions about the logical status and consistency of Participant
Observation (PO) methods were placed on the agenda.   The trans-
mission, by the NDC and other agencies, of the writings of PO
practitioners from the USA inculcated something of a methodological conscience into students of subcultures: a group of texts
converged to provide some codification of fieldwork procedures
and analysis, associated with the practical PO achievements of
Howard S. Becker (1971), Norman Denzin(1970 and ed., 1970),
Herbert Gans (1963 and 1968), Blanche Geer (1964 and 1970),
Barney Glaser and Anselm Strauss (1965, 1968 and 1975), and
Leonard Schatzman (1973).   The range, and the limitations, of
this codification are exemplified in the authoritative 'Text and
Reader' of McCall and Simmons eds. (1969); while Denzin (1971)
indicates the organic connection of PO methodology with the
efforts to formulate systematically the theory of Symbolic
Interactionism made by Rose   (1962), Strauss (1959), Blumer
(1969) and Meltzer et al (1975).   Since the later Sixties,
there has been an increasingly confident suggestion that PO
practised under the aegis of Symbolic Interactionism constitutes
a 'Paradigm' of theory and methods to rival the positivist/
functionalist approach.   The aim of this article is to examine
in some detail the 'methodological rulebook' which has been
written for the 'Participant Observation Paradigm' (POP) and
discuss the points of tension arising from the implementation
of principles and rules, in the light of the assertion made by
Brian Roberts (above) that the opposition between positivist
sociology and POP is a very mediated one, involving the
contamination of the latter by the former.   As other parts
of this journal show, there has been a serious interest among
members of the Subcultures Group in the approaches of phenomenology, structuralism and historical materialism, in addition to
'naturalistic sociology'. My argument here is intended to assist,

in a ground-clearing way, in the continuing search for ways of incorporating the best features of documentary and PO methods within a new approach for the sociology of culture, less susceptible than earlier paradigms to 'ideological closure' of the field of enquiry.

I Empiricism and inductive methods

(a) POSITIVIST SOCIOLOGY AND THE NATURAL SCIENCE IDEAL

Many sociological textbooks offer an account of the 'general rules of empiricism' as a foundation for their argument: a recent example is Krausz and Miller (1974). The assumption is that there is a universal model of scientific procedure and reasoning, derived from the achievements of the physical sciences; and that the cultural or social sciences must find ways of formulating their problems which provide for the possibility of the same order of procedurally guaranteed certainty in the results of their enquiry. This is quite misleading, for there is raging controversy over the status of the presuppositions, metaphors and methods which inform the logic -of-enquiry of natural scientists. (For some interesting recent contributions, see Hindess, 1973a: 51-58 and Lecourt, 1975.) The notions of systematic theory based on a hierarchy of axioms and theorems within an architectural whole, and of testing hypotheses against the canons of classical logic, which are sometimes called in to legitimise sociological work, belong to a peculiarly hybridised 'philosophy of science' which joins rationalism with empiricism: they are in any case inappropriate to the kind of theorising which includes propositions like 'the more of x, the more frequent y', and 'the combination of p and q is often accompanied by a certain incidence of y'. A recent book by David and Judith Willer (1973) has documented some of the ways in which specific methodological myths lead sociologists to make unwarranted claims for the kind of knowledge which vulgar positivist methods produce under the banner of 'scientific empiricism'. These include:

(i) The idea that there is 'out there' an objective social reality which has the ability to represent itself directly to the experience of a clear-minded and careful observer. (It is the 'representing' which is problematical.)
(ii) The idea that scientific knowledge is produced by a Subject (the scientist) who addresses his attention to a really-existing Object *about which* he theorises in terms which include a convenient name-for-the-Object. (More sophisticated philosophers, such as Bachelard - see Lecourt, 1975 - recognise that the scientist tries to *make* some of the forms in which he wants to represent the phenomenal world, not just *register* pre-given forms.)

254

(iii)   An account of how 'induction' works, as the reasoning
technique upon which scientific study and theorising of
every kind depends: this account originates from John Stuart
Mill, to whom Willer and Willer devote a chapter.   What
Mill called the "hypothetico-deductive method" involves
both deduction (predicting events which should follow from
certain starting conditions and rules) and induction (infer-
ring from observed events that a hypothesis has been
exemplified or borne out, given the validity of certain rules);
but the general direction of empiricist enquiry he characterised as inductive.

Willer and Willer show that when sociologists put their faith
and practice at the disposal of these myths, their work often
resolves into a search for economical ways of summarising
descriptions of social organisation and cultural form; and that
truly theoretical work requires that a mode of reasoning different
from induction be brought into play during the analysis and
criticism of empirical 'facts'.   Brian Roberts has indicated
above that PO was sponsored by the Naturalist revolt against
vulgar positivism: it remains to examine how successful PO
practitioners have been in their search for a logic-of-enquiry
which breaks with the deeper-lying 'general rules of empiricism'
for which positivist sociology provides only one style of implementation.

(b)   ALTERNATIVE MODELS OF SOCIOLOGICAL ENQUIRY

I am going to concentrate on the moment of *analysis of data*
in this brief round-up of the modes of reasoning which have
served the purposes of qualitative sociological research.
This runs parallel with the third of the myths listed, to the
effect that inductive reasoning = scientific method.   Of course,
definitions of phenomena and their world, and conceptions of the
process of empirical investigation should also be treated in any
thorough review of logics of enquiry, but I shall touch on them
only tangentially.   Here I present four alternative types of
analytic strategy, and comment on the mode of reasoning through
which each is mobilised:

Type I: "Appreciative understanding"

Classical social anthropology based its theorising on the
preliminary organisation of fieldwork data in *ethnographic
description* which "mapped" the meanings of custom, role and
social structure within a presumed closed cultural system.
PO research still produces much ethnographic description;
but its keynote has shifted to a more 'phenomenological' register, in which the texture of symbolic exchange is highlighted
in order to display the practical commitment of individuals to
making their own sense out of their social encounters.   The

255

quest for appreciative understanding of 'lived meanings' in subcultural situations is not purely arbitrary: Bruyn (1966) has explicated some of the techniques involved in this form of induction. But this style of reasoning contains strong 'intuitive' elements, and does not lead of itself to the production of a theoretical analysis.

Type II: Analytic induction

Alfred Lindesmith (1947) believed that opiate addiction was a phenomenon so 'crystallised' that drug-users' careers could be analysed to yield high-level generalisations about the properties of opiate-using as a cultural form. Employing Znaniecki's strategy (Znaniecki, 1972) of analytic induction, he tried to abstract out from local contexts the main patterns of hard-drug using behaviour, while - he hoped - preserving significant subcultural variants, and by trial-and-error elaborated partial models of the cultural features of addiction. He then had to reconcile all his partial models or hypotheses to one another, and to all the data: if any contrary evidence emerged, the relevant model had to be changed to account for it. The end result was a welding together of all his remaining propositions into a rather tortuous 'total hypothesis': an explanatory account, loaded with qualifications and detours, of the real character of the phenomenon. This inductive strategy combines the systematic coding and mapping of evidence with a more creative scanning of the data in the search for plausible and testable sub-models. Its disadvantages (definitively discussed in Turner, 1953) are that it can work only on a restricted number of sociological problems; and, more seriously, that it does not generate true 'universals' vested in a scientific theory, but only a perspectivisation and patterning of widely observed 'facts' of certain cultural forms.

Type III: The constant comparative method

This analytic strategy also seeks to generate widely-applicable models by coding and scanning data in order to build up clusters of hypotheses. But here the purposes of systematic comparison are more clearly spelled-out, and are integrated with the strategy for collecting and coding observations in the PO fieldwork. The assumption is that selecting contexts in which to seek significant data within a problem-area can be best guided by the emergent analysis, which is produced concurrently with fieldwork note-taking and reflection. There is a spiral process of "theoretical sampling" (as opposed to statistical sampling) of locales and events; recording and coding observations; writing trial hypotheses into "analytic memos"; and providing for more detailed and focussed comparisons of data with data, and data with concept or hypothesis, through further, and now more sociologically-informed sampling.

The categories of social type, interpersonal transaction and ideological form which are thus identified must now be cross-compared, and related to their place of residence within esta-blished patterns of social organisation: this is the task of the method of constant comparisons, as explained by Glaser (1965). The focus is always on the difference made by the introduction of a new analytic dimension to the relations between sub-groups of incidents, persons or social forms, given that the distinc-tions imposed by this new dimension will cross-cut and regroup them. The procedure and its logic are very similar to those developed by Paul Lazarsfeld for the 'multivariate analysis' of survey statistical data (see Lazarsfeld et al, eds, 1972: 119-217). But it is addressed specifically to qualitative data because Glaser and Strauss (1968), its authors, are concerned to avoid pre-selecting ready-defined 'variables', before the enquiry has entered the field. The method is oriented towards generating hypotheses ('discovering grounded theory') rather than testing them.

The strategy looks towards the establishment of law-like generalisations about cultural forms within narrowly limited social and historical locations. These generalisations are not obtained immediately, but only after the revision and hierarchical organisation of a series of provisional hypotheses or partial models. Its mode of analytic inference falls close to that which C. S. Pierce characterised as *abduction* (see Habermas, 1972: 334): starting with a surprising result (an anomalous incident), the analyst searches for a rule (sociologi-cal hypothesis or model) which will explain the case (incident plus the already-understood context). But, as Habermas points out, there is considerable doubt as to how abduction really works.

Type IV: The progressive-regressive method

An important weakness of the constant comparative method is that it fails to acknowledge the ways in which pre-given theory provides a framework of rules for analysing: Glaser and Strauss's theorising cannot be independent of syntax and stylistics. Jean-Paul Sartre (1963) confronts this problem with respect to marxist cultural studies. He notes that the marxism of Stalin's day selected materials for study solely for their (presumed) capacity to illustrate the dialectical laws of historical materialism. Critical enquiry was restricted to speculation about the variant forms of expression of these laws in different cultural-historical contexts. This 'placing' of phenomena within theory he dubs the *regressive* moment of analysis; but he acknowledges it as a necessary moment, since

257

topics have to be selected according to theoretical preferences within the limitations of the current state of theory. But once the analysis has entered into a concrete engagement with the phenomenon, to which the analyst must freely submit his sensibility, the movement shifts to a *progressive* tracing of the causal and cultural connections ("mediations") between human experience and the social processes which go on behind the backs of us all.

By questioning the provenance and pertinence of more and more determinations of a phenomenon, this tracing of mediations constantly re-opens issues which the starting theory pigeonholed. The ensuing knowledge of levels and types of mediation first enriches, then - in a new regressive movement - restructures the theory. Sartre's programme for cultural studies requires a mode of reasoning which will sustain repeated movements between progressive and regressive analysis: this is the theme of his major (unfinished) methodological work (Sartre, 1960). His method is founded on a 'historicist' conception of the inter-play of contradictory cultural forces which stresses the heuristic value of moments of refusal of the dominant meanings of a social order. Whereas the constant comparative method treats such moments even-handedly as part of the pattern of human organisation, Sartre's analytic strategy assumes that cultural forms and social forces are related to one another a-symmetrically. I will return to the discussion of this 'break' between the two analytic modes in a later section.

2 Some general principles of naturalistic field research

Field research is an 'umbrella' of activities united by the perspective and spirit in which the research strategy is thought. The PO researcher must be, says Schatzman (1973: 14), "a pragmatist, all the more so because he is not constrained to articulate in advance a specific technique or a specific problem." This view of the open-ended character of field research is more radical than that of pragmatism's classical spokesman, John Dewey (1938), who simply explored the quasi-experimental features of all enquiry. It acknowledges - and embraces - the psycho-social dynamics of researcher-host relationships. It permits the observer to help along the processes he is studying, or even deflect them. It requires the researcher to draw out the private meanings of the host's experience by empathically appropriating them to his own consciousness. It encourages the student of subcultures and deviance to submit his own character to the re-socialising agency of ethnographic study, to re-write himself with the articulation of his analysis. I shall note here just a few selected 'general principles' of method within the naturalistic orientation, under headings that refer to 'stages' in the research trajectory: but bear in mind

258

that the stages are not fixed steps in an unalterable sequence. The remaining sections of this article examine some of the rules of method through which these general principles are implemented, according to my reconstruction of the POP primer.

(a)   *Making fieldwork relationships*: Relationships with hosts have to be negotiated in an open and reciprocal fashion, in which the researcher will give some account of his identity and purposes.   But the effort put into the negotiation of a particular relationship will depend on the plan for 'theoretical sampling', and the estimated fruitfulness (in amount and quality of data) of contact with a prospective informant.

(b)   *Working up the research plan*:   The researcher should enter the field with a definite conception of the topic(s) available to him, and their sociological interest; but the focus and strategy of the fieldwork must be evolved through exploration of the patterning and properties of field incidents, and attentiveness to hosts' accounts of what in their situations is problematical to them.

(c)   *Managing fieldwork processes*: The researcher must handle his field encounters and relationships so as to ensure a manageable combination of the instrumental (using the flow of data to help him generate hypotheses), the interventionary (setting up new situations to illuminate or catalyse a natural-setting process), and the merely sociable (making friends out of 'hosts'):   the humanistic code requires that all three be essayed.

(d)   *Analysing qualitative data*: The analytical phase is directed towards the production of coherent, defensible theory: it will therefore exert some retroactive control over the pragmatism of the PO fieldwork style.   When the researcher is confident, within his own perspective, that the emergent theory is cogent and adequately grounded in the factual content of the data, he will conclude his analysis; and - whenever possible - publish it fully, without showing fear or favour to the parties which might wish to exploit or suppress it.

3 Strategy for entering

W. F. Whyte's famous Appendix to *Street Corner Society* (1955) shows how much power lies with the first field relationships, to make or break the research; and Herbert Gans (1968) testifies to the continuing difficulty of this moment in a PO project. Once the research topic has been defined (and we will return to this in the next section) the negotiation of access to people, places and information determines much of the research.   This negotiation depends on the researcher's competence in

(i) casing the joint; (ii) assuming an appropriate master-role;
(iii) predicting the main variants of the master-role he needs
to deploy and (iv) preparing cover-stories which can be
traded with the accounts of "hosts" in getting to know individuals personally.

(i)   Schatzman (1973: 19-21) tells us that joint casing is done
to produce judgements about sites for observing (which are the
best pubs for listening to homosexual *argot* in London?); about
the feasibility of tasks (how much dancing ability is expected
of the taxi-dance hall client?); and about the suitability of
entry ploys (can a hospital be entered through its director?
Or a religious sect through its leadership?).   The techniques
for joint-casing derive largely from the obvious analogies with
the practice of private-eyes, conmen and other allied trades:
the main requirement is that the researcher develop a nose for
workable field situations, rich in materials, and offering
openings for the decoding of host language systems.   (Worka-
bility has to be related to the overall research strategy, which
is discussed in the next section.)

(ii)   Buford Junker has characterised the four "master roles"
for PO research, and these are clearly summarised by Raymond
Gold (1958).   The *pure observer* stands on the sidelines and
passively records the scene from a safe distance.   The *observer-
as-participant* engages in brief encounters with host subjects,
but he departs from the rules of 'focussed interviewing' by
suggesting a more positively affective and flexible conversation/
relationship, making his 'interview' open to development to an
undetermined degree.   The *participant-as-observer* plunges more
boldly into the action.   He joins with his subjects in some
common enterprise, and also tries to allow them some participation in his research enterprise.   The limiting case of this role
is in classic social anthropologist fieldwork where the whole
framework of host-group norms, roles and beliefs circumscribes
the researcher.   He must, however, preserve his estrangement
from his hosts' "vocabulary of motives" so as to prevent
himself losing control over fieldwork strategy.   (Albert Reiss,
1968, gives an account of an observer at a precinct police-
station who 'went native' to the point of demanding to be allowed
to work over the next negro suspect brought in for questioning.)
The *complete participant* is a surreptitious investigator,
secretly observing and recording on the sly.   Serious difficulties attend this role; and it clearly overlaps with another mode
of research, involving the writing of one's own life history
within a cultural studies perspective.

(iii)   Various theoretical, practical and ethical criteria bear
upon the selection of a master-role; but once chosen, the possible variant ways of playing it have to be attended to.   These
will follow from the *types of informant* which the researcher
constructs on the basis of his early 'mapping' work.
John Dean et al (1967) offer a taxonomy which includes the

naive informant, who will tell you all he knows, for what it's worth; the politically frustrated (the out-of-office); the old hand; the dogsbody; and the neurotic greedy for conversational recognition. The competent PO researcher can manipulate each type's responses to his own self-presentation, if he understands the basic principles of role-playing (see E. Goffman 1959, 1963 and 1969).

(iv) Cover-story tactics have to be *tested*: they are best tried out first in rehearsals of lines of conduct with hosts not crucial to the main access issues. Where the researcher infers from the tone of his transactions that 'good rapport' has been established in these dry runs, he will retain those aspects of his cover (e.g. versions of his past biography) which seem to have contributed most positively. This is very much a 'commonsense competence'.

The logical problems of the entry phase whose techniques we have sketched arise from the problematical character of 'the access bargain': what is being traded for what, when the researcher gives incentives for his hosts to allow him sufficient field access to explore the inner connections of the phenomena which interest him? The central practical dilemma is this:

> "The field researcher needs to create situations which invite visibility and disclosure for others" (Schatzman, 1973) while conserving the indeterminacy of his own role, so as to allow scope for further influencing others' orientations to him; how can he close the deal on access without being tied down at later stages by obligations arising from his side of the entry bargain?

The rules which enable him to traverse this dilemma are drawn from the armoury of Symbolic Interactionist knowledge. He must try to persuade others to fall into role-*taking* behaviour while he undertakes role-*making*, during the four phases of role development outlined by Ralph Turner (1962). This entails working on the separation of 'researcher roles' from 'life roles' so as to maintain ego-detachment and instrumentality as the researcher's primary mode of consciousness: see Olesen and Whittaker (1967). He must preserve freedom to manoeuvre in his self-presentation by suggesting - through dress and demeanour - a marginal social status for himself, halfway between bureaucratic office holder and card-carrying subculture member ("research student" often does nicely). He must bargain for access one stage at a time, always showing concern for hosts' feelings, so that they will gradually relax

261

their interdiction on information about their private affairs. Restrictions accepted initially must be understood as "renegotiable at later, more propitious times" (Schatzman, 1973). The logical skills required in the implementation of these rules are of a zero-sum-game-playing order. Ned Polsky acknowledges the overlaps between his occupational skills as a sociologist and those of his subjects in his study of pool-room hustlers, although he vigorously denies the suggestion that his immersion in the field made him more of a con-man than a social scientist (Polsky 1971: 115-147).

Commentary

The status of the competences implied by these rules seems fairly obvious, in view of their parentage. Instrumental pragmatism is in command. Goffman's dramaturgical perspective reminds the researcher of the role preparation to be done in, "the back room" and the stratagems for controlling self-presentation "on stage" (see Messinger, 1962). Scheff's account of the ways in which professionals retain the initiative in negotiating "definitions of reality" with their clients reveals the pertinence of power in the negotiation of moral and epistemological order (Scheff, 1968). But these "background relevances" suggest the crucial importance of *metaphor* in shaping our understanding of what is at stake in the researcher's rule-following, both practically and philosophically. *Two* metaphors collide in this account of "strategy for entering the field". The *strategic interaction* metaphor reminds us that the hosts have powers of discretion and initiative too (otherwise no access problems) and that they may win some rounds in the poker game, through counter-strategies within access bargaining: the analogy is with the crime scene, in which quite a proportion of wrong-doing is not detected and 'solved'. Erving Goffman's discussion (Goffman, 1969) begs the question of what conditions enable one party to a set of knowledge-trading transactions consistently to make a profit, as the CIA has generally done in South America; but his games-theory orientation allows only for the contingent maintenance of a 'winning streak'. Alternatively the *surplus appropriation* metaphor provides a much more complete account of how, within a formal system of encounter and exchange, one party may *without risk of failure* ensure the creation and realisation of the 'surplus product'. M. Godelier (1966) shows how Levi-Strauss's analysis of the exchange of women through aboriginal kinship systems and Marx's analysis of the exchange of living labour-power against the dead labour of wage-commodities are analogous in form. The making and mobilising of researcher-host relationships seems to be of the same order, which explains the close attention paid by POP methodologists to the problems of entry: the rules dealing with the central dilemma of access bargaining (how to profit from a fair exchange of cultural sign/commodities) are as important to PO research as the rules of book-keeping are to capitalism. This is

262

not intended as a conclusive moral criticism, for it is difficult
to see how any progressive development of knowledge in the human
sciences can avoid founding itself on such structural 'unequal
exchange'. My point is rather that the interactionist metaphor
fails to explicate the deeper process behind PO access-bargaining;
and this failure suggests that PO research has a mystified
consciousness of its own practice.

4 Strategy for developing the research design

Socio-cultural studies have few axioms or theorems already
generally accepted, and no standardised canons for testing
hypotheses which claim to resolve outstanding theoretical
'puzzles' in Kuhnian fashion[1]. POP trades on this absence of
'normal science' by asserting that:

(a)   the suggestion of plausible, data-related hypotheses,
preferably within a group of simultaneously-presented and
linked hypotheses, is far more worthwhile than meticulous
testing of existing ideas;

(b)   the cogency or credibility of hypotheses generated
through the joint collection, coding and analysis of
qualitative data may be esteemed (under certain conditions)
just as highly as scientifically verified ones.

On these premises, POP prescribes that the place for formulating
the details of research design should be a movable feast, and in
any case, some way into the pathway of the research process.   Only
when the research plan grows out of the exploration of new empirical terrain, and then modifies itself in the light of emergent
fieldwork insights, can we attain reflexive sensitivity to the
reality of the phenomena being addressed.   So the researcher's
first days in the field must be spent on mapping exercises which
will determine the design decisisons: where to go, what to look
for, whom to relate with.   Glaser and Strauss (1968) argue that
these decisions must encourage the constant searching-out of
suitable sites for exploring the properties or dimensions of the
categories whose preliminary definitions frame the research topic.
Some categories will be taken from everyday experience - e.g.
Jock Young's (1972) marijuana busts - while others will derive
from scientific discourse ("collective paranoia").   The process
which the evolving design commands is called theoretical sampling,
which leads in turn to the method of constant comparisons in the
analysis phase.   Since design, data-collection, coding and
analysis are all interpenetrative, new comparative samples of events or personal accounts or documents can be written into the
design at any point where the elaboration of the piecemeal-
constructed analysis suggest a need for corroboration.
The central dilemma for the research design is this:

Commitment to certain sensitising concepts, and to hunch-hypotheses about the working of their properties, determines the trajectory of the search for comparable data. How can the researcher avoid using his first days in the field as a way of convincing himself that his hunches are taking him along the right track?

The standard gloss on the first days in the field is that they provide culture shocks and stimulate acute phenomenological aware- ness so that the researcher is drawn almost unconsciously to penetrate the commonsense or in-group accounts of interaction- events, and to pose upsetting questions on what is going on.   In a classic article, Blanch Geer (1964) conducts a tour of her first three weeks' field notes (and some of her colleagues') from a PO study of student life at Kansas State University.   The research began with the assumption that a middle-class, mid-western campus would be governed by the social convention that university was a necessary port of call for young people who would only become serious about their everyday activities when they settled to a job: but notes from interviews, participant observation and official briefings during the Freshmen's Conference led to a discussion of the dimensions of student seriousness about being at university: academic competition for grades was found to be a central point of reference and negotiation for every type of student.   This insight, together with further ideas about methods, which were crystallised in the "analytic recess" after the hectic first days period, set the course for the rest of the research. The study turned into a critical account of the campus system of academic stratification and its effects, which concluded with a policy recommendation that grading be abolished altogether.

The basic rules for handling our dilemma seem to be: (1) always use the experience of first days in the field as a resource for overhauling preliminary ideas about the research problem itself, as well as the nature and possible sources of data; and (2) em- ploy the device of theoretical sampling in order to ensure the fitting of conceptual categories with evidence of their empiri- cal forms of manifestation, and with categories which may be related with them, through the development of further hypotheses. Explicit coding is an important aid in the second process.   As the researcher discovers new properties of his concepts, or new links between phenomena, he works through his field notes, scan- ning the observational notes and theoretical notes for further samples.   Items in the notes may therefore be coded and recoded, and the whole coding apparatus moves along with the emerging analytic scheme: so clearly it is important that the notes taken during first days be sufficiently extensive to allow for fairly elaborate coding.

But the accounts of Glaser and Strauss (1968) Becker (1958)
and Geer (1964) leave doubt about how far research designs are
ever criticised in ways which invoke a change of perspective on
the problem area they start with. Most work on the labelling
of subcultural deviance has failed to look for, let alone produce,
an account of where the labels come from which goes beyond Becker's
early notion of "moral entrepreneurs". Probably the tasks of
design and constant comparison are implicitly understood by POP
researchers as tightly constrained within a well-established
repertoire of perspectives and imagery. Certainly,Geer's student
study, once it had shifted its focus onto academic work and
grading, generated a very predictable analysis, in which labelling of students by lecturers was accounted solely in terms of the
negotiation of tasks and criteria within a system which allows
the academics to retain the initiative: the larger questions
of the sociology of academic knowledge and of intellectual
experience were left untouched.

5 Managing fieldwork processes

PO fieldwork imposes on the researcher three sets of require-
ments:
(i)   He has to maintain an impressionability of outlook, and an
accessibility to insight, against the grain of the tendency to
routinise established PO work. He may do this simply by practi-
sing a childlike "open gaze" of attentiveness; or by repeatedly
shifting his observational site; or by taking every opportunity
to imaginatively "take the role" of the others he encounters.
(2)   He must constantly develop his "grounds for watching" what
he is working on, so as to discover more in it, or alongside it.
He may do this by regularly considering: (a) whether he needs to
flesh-out concepts by spending more time on looking for their
properties; (b) whether he has come across a person or situation
which needs to be referred back to some previous observation;
(c) whether he has a clear rationale for looking at events, in
terms of an appropriate perspective which will help to characterise them; (d) whether he needs to firm up a 'theoretical lead' by
changing the focus and purpose of his PO; and (e) whether he
needs to move quickly to the precise formulation of a hypothesis
or model, and then drop other work in favour of a systematic
search for confirming evidence (and possible disconfirming
evidence). Schatzman (1973: 53-58) presents a clear account
of the reasons for moving from one to another of these grounds
for watching in various phases of fieldwork; but remarks that
knowing when to shift emphasis is, in the end, a matter of the
researcher's judgement.

(3)   He must find tactics by which to implement his basic
master role. Within the participant-as-observer role, for
example, he may choose "limited interaction" waiting until

invited to get further into the action of conversation; or
he may use his "tolerated" position to engage hosts in a
tightly-controlled interview. Which he tries depends on his
judgement of the potentialities of a situation, in the light
of the overall plan: Donald Roy (1970) describes how he moved
from one to another during a PO study of a trade union recruiting
campaign.

But while experienced fieldworkers have a sense of how to
change pace, and when to deploy their imagination so as to
integrate disparate pieces of observational work, there remains
a major dilemma for all fieldwork management:

How can the researcher test and judge the validity and
originality of his "partial models" or hypotheses while he
is enclosed within his fieldwork strategy and perspective?

The implications of this dilemma run far. The presence of the
observer may have one of a number of types of disturbance-effect
on the hosts: he may (in their view) be incorporated as a useful
supernumary; he may be bracketed as a distrusted nuisance (but
thus available to the lonely and disaffected); he may become a
passive catalyst encouraging conversation previously suppressed;
he may play an interventionary role, leading new action; and he
may become a storm-centre for dissent and strife, with catastro-
phic effects on the scientific purposes of the research. The
textbooks offer little advice on the management of these forms
of "disturbance" once initiated: they simply require that
field researchers should lie on the beds they make for themselves.
"The paradoxical issue of change and not-change .... should pre-
occupy neither us nor our model fieldworker. The latter ... has
no other recourse than to act as a field researcher might be expected to act ..." (Schatzman, 1973: 64). But even if this were
true, the researcher must use his awareness of field contingencies
to guide an internal calculus of researcher-effects on the action-
scene, both to judge how things would have been if undisturbed,
and to use the observed results of his intervention as though
these were the data of an experimental investigation. The logic
of such a calculus should be crucial to the process of data-
collection, coding and analysis; yet there seems to have been
little advance in this methodological sector since Weber discussed
the logic by which historians might assess the effects of the
Battle of Marathon (Weber, 1949: 171-174).

The procedural means which have been explicitly provided for
gaining some critical distance from the interpretative hurly-burly
of fieldwork lie in the area of recording field observations and
reflections, and organising fieldwork notes. Fieldwork notes

266

are the medium through which the dialectic of involvement and detachment is played through. The more notes written, the more detachment is possible, through the later scanning and checking of observations and codings. In a team project, exchange and criticism of the daily field notes form the principal ground of development of research strategy. Extensive fieldwork is always punctuated by "methodological recesses" in which researchers go into conference, circulate and debate "analytic memos", and review alternative programmes for linking up their hypotheses and data-patterns. Schatzman illustrates the different slants of three kinds of field note: *Observational*, *Methodological*, and *Theoretical*, and shows how each contributes to later analytical work. Glaser and Strauss (1975) have recently published detailed instructions on how to write an analytic memo, and how to use it to reshape fieldwork activities.

Commentary.

The crux of the process of 'objectifying' field experiences is the de-construction of the role-making and meaning-exchanges which were achieved in the synthesising negotiation of fieldwork encounters. The researcher must *abstract* from these experiences knowledge of social processes (or knowledge of how to address their forms of appearance). He does this by 'wrapping up' what he got out of encounters with hosts - in his role as social scientist - in a tightly-worded package. Schatzman says: "The package is so prepared as later to be scanned and comprehended at a glance .... The recorder disciplines himself to think in terms of *units of information,* whatever their content" (1973). Although the logic of recording, coding and scanning has still not been explicated, we can now see its essential operative condition: the ambiguous and thought-provoking character of field encounters must be *reduced* to units of information which have a specific content, a directional value for the constant comparisons of the research plan. This is the point within POP research at which the freewheeling, humanistic pragmatism of Mead and Dewey has to settle accounts with the rationalism of the nineteenth-century natural science tradition. It is at this point that the logic of inductive reasoning is firmed-up to meet the criteria of J. S. Mill's hypothetico-deductive method, securely anchored in the procedures of syllogistic demonstration and experimental proof (see Willer and Willer, 1973: ch. 4).

6 Analysing qualitative data

Analysis always involves the re-organisation of propositions which already include an interpretation, a re-presentation of the forms of social reality; for it would be impossible within the field of sociocultural studies to avoid using and extending the currency of metaphorical 'ways of seeing'. What is at issue

here? It is the question of whether a particular strategy for
analysis of PO data is likely to generate a theoretical account
which gives the reader a view of the relations between and
beneath the cultural forms in which the metaphorical discourse
is *either* shriven, *or* securely appropriated to a rigorous language
-for-theorising. The four types of analytical reasoning identified in Part 1 offer three variant responses to this question.
Firstly, appreciative understanding explicitly aims to preserve
the metaphorical texture of cultural forms in their original
quality, reflecting as far as possible the manner in which they
are lived by their subjects. The analytic process is necessary
even here, but it limits its objectives to the *finding of patterns*
in the data, so that the researcher's PO materials may be presented in a form which is ethnographically cogent: the metaphors and
images of the host culture (or subculture) are regrouped, but
remain untranslated. Secondly, the researcher may seek to impose
a master metaphor on those indigenous to his material: this is
the strategy of *building models* to which both analytic induction
and constant comparisons belong. Analytic induction's commitment
to the construction of a closed and unitary model which accounts
for supposedly universal features of a cultural phenomenon makes
of its strategy a limiting case which (in view of Turner's 1953
critique) I will leave aside. I will examine the strategy of
constant comparisons to elucidate the main steps in the model-
building process, and criticise the arbitrary relationship between
the "grounded theory" model it produces, and the model's "domain of
interpretation". Thirdly, I will argue that one possible interpretation of Sartre's progressive-regressive strategy entails
searching for structural/historical mediations, a mode of analysis
which might enable us to surpass some of the contradictions of the
constant comparative method.

All four types of analytic strategy face the same central dilemma; although the first denies its premise, and refuses a relation to the unobservable elements of social reality (see H. S.
Becker, 1971: v-vi). The dilemma is this:

Given that the analyst must subsume observational
statements within the propositions of a theoretical account
of the inward relations of cultural forms, how should he
conserve and display his grasp on the concrete properties
of social scenes which are imprinted on his data?

a.   THE CONSTANT COMPARATIVE METHOD

Glaser and Strauss first presented their strategy in an article
(1965) which stressed the speed at which research could move
through the comparison of groups, when these were specially

268

selected to yield categories for particular model-building purposes, and the 'credibility' which constant comparisons gave to hypotheses generated through joint collection, coding and analysis of data. Their later book (1968) gives a more extended account of the rationals for theoretical sampling of groups and incidents; and also tries to codify the main tasks of the analysis stage. In a recent sequel (1975) they show how the practicalities of fieldwork and memo-writing are governed by the requirements of their analytic strategy. Key terms in their accounts are "properties" and "linkages". First days in the field focus the research on sensitising concepts which lead the researcher to posit the effective existence of certain *categories*. These are socio-cultural syndromes whose properties must be discovered through the comparative enquiry; only when all the loose ends of data, in the skein of materials judged relevant to a category, have been classified and inter-related does the researcher assume that "theoretical saturation" of his categories by their properties has been achieved. In the course of searching for properties, the researcher constructs hypotheses with the intention of finding thematic connections between them which will help him to build a sociological model for the phenomena at issue. Thus, gradually, the field open to constant-comparative exploration is narrowed and closed; as Schatzman (1973: 111) puts it: "Once the analyst gains a Key Linkage - that is, a metaphor, model, general scheme, overriding pattern or story-line - he can become increasingly selective of the classes (of persons or events) he needs to deal with." Eventually, all the retainable hypotheses will have been organised, hierarchically, within this metaphor or model, and the so-called theoretical saturation of categories will have been complemented by a saturation of the model in the data obtained. The resulting "grounded substantive theory" will have been data-dyed in colours whose combination articulates the architectural tonalities of a double-fitting of data to concepts, and concepts to model. Four phases of analysis take us from early fieldwork to model completion: *comparing incidents* as a means to clarify and elaborate categories; *integrating the discovered properties* into category definitions (a sub-routine borrowed from analytic induction); *delimiting the theory* by linking and merging hypotheses to reduce complexity; and, in a final withdrawal from fieldwork, *writing up* the fully-organised theory/model in an account that is satisfying aesthetically and sociologically. Glaser and Strauss give a useful step-by-step illustration of the practical operation of this sequence in the research they did on the ways in which contingencies in the nursing of dying people were handled through the nurses' occupational subculture (1968: 105-114).

Commentary

Studies of occupational subcultures or organisational underlife

produced according to the rules of the constant comparative method
manifest a palpable cogency and credibility: (see, for example,
Strauss et al 1964; Glaser and Strauss, 1965; and Becker et al
1968). But this simply begs the question of what constitutes a successful negotiation of our dilemma of analytic strategy.
I believe that the credibility achieved depends on a short-circ-
uiting of the rational criteria for the criticism of theoretical
knowledge. Glaser and Strauss aver:

> The evolving systematic analysis permits a fieldworker quite
> literally to write prescriptions so that other outsiders could
> get along in the observed sphere of life and action ... Not
> infrequently people successfully stake their money, reputations
> and even lives, as well as the fate of others, upon their inter-
> pretations of alien societies. What the fieldworker does is
> to make this *normal strategy* of reflective persons into a
> successful *research strategy*. (1968: 226-227)

This pragmatic conception of the prescriptive functions of
model-building assumes that grounded theory will be consumed by
a readership competent in the codes which carry both the model
and its analytic subroutines: the Projection upon which this
'cognitive mapping' is predicated, is not itself available to
critical testing. In this way, the canons of rational demonstration and proof are side-stepped: in order to make sense of the
model, the reader must imprison himself within its domain of
interpretation. (In addition, it has been argued persuasively
by Barry Hindess, 1973b: 242-247, that sociological model-building cannot be related to general social theory by a rigorous set
of semantic rules, as mathematical models can be set against
their formal systems: grounded theory is more a matter of style
than of grammar.) The constant comparative method maintains
its self-validating privilege partly by parcelling out its interpretative domain into substantive problem areas which are restricted in space and time to the particular phenomena for which the
researcher has cornered the sociological market. Colin Fletcher
(1974) suggests that the tradition of 'to each anthropologist his
own tribe' has vitiated the capacity to support truly critical
theorising. He might have cited as evidence the study of academic assessment in a mid-western university by Becker et al,
(1968) which culminates in a recommendation to abolish the whole
grading system. Their appeal for the ending of an oppressive
labelling practice is presented so abstractly that there was
little danger that it would be construed as a real political
intervention into the arena of struggles over cultural classification.

b. THE SEARCH FOR STRUCTURAL/HISTORICAL MEDIATIONS

Sartre's strategy attempts a round-trip passage from a presump-
tive theory of the whole social order, to the level of the
negotiated cultural nexus in which individuals make and live their

270

experience, and back to the totality, carrying now some means to criticise the original account.   Any judgement on the adequacy of this strategy for dealing with our dilemma must assess the researcher's management of both the regressive and the progressive moments in the analysis.   The formulation of the research topic will from the start entail that phenomena be situated within an explicit conception of the central structures and dynamics of a whole society (regressive moment).   The exploration of the research topic will require a continuous elaboration and re-working of empirically traced connections between processes belonging to the 'levels' of biography, family and neighbourhood, community, economy and nation-state (progressive moment).   Often the empirical connections suggest the existence of processes at work in dimensions of social reality which lie skew to these levels, as is the case with 'delinquent' youth styles and the discourse of law-and-order.   Such a point was encountered during the analysis of materials on The Mugging Phenomenon;   see Clarke et al.(1975).   Here, POP methods - knowledge of a local community acquired through work in a neighbourhood advice and action centre; analysis of newspaper stories and other documents;   intervention in an Appeal Court campaign - could be seen as a 'necessary poison' used within a progressive-regressive study whose aim was to open up and reorganise the received account of monopoly capitalist hegemony in postwar Britain, so as to accommodate a new social history of law-and-order versus 'delinquency' in the theatres of ideology and politics during the passage from the conjuncture of the mid-sixties to that of the mid-seventies.

When a rich tract of materials throws into relief a new complex of mediations, much of the framework of a study is brought in question and the effort to achieve a new theoretical totalisation before the research strategy falls apart is hazardous.   This 'deconstructive' moment raises methodological problems, whose centre of gravity is clearly exposed, in Stuart Hall's recent discussion of Marx's ideas on methods (Hall, 1974b:150-160), as the tension between *historicist* ways of studying a total social formation and those of a *structuralist* approach.   In the first, the relation between one specific social process and another is referred to a genetic account of the overall historical movement which bears them both: in our example, the amplification of 'mugging' incidents and responses to them is situated within an account of a deepening crisis of 'Consensus' ideology and politics in late-sixties Britain.   In the second, the exposure of media-tions leads to the elaboration of an anatomical account of a complex of contradictions, "structured in dominance":   the ideo-logical plane of judicial and social administration is shown as intersecting that of youth culture so as the generate 'structu-rally' a mutual interference in each other's discourse.   The central problem is, then, to find a way of documenting the ideological practices of youth culture (etc.) which leads to an understanding of the 'structural effectivity' of the complex of

271

contradictions in which they have their determination, while
simultaneously opening a road to the identification of the
processes of historical movement in which this effectivity is
only a conjunctural moment.

Commentary

Sartre's exposition of his analytic strategy emphasises the
need to place in command the characterisation of historical
movement, so as to allow for a genuinely critical totalisation in
the account of cultural phenomena, and to reveal the possibilities
for transcending the present state of affairs. But he is vague
on the crucial question of procedural and theoretical controls
over the construction of such accounts. These controls are not
so much a matter of logic in general, although logical rules cannot be evaded, as a question of the social and cultural forms
through which we may apprehend the working connections between
the deepest structures of class societies: mode of production,
hegemonic ideologies and their combinatory repertoire, the 'modes'
of political power. The Mugging Phenomenon project, and the
work of the Subcultures group in general, has yet to find ways of
anchoring ideology-critique in the results of an adequate economy-
critique (thus modifying both); and even then it has to carry
the whole account into the further level of the analysis of the
political conjunctures - an analysis which confronts the real
possibilities for intervention in actual struggles between groups
and, ultimately, class alliances. Meanwhile, these dimensions
are better treated by historical analogy and metaphor than not at
all, as in the professional sociologist's attempts to 'discover'
a strictly delimited grounded theory of localised subcultures and
deviants.

7 Conclusion

I have pointed out some weaknesses in the logic-of-enquiry of
the Participant Observation Paradigm, as this is represented in
leading methodological texts: significantly, the weaknesses appear at just those places where the texts provide rules for the
management of procedural and theoretical dilemmas. I have suggested that critical studies of cultural formations might
fruitfully adopt a version of Sartre's progressive-regressive
method - a version modified so as to replace his loose, if
imaginative, historicism with a more complete synthesis of
historical and structural methods. But I have not been able,
here, to offer an account of such a methodological approach which
goes beyond the uneven achievements of the recent work of the
Subcultures Group, whose results are recorded in Section One,
above. What is at stake here is not a universal 'logic' of
sociological enquiry, but the *specific logics* of the different
techniques by which critical cultural studies can lay hold on

the connections between different types of element in the socio-historical formation, and the articulations through which it achieves its complexly structured determinacy. The work of developing methods of study cannot proceed in abstraction, but will bear fruit to the extent that ways are found to do justice to the contradictions of our society in an adequate confrontation of the theoretical and political problems which they pose[2].

FOOTNOTES

1. Thomas Kuhn's account of the production of natural science knowledge turns on the fact of the domination for much of the time of the scientific enterprise by a consensual Paradigm of axioms, concepts and methods, which dictates what is to be studied, and how. In such periods of 'normal science' the paradigm's supporters claim to have settled the central questions about how the world is constituted, and attention is directed to the fine detail of residual 'puzzles' at the periphery of scientific knowledge, where practical research continues according to institutional rules.

    Before a scientific field shifts into 'normal science' for the first time, there is open competition between 'Pre-paradigms' which contend for the first place in the preference of would-be professional scientists. If we were to attempt to apply Kuhn's model (which has largely allegorical status) to the social sciences, then we might identify 'positivistic' and 'naturalistic' sociology as ranking pre-paradigm contenders. In anticipation of victory, the naturalists may have written up their methodological rulebook as though it carried the canons of a normal science paradigm. Ironically, though, Kuhn's account debunks both the authority and the romanticism of established scientific practice:

    > "No part of the aim of normal science is to call forth
    > new sorts of phenomena; indeed those that will not
    > fit the box are often not seen at all. Nor do
    > scientists normally aim to invent new theories, and
    > they are often intolerant of those invented by others.
    > Instead, normal-scientific research is directed to
    > the articulation of those phenomena and theories that
    > the paradigm already supplies."
    > (Kuhn, 1970: 24)

2. I was introduced to the topic of the logic-of-enquiry of sociological methods through the work of Professor Gi Baldamus of the University of Birmingham, which points out the contradiction within much sociological practice between logical rigour and theoretical import. This article has benefited from many criticisms and suggestions made by Rachel Powell of CCCS.

References

ABRAMS, M. 1959. *The Teenage Consumer*. London Press Exchange Ltd.

ABRAMS, M. 1969. *Must Labour Lose?* Penguin Special

ADDAMS, Jane. 1972. *The Spirit of Youth and the City Streets*. University of Illinois Press (originally published, 1909).

AHIRAM, E. 1966. "Distribution of Income in Trinidad-Tobago and Comparison with Distribution of Income in Jamaica." *Social and Economic Studies*, vol.15. Institute of Social and Economic Research, University of the West Indies.

AKERS, R.L. 1967. "Problems in the Sociology of Deviance: Social Definitions and Behaviour." *Social Forces*, 46.

ALTHUSSER, L. 1969. *For Marx*. Allen Lane, Penguin Press.

ALTHUSSER, L. 1971. "Ideology And The State." In *Lenin And Philosophy, & other Essays*. New Left Books.

ANDERSON, P. 1964. "Origins of the Present Crisis". *New Left Review*, 23. Reprinted in P. Anderson and R. Blackburn, eds. (1965).

ANDERSON, P. 1965a. "The Left and the 50's". *New Left Review*, 29.

ANDERSON, P. 1965b. "Socialism and Pseudo-Empiricism." *New Left Review*, 35.

ANDERSON, P. and BLACKBURN, R. (eds.) 1965. *Towards Socialism*. Fontana.

ANDRESKI, S. (ed.) 1974. *The Essential Comte*. Croom Helm.

ARMISTEAD, N. (ed.) 1974. *Reconstructing Social Psychology*. Penguin.

ARNOLD, D.O. (ed.) 1970. *The Sociology of Sub-Cultures*. Glendessary Press.

AULD, J. 1973. "Cannabis: the Changing Patterns of Use" *New Society* (6th September).

BACRACH, P. & BARATZ, M. 1962. "The Two Faces of Power." *American Political Science Review*, No.56.

BADEN-POWELL. 1930. *Scouting for Boys*. C. Arthur Pearson Ltd. (first published 1908).

BAILEY, R. 1973. *The Squatters*. Penguin.

BAILEY, R. and YOUNG, J. (eds.) 1973. *Contemporary Social Problems in Britain*. Saxon House.

BANTON, M. 1967. "Integration into what Society?" *New Society* (9th November).

BARKER, P. and LITTLE, A. 1964. "The Margate Offenders: a Survey." *New Society* (30th July). Reprinted in T. Raison, ed. (1966).

BARTHES, R. 1971. "Rhetoric of The Image." *Working Papers in Cultural Studies*, No.1 (Spring). CCCS, University of Birmingham.

BECKER, H.S. 1958. "Problems of Inference and Proof in Participant Observation". *American Sociological Review*, 23 (December).

BECKER, H.S. 1963. *Outsiders: Studies in the Sociology of Deviance*. Free Press, Glencoe.

BECKER, H.S. 1967. "Whose side are we on?" *Social Problems*, 14. Reprinted in J. D. Douglas, ed. (1972).

BECKER, H.S. 1971. *Sociological Work: Method and Substance*. Allen Lane.

BECKER, H.S. (ed.) 1964. *The Other Side: Perspectives on Deviance*. Free Press, Glencoe.

BECKER, H.S. and GEER, B. 1957. "Participant Observation and Interviewing: a Comparison." *Human Organisation*, 16, 3. Reprinted in G. J. McCall and J. L. Simmons, eds. (1969).

BECKER, H.S. et. al. 1961. *Boys in White*. University of Chicago Press.

BECKER, H.S. et.al. 1968. *Making the Grade*. John Wiley.

BECKER, H.S. et. al. (eds.) 1968. *Institutions and the Person*. Aldine, Chicago.

BERGER, B.M., HACKETT, B.M. & MILLAR, R.M. 1972. "Childrearing Practices in the Communal Family". In H. P. Dreitzel, ed. (1972).

BERRY, Lynda. 1974. "Women in Society - 1. A Discussion on Female Violence." *The Listener* (7th November)

BEYNON, H. 1973. *Working For Ford*. Penguin Sociology.

BLACKBURN, R. (ed.) 1972. *Ideology in Social Science: Readings in Critical Social Theory*. Fontana.

BLACKBURN, R. and COCKBURN, P. (eds.) 1969. *Student Power*. Penguin.

BLOCH, E. 1970. *A Philosophy of the Future*. Herder and Herder.

BLOCH, E. 1971. *Man on his own*. Herder and Herder.

BLUMER, H. 1954. "What is Wrong with Social Theory?" *American Sociological Review*, 19. Reprinted in N. K. Denzin, ed. (1970).

BLUMER, H. 1956. "Sociological Analysis and the Variable." *American Sociological Review*, 21. Reprinted in P.F. Lazarsfeld et.al., eds. (1972).

BLUMER, H. 1969. *Symbolic Interactionism*. Prentice-Hall.

BOGDANOR, V. & SKIDELSKY, R. (eds.) 1970. *The Age of Affluence*. Macmillan Papermac.

BOOKCHIN, M. 1971. *Post-Scarcity Anarchism*. Ramparts Press.

BOOKER, C. 1969. *The Neophiliacs: a Study of the Revolution in the English in the Fifties and Sixties*. Collins.

BOOKHAGEN, C. et.al. 1973. "Kommune 2: Childrearing in the Commune." In H. P. Dreitzel, ed. (1973).

BOYD, J. 1973. "Discussion contribution on Trends in Youth Culture". *Marxism Today* (December).

BRAKE, M. 1973. "Cultural Revolution or Alternative Delinquency." In R. Bailey and J. Young, eds. (1973).

BRUYN, S. 1966. *The Human Perspective in Sociology*. Prentice-Hall.

BUFF, Stephen. 1970. "Greasers, Dupers and Hippies: Three responses to the Adult World." In L.K. Howe, ed. (1970).

CARPENTER, M. 1968. *Reformatory Schools for the Children of the Dangerous and Perishing Classes and Juvenile Offenders*. Woburn Press of London (originally published 1851).

CHAMBERLAIN, C. & MOORHOUSE, H. 1974. "Lower Class Attitudes to The British Political System". *Sociological Review*, 22, No.4 NS (November).

CHAMBERS, I. 1974. "Roland Barthes: Structuralism/semiotics." *Working Papers in Cultural Studies*, No.6 (Autumn). CCCS, University of Birmingham.

CLARKE, J. 1973. "Skinheads and Youth Culture". *Stencilled Paper*, No.23, CCCS, University of Birmingham.

CLARKE, J. 1974. "Reconceptualising Youth Culture." Unpublished MA Thesis, CCCS, Birmingham University.

CLARKE, J., HEBDIGE, D. & JEFFERSON, T. 1974. "British Youth Cultures 1950-1970". *Instituto Universitario Orientale, Annali,*

Sezione Germanica, Anglistica XVII (i) and (ii). Also available
as CCCS *Stencilled Papers,* Nos. 14, 22, 20 and 23.

CLARKE, J. and JEFFERSON, T. 1974. "Working Class Youth Cultures."
CCCS *Stencilled Paper,* No.18. Reprinted in G. Mungham and
G. Pearson, eds. forthcoming.

CLARKE, J. et.al. 1975. "Mugging and Law 'n' Order." Paper
presented at National Deviancy Conference, University College,
Cardiff. (April.)

CLEAVER, E. 1970. *Soul on Ice.* Panther.

CLOWARD, R. & OHLIN, L. 1960. *Delinquency and Opportunity: A
Theory of Delinquent Gangs.* Free Press, Chicago.

COHEN, A. 1955. *Delinquent Boys: The Culture of The Gang.*
Free Press, Chicago.

COHEN, P. 1972. "Sub-Cultural Conflict and Working Class
Community". *Working Papers in Cultural Studies,* No.2
(Spring). CCCS, University of Birmingham.

COHEN, S. (ed.) 1971. *Images of Deviance.* Penguin.

COHEN, S. 1973. *Folk Devils and Moral Panics.* Paladin.

COHEN, S. 1974. "Criminology and the Sociology of
Deviance in Britain." In P. Rock and M. McIntosh,
eds. (1974).

COHN, N. 1970. *The Pursuit of the Millenium.* Paladin.

COLEMAN, A. 1961. *The Adolescent Society.* Free Press,
Glencoe.

COOPER, D. 1967. *Psychiatry and Anti-Psychiatry.* Paladin.

COOPER, D. 1972. *The Death of the Family.* Pelican.

COOPER, D. 1974. *The Grammar of Living.* Allen Lane.

CORRIGAN, P. forthcoming. *The Smash Street Kids.* Paladin.

COUSINS, J. & BROWN, R. 1972. "Patterns of Paradox: Shipbuilding
Workers' Images of Society." Paper presented to SSRC
Conference on the Occupational Community of the Traditional
Worker, University of Durham.

CRITCHER, C. 1975. "Football Since the War: a Study in
Social Change and Popular Culture." CCCS, *Stencilled
Paper,* No. 29, University of Birmingham.

DANIEL, S. & McGuire, P. (eds.) 1972. *The Paint House.* Penguin.

DAVIS, F. 1970. "Focus on the Flower Children: why all of us
may be Hippies some day." In J. Douglas, ed. (1970).

DEAN, John P. et. al. 1967. "Participant Observation and Interviewing". In John Doby, ed. (1967).

DENZIN, N.K. 1970. *The Research Act.in Sociology.* Butterworths.

DENZIN, N.K. (ed.) 1970. *Sociological Methods: a Sourcebook.*
Butterworths.

DENZIN, N.K. 1971. "The Logic of Naturalistic Enquiry". *Social
Forces,* L,2.

DEWEY, J. 1938. *Logic: the Theory of Inquiry.* Holt, Rinehart
and Winston (NY).

DOBEY, John (ed.) 1967. *An Introduction to Social Research.*
Meredith Publishing Company, NY/Appleton-Century-Crofts, London.

DOUGLAS, J.D. (ed.) 1970. *Observations of Deviance.* Random
House.

DOUGLAS, J.D. (ed.) 1972. *The Relevance of Sociology.*
Appleton-Century-Crofts.

DOWNES, D. 1966. *The Delinquent Solution.* Routledge and
Kegan Paul.

DOXEY, G.V. 1969. *Survey of the Jamaican Economy* (Govt.Report)

DREITZEL, H.P. (ed.) 1972. *Recent Sociology No.4: Family, Marriage, and the Struggle of the Sexes.* Collier-Macmillan.

DREITZEL, H.P. (ed.) 1973. *Recent Sociology No.5: Childhood and Socialization.* Collier-MacMillan.

DUNNING, E. (ed.) 1971. *The Sociology of Sport: a Selection of Readings.* Cass.

EASTHOPE, G. 1974. *History of Social Research Methods.* Longman.

EISEN, J. (ed.) 1970. *Altamont.* Avon Books.

ERIKSON, K.T. 1962. "Notes on the Sociology of Deviance." *Social Problems,* 9 (Spring). Reprinted in H.S. Becker, ed. (1964).

ERIKSON, K. 1966. *Wayward Puritans.* John Wiley.

FARIS, R.E. 1967. *Chicago Sociology: 1920-1932.* University of Chicago Press.

FLETCHER, C.L. 1966. "Beats and Gangs on Merseyside." In T. Raison, ed. (1966).

FLETCHER, C.L. 1974. *Beneath the Surface.* Routledge and Kegan Paul.

FOSTER, J. 1974. *Class Struggle and Industrial Revolution.* Weidenfeld and Nicolson.

FRANCIS, O.C. 1963. *The People of Modern Jamaica.* Department of Statistics, Kingston, Jamaica.

FRITH, S. Forthcoming-a. "Cum on Feel the Noize - Slade Alive" In M. Gold, ed. (forthcoming).

FRITH, S. Forthcoming-b. "Socialisation and Rational Schooling: Elementary Education in Leeds, 1800-1870." In W.P. McCann, ed. (forthcoming).

FYVEL, T.R. 1963. *The Insecure Offenders.* Chatto and Windus.

GANS, H. 1963. *The Urban Villagers.* Free Press, New York.

GANS, H. 1968. "The Participant Observer as a Human Being: Observations on the Personal Aspects of Fieldwork." In H.S. Becker et.al. eds. (1968).

GEER, B. 1964. "First Days in the Field". In P. Hammond, ed. (1964). Reprinted in G.J. McCall and J.L. Simmons, eds. (1969).

GEER, B. 1970. "Studying a College" In R. Habenstein, ed. (1970).

GIBBS, J. 1966. "Conceptions of Deviant Behaviour: the Old and the New." *Pacific Sociological Review,* 9 (Spring).

GILLIS, John R. 1974. *Youth and History: Tradition and Change In European Age Relations 1770 - Present.* Academic Press.

GILLMAN, P. 1973. "I Blame England." *Sunday Times* Magazine (30th September).

GLASER, B. 1965. "The Constant Comparative Method of Qualitative Analysis." *Social Problems,* Vol.12. Reprinted in G.J. McCall and J.L. Simmons, eds. (1969).

GLASER, B. and STRAUSS, A. 1965. *Awareness of Dying.* Aldine, Chicago.

GLASER, B. and STRAUSS, A. 1968. *The Discovery of Grounded Theory.* Weidenfeld and Nicholson.

GLASER, B and STRAUSS, A. 1975. *Theoretical Sampling.* Aldine, Chicago.

GLYN, A. and SUTCLIFFE, B. 1972. *British Capitalism, Workers, and the Profits Squeeze.* Penguin.

GODELIER, M. 1972. "Structure and Contradiction in *Capital*". In R. Blackburn, ed. (1972).

GOFFMAN, E. 1959. *The Presentation of Self in Everyday Life.* Doubleday, NY. (Penguin edition, 1971.)

GOFFMAN, E. 1961. *Asylums*. Doubleday (NY). (Penguin edition, 1968.)

GOFFMAN, E. 1963. *Behaviour in Public Places*. Free Press, New York.

GOFFMAN, E. 1968. *Stigma*. Penguin.

GOFFMAN, E. 1969. *Strategic Interaction*. Basil Blackwell.

GOLD, M. (ed.) forthcoming. *Rock in Performance*. IPC and Phoebus.

GOLD, R. 1958. "Roles in Sociological Field Observations." *Social Forces*, 36 (March). Reprinted in N. Denzin, ed. (1970).

GOLDTHORPE, J.H. and LOCKWOOD, D. 1963. "Affluence and the British Class Structure." *Sociological Review* Vol.11, No.2.

GOLDTHORPE, J.H. et. al. 1968. *The Affluent Worker: Industrial Attitudes and Behaviour*. Cambridge University Press.

GOLDTHORPE, J.H. et.al. 1969. *The Affluent Worker in the Class Structure*. Cambridge University Press.

GORMAN, G. 1972. *Making Communes*. Whole Earth Tools.

GOSLING, R. 1962. *Sum Total*. Faber.

GOULDNER, A. 1968. "The Sociologist as Partisan: Sociology and the Welfare State." *The American Sociologist* (May). Reprinted in J.D. Douglas, ed. (1972).

GRAMSCI, A. 1971. *Selections From the Prison Notebooks*. Lawrence and Wishart.

HABENSTEIN, R. (ed.) 1970. *Pathways to Data*. Aldine, Chicago.

HABERMAS, J. 1972. *Knowledge and Human Interests*. Heinemann.

HALL, Stanley. 1905. *Adolescence: its Psychology and its Relations to Physiology, Anthropology, Sociology, Sex, Crime, Religion and Education*. Sidney Appleton (London edn.).

HALL, S.M. 1973. "Encoding and Decoding in the Media Discourse." *Stencilled Paper*, No.7, CCCS, Birmingham University.

HALL, S.M. 1974a. "Education and the Crisis of the Urban School." In J. Raynor, ed. (1974).

HALL, S.M. 1974b. "Marx's Notes on Method." *Working Papers in Cultural Studies*, No.6 (Autumn), CCCS, Birmingham University.

HALL, S.M. and WHANNEL, P. 1964. *The Popular Arts*. Hutchinson.

HAMBLETT, C. & DEVERSON, J. 1964. *Generation X*. Tandem Books.

HAMMOND, P. (ed.) 1964. *Sociologists at Work*. Basic Books (NY).

HARPER, P. (ed.) Forthcoming. *Alternative Technology*. Wildwood House.

HEBDIGE, D. 1974. "Aspects of Style in the Deviant Sub-Cultures of the 1960's". Unpublished MA Thesis, CCCS, Birmingham University. Available as CCCS *Stencilled Papers*, Nos. 20, 21, 24 and 25.

HEINLEIN, R. 1965. *Stranger in a Strange Land*. New English Library.

HENRY, Jules. 1963. *Culture Against Man*. Random House. (Penguin edition, 1973.)

HERMAN, G. 1971. *The Who*. Studio Vista.

HILLIER, P. 1975. "The Nature and Social Location of Everyday Conceptions of Class." *Sociology*, 9(1).

HINDESS, B. 1973a. *The Use of Official Statistics in Sociology*. MacMillan.

HINDESS, B. 1973b. "Models and Masks." *Economy and Society* Vol.2, No.1 (February).

HINES, V. 1973. *Black Youth and the Survival Game in Britain*. Zulu Publications.

HIRO, D. 1973. *Black British, White British*. Pelican.

HOGGART, R. 1958. *The Uses of Literacy*. Pelican.

HOURIET, R.   1971. *Getting Back Together.* Abacus.

HOWE, L.K. (ed.) 1970. *The White Majority: Between Poverty and Affluence.* Vintage Books.

HURT, J. 1972. *Education in Evolution.* Paladin.

HUTT, C. 1973. *The Death of the English Pub.* Arrow.

JACOBY, R. 1973. "The Politics of Subjectivity". *New Left Review,* 79.

JEFFERSON, T. 1973. "The Teds: a Political Resurrection." CCCS *Stencilled Paper,* No.22.

JEFFERSON, T. 1974. "For a Social Theory of Deviance: the Case of Mugging, 1972-3."   Unpublished MA Thesis, CCCS, University of Birmingham.

JEFFERSON, T & CLARKE, J. 1974. "Down these Mean Streets: the Meaning of Mugging." *Howard Journal,* Vol.XIV, No.1. Available as CCCS *Stencilled Paper,* No.17.

JOHNSON, P. 1964. "The Menace of Beatlism". *New Statesman* (28th February).

JOHNSON, R. 1970. "Educational Policy and Social Control in Mid-Victorian England." *Past and Present,* vol. 49.

KALLYNDYR, R. & DALRYMPLE, H. *Reggae, A Peoples' Music.* **Carib** - Arawak Publications. (From 109 Deacon Road, Willesden, London N.W.2, Price 20p.)

KASSCHAU, P., RANSFORD, E. & BENGTSON, V. 1974. "Generational Consciousness and Youth Movement Participation: Contrasts in Blue Collar and White Collar Youth." *Journal of Social Issues,* 30 (3).

KAUFMAN, M. 1971. "The New Homesteading Movement." In S. Teselle, ed. (1971).

KEROUAC, J. 1958. *On the Road.* Andre Deutsch.

KERR, M. 1958. *The People of Ship Street.* Liverpool University Press.

KITSUSE, J.I. 1962. "Societal Reaction to Deviant Behaviour: Problems of Theory and Method." *Social Problems, 9* (Winter). Reprinted in H.S. Becker, ed. (1964).

KRAUSZ, E. and MILLER, S. 1974. *Social Research Design.* Longman (social research series).

KUHN, T. 1970. *The Structure of Scientific Revolutions.* University of Chicago Press.

LAING, D. 1969. *The Sound of Our Time.* Sheed and Ward.

LAING, R.D. 1967. *The Politics of Experience and The Bird of Paradise.* Penguin.

LANE, T.   1974 . *The Union Makes Us Strong.* Arrow.

LAUFER, R. & BENGTSON, V. 1974. "Generations, Aging and Social Stratification: on the Development of Generational Units." *Journal of Social Issues* 30(3).

LAZARSFELD, P.F. et al. (eds.) 1972. *Continuities in the Language of Social Research.* Free Press, New York.

LEARY, T. 1970. *The Politics of Ecstasy.* Paladin.

LECOURT, Dominique. 1975. *Marxism and Epistemology.* New Left Books (Cheaper from NLR Editions).

LEMERT, E.M. 1967. *Human Deviance, Social Problems and Social Control.* Prentice-Hall (NY).

LESSING, D. 1969. *The Four Gated City.* Panther.

LEVI-STRAUSS, C. 1966. *The Savage Mind.* Weidenfeld and Nicolson.

LEVI-STRAUSS, C. 1969. *Totemism.* Penguin.

LINDESMITH, A. 1947. *Opiate Addiction*. **Principia Press** (Bloomington).

LOCKWOOD, D. 1966. "Sources of Variation in Working Class Images of Society." *Sociological Review* 14(3).

LOWENTHAL, D. 1972. *West Indian Societies*. Oxford University Press.

LUKES, S. 1974. *Power: a Radical View*. Studies in Sociology Series, MacMillan Papermac.

McCALL, G.J. and SIMMONS, J.L. (eds.) 1969. *Issues in Participant Observation*. Addison-Wesley.

McCANN, W.P. (ed.) forthcoming. *Popular Education and Socialisation, 1800-1900*. Eyre-Methuen.

McDERMOTT, J.J. 1971. "Nature, Nostalgia and the City: an American Dilemma". In S. Teselle, ed. (1971).

McGLASHAN, C. 1973. "Reggae, Reggae, Reggae." *Sunday Times* **Magazine (4th February)**.

MacINNES, C. 1957. *City of Spades*. MacGibbon and Kee.

MacINNES, C. 1961. *England, Half-English*. McGibbon and Kee.

MAILER, N. 1968. "The White Negro" in *Advertisements for Myself*. Panther.

MANKOFF, M. 1971. "Societal Reaction and Career **Deviance**: a Critical Analysis." *The Sociological Quarterly*, 12 (Spring).

MANN, M. 1973. *Consciousness and Action among the Western Working Class*. Macmillan.

MANNHEIM, Karl. 1952. "The Problem of Generations." In *Essays in the Sociology of Knowledge*. Routledge and Kegan Paul.

MANNHEIM, K. 1972. *Ideology and Utopia*. Routledge and Kegan Paul.

MARCUSE, H. 1964. *One Dimensional Man*. Routledge and Kegan Paul.

MARCUSE, H. 1969. *An Essay on Liberation*. Allen Lane, Penguin Press.

MARCUSE, H. 1970. *Eros and Civilization*. Sphere.

MARSHALL, T.H. 1963. "Citizenship and Social Class". In *Sociology at the Cross Roads*. Routledge and Kegan Paul.

MARX, K. 1951. "The Eighteenth Brumaire." In *Marx-Engels Selected Works*, vol.I. Lawrence and Wishart.

MARX, K. 1964. *The Economic and Philosophical Manuscripts of 1844*. Lawrence and Wishart.

MARX, K. 1970. *The German Ideology*. Lawrence and Wishart.

MATZA, D. 1961. "Subterranean Traditions of Youth". *Annals of the American Academy of Political and Social Science*, 338.

MATZA, D. 1969. *Becoming Deviant*. Prentice-Hall.

MATZA, D. & SYKES, G. 1961. "Juvenile Delinquency and Subterranean Values". *American Sociological Review*, 26.

MAYS, J.B. 1954. *Growing up in the City*. Liverpool University Press.

MEAD, G.H. 1934. *Mind, Self and Society*. University of Chicago Press.

MELLY, G. 1972. *Revolt into Style*. Penguin.

MELTZER, B.N. et.al. 1975. *Symbolic Interactionism: Genesis, Varieties and Criticisms*. Routledge and Kegan Paul.

MELVILLE, K. 1972. *Communes in the Counter Culture*. Morrow Paperback.

MERTON, R.K. 1968. *Social Theory and Social Structure*. Free Press, New York (Enlarged Edition).

MESSINGER, S. 1962. "Life as Theater: Some Notes on the Dramaturgic Approach to Social Reality". *Sociometry*, 25. Reprinted in M. Truzzi, ed. (1968).

MILIBAND, R. 1961 *Parliamentary Socialism*. Allen and Unwin.

MILIBAND, R. and SAVILLE, J. (eds.) 1965. *The Socialist Register, 1965*. Merlin Press.

MILLER, W. 1958. "Lower-class Culture As a Generating Milieu of Gang Delinquency." *Journal of Social Issues, 15*. Reprinted in D.O. Arnold, ed. (1970).

MILLS, C.W. 1966. *Sociology and Pragmatism*. Galaxy Books (NY).

MITCHELL, J. 1971. *Woman's Estate*. Pelican.

MITCHELL, J. 1974. *Psychoanalysis and Feminism*. Allen Lane (Penguin paperback, 1975).

MONOD, J. 1967. "Juvenile Gangs in Paris: Towards a Structural Analysis." *Journal of Research on Crime and Delinquency*, vol.4.

MOORHOUSE, H.F. and CHAMBERLAIN, C.W. 1974. "Lower class attitudes to Property: Aspects of the Counter Ideology." *Sociology*, 8 (3).

MORAN, Ld. 1968. *Winston Churchill*. Sphere.

MORRIS, T. 1957. *The Criminal Area*. Routledge and Kegan Paul.

MUMFORD, L. 1922. *The Story of Utopias*. Boni and Liveright, N.Y.

MUNGHAM, G. and PEARSON, G. (eds.) forthcoming. *British Working Class Youth Cultures*. Routledge and Kegan Paul.

MURDOCK, G. 1973. "Culture and Classlessness: the Making and Unmaking of a Contemporary Myth". Paper delivered to *Symposium on Work and Leisure*, University of Salford.

MURDOCK, G. 1974. "Mass Communication and the Construction of Meaning." In N. Armistead, ed. (1974).

MURDOCK, G. Forthcoming. "Youth and Class: the Career of a Confusion." In G. Mungham and G. Pearson, eds. (forthcoming).

MURDOCK, G. & McCRON, R. 1973. "Scoobies, Skins and Contemporary Pop." *New Society*. No.547.

MUSGROVE, F. 1968. *Youth and the Social Order*. Routledge and Kegan Paul.

MURGROVE, F. 1974a. "The Curriculum for a World of Change." In P.H. Taylor and J. Walton, eds. (1974).

MUSGROVE, F. 1974b. *Ecstasy and Holiness: Counter Culture and Open Society*. Methuen.

NAIRN, T. 1964a. "The British Political Elite." *New Left Review*, 23.

NAIRN, T. 1964b. "The English Working Class." *New Left Review*, 24. Reprinted in R. Blackburn, ed. (1972).

NAIRN, T. 1964c. "Anatomy of the Labour Party" Pts. 1 and 2. *New Left Review*, 27 and 28.

NAIRN T. & QUATTROCCHI, A. 1968. *The Beginning of the End*. Panther.

NEEDLEMAN, J. 1971. *The New Religions*. Doubleday.

NETTLEFORD, R. 1970. *Mirror, Mirror*. William Collins and Sangster (Jamaica), Ltd.

NEVILLE, R. 1971. *Play Power*. Paladin.

NEWSOM, Sir J.H. 1948. *The Education of Girls*. Faber.

NEWSOM, Sir J.H. 1963. *Half Our Future; a Report*. HMSO. London.

NICHOLS, T. 1974. "Labourism and Class Consciousness: the 'Class Ideology' of some Northern Foremen." *Sociological Review*, 22(4).

NICOLAUS, M. 1969. "The Professional Organization of Sociology:

a View from Below." *Antioch Review* (Fall). Reprinted in
R. Blackburn, ed. (1972).

NUTTALL, J.   1970. *Bomb Culture*. Paladin.

OGILVY, H & OGILVY, J.   1971. "Communes and the Reconstruction of
Reality." In S. Teselle, ed. (1971).

OLESEN, V and WHITTAKER, E. 1967. "Role-making in Participant
Observation: Processes in the Researcher-actor Relationship."
Human Organisation 26. Reprinted in N.K. Denzin, ed. (1970).

ORTEGA Y GASSET, Jose. 1931. *The Modern Theme*. C. W. Daniel
Company. (Originally published 1920-1)

PARK, R.E. and MACKENZIE, R.D. (eds.) 1967. *The City*. University
of Chicago Press.

PARKER, H.J. 1974. *View from the Boys*. David and Charles.

PARKER, T. 1969. *The Plough Boy*. Arrow.

PARKIN, F. 1971. *Class Inequality and Political Order*.
McGibbon and Kee.

PARSONS, T. 1942. "Age and Sex in the Social Structure of
the United States." Reprinted in 1964 in *Essays in Sociological Theory*. Free Press (paperback edition).

PATRICK, J. 1973. *A Glasgow Gang Observed*. Eyre-Methuen.

PATTERSON, O. 1964. "Ras Tafari: Cult of Outcasts." *New Society*
(12th November).

PAUL, JIMMY AND MUSTY SUPPORT COMMITTE. 1973. *20 years*. Available
from the Action Centre, 134 Villa Rd., Handsworth, Birmingham 19,
price 15p.

PEARSON, G. 1975. *The Deviant Imagination*. MacMillan.

PEARSON, G. & TWOHIG, J. Undated. *Becker, Marijuana and the
Sociology of Fun*. Unpublished mss., University of Cardiff.

PEARSON, J. 1973. *The Profession of Violence*. Panther.

PINTO-DUSCHINSKY, M. 1970. "Bread and Circuses: the
Conservatives in Office, 1951-64." In V. Bogdanor and R.
Skidelsky,eds. (1970).

POLSKY, N. 1971. *Hustlers, Beats and Others*. Penguin.

POULANTZAS, N. 1966. "Marxist Political Theory in Great
Britain." *Les Temps Modernes* (March). Translated in
1967 in *New Left Review*, 43.

POULANTZAS, N. 1973. *Political Power and Social Classes*. New
Left Books and Sheed & Ward.

POWELL, R. 1972. *The Background of West Indian Children*.
Unpublished Report to the Schools Council.

RAISON, T. (ed.) 1966. *Youth in New Society*. Hart-Davis.

RAYNOR, J. (ed.) 1974. *Issues in Urban Education*. Open
University Press (Urban Education Block 1).

REICH, Charles, A. 1972. *The Greening of America*. Penguin.

REICHE, R. 1968. *Sexuality and Class Struggle*. New Left Books.

REISS, A.J. 1968. "Stuff and Nonsense about Social Surveys and Observation".
In H. S. Becker et.al., eds. (1968).

REX, J. (ed.) 1974. *Approaches to Sociology*. Routledge and Kegan
Paul.

RICHMOND, A.H. 1954. *Colour Prejudice in Britain: a Study of
West Indian Workers in Liverpool, 1941-1957*. Routledge and
Kegan Paul.

RICKMAN, H.P. (ed.) 1961. *Pattern and Meaning in History*.
Allen and Unwin.

RIGBY, A. 1974a. *Alternative Realities*. Routledge and Kegan
Paul.

RIGBY, A. 1974b. *Communes in Bri   ⁊.* Routledge and Kegan Paul.
ROBERTS, R. 1971. *The Classic Slum.* Manchester University Press.
ROCK, P. and COHEN, S. 1970. "The Teddy Boy". In V. Bogdanor and R. Skidelsky, eds. **(1970)**.
ROCK, P. and McINTOSH, M. (eds.) 1974. *Deviance and Social Control.* Tavistock.
RODNEY, W. 1969. *The Groundings with my Brothers.* Bogle-L'Ouverture Publications.
ROSE, A. (ed.) 1962. *Human Behaviour and Social Processes.* Routledge and Kegan Paul (paperback, 1971).
ROSZAK, T. 1972. *Where the Wasteland Ends.* Faber.
ROWBOTHAM, S. 1973. *Woman's Consciousness, Man's World.* Pelican.
ROWNTREE, J.& ROWNTREE, M. 1968. "Youth as Class: the Political Economy of Youth." *Our Generation,* Vol.6, Nos.1-2 (May/July).
ROY, Della & ROY, R. 1972. "Is Monogamy Outdated?" In H. P. Dreitzel, ed. (1972).
ROY, Donald. 1970. "The Study of Southern Labor Union Organizing Campaigns." In R. Habenstein, ed. (1970).
RUNCIMAN, W.G. 1966. *Relative Deprivation and Social Justice.* Routledge and Kegan Paul.
RUSCOE, G.C. 1963. *Dysfunctionality in Jamaican Education.* University of Michigan, School of Education, Ann Arbor.
SANDILANDS, J. 1968. "Whatever happened to the Teddy Boys?" *Daily Telegraph Magazine,* No.217 (29th November).
SARTRE, J-P. 1960. *Critique de la Raison Dialectique.* Gallimard, Paris - translation by Hazel Barnes forthcoming from Methuen.
SARTRE, J-P. 1963. *The Question of Method.* Methuen. Reprinted in 1968 as *Search for a Method,* Vintage Books.
SCHATZMAN, L. 1973. *Field Research: Strategies for a Natural Sociology.* Prentice-Hall.
SCHEFF, T. 1968. "Negotiating Reality." *Social Problems,* 16.
SCHUMACHER, E.F. 1974. *Small is Beautiful.* Abacus.
SILBER, I. 1970. *The Cultural Revolution: A Marxist Analysis.* Times-Change Press, N.Y.
SIMEY, T.S. 1946. *Welfare and Planning in the West Indies.* Clarendon Press.
SMITH, A.C.,BLACKWELL, T. & IMMIRZI, E. 1975. *Paper Voices.* Chatto and Windus.
SMITH, M.G. 1956. *Labour Supply in Rural Jamaica.* Institute for Social and Economic Research. U.C.W.I., Kingston, Jamaica.
SMITH, M.G. 1965. "Educational and Occupational Choice in Rural Jamaica." In *The Plural Society in the West Indies.* University of California Press, Berkeley.
SMITH, M.G., ANGIER, R. & NETTLEFORD, R. 1960. *The Ras Tafarian Movement in Kingston, Jamaica.* Institute for Social and Economic Research, U.C.W.I., Kingston, Jamaica.
SPRINGHALL, J.O. 1971. "The Boy Scouts, Class and Militarism in relation to British Youth Movements 1908-1930." *International Review of Social History,XVI.*
STATERA, G. 1975. *Death of a Utopia.* Oxford University Press.
STRADLING, R. and ZURIEK, E. 1973. "Emergence of Political Thought among Young Englishmen: a Conflict Perspective." *Political Studies,* XXI(3).
STRAUSS, A. 1959. *Mirrors and Masks: the Search for Identity.* Free Press, N.Y.
STRAUSS, A. (ed.) 1965. *George Herbert Mead on Social Psychology.* Chicago University Press/Phoenix Books.

STRAUSS, A. et.al. 1964. *Psychiatric Ideologies and Institutions.* Free Press, New York.

TAYLOR, I. 1971a. "Soccer Consciousness and Soccer Hooliganism". In S. Cohen, ed. (1971).

TAYLOR, I. 1971b. "'Football Mad' - a Speculative Sociology of Soccer Hooliganism". In E. Dunning, ed. (1971).

TAYLOR, I., WALTON, P. & YOUNG, J. 1973. *The New Criminology.* Routledge and Kegan Paul.

TAYLOR, I., WALTON, P. & YOUNG, J. (eds.) 1975. *Critical Criminology.* Routledge and Kegan Paul.

TAYLOR, L. and TAYLOR, I. (eds.) 1973. *Politics and Deviance.* Penguin.

TAYLOR, P.H. and WALTON, J. (eds.) 1974. *The Curriculum: Research, Innovation and Change.* Ward Lock Educational.

TESELLE, S. (ed.) 1971. *The Family, Communes, and Utopian Societies.* Harper Torchbooks.

THOMAS, M. 1973. "The Wild Side of Paradise." *Rolling Stone* (July 19th).

THOMPSON, E.P. 1960. "The Long Revolution". *New Left Review,* 9 and 10.

THOMPSON, E.P. 1963. *The Making of the English Working Class.* Victor Gollancz. (Revised Pelican edn., 1968).

THOMPSON, E.P. 1965. "The Peculiarities of the English". In R. Miliband & J. Saville, eds. (1965).

THOMPSON, Hunter, S. 1967. *Hell's Angels.* Penguin.

THRASHER, Frederic. 1927. *The Gang.* University of Chicago Press.

TITMUSS, R.M. 1962. *Income Distribution and Social Change.* Allen & Unwin.

TREMENHEERE, H.S. 1844. *Report on the Disturbances in the Mining Districts.* Parliamentary Papers Cmd.592.

TROW, M. 1957. "A Comment on 'Participation Observation and Interviewing: a Comparison'." *Human Organisation,* 16,3. Reprinted in G.J. McCall & J.L. Simmons, eds. (1969) - followed by Becker & Geer's Rejoinder.

TRUZZI, M. (ed.) 1968. *Sociology and Everyday Life.* Prentice-Hall.

TURNER, R.H. 1953. "The Quest for Universals in Sociological Research". *American Sociological Review,* 18 (June). Reprinted in N.K. Denzin, ed. (1970).

TURNER, R.H. 1962. "Role-taking: Process versus Conformity". In A. Rose, ed. (1962).

WALVIN, J. 1975. *The People's Game.* Allen Lane.

WEBER, M. 1949. *The Methodology of the Social Sciences.* Free Press, New York. (Edited by E. Shils.)

WESTERGAARD, J. 1965. "The Withering Away of Class. "In P. Anderson and P. Blackburn, eds. (1965).

WESTERGAARD, J. 1974. "Some Aspects of The Study of Modern British Society". In J. Rex, ed. (1974).

WHITE, G. 1967. "Rudie, oh Rudie". *Caribbean Quarterly,* Vol.13, No.3. Univ. of West Indies, Extra-Mural Dept., Kingston, Jamaica, and Port-of-Spain, Trinidad.

WHYTE, W.F. 1955. *Street Corner Society.* Chicago University Press (revised paperback edition).

WILKINSON, P. 1969. "English Youth Movements: 1908-1930." *Journal of Contemporary History,* 4(2).

WILLER, D. and WILLER, J. 1973. *Systematic Empiricism: Critique of a Pseudoscience.* Prentice-Hall.

WILLIAMS, R. 1973. "Base and Superstructure". *New Left Review,* 82.

WILLIS, P.E. 1971. *Non-Participation in Elite Culture: a Case Study of Young Participation in the Culture of Popular Music.* A report to UNESCO social sciences division.

WILLIS, P.E. 1972. *Pop Music and Youth Groups.* Unpublished Ph.D., CCCS, University of Birmingham.

WILLIS, P.E. 1974. "Symbolism and Practice: a Theory for the Social Meaning of Pop Music." CCCS *Stencilled Paper,*No. 13.

WILLIS, P.E. Forthcoming. *Profane Culture.* Chatto and Windus.

WILLMOTT, P. 1969. *Adolescent Boys of East London.* Penguin.

WOLFE, T. 1966. *The Kandy-Kolored Tangerine Flake Steamline Baby.* Jonathan Cape.

WOLFE, T. 1969a. *The Electric Kool-Aid Acid Test.* Bantam.

WOLFE, T. 1969b. *The Pump House Gang.* Bantam.

WOLFE, T. 1971. *Radical Chic and Mau-Mauing the Flak-Catchers.* Bantam.

WOLFF, K.H. (ed.) 1964. *The Sociology of Georg Simmel.* Free Press, New York.

YOUNG, J. 1970. "The Zookeepers of Deviance". *Catalyst, 5.*

YOUNG, J. 1972. *The Drugtakers: the Social Meaning of Drug Use.* Paladin.

YOUNG, J. 1973. "The Hippies: an Essay in the Politics of Leisure." In L.Taylor & I.Taylor, eds. (1973).

ZICKLIN, G. 1973. "Communal Childrearing: a Report on Three Cases". In H. P. Dreitzel, ed. (1973).

ZNANIECKI, F. 1972. *Florian Znaniecki on Humanistic Sociology.* Chicago University Press/Phoenix Books.

ZWEIG, F. 1961. *The Worker in An Affluent Society.* Heinemann.

INDEX OF KEY TERMS

and hegemony, 38–40, 193–5, 202, 231
and women, 226
and youth sub-cultures, 32, 45–8

Methodology
naturalistic, 119–22, 124–5, 243–70
positivistic, 243–6, 253–5
structural/historical, 30–5, 203–7, 232–3, 235–9, 257–8, 270–3
and stratification, 200–3
Middle Class
counter cultures, 57–71, 198–200
and youth, 192–5
See also Culture
Mods, 14, 32–4, 48, 54–5, 72–4, 76, 87–96, 147–9, 178–84, 187–90, 204, 212, 214–15, 217–18, 229
Mugging, 73, 77, 79, 167–73, 271–3

Politics
and youth culture, 71–9, 173, 192–5, 206–7, 231–9, 272–3
Problematic, 15, 29, 48–9, 69–71

Rastafarianism, 56, 138–40, 143, 146, 150
See also Reggae, Rudies
Reggae, 140–53
See also Rastafarianism, Rudies
Rockers, 14, 54, 76, 179–84, 212, 216–17
Rudies, 56, 144–7, 184
See also Rastafarianism, Reggae

Scouts, 193–5

Skinheads, 14, 32–4, 48, 53–4, 72, 99–102, 149–52, 180–1, 184–6, 190–1, 202, 204, 214–15, 229
Social Reaction
control culture and media, 75–9
theory, 248–52
to mugging, 167–8, 271–2
to working class, 176, 233–9
to youth, 64–8, 71–4, 182, 184–91, 193–5
Socialism, fear of, 192–5
Style, 20–1, 30
meaning of, 52–7, 92–4, 175–91, 203–7, 237–8
See also Hippies, Mods, Rastafarianism, Reggae, Rockers, Rudies, Skinheads, Teds

Teds, 14, 27–8, 48, 53–5, 72–3, 81–6, 178–80, 182, 204, 212–14

Working Class
leisure, 50–1, 175–7, 198–9
neighbourhoods, 28, 43
resistance, 26, 232–3
responses to post-war change, 35–8
See also Culture

Youth Culture, 9–10, 15–22, 27, 185–91, 197, 231–2
Youth Sub-Cultures
definition of, 13–17
theories of, 28–57, 232, 243–52
and relation to black music, 161–7
See also Girls, Middle Class, Style